The History of Furniture

The History of FURNITURE

Introduction by
SIR FRANCIS WATSON

CRESCENT BOOKS New York

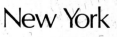

Frontispiece: Room by William Morris dated 1866
(Victoria & Albert Museum, London)
Endpapers: Illustration of furniture manufacture from
Diderot's Encyclopédie *(1751)*

EDITORIAL CONSULTANT Jonathan Bourne
EDITOR Anne Charlish
PICTURE EDITOR Faith Perkins

© 1976 by Orbis Publishing Limited, London
All rights reserved
This 1982 updated and revised edition is
published by Crescent Books
Distributed by Crown Publishers, Inc.
Printed in Jugoslavia by Mladinska Knjiga, Ljubljana
ISBN: 0-517-37742X
h g f e d c b a

Library of Congress Cataloging in Publication Data
Main entry under title:

The History of furniture

    Bibliography: p.
    Includes index.
    1. Furniture-History.
NK2270.H55   1982   749.2   82-2456
ISBN 0-517-37742-X (Crown)   AACR2

CONTENTS

FOREWORD

by Sir John Pope-Hennessy
Director, The British Museum

This book describes the way in which people in the past have lived. It deals not with social attitudes, but with the appurtenances of living through which social attitudes are commonly expressed. If you are furnishing a house today, you can adopt one of two points of view. You can say to yourself that tables and chairs and cupboards are articles of convenience and nothing more, and that their appearance is of no consequence provided the tables are solidly constructed, the chairs can be sat on without discomfort, and the cupboards are sufficiently commodious to take the things you wish to keep in them. Alternatively, you may recognize that a great part of your future life will be lived in close association with the furniture you buy, and that its purpose is not simply functional; that it can, through its design and workmanship contribute a dimension of enjoyment to your daily life and enhance your peace of mind. If you take the first of these two views, this book is not for you. You will regard the furniture it illustrates, whether it was made in Egypt or in France in the late eighteenth century, as an example of conspicuous waste. But if you take the second view, you will welcome the book enthusiastically, because it shows how, over the centuries, prevalent style concepts have influenced the scenography of living, and how artists have been encouraged by perspicacious patrons to develop the prosaic trade of cabinet-making into an art form in its own right.

In museums pieces of furniture are generally shown in isolation. But this was not the way in which most of them were planned. As we know from frescoes of Renaissance rooms by Ghirlandajo, or paintings of Dutch seventeenth-century rooms by Terborch and Vermeer and French eighteenth-century rooms by De Troy, or from real rooms by Kent

Left: Mme de Sérilly's boudoir, 1778–9 (Jones Collection, Victoria & Albert Museum, London)

at Houghton and Adam at Osterley in which the original furnishings have been preserved, they were components or properties in a stage set occupied by people fairly like ourselves. This book forms a corrective to the museum view, in that it reinstates much of the furniture in the context for which it was intended, and in which, at least in the imagination, it must be seen. But though the setting not unnaturally reflected the architectural forms and ornament and therefore more generally the thinking of the age in which it was produced, the purpose for which each piece of furniture was made deviates only marginally from purposes we recognize today. Through it we can gain some impression of how people in the past went about the domestic tasks and social duties we still perform.

Until comparatively recently a line used to be drawn between the fine arts — painting, sculpture and architecture — and the decorative arts, headed by furniture. Research into the fine arts was pursued with sophistication and intelligence, while study of the decorative arts remained cruder and more approximate. In recent years this situation has undergone a change. The study of French furniture in the eighteenth century has become a complex academic discipline, and the documentary background of English furniture has also been very thoroughly investigated. As a result makers of furniture have come to be looked on as what, in the fine arts, are called artistic personalities. They are no longer names which are attached generically to certain types of furniture; they are artist-craftsmen whose style and evolution and aesthetic preferences are reconstructible. This advance is evident throughout the present book. On the one hand, it can be commended to any reader who is responsive to the quality, indeed to the imaginative fantasy of many of the works with which it deals. On the other, it offers proof of the significant advance that has been made in rewriting the history of furniture.

7

INTRODUCTION

by Sir Francis Watson

In 1801, the French diarist P-L Roederer wrote of a wealthy man who, having been to a firm of interior decorators, was congratulated on possessing the most complete collection of furniture in the fashionable neo-classical taste that had yet been formed. But the fortunate owner of this unique assemblage of furniture replied, 'I am not interested in this furniture at all. It is heavy, hard, ugly and uncomfortable. To be able to lie or sit in comfort, that is all I ask of my bed and my armchair.' To the consternation of his listener, he continued, 'They aim at representing the room of Themistocles or Cimon for me, whereas my purpose is that they should furnish my own room. . . . God preserve us nowadays from the temptation of letting oneself drop into an armchair; one would run the risk of breaking oneself to pieces.' This would seem a very simple and obvious view, but the speaker was clearly not representing the conventional taste of his time.

The Napoleonic era was not a period in which comfort was looked for from furniture. The omnipresent soldiers, tightly buttoned into uniforms stiff with gold braid, their legs restricted by skin-tight breeches of buckskin and high leather boots, actually needed the stiff forms of Empire furniture to provide adequate support for their bodies. To fling themselves into a well-upholstered sofa or armchair would have been neither dignified nor physically possible. The ladies of the period, too, in their high-waisted classical dresses, had no wish at all to relax into chairs and sofas. They were more concerned that they should be able to recline or sit in the elegant poses inspired by scenes depicted in Greek vase paintings.

Thus the form of the furniture reflects the demands of society at any given moment. To a considerable degree it is dictated by the social customs of the time, but furniture also has its own internal demands. It might be suggested that the distinguishing features of all good furniture are solidity, utility and decorativeness, but these three qualities do not necessarily appear at the same time in any one piece. At different periods one quality has predominated or even excluded the others altogether.

It may seem surprising today that comfort has only been required of furniture intermittently and has only become a necessity relatively recently. Decoration and display have always played a far more important role than comfort in the history of furniture. Ostentation was expressed through furniture as early as ancient Egypt—when chairs, for example, were symbols of honour found only in noble households. A similar attitude was very marked during the Baroque period in the seventeenth and eighteenth centuries, and was particularly clearly reflected in the etiquette which gave rise to so much squabbling at the court of Louis XIV where chairs were reserved for the use of the King and a few Princes of the Blood alone. At court, only duchesses were allowed to seat themselves in the presence of the sovereign, and even they were only allowed a stool. The rest of the company stood. The hierarchical role of the throne itself is a clear example of this approach to furniture.

Pure utility or functionalism as it was preached at the Bauhaus in the 1920s has remained an undercurrent of furniture design ever since, but it is a rarity in the history of furniture. Even in the Middle Ages when portability and utility were dictated by the itinerant nature of everyday life, the simplest pieces were usually given some embellishment. Where there was no carving, metal hinges and strengthening bands were usually given simple decorative shapes. The proliferation of gilt-bronze mounts, which is such a feature of French eighteenth-century furniture, originated merely from the need to protect the more vulnerable parts of a wooden construction such as the corners.

Nevertheless, even in the elegant and highly sophisticated society of eighteenth-century Paris, pure utility sometimes obtruded in strange ways. The forecorners of most Louis Seize chairs are square and quite sharply shaped. But examination of those made for

Below: Mme Récamier by J-L David, 1800 (Louvre, Paris)

the use of the French Crown in the decade preceding the French Revolution in 1789 will reveal that a large number, generally those made for the card-rooms of the various royal palaces, are rounded. The reason is distinctly curious. The King was short-sighted and clumsy, and as he blundered about he frequently knocked his shins against the sharp corners of the chairs in his path. His officials therefore instructed the royal chair-makers to round the corners of the seats of the chairs.

Strength is of course a permanent requirement of all furniture. A chair which collapses under the weight of the human body is clearly of little use, however decorative it may be. But strength has sometimes had to be supplied at the expense of other qualities. Mediaeval benches and chairs were always solid and comfortable, but they tended to lack decorative qualities. Certain forms of contemporary chair have no form or strength at all until shaped by the human body. Intermediate between these two extremes come the sophisticated constructional methods which enabled the stretcher linking the legs of seventeenth- and early eighteenth-century chairs to be dispensed with. But such technical advances were often abandoned in the nineteenth century in the interest of economy, and many small chairs and tables made for the middle classes of the Victorian period are neither strong nor stable.

These points illuminate not merely the history of furniture but history itself. The two disciplines are complementary. It is this which makes the studies with which this book is concerned so important. Unhappily, the serious study of the history of furniture is a comparatively recent phenomenon which only appeared late in the nineteenth century. It therefore lags behind social history as a scholarly discipline.

It is no chance matter that the serious study of furniture should have begun in France. A wealth of information about historic furniture is available there which is entirely lacking in other countries. In England, for example, evidence has to be quarried from the account-books of individual country-houses or through records of transactions in the numerous offices where they have been deposited. Over the past three or four decades, scholars—including a number of the contributors to this volume—have been able to use such documents to illuminate our picture of the past considerably. But the information available varies from country to country, and much of what is known is dispersed in learned periodicals and obscure books in half a dozen languages. It is the merit of this book that it gathers together so much of this information and makes it a coherent story, full of interest to the historian of furniture, the social historian and the general reader alike.

THE ARCHAEOLOGICAL RECORD
Ancient and mediaeval furniture

Until comparatively recently, elaborate furniture was available only to the households of royalty and their wealthiest subjects. A peasant or town-dweller might construct a crude stool or bench but would sleep on the floor and fashion only the meanest of household objects. It is natural, therefore, that the earliest surviving pieces of furniture should concern us with the ruling classes and their way of life.

Egypt

The idea of sheer comfort is relatively modern; furniture of the early civilizations through to the mediaeval period fulfilled two basic roles, ostentation or utility. The treasures of King Tutankhamun, now in the Cairo Museum, sumptuously decorated though they are, have no pretension to the comfort we expect of furniture today. The interiors of Egyptian palaces and Roman villas were decorated with elaborate murals and their furniture studded with precious materials, but their vast spaces would have seemed stark compared with the collected clutter of a modern house. The furniture of any civilization must reflect its pattern of daily life as well as being regarded as an art form in itself. Relatively few pieces of early furniture have survived intact, and a great deal of our knowledge therefore has to be culled from other contemporary sources such as wall- and vase-painting, manuscript

illumination and sculpture. The picture is far from complete and one must be wary of drawing facile conclusions.

In Ancient Egypt it is only from the time of the New Kingdom (about 1567 to 1320 BC) that furniture survives in any quantity although it is clear that furniture was well known as far back as the third millennium BC. This knowledge has been made possible by the custom of burying treasures with their owner — the most famous example being the tomb of Tutankhamun (c.1361–1352 BC) discovered in 1922. Tutankhamun lived in the former palace of Amenophis III on the west bank of the Nile while his administration was based in Memphis. He is known to have made lavish gifts to the treasuries of the temple of Amun. His tomb and its treasures survive almost intact because the dry climate of the Valley of the Kings preserved the wood and the Egyptians were careful to obscure the tomb from looters. An indication of the quantity of gold used for royal possessions can be gauged from the fact that Tutankhamun's gold inner coffin weighed more than one ton.

Not only was treasure buried, but furniture was often made expressly as equipment for the afterlife. The principal woods used by Egyptian craftsmen were the local acacia, sycamore, cedar imported from Syria and Lebanon, and ebony. They were also skilful in the art of veneering and intricate inlay in lapis lazuli, ivory, glass and faience (decorated earthenware).

Seat furniture is the dominating and most interesting form in this period and had a lasting importance for later civilizations. The chair has frequently been recognized as a symbol of honour and in Egypt it was only used in noble households. Chairs had legs carved as bull's hooves or lion's paws or were left unadorned with square, slightly curving and usually sloping backs and with seats of plaited rushwork or leather. Occasionally the seat was quite near the ground and the occupant would have squatted rather than have adopted the normal sitting position. The armchair was less common and was used for

important ceremonial occasions. The best known examples are the gold-covered thrones of Queen Hetapheres and Tutankhamun himself. The influential folding-stool appears to have been introduced during the Middle Kingdom with two frames turning on metal bolts forming an X-shape and usually terminating in duck's heads. A very similar folding-stool dating from about 1200 BC was found in Jutland which raises the interesting possibility of intercourse between Egypt and northern Europe. The most common seat, however, was the easily movable painted rectangular stool with strutted supports and a top of leather or wood, often curved. The peasant classes would have used small rush-seat stools.

A great deal is known about the layout of the interior of a typical, affluent Egyptian town-house from the excavations at El-Amarna. The central hall was the main living area with portable furniture arranged as the occasion demanded while the walls were brightly painted. Other excavations and tomb finds reveal that most non-royal furniture consisted of simple but solidly constructed stools and chests. The latter, of varying shapes, are often quite ornate with painted geometric and floral patterns.

Tables were purely functional but in general use; they were easily portable and may have served as trays. Otherwise three-legged *jardinières* — ornamental display stands — and occasional tables fulfilled the carrying function. As with painted stools the strutted-support construction was favoured. Possessions were stored in chests or baskets; there were over 30 chests in the tomb of Tutankhamun. As well as larger decorative linen-chests which came in all shapes and sizes, several miniature jewellery and toilet caskets survive which were made of ivory and ebony and these often had drawers. Beds were a luxury afforded only by the very rich; early examples sloped downwards towards the footboard. Tutankhamun's beds were very high off the ground and would have needed a mounting-block. Linen was used sparingly in such a hot climate and curious crescent-shaped headrests acted as pillows. It may be presumed that cushions were used on seats and beds.

Mesopotamia

Contemporary with the civilization of Ancient Egypt was that of Mesopotamia. The difference in the climate and construction of their tombs has meant that only a few ornamental fragments have survived although there are a large number of representations of furniture on sculpture and seals. The Sumerian civilization was centred on Ur, Nippur and Lagash. Important excavations at Ur earlier this century included the discovery of the 'Royal Tombs' dating from about 2600 BC where the jewel-like 'Standard of Ur' was found. Antedating these tombs are a great number of cylindrical stone seals whose depictions of furniture made of reed and wood show stools and sideboards of lattice construction, the earliest of which probably dates back to the fourth millennium BC, before the first dynasty of Egypt. The emergence of the folding-stool in about 2300 BC also occurred probably earlier than in Egypt. Slightly later, chairs and thrones with curving scrolled backs and bull's legs appear.

During the course of the Assyrian and Babylonian eras (c.1350–539 BC) types of furniture appeared with a new emphasis on the use of precious materials such as ivory, ebony and gold. Particularly notable are the impressive sculptured reliefs in the palaces of such kings as Ashurbanipal at Nineveh in the ninth century BC, Sargon II (721–705) at Khorsabad and Sennacherib (704–681) at Nimrud. These reliefs commemorating new territorial conquests show a variety of heavily ornamented thrones, couches and tables often being carried by slaves.

Greece

The emergence of the Greek civilization is one of the most remarkable phenomena of the pre-Christian era, particularly in the field of the decorative arts. As in earlier civilizations

Left: Ebony and ivory gaming-board found in Tutankhamun's tomb. It stands on four paw feet on an unusual sledge base. (Cairo Museum)

Above: A limestone relief taken from the palace of Nineveh, showing Ashurbanipal, King of Assyria in the seventh century BC. All the furniture is shown with intricately carved legs and stretchers. (Courtesy of the Trustees of the British Museum, London)

Right: This Greek vase painting shows the gods feasting. The couches with their small painted volutes and rectangular legs are covered with mattresses. The three-legged side-table on the right would have been pushed under the couches after the meal. (Museo Nazionale, Naples)

very few pieces of furniture survive, but we may rely on 'second-hand' representations on vase-paintings, coins, reliefs and terracotta models. Depictions on funerary stelae are the most useful as they give an idea of the third dimension on a large scale that the necessarily flat treatment of vase decoration cannot. There are also many evocations in heroic literature of the splendour of the Greek interior.

In vase-painting the gods, dead heroes and important mortals sat on thrones *(thronoi)* although the difference between a throne and a chair is often indistinguishable. Early or Archaic examples have animal feet, swan-head finials on low backs with carved side aprons. In the fifth century BC a new type emerged with either turned or rectangular legs, the latter with incised patterns topped by rosettes and volutes, and aprons with carved or painted mythological scenes. Then the throne with a solid back and sides appeared, usually in marble, and was especially popular in the Hellenistic and Roman periods. This was chiefly for ceremonial or theatrical use.

The Greeks' most startling creation ranking high in the history of early furniture design was the *klismos*, a beautifully simple chair much favoured by classical artists. The peak of its popularity was in the latter half of the fifth century BC. It is typified by the elegant splayed legs, with an enclosing backrest and a lack of surface decoration as seen in the

Hegeso stele example. There are many variations in its design and dimensions; from the fourth century the proportions became heavier and more exaggerated with a resulting loss in much of its earlier beauty. The klismos was clearly a most refined and original article whose elegant curves lead one to suppose that the technique of steam-bending was understood from an early stage. The seat was usually plaited and a cushion or piece of leather placed on top.

The easily portable backless and armless rectangular stool with turned legs, known as the *diphros*, was the usual form of seat for deities and mortals alike, as in the Parthenon frieze, and in basic form originates from Egypt and Assyria. The ubiquitous folding-stool or *diphros okladias* is usually shown carried by slaves for their masters' convenience. These were often highly decorated with either fixed or collapsible legs. They fall into two types, one with plain, straight legs, the other with inwardly curving legs and animal feet. Footstools usually accompanied seat furniture as the natural accessories to couches, thrones and chairs.

Banquets of the gods are among the more popular scenes on vase-paintings and in these the couch *(kline)* and table *(trapeza)* play an important part. The couch fulfilled a dual role, being used both for sleeping and eating; as a bed it loses the Egyptian slope and

Left: Roman bas-relief showing Persephone seated on a low-backed armless chair with curiously turned concave legs. Persephone appears to be opening her jewel-casket, which is made of rushes mounted on a wooden core. The simple table has rectangular supports and a marble top with scrolled over-ends and egg-and-dart banding. (Museo Nazionale, Reggio Calabria)

Right: Beautifully cast Roman bronze tripod stand from the Temple of Isis at Pompeii with elegantly curving legs; the tops are formed as winged sphinxes and are joined in the centre by a series of delicate scrolls. (Museo Nazionale, Naples)

Left: Etruscan painted terracotta sarcophagus, of about 500 BC, showing a low couch with a painted and incised decorative frieze of acanthus and palmettes. The dead couple are depicted reclining on two pillows and a long mattress which is enclosed by a sheet. In classical times, couches were often wide enough for two people. (Louvre, Paris)

footboard and gains a pillowrest of more natural form. Couches with animal legs deriving from the Egyptian model are found mainly in the sixth century BC. Examples with turned legs appear from the Archaic period, and some bronze-mounted ones have survived. Scrolled headboards or pillow-rests dating from the fourth century BC are of great importance for Roman developments. There are also couches with rectangular legs with carved and incised decoration similar to that on thrones. Some of these were evidently long enough for two people. Banqueting scenes show couches placed end to end against a wall with side-tables for carrying food and wine which were pushed under the couches afterwards. The less wealthy appear to have sat on diphroi at a large table — it was a mark of distinction to recline at a meal rather than sit. Side-tables were rectangular with three legs in the Egyptian manner, with feet that were often fluted and tapered towards lion's paws. The four-legged table was much less common and there are rare representations of small pedestal tables. From the fourth century BC the round-topped tripod-table with animal and foliate designs became increasingly popular and served as the prototype for Roman usage. One found in Luxor is now in the Brussels Museum. The linen-chest (*kibotos*), again following the Egyptian pattern, is often found in paintings of ladies' boudoirs. From the Greek word *kiste,* generally meaning casket, are derived the Latin *cista* and the English *chest.*

Etruscan furniture from the seventh to the third centuries BC mainly comes from graves, but the evidence is rather fragmentary. Most forms seem to correspond to those of contemporary Greece and these provided another source for Rome to copy. Coloured terracotta models show typical Greek couches.

Rome

Developments in Greece during the later Classical and Hellenistic periods, tending towards luxury as well as practicality, are the stepping-off point for a study of the furniture of Ancient Rome. The spread of the Roman way of life throughout the Empire from Africa in the South to Britain in the North is seen in the remarkable uniformity of furniture styles. The wall-paintings at Pompeii together with many finds from villas and palaces, the use of bronze and marble as basic materials and the evidence of contemporary literature provide us with a variety of information not surviving from earlier civilizations. Roman furniture forms were surprisingly restricted in number, however; the idea of the ostentatious interior was more important than that of comfort or convenience — and it was Roman ornament that was re-employed in later centuries rather than structural designs.

Tacitus considered the dining-room and baths as the hallmarks of civility and the social centre of Roman life. Family meals were often taken in the enclosed courtyard (*atrium*) with the paterfamilias alone reclining on a couch, his wife on a chair beside him and the children on stools by the table, with a separate table for the slaves. Citron and maple were particularly prized materials for which high sums were paid by leading personalities. The Romans were also fond of elaborate veneers and inlay in wood, ivory and precious metals.

As in Greece the couch (*lectus*) was an important and desirable article of which several survive. Of special note are the large number of bronze and ivory ornaments for foot and headboards (*fulcra*) of exquisite workmanship. The most common variety was the long couch with turned legs, which was popular in the late Republican and early Imperial periods. Bronze examples from Pompeii show a multitude of turnings of no structural importance; bone and ivory were used as main supports. The height of the couch varied according to its purpose; in the dining-room couches were arranged in threes at right-angles to one another. The highly decorated couch must have been the most expensive item of furniture in the villa.

The throne (*solium*) is found in representations of deities and their followers, close to

15

bronze or marble round-topped tripod-table of which several were found at Pompeii. The pedestal table with a central marble support and bronze mounts were also used. Often tables for specific use in the dining-room had semi-circular tops to fit the couch base. Large rectangular marble tables with two carved slab supports were mainly used outdoors and these designs were re-used in the Renaissance.

Byzantium and the Middle Ages

The decline in living standards following the collapse of the Roman Empire had an immediate and lasting effect on the function and importance of furniture in Western European society, while the foundation of

Above: This painting from the Codex Amiatinus (AD 689–716) depicts the prophet Ezra writing. He is seated on a low bench with painted edges; his feet rest on a simple stool with a pegged stretcher. The panelled cupboard has two doors—rare at this time. (Laurentian Library, Florence)

Above right: The 'Throne of Dagobert', probably ninth century, is an outstanding example of early mediaeval bronze-casting from the Court School of Charlemagne. (Bibliothèque Nationale, Paris)

the Greek pattern but with a greater elaboration of turned members and a general increase in proportions. Thrones with solid sides became popular for ceremonial occasions with high, rounded backs and stepped sides (hardly suitable as armrests) and two solid end-supports carved with palmettes, scrolls and winged lions. The high-backed, all-enclosing wicker chair found favour with ladies at their toilet. The klismos assumed heavy, unbalanced proportions with thick legs and wide, curving backrests and was favoured in representations of female deities. The stool, especially the folding variety, was the most common seat form, attaining special significance as the *sella curulis* used by senators and magistrates.

As in the modern idiom the Romans used tables as permanent stands for displaying possessions, and of particular note was the

Constantinople and the Empire in the East assured the continuation of the classical tradition. At the same time the spread of Christianity, and in particular its off-shoot, monasticism, provided the basis for the pursuit of learning and the development of the arts. It was the achievement of the Frankish dynasty under Charlemagne to emerge as the dominant force and partially re-kindle the flames of Ancient Rome with a Christian spirit, setting a seal on the course of early mediaeval history in the West. Internal squabbles, however, and Viking raids from outside the Empire, made for a constantly changing map of Europe.

It is this background of territorial uncertainty from which the fabric of mediaeval society evolved—a society consisting of a small ruling class with a vast majority of serfs and peasants, the former geared for war and always on the move, the latter bound to the land eking out a bare subsistence. Through necessity, therefore, articles of furniture were scanty and essentially portable; of course virtually nothing has survived. The wealth of the king was either transported along with his retinue or stored for safe keeping in monasteries.

Many fine works of art remain from the early mediaeval period to testify to the high standard of craftsmanship and quality of materials used. It is from such objects as jewel-caskets, reliquaries and other sacred receptacles that we may assume that elaborate pieces of furniture existed. Manuscript illumination and occasionally monumental sculpture give us an insight into the world of the royal and monastic scriptoria. Characteristic artistic styles developed throughout Europe, notably under the patronage of the Holy Roman Emperor.

There are representations of kings seated on the most elaborate architecturally-contrived thrones with painted canopies and cushions. Whether these were the artists' fanciful creations or not is open to question. It is clear, however, that only royal personages could expect to be associated with furniture of any size or quality. Such is the bronze 'Throne of Dagobert' which probably dates from the early ninth century and has tenuous connections with King Dagobert (AD 622–638), the supposed founder of the Abbey of Saint Denis. The folding legs with their lion's heads and paws are typical of late antique work; it is possible that it does date from the seventh century, but is more likely to be a good example of the resuscitation of classical motifs after the time of Charlemagne.

The folding-stool is certainly the most illustrated piece of furniture in the early Middle Ages, examples being found on ivory panels, in manuscript borders and on cathedral façade sculpture. It usually had a regal connection or at least indicated the secular or religious significance of the sitter depicted. Its social importance of course dates back to Ancient Egypt. There is a richly decorated example from Styria, now in Vienna, dating from about 1200.

That a high standard of craftsmanship was maintained in Byzantium at the same time is indicated in the series of ivory panels attached to the throne of Archbishop Maximianus of Ravenna (AD 545–556) in which one sees the ultimate flowering of the Hellenistic style. Byzantine manuscripts of saints and scholars show that the lectern was a favoured article, often with a cabinet beneath for storing books. And the mosaics of the churches of Ravenna reveal a taste for elaborate hangings and interior decoration in the Eastern Empire not seen elsewhere till the fourteenth century.

There is no doubt that living conditions at this time were squalid and uncomfortable. Life was centred on the great hall which was used for meals, entertainment, the administration of justice and all daily business. It was sparsely furnished with trestles, benches and stools strewn with mattresses or pillows, with only the one chair or folding-stool for the king or lord. The walls might be hung with tapestries; in the epic poem, *Beowulf*, there is mention of hangings inwoven with gold used for ceremonial occasions. And the Bayeux

Below: The ivory throne of Maximianus, early sixth century AD. *The ivory panels attached to the wooden core show the final stages of the Hellenistic style in Byzantium. The five figures in the front panels represent John the Baptist and the four Evangelists. (Museo Nazionale, Ravenna)*

tapestry as well as providing evidence of royal furniture gives one an idea of the quality attained in eleventh-century textiles with its variety of colours and animated depiction of the Norman Conquest of Britain.

The essence of mediaeval furniture was its portability to suit the itinerant nature of everyday life. Although sacred caskets and reliquaries do not fall under the general category of furniture, they do have a family connection with travelling-chests which could have been carried under the arm or on horseback. These were either simple wooden boxes or more often were made of leather bound with iron. Such items as trestles, benches and large

chests would have remained in the hall or monastery. Treasure chests and less decorative or valuable pieces would have accompanied the retinue. Not unnaturally most of the surviving examples of the ubiquitous chest, at any rate until the later fourteenth century, have a history of Church ownership as they have tended to remain *in situ*. Decoration on such chests frequently relies on architectural motifs such as arcades, columns and decorative mouldings, notable examples of which are the chests or *standards* from Valère in Switzerland with their cloister-like arcades and geometric patterns.

Among the more important types of 'static'

Right: The Great Hall, Penshurst Place, Kent, dating back to 1340, is one of the best surviving examples of a mediaeval hall. The main points of interest are the great screen and magnificent roof. The screen is composed of elaborate panels of Perpendicular tracery with ogees and trefoils topped by crenellations. (By Courtesy of Viscount de L'Isle, Penshurst Place, Kent)

Left: Twelfth-century chair from Tydal, Norway. Much of the surface is covered with interlacing foliage inhabited by beasts in typical Scandinavian style. It has a simple mortise-and-tenon structure with a cross-shaped back, curves in the top and side-rails, and carved stretchers and struts, while all round the edges is twisted dog-tooth decoration. (Oslo University)

18

that the artisan, as opposed to the carpenter, would have come. It was only after the organization of the craftsmen's guilds in the thirteenth century that the cabinet-maker's art was separately identified.

After about 1250 it becomes easier to date existing pieces of furniture with a degree of certainty as the Gothic style gained a firm and lasting grip on the applied arts throughout Europe. It was an exuberant style with great decorative potential that went hand in hand with the new age of chivalry and heraldry, the rise of the merchant classes, the emergence of

Above: A mid-fifteenth century master-carver's workshop. The bench-front has linenfold panels. (Ecole des Beaux Arts, Paris)

Above right: The Blessed Agnes attending a sick man by Nicholas Puchner. The simple bed is constructed of planks within a double frame formed of solid beams. (National Gallery, Prague)

furniture are also those ceremonial chairs and thrones, both secular and ecclesiastical, such as Charlemagne's throne at Aachen, the episcopal thrones at Bari and Canossa, Saint Augustine's chair at Canterbury and the sanctuary chairs at Beverley and Hexham, all made of stone or marble and of varying degrees of sophistication.

The ordered and relatively sedentary life of the monastery and cathedral no doubt required certain specific types of furniture such as lecterns, choir stalls and of course altars of which there are some beautifully sculpted survivors, notably that of Avenas in Burgundy. And it was largely from ecclesiastical *ateliers*

the city-state and secular artistic patronage rivalling that of the Church.

Later mediaeval furniture and interior decoration reflects a new distribution of wealth. A glance at the sumptuously painted *Très Riches Heures du Duc de Berry* gives a vivid impression of the richness and colour of court life with its fairy-tale architecture and wealth of hangings and textiles complementing articles of furniture. In England Edward III created the office of King's Tapestry-Maker and such fourteenth-century work was renowned throughout Europe as *opus anglicanum*. From the late thirteenth century onward we find wills and inventories that specifically mention furniture in lists of chattels; the lack of earlier documentation has led to the conclusion that furniture was hitherto held in low esteem, although representations of elaborate royal furniture would seem to negate this notion. The earlier dominance of the great hall as the social centre gradually gave way to the smaller chamber with the result that functional furniture with a degree of comfort became necessary. In Italy, however, the Gothic style did not find favour and furniture there was painted, rather than carved, with scenes of city life and relatively few architectural motifs.

The beginnings of the Gothic style can be traced well back into early twelfth-century architectural developments in France, the various stylistic and constructional elements fusing in the 1140s in such buildings as the abbey of St Denis and the cathedrals of Sens and Noyon. It is this fresh array of detail that became the basis of mediaeval furniture decoration, the most widely used motifs being the pointed arch, multi-foil shapes and tracery patterns. These details did not appear in

Below: Detail of a mid-fifteenth century interior by Lyedet showing a testered bed in the left-hand corner covered in rich blue cloth with gold embroidery. At the side is a green-covered couch with a low back, collapsible sides and a panelled front. (Bibliothèque de l'Arsenal, Paris)

pieces of furniture immediately, however, as the Romanesque tradition was still very strong in the non-architectural field in the twelfth and thirteenth centuries. The architectural origins of later medieval furniture design were often openly displayed in their construction; for example, many chests have buttress-shaped corner- and side-strengthening members. Master craftsmen were able to translate what they saw in stone into the medium of wood. Indeed, there is every reason to suppose that the carver working on a stone altar-screen or sculptured façade would also

execute furnishings such as choir stalls and episcopal thrones. Certainly during the fourteenth century an interest in delicate Gothic forms led to a much more economical use of materials and constructional methods, with less reliance on the simple slab or plank of wood. This was also achieved by the breaking-up of the surface by the use of pierced forms and elegant overall patterns.

The chest was still the most widespread article of domestic furniture in the later Middle Ages. Thirteenth-century examples from France reveal a taste for attached iron scroll-work and also raised feet with chip-carved geometric and foliate ornament. From the early fourteenth century architecturally-contrived chests appear with blind arcading, crockets, ogival tracery patterns and pinnacles of the type found on the 'flamboyant' façades of French cathedrals such as Strasbourg and Rouen, and Perpendicular elevations in England like the nave of Canterbury. Another tradition was the representation of jousting scenes, the lives of the saints and animal life. In Spain profuse and complex Moorish ornament was combined with Gothic to produce an encrusted wedding-cake effect. One of the finest vehicles in furniture for elaborate tracery was the ceremonial throne, two notable examples being the coronation chair in Westminster Abbey completed for Edward I in 1300–1, and the splendid silver-gilt throne of King Martin of Aragon, now in Barcelona, dating from the second half of the fourteenth century.

As the guilds recognized the trade of the cabinet-maker so a fresh variety of woods were employed. Oak and beech were the principal materials in northern Europe while walnut, cypress and fruitwoods found favour in the Mediterranean lands.

Linen-fold panelling is of fifteenth-century Flemish origin and became popular in northern Europe not only in the decoration of furniture but also for the wainscoting of chambers in whose corners a bed with a canopied tester might be fitted. The origins of specialized writing-desks as boxes with sloping, hinged lids date to earlier centuries and vary in size from those held in the laps of the figures of Aristotle and Pythagoras from the mid-twelfth century Portail Royal at Chartres to substantial fifteenth-century examples which would have been placed on a table. Trestle tables remained the main dining-room furnishing and there are Flemish paintings showing occasional tables of various shapes. Cupboards, sideboards and presses dating from the fifteenth century for storing and displaying plate, clothes and books have a wealth of delicate ornament, often in bands because of their size. There are earlier examples with a specific function such as the sacristy cupboard in Halberstadt Cathedral dating from perhaps the twelfth century.

The impact of the Italian Renaissance was relatively slow to affect furniture north of the Alps, notably in England where the tradition of Gothic was deeply entrenched and thrived for the next four centuries. Indeed in the nineteenth century the decorative impact of the 'Early English' style was the basis for the school of design of Gothic ornament fostered by A W N Pugin and his circle which so dominated Victorian taste.

THE CLASSICAL REVIVAL
Europe's Renaissance

In the mid-thirteenth century when Villard d'Honnecourt was sketching details of buildings — towers, flying buttresses, choir stalls and windows — into his now famous album he thought of no other style than Gothic. It was the style which fashioned the great cathedrals, created to soar upwards in linear and vaulted complexity. They proclaimed throughout Europe the church, powerful and triumphant, and provided a vivid and visually exciting experience to those who moved forward through long nervous lengths of grey stone, and coloured imagery in leaded glass. At Amiens, Strasbourg, Milan, and other cathedrals, the choirs were filled with filigree wooden stalls and bedecked organ cases, with polychromatic saints in stiff array in the scented gloom. Joiners and carvers, not yet tightly bound to guild tradition, found their most sympathetic, yet demanding, patrons among the Prince Bishops.

The feelings of greatest moment and enquiry seem to have arisen in the city of Florence, and within the circle of its most talented architect Filippo Brunelleschi (1377–1446). He was to surmount the Gothic cathedral with a great dome which eschewed the normal use of timber centering for its construction. In its majestic proportion it was a fitting statement of what the age was to be about. He initiated the mathematical formulae governing perspective which his friend the young painter Masaccio used to powerful effect in the late 1420s. Groups of engravers in Germany and France later scribed its intricacies for editions of architectural and decorative prints which were to interest furniture-makers, goldsmiths and sculptors throughout Europe.

In the experiments which artists carried out the rigours of International Gothic were finally abandoned. For too long this style had dictated that what the court painter to the Dukes of Burgundy did would look similar to work produced for imperious masters in Florence or Mantua. In the Netherlands in 1434 Jan van Eyck painted the Italian merchant Giovanni Arnolfini and his wife. They were depicted standing before the bed, chair, and mirror of a real and recognizable room rather than in a stylized sacred setting. But in achieving freedom from tyranny of style, artists and craftsmen became subordinate to the particular school of painting or craftsmanship in their town or region.

The status of the house was also changing. The hall, with its large carved wooden screen, became the entrance to the great English house rather than the hub of its existence. The dining-room and parlour were created with a corresponding demand for furniture. Money once spent on fortification of an Italian town-palace could be spared for gilded beds, inlaid tables, chairs with reclining backs, and pedimented cupboards with reclining figures.

25

There were also the variations created by the use of different woods. In the north oak was easily available and it could be chiselled with precision to form panels in high relief: in the south it was necessary to work in soft woods such as pine and larch and this gave a flatter quality to all that was decorated. The techniques of inlay and marquetry developed as the trade guilds trained and supervised the system of apprenticeship. They produced the men to create the cabinets of wonders, encrusted with precious stones, and the men who created the simple 'best bed' described in many a yeoman's inventory. The grammar of ornament which the Renaissance had spread substituted classicism for Gothic detail. The men who created furniture were, within a hundred years or so of Michelangelo's birth, to be looked on as artists themselves and furniture itself at last shook off its mediaeval origins.

Italy

In 1386 on the orders of Gian Galeazzo Visconti the Gothic cathedral at Milan was begun. Across the succeeding years and as late as the sixteenth century French, German, and Italian master-masons directed its erection—a wonder of white marble gables, pinnacles, belfries, rose-windows and statues. But it was almost alone in Italy in its portrayal of the pointed style of Gothic architecture. Gothic stone tracery, thin and strong in its arch formation, allowed for large areas of glass to be disposed within a frame. To Italians intent on restricting bright hot sunlight entering their buildings this was a disadvantage. Instead they painted in fresco the coloured pictures which enlivened the wall spaces between any small windows. As a

Left: With its lion paw feet and painted panels, this Florentine cassone or marriage-chest of about 1492 is an outstanding example of the gilder's and painter's art. The narrative panels are painted in tempera on gesso. The Bible, Italian literature and classical mythology provided the most frequently used sources of inspiration for such panels. Many cassoni were executed in famous workshops such as those led by Uccello and Ghirlandajo. (Courtauld Institute of Fine Art, London) result Italian schemes of decoration and furniture owed little to Gothic.

It made its brief appearance most effectively as the International style and is seen in the structure of the great wooden altarpieces of the early fifteenth century. Two examples in the Uffizi Gallery in Florence are typically grand and flamboyant. Lorenzo Monaco's *Coronation of the Virgin* (signed and dated 1413) shows how persistent the archaic styles were, even as the Renaissance was about to dawn. The polyptych has pinnacles, pilasters and is set as usual on a pierced and painted platform known as a *predella*. Ten years later Gentile de Fabriano painted his *Adoration of the Magi* for a powerful patron, Palla Strozzi. The altarpiece is triple arched with superb decorated finials and elaborately pierced columns, thickly encrusted with gold leaf. As International Gothic came to its end it produced these richest and most splendid creations, with Lorenzo Monaco's influence on this style being of paramount importance.

There are few ways of ascertaining what furniture was in certain rooms at various periods other than to examine a wide range of paintings which show interiors. It is necessary to take into account that they sometimes depict an ideal world, or one distorted by symbolic and allegorical allusions. Allowing for this and for a certain time-lapse, the furniture bears some relationship to what was familiar to the artist and his contemporaries.

In 1491 Domenico Ghirlandajo completed a wall-painting of the *Birth of the Virgin* in the church of Sta Maria Novella, Florence. It is concerned with the birth of the Virgin Mary and several relatives of her mother St Anne coming to visit her to offer greetings and congratulations. The room has a classical frieze of riotous *putti* (or cherub-like infants), an elegant staircase at the left, correctly drawn in perspective, and four richly decorated, Ionic capped, square columns. The wainscoting is decorated in intarsia — a form of decorated wood inlay — and St Anne is seated on a version of a *cassapanca* — a chest to which there is a back and the seat of which opens to reveal a storage space. Vittore Carpaccio's *Dream of St Ursula* in the Accademia, Venice, of some four years later shows a very sparsely furnished room. With its double-arched window, the room is dominated by a bed on a decorated plinth, with slender turned posts, a Gothic chair with pointed back and scrolled arms, the ubiquitous splayed stool, a small square table covered with a fringed cloth and a small cupboard. The rare appearance of Gothic, and the Renaissance interest in perspective, is exemplified in Perugino's *The Virgin appearing to St Bernard* of about 1490 (now in the Alte Pinakothek, Munich). Six figures are ranged in two groups of three, with St Bernard seated on a simple square bench at a small desk with a plain lectern on top and a diamond lozenge motif on its sides. Triple arches frame the simple landscape. It indicates in stark symmetry the marked paucity of furniture even when the architectural setting itself is magnificent and imposing.

If by contrast with Gothic detail one explores the grand sweep of only one Renaissance house — the Palazzo Farnese in Rome — differences are apparent. It housed the rich collections of antiques and works of art gathered by the Farnese family. There were grand salons decorated in paint and gold by the Carracci studio, but little furniture — the great table of inlaid marble (now in the Metropolitan Museum, New York) stood in the *sala degli imperatori*, named after the twelve busts of Roman emperors which were

ranged along its walls. The second-floor rooms were filled with tapestries, services of plate, and rock crystal, and the libraries of the Farnese and Orsini families.

Much early Italian furniture was itself painted rather than carved and its highest expression was in the wedding-chests or *cassoni*, created particularly in Florence. Continuity and rank were cemented in the marriage alliances between great families, who attached considerable importance to the grandeur of the marriage ceremony as a result. To produce the chests in sufficient number was reason enough to avoid any unusual techniques – the Florentines in any case well understood painting on prepared wood panels, or decorating in a stucco relief which was composed of sand, marble dust and gypsum. The long panels of the cassone were admirably suited to spatial and perspective compositions in miniature and famous artists became adept in their decoration.

The sixteenth-century Italian architect and painter Giorgio Vasari explained to his readers that earlier artists had felt no concern at employing themselves in the painting of furniture. They had still to acquire a unique and decisive status and were versatile enough to vary their accomplishments. The great Florentine artists — Botticelli, Uccello, the sculptor Donatello and Pollaiuolo — all worked on cassoni in the first half of the fifteenth century.

This was the period when important families dominated Italian life and vied with each other for power, possessions, and the right to bestow patronage or misery. The riches of the

Below: This fifteenth-century Florentine cassone *has a simple, rough construction with three painted panels. Compared with the grand examples produced in the best workshops, it is obviously an inferior piece, but it shows the sort of cassone that the more modest families might wish to possess. (Palazzo Davanzati, Florence)*

Above: In St Augustine in his Study by Vittore Carpaccio, the flamboyant chair and scrolled lectern on the left owe much to the combined skills of carver, embroiderer and leather-worker. With swooping scrolls and splayed legs they are tasselled and studded, set on their own covered kneeling platform and are en suite with the furniture in the room. The Saint sits working at an elegant thin table, again with a covered and studded top. (San Giorgio Maggiore, Venice)

Medici, the Sforza and the Gonzaga raised art to an intense level. Lodovico Gonzaga, Duke of Mantua (1414–78) had a wide-ranging ability which encompassed that of action and scholarship. He persuaded Mantegna to become his court-painter, he employed Alberti as his architect, and collected the writings of Dante, Petrarch, Boccaccio and the earlier classical authors. The cassoni painters found it expedient to paint scenes from such authors — the *Decameron* was popular. Their virile depiction enhanced an object which had been created in strict accordance with classical rules of proportion. The knights and ladies of an age of chivalry which are found on a cassone of the late fourteenth century, now in the Victoria & Albert Museum, London, were in keeping with the ideas which emanated from Mantua with the residence, in the time of Lodovico's father, of the great humanist Vittorino da Feltre.

The subjects depicted on cassoni were wide-ranging. While the spirit of rivalry between neighbouring states often erupted into violent war, the cassoni rarely portrayed this. There are some tournament scenes, with prancing horses and tilted lances, and also classical subjects with a violent theme, for example Cephalus hurling his spear and killing his wife, or the equally tragic death of Actaeon torn to pieces by his own hounds. Much more acceptable were the paintings, sometimes erotic, based on the many love-poems by Ovid, even if they were denounced by Savonarola, whose own love-suit in the 1470s of a member of the Strozzi family was treated with a disdain sufficient to cause him to enter the church.

What is slightly more puzzling are the large panels in cassone style which are obviously too large to be so used. When Schubring issued his two-volume work on the marriage-chests in 1923 he indicated that the panels were fixed to the walls of rooms above the painted wainscoting. With parts of the whole wall to work on it was possible for an artist to imitate his peers who had covered all before them with a painterly virtuosity. The cassoni became a small part of a greater whole, but remained important statements about Italian life and manners. As the Renaissance gained momentum they were created as classical monuments in sarcophagus form, carved in

29

high relief in walnut. They displayed classical motifs of urns, griffins, leaves and flowers, or were decorated with an intarsia of exotic woods.

At the beginning of the sixteenth century in Italy — a period when Bramante, Michelangelo, Leonardo da Vinci, Raphael and Titian were at work — the role of the artist underwent a change. No longer was he a craftsman content to paint a chest but a person capable of keen enquiry and observation of anatomy, natural laws and mathematics. The courts were seeking prestige one above the other, and were wise in their investments, often to the exclusion of aesthetic considerations in what they bought. Michelangelo had begun his long acquaintance with the Sistine Chapel works, the tomb of Julius II and St Peter's. Giulio Romano was to spend the 1520s erecting the Palazzo del Te at Mantua for the Gonzagas, and Alessandro Farnese (later Pope Paul III) strained his vast fortune for 40 years with the erection from 1514 of the Palazzo Farnese. These buildings created luxurious settings for paintings by the Carracci and others, which in riots of exuberant colour portrayed the mythological amours of unconsidered hordes of gods and goddesses.

One of the noblest acts of creation was the decision by Pope Leo X — a Medici — to continue the work on St Peter's and the Vatican under the supervision of Raphael. Raphael worked from about 1515, with his assistants, Giulio Romano, Giovanni da Udine and his associate Baldassare Peruzzi at the Villa Madama for the Pope's cousin, Cardinal Giulio de' Medici. It was work in stucco and paint which was to have an important influence on the decoration of Fontainebleau for the French king, François I. Vasari in his near-contemporary *Lives of the Artists* says that Pope Leo was well pleased with Raphael's work in the *stanze* of the Vatican 'and to make the panelling worthy of the paintings he sent to Monte Oliverto di Chiusuri in the Siena district for Fra Giovanni da Verona, who in those days was a great master of perspective-views in wood inlay. Fra Giovanni executed not only the surrounding panelling but also some very fine doors and chairs, with perspective studies, which won him generous praise and rewards from the Pope.'

The expenditure of vast sums on such decorative richness seems, however, to have prevented too much expenditure on furniture. Carpets and luxuriant cut velvets, and tables holding bronzes, and vessels of gold and silver were there in profusion. The *studiolo* of Francesco I de' Medici, a room designed in the 1570s by Vasari, has walls and ceiling covered with paintings, and has bronze statuettes in niches. Of furniture it only had enough to form a proportioned central feature. No great sixteenth-century bed survives in Rome or

Venice, although they appear in paintings, with Corinthian capitals to the posts and a classical frieze to the canopy. Furniture that was rough and practical could be rendered fit to set on the marble patterned floor of the *piano-nobile* (the main floor) simply by covering it with a Turkish carpet or a damask cloth. Even Raphael's famous painting of Pope Leo X, painted in 1518, shows the Holy Father seated in a red tasselled and upholstered armchair at a table covered with a scarlet cloth.

We have mentioned intarsia decoration on cassoni, and there is also a splendid room,

Above: This sixteenth-century Florentine credenza is more than usually architectural, with the grotesque masks and caryatid figures contained within a frieze supported by three pilasters. (Villa Medici, Florence)

the Studiolo of Federigo de Montefeltro in the Ducal Palace at Urbino, of about 1470, with superb intarsia decoration by an unknown artist. As an art it attracted its own groups of craftsmen. One of the best known was Fra Giovanni da Verona, whom we have noted working for Pope Leo X under Raphael's supervision. He also decorated choir stalls and library cupboards with double-panelled doors. The cupboards were decorated with urns, arches and *trompe l'oeil* depictions of enigmatic open cupboards. The side panels of foliate decoration and a classical ornament in the frieze completed an object at once practical and imposing. Walnut was used frequently for the manufacture of cassoni and for sideboards, *credenza*, which replaced the simple tables covered with rich cloths. They were at once architectural in form, but were plain by comparison with the tables and caskets created in a moment of high Mannerist eccentricity.

The greatest of the palaces in Rome needed objects which would not be completely subordinated by rich decoration. The Farnese table of 1570 with its carved marble supports

31

and inlaid marble top was possibly designed for the Palazzo Farnese by the architect Vignola. Carved wood tables of the period also have boldly sculptured supports which show the fantasies of Mannerism. It is a style which defies quick analysis, but in essence was the result of an excessive addiction to a distinctive style which had evolved in courtly circles. Painted and sculptured figures were produced in a manner which betokened a poise and refinement capable of resolving all difficulties, but which was grounded deep in the philosophy of the age, particularly neo-Platonism. Some of the figures on Michelangelo's Sistine Chapel ceiling, or *The Dying Slave* (1513), have the new abstraction about them. His marble sculptures affected the work of silversmiths and furniture-makers in awakening them to adornment with figures. Cellini, too, had employed the Mannerist style in his *Perseus with the Head of Medusa* (1545) in Florence, and when the Farnese casket (now in the Museo di Capodimonte, Naples) was created a few years later in rich

silver gilt it bore small figures in caryatid form as on the marble and bronze base of the Cellini *Perseus*.

While exact references are not possible, it is nevertheless sensible to bear in mind that the decorative arts followed the social scene. The moderates in the church had fought to see that at the 1563 Council of Trent the visual arts were defended from the extremists. The resulting pursuit of simplicity, clarity and avoidance of the nude figure were contrary to the spirit of Mannerism, and they diverted attention from the essays in flamboyance, into which category fell the lavish creations in *pietra dura* — hard-stone. In 1580 Francesco I de' Medici summoned craftsmen from Milan to set up a hard-stone workshop — the *Opificio delle Pietre Dure* in Florence. The aim was to have within his patronage a means of adding works to his own extensive collections, and to have an easy facility for providing gifts to those whose support and friendship he earnestly desired. When John Evelyn visited the Opificio in 1644 he saw: 'divers incomparable

Above: The Sala dei Pappagalli provides an elaborate setting for a fine bed with finials to its posts, a carved headboard, draperies and valances. A leather upholstered elbow chair with brass studs stands against the wall. (Palazzo Davanzati, Florence)

Above right: Contained in four panels below a Roman lettered frieze, this late sixteenth-century grand chest exemplifies Renaissance furniture at its best and most formal. (Palazzo Davanzati, Florence)

scene in Europe. But the estates were built on the many smaller houses and the devoted work of humbler men and women. They used simple rush-seated ladderback chairs, benches and stools which were made across the centuries with little variation. In the larger towns the shopkeepers were numerous and powerful, and, by forming their own guilds, they guarded jealously their customs and enhanced their own status. This produced the demand for a more sophisticated form of furniture in which the ladderback chair was upholstered, the bellows covered with crimson velvet and carved in relief, and the pinewood mirrors gilded. There was also a church which each guild patronized, with a steady demand for seats, small altars and chapel furniture. Plague and fever might frequently visit the houses of the poor but religion was a purging grace which gave secular strength, and hopes of a status with possessions to match.

Below: Grand cabinet with architectural compartments containing bronze statuettes. The panels of pietra dura, made fashionable in Florence from the end of the sixteenth century, are of fruit and flowers, with incrustations of lapis lazuli. The base has eight legs in four conjoined pairs, and the cabinet has a galleried top. (Museo Stibbert, Florence)

tables of Pietra Commessa, which is a marble ground inlayed with several sorts of marbles and stones of divers colours, in the shapes of flowers, trees, beasts, birds and Landskips like the natural.' With commendable perception, a splendid table made in about 1640 had been put in the Tribune of the Uffizi to catch the eye of visitors on the Grand Tour, such as Evelyn, who journeyed to Italy from all over Europe. It was perhaps similar to the one, still in the Opificio museum, designed by Jacopo Ligozzi and Bernardino Poccetti for Ferdinando de' Medici in 1633–49. The top is composed of a mosaic of semi-precious stones —jaspers, agates, lapis lazuli—set into a ground of black marble with a dexterity that defies comprehension.

In the presence of studied opulence in furniture it is easy to find further examples. The gems in the Medici collection were priceless and the Grand Duke of Tuscany was said to have lavished a fortune on a table and a desk, both richly set with precious stones. Caskets housed precious relics and in themselves were small expressions of wealth and the acquisitive urge. They were fashioned with ebony and ivory inlays, contrasting dark and light woods and overlaid with silver, silver gilt and precious and semi-precious stones. A Milanese cabinet of drawers in the Wallace Collection, London, of the late sixteenth century, is of pine, veneered with ebony. The walnut drawers are faced with ebony which frames embossed steel plaques damascened in gold with mythological subjects of Orpheus, Venus, Cupid and Mars. Furniture such as this had reached a position where it was venerated as much as the relic caskets and tapestries of a mediaeval court.

Mediaeval and Renaissance Italy has long been known for the contributions its great families made to the political and financial

France

The brilliantly coloured world exemplified in
the International Gothic style was not only
portrayed by Italian artists of the fourteenth century but was precisely drawn by
German and Flemish engravers. In the early
years of the fifteenth century, the Franco-
Flemish style of the lavish courts of the
Dukes of Burgundy and the Dukes of Berry
was most influential. The courts encouraged
important contributions to the arts of miniature painting and illumination including
the famous *Books of Hours* created for Jean,
Duc de Berry, in the 1420s by Pol, Hennequin
and Herman de Limbourg. Work inspired by
the Flemish style also made its appearance in
Angers and Provence, areas which were under
the rule of René of Anjou, King of Sicily, an
ardent patron of Flemish artists. Philippe le
Bon, Duke of Burgundy, also owned paintings
by the van Eycks — Jan van Eyck was his
court painter in about 1425 — and Roger van
der Weyden.

It was a period in France for flamboyant
furniture designed for display, both within its
complex ornamentation and for the showing
of gold and silver plate. The *buffet* or sideboard
during the Gothic years resembled architecture in miniature — rich tracery ornament
above, cusping and linen-fold panelling below,
with a locking compartment for valuable plate
and upper and lower shelves for display of
various pieces. The observance of architectural
forms was the result of the furniture-makers
copying work by regional schools of stone-
masons, and being inspired by the great
Gothic structures, such as Milan Cathedral,
being built at about this time.

As early as the thirteenth century the
wooden chest had shown this preoccupation
with architecture and carving in high relief.
A chest of this date in the Musée de Cluny,
Paris, shows a relief carving of 12 knights
in armour, and other examples have elaborate
banding in metal. They depicted status and
this was taken to extreme lengths in the
frequent possession, by personages such as
Margaret of Flanders, of two cradles — one
for the child, one for ceremonial parade. Such
cradles frequently had what became a common
element in display furniture — the canopy.
This was equated with rank and high office
and was frequently depicted in paintings and
engravings — surmounting the throne of a
heavenly or temporal ruler. They were also
used as temporary erections of timber and
fabric for important state occasions, and in
varying forms were adapted as testers for
beds, and over buffets — the *dressouer de
parement* which appears in fifteenth-century
inventories.

At the meeting-point of European influences,
French furniture soon came under the subtle,
influential spread of classicism. The process

was helped to a high point of achievement
by the advance into Italy in 1494 of Charles
VIII of France, intent on conquering Naples
and recovering Angevin possessions elsewhere
in northern Italy. Italian ideas began to
interest seriously those young, ardent intel-
lectuals who saw, beyond the sword-point, a
world which had known, which had almost
created, symmetry and order in architecture
and decoration.

Charles VIII had been born in the Château
of Amboise — he also died there — and was
intent, even prior to his Italian campaign, on
improving it. From Italy he brought back the
Modenese sculptor, Guido Mazzoni, masons
proficient in the 'antique style', decorators
and garden architects. While hardly anything
survives of their work their presence was an
important means of diffusing Renaissance
ornamentation throughout France. Abbot
Antoine Bohier returned to Fécamp with
Italian sculptures and later craftsmen to work
on his church. The carved stone screens, made
in about 1518, show in their pierced scrolling

*Above: Le Bourgeois from
the Four States in the Life
of Man by Jean
Bourdichon (c. 1457–1521).
The dresser with carving
of Corinthian capitals,
base and frieze is in the
Italian style, imported
into France during the
wars of François I. The
seat has an unusual
reclining back as opposed
to those derived from the
upright Gothic rigidity,
and the canopied fireplace
on the twin column
supports is reminiscent of
those over mediaeval tombs.
(Ecole des Beaux Arts,
Paris)*

and acanthus-type relief foliage the preoccupation with a new ornamental form. The
work is paralleled at many other French
churches and in the decoration of tombs. It
was pursued with royal obsession — imperious
and demanding — by François I at Blois,
Chambord and Fontainebleau. He succeeded
Louis XII in 1515, and commissioned the
Italian sculptors Antonio and Giovanni Giusti
to provide, over the next 16 years, the splendid
arched tomb at St Denis for his predecessor.
All traces of Gothic were now banished, and
courtly life at Amboise took on the mantle of
the Italian Renaissance, with Leonardo da
Vinci spending the last years of his life there.
But François was concerned that the residence
of the kings should be centred at
Fontainebleau, and that power should be
moved nearer to Paris rather than being
wielded from the Loire valley.

The ideal was, however, somewhat removed
from its realization. François I was defeated
by the Holy Roman Emperor, Charles V, at
Pavia in 1525 and imprisoned in Spain. After

his return from Madrid and his reconciliation
with the Emperor, François identified himself
with the Catholic faith and the Papal alliance,
with the active support of his sister,
Marguerite de Navarre. He also set about
making Paris his centre and in an elaborate
building programme at several châteaux
entrenched the Italian style — notably at the
Château de Madrid, begun in 1528, and in a
second phase of activity at Fontainebleau and
Villers-Cotterêts. We only know what 'Madrid'
looked like from the engravings of du Cerceau,
whose depiction of a mantelpiece at the
château shows it adorned with classical
figures flanking armorials — motifs which
lent themselves to Mannerist interpretation.
This work was complex and flamboyant, and
in contrast, the work of 1528 to 1540 at
Fontainebleau may be seen to portray classical
simplicity. It was almost entirely realized in
the interior decoration by two major Italian
artists, Francesco Primaticcio and Giovanni
Battista Rosso. Primaticcio had trained and
worked under the supervision of Raphael's

pupil, Giulio Romano, and Rosso had worked in Florence and Rome.

It is the Galerie François I, Rosso's main creation, which survives—most of the stucco-work by Primaticcio having disappeared. If, however, one looks at the splendid mantel-piece in the Chambre de la Reine by Primaticcio, on its two Corinthian columns, and with sphinx-like and caryatid figures, it is easy to see how such motifs in all their promise of movement and elegant stance affected the furniture-makers. Rosso's Galerie has been much altered but as a room it is divided along its vertical surfaces almost equally by panelling (carved by an Italian, Scibec de Carpi), and in the upper part by painting and stucco figures. The intertwined strapwork, cut into elaborate stucco-shapes and based on Italian engravings, was an important decorative theme which spread throughout Europe.

The influence of the Fontainebleau decoration was well set out by the engravers and there is a remarkable series of dressers which follows drawings by Hugues Sambin and Androuet Du Cerceau. That in New York (in the Frick Collection) has caryatid figures at each corner and flanking the centre upper section, and has flamboyant scrolls terminating in lion's feet. An example in the Philadelphia Museum of Art has the figure of Minerva on the upper door, and five caryatid figures on the upper and lower stages. In France, a cabinet of about 1600 (Conservation des Musées, Tours) from the Château of Azay-le-Ferron is similar to an example now in the Wallace Collection, London. Both have an elaborate broken pediment with reclining figures, flanking a smaller, pedimented arch. All four doors are richly carved in relief and disposed within architectural columns or pilasters. This formality may have owed, in its title-page rigidity, just a little to Sebastiano Serlio, who had come from Italy in the 1540s to the court of François I's successor, Henri II. He was put in charge of works at Fontainebleau but his international reputation was to be secured by his important treatise on architecture which was widely disseminated and translated throughout Europe.

It is never wise in the documentation of French furniture of the Renaissance period to pay too much attention to regional variations. Many of them were led by the influence of the main centres and by Du Cerceau's engravings. Jean Goujon was partly responsible for the distinctive style of Normandy and Hugues Sambin of Dijon was known as the creator of the flamboyant and splendidly-fashioned furniture and carving for the allies of the Dukes of Burgundy. But these exceptional cases of regional originality led the field and were many years ahead of the anonymous host.

In 1539 there was published in Lyon a small

Left: A royal bedroom in the Château de Blois, France, one of a suite designed for François I between 1515 and 1524. The king developed a passion for building and decorating at a time when Italian influence was predominant. The bed has tapered, fluted posts of walnut and the mattress is set on a wooden platform. The tester is arranged so that the embroidered hangings can be fastened to its inner side and also suspended at the head of the bed. In this way, and almost for the first time, the bed could be totally enclosed overnight. (Château de Blois)

37

book by Gilles Corrozet, *Les Blasons Domestiques*. It set out a description of the furnishing of a gentleman's house, although it would be wrong to regard the observations on furnishing as typical of what was available. Corrozet thought that the *salon* should contain a bed, a buffet, a table and a chest as well as a great chair and several stools — there should be a concern for domestic comfort, rather than austere architectural forms. In particular the gradual disappearance of the chest — long a symbol of authority and importance — took place, to be replaced by the wardrobe, or *armoire*, which was sometimes incorporated into the panelling of the room in the way that corner-beds had been in earlier times. It was the older buffet in a new guise. Rooms were also changing their style and size, as they were required for dining and entertaining by smaller groups. This allowed the use of a smaller table than the long imposing ones made for refectory and great hall use, and it gradually took up its position at the centre of the room. Each person also had his own stool, with a chair provided for the head of the family. An inventory of the Hôtel de Montmorency, home of Anne de Montmorency, taken in 1556 lists 'four dozen escabelles serving for all the house—eight demi-tables serving both for the said chamber of the king and for elsewhere'. The age of completely portable furniture, moved from room to room as needed, had come. The 'escabelle' was a low short bench, and had also appeared in the 1514 inventory of the possessions of Cesare Borgia, the warlike son of Pope Alexander VI, who had married a Frenchwoman.

The latter half of the sixteenth century in France was a period torn by religious wars—a bitter struggle between Catholics and Calvinists. The houses of Lorraine and Bourbon ranged in opposite camps and the violence registered itself in the arts of the period. The attitudes at the court of Henri III, however, continued to embrace cultural activity and in furniture appeared as an advanced form of Mannerism. The engravings of the elder du Cerceau and Hugues Sambin, the sculptures of Germain Pilon which reflected the earlier example of Cellini, and the paintings of Antoine Caron, Jean Cousin the Younger and the portrait-painters made important contributions. It might be said that furniture, useful, sophisticated and on occasion elevated to a high art, merely shook off the trappings of Gothic for the thin precise cloak of classical ornament. That would deny, however, the achievement of those, Sambin among them—his Maison Milsand at Dijon of about 1561 shows him as an accomplished architect—who created furniture in a conscious architectural form with its own decorative repertoire.

When Henri IV entered Paris as king in 1594 it was as head of a France worn out by civil war and strife with the Spaniards, and also uneasy under heavy taxation. Within four years he had secured relief from the invaders and his Edict of Nantes established a religious toleration that was to last to the late years of the seventeenth century. From 1598 there was the chance to give time to reviving trade and industry, and to the reconstruction of Paris by many ambitious town-planning projects. The crafts were given their own impetus by the setting-up in 1608 of workshops in the Louvre, with royal patronage and protection for artisans. The architect Salomon de Brosse, steeped in classicism, needed them for the decoration of châteaux and royal palaces. Progress halted and was then uncertain in the troubled period when the King was assassinated in 1610.

Henri had devoted considerable time and money to his residences, patronizing, in effect, the Second School of Fontainebleau. When he was killed the future Louis XIII was a minor and power passed for a short time to Marie de' Medici, an Italian with a taste for Flemish art and the skills of Rubens. Great mansions such as the Hôtel Chalois-Luxembourg and the Hôtel de Sully were erected for rich financiers and ministers—Sully was in the service of Henri IV. With precise inner courts and beamed ceilings (known as *plafonds à la française*) they reflected the architectural achievements of a new age which needed rich trappings to fill them. The state apartments of the long gallery or *galerie des fêtes* dazzled the eye, with mirrors, paint, stucco, gilding and silk fabrics. None more so than at Richelieu where the King's minister, Cardinal Richelieu, gathered around him treasures of furniture, painting and sculpture, which rivalled those of his royal master.

Under Richelieu, and more particularly his successor, Cardinal Mazarin, the middle classes increased their financial power and influence. This in turn filtered down to craftsmen in the form of commissions for paintings, furniture and works of art. Many

French artists went to Italy — Mazarin was Italian — and the taste of the Queen, Anne of Austria — Spanish by birth — was also affected by Mazarin's ideas and by the work of his compatriots. Marquetry inlay of tortoiseshell and pewter was to be highly developed. It reached a supreme point under Louis XIV by the work of the eminent André-Charles Boulle (1642–1732). The art of veneering in ebony was to be found in the work of Jean Mace who had been recalled from the Netherlands by Marie de' Medici. There was also a keen demand for furniture with legs and stretchers turned on the lathe in various complex forms. Upholstery was becoming more popular and was fringed and brass-nailed into subjection. When an inventory was drawn up for Mazarin in 1653 he had, in a bedroom, no fewer than 14 chairs of various kinds, of which the two armchairs were entirely covered with velvet nailed to the wooden frames. The rest of the bedroom was equally impressive, with bed-curtains and draperies for the bases and posts of the bed. Elsewhere in the house were 22 cabinets of ebony or tortoiseshell which had been made in Italy, the Low Countries or Germany. There were also Venetian mirrors and tables with

pietre dure inlays which stood beneath painted ceilings with Renaissance motifs.

France had lived through a long period of austerity and the underprivileged sections of the nobility and bourgeoisie endeavoured to right their position in a series of bitter struggles. The opposition group known as the Fronde, however, collapsed in confusion in 1653. With the power of the nobility thus eroded Louis XIV could divert them with the grandest of schemes — the settling of the court at Versailles. The King was 23 at Mazarin's death in 1661, and was ready to introduce all France to the rise of classicism in a series of great galleries and *salons*. They survive as witness to the fact that he achieved his aim in a style of complete grandeur.

Germany and Scandinavia

By the thirteenth century the Gothic style was dominant throughout Europe and had penetrated as far to the north and south as Norway and Portugal. It had spread rapidly and had also put its linear and patterned mark on metalwork and furniture. As very little German mediaeval furniture has survived even from the fourteenth century, it is difficult

Above: Detail from The Peasant Wedding by Peter Breughel the elder (c. 1525–69). This simple composition depicts a way of life in sixteenth-century Flanders unaffected by Italian ideas and status. The long refectory tables of joined planks of oak are flanked by long benches with splayed turned legs fitted into the upper seat. Such furniture was the creation of a joiner with a basic skill rather than a sophisticated repertoire of knowledge of ornament and design. (Kunsthistorisches Museum, Vienna) to establish how rooms were furnished. It may be assumed that the poor used expediency and no small amount of ingenuity to provide simple necessities — tables, benches and stools — which always have a certain dateless anonymity and span the years. They are found in the Flemish paintings of country scenes by Peter Breughel the elder — his *Peasant Wedding* (in the Kunsthistorisches Museum, Vienna) shows a typical bench and stool with splayed legs, strong, unpretentious, and in consequence disregarded.

In 1969 Max Piendl discovered a careful inventory dated 1376 in the archives at Ratisbon listing the property of Erhard der Rainer who lived in Lower Bavaria. He owned three benches and four trestle-tables, all with cushions; a round table and a bench; eight chests of maple, spruce, pine and limewood; eleven cupboards together with two store cupboards, one of which was of oak. There were also nine small letter-boxes, three of maple. We may assume that Rainer had beds but the inventory page is missing — he had mattresses and bed-linen enough for all the servants as well as the family. Very little of his furniture was of oak, which was not often used in southern Germany. Carved limewood and light-coloured maple of good grain served instead. With bright fabrics and a brocaded cloth threaded with gold for the table, the furniture in Rainer's house represented a good standard of living, and a sharp contrast to the peasant style.

By 1400 changes were taking place in Germany as a result of political, religious and economic expansion. The countries which now form Scandinavia, for example, relied on their trade connections with the ports of Hamburg and Bremen. There was a chance for itinerant craftsmen to succeed. Vert Stoss who lived for most of the latter half of the fourteenth century at Nuremberg was commissioned to provide a great carved altar in 1477 for the Polish city of Cracow. In triptych form it depicts the death of the Virgin Mary, surrounded by the twelve apostles. The two wings carry six representations of important moments in the life of the Virgin — carved with great virtuosity. It was this precise German skill which led to an even more important event than any altar by Vert Stoss — the invention in the mid-fifteenth century of printing. It was then possible with

Gutenberg's work with movable letters to combine them with impressions from wood-blocks, and later copper plates, to issue patterns and pattern-books. Artists learned of each other's ideas — furniture-makers could copy from the work of the Masters HS and HG, Peter Flötner and others.

Recent research by Simon Jervis has done much to clarify the importance of printed furniture designs prior to 1650. They are essential documents for the understanding of the development of furniture in an obscure period, although many of the designs were also destined to be used by a wider range of craftsmen such as goldsmiths and embroiderers. Those that portrayed perspective were of more use to the furniture-maker and the inlayer. He could of course widen his practical experience, as Vert Stoss had done, by travel. It has been shown that of some 400 foreign craftsmen who had come to London between 1511 and 1621, several were from Germany — 12 from Cologne. There were also other artists, such as Dürer, heir to the great Gothic artistic traditions, who journeyed abroad — in his case to northern Italy and later to Venice — thus coming into contact with Renaissance philosophy and art. The

German engravers soon turned to classical ornament and the supremacy of Gothic declined in favour of the Italian examples. Peter Flötner of Nuremberg may have made two journeys to Italy in the 1520s and he became one of the principal exponents of the Renaissance style in Germany. His design for a wooden door of about 1540 is a flamboyant affair with richly decorated pilasters, a tympanum of swirling foliation, and urns and cherubs over all — fit for a Medici palace. His beds are equally grand, four-posted in the Corinthian style.

Presses and cupboards of various specialized kinds survive from the fifteenth century in some profusion. In southern Germany there was a two-tiered cupboard used in church sacristies as a secure place to keep plate and precious books. In the north the *Schenkschieve* was a four-doored cupboard, but was used in sideboard fashion to store plate and documents and, in versatile form, to serve drinks to guests. Made in maple, pine, larch and limewood, they have foliated friezes in strong vertical and horizontal bands and are sometimes covered with coloured leather.

There were of course variants of the two-tier cupboard evolved in south-west Germany,

Above: This painting by Bartholomew Bassen is an attempt to carry the Renaissance beyond the Alps — there are vistas through the architectural screens on the left and a wonderful fireplace with an elaborate overmantel. The two-stage dresser on the right is Gothic in origin, but the coffered ceiling and the caryatid figures flanking the intricate door indicate the pervading influence of Italianate decoration. (Hessisches Landesmuseum, Darmstadt)

Bavaria and Austria. The Austrian cupboards have ornament in low relief, and shallow carving is also found on Bavarian examples — lines of flowers in precise *paterae* formation. The cupboard was universally useful and had its counterpart in the horizontal, long chest which was used for storing linen and, on occasion, food. It was usually raised on a Gothic pierced plinth with two carrying handles, a hinged lid, and often a brightly coloured interior of green, red, or blue. Salzburg was an important centre for their manufacture, with panels of rich elaborate tracery being executed in limewood and inlaid with oak and maple. The origins of the decoration may be traced to northern Italy up to the southern edge of the Alps — a natural transfer-point for decorative detail.

Solid tables in limewood, pine and maple disposed together in the same piece are common — the *Wangentisch* of about 1500. The legs are splayed at an angle with a low surrounding stretcher which gives great stability. A rarer type *(Schragentisch)* had cylindrical legs, turned or carved, placed diagonally. Four of the tables listed in Rainer's house in Bavaria were of this type.

Beds of the Gothic period are unusually rare apart from their depiction in engraved form. The mediaeval bed was usually a part of a small separate room, built into the wainscoting. Another kind has a tester or canopy which hangs from a tall backboard and is architectural in form, in that the tester has timber 'vaulting' in architectural style. The use of different woods affected the decorative treatment. The north German use of oak allowed for deep carving with expert use of the chisel. The south German blend of various soft woods, often in the same object, dictated a low relief, two-dimensional carving. Its flatness demanded accentuation by the use of colour and the selection of woods with attractive grain.

The highest forms of German furniture in respect of style and skill were undoubtedly the elaborate writing-desks or cabinets and the works in chiselled steel, produced at Nuremberg and Augsburg. German cabinets were exported in considerable numbers in the late sixteenth and early seventeenth centuries. The trade was monopolistic and affected the Spanish furniture market in particular, to such an extent that Philip III in retaliatory spirit banned further imports of Nuremberg cabinets into Spain and Portugal. In form the cabinet developed from the *vargueño*, which has a fall-front serving as a writing area, to one with hinged central doors. These enclosed from immediate view a variety of smaller drawers which could be utilized for the safe keeping and distribution of all those items beloved of collectors — coins, medals, jewels, miniatures. Wood was used but the precious

and semi-precious stones and filigree metal played no small part, the latter being an especial feature of Augsburg cabinets.

One of the most famous of the Augsburg cabinets, the *Kunstschrank*, was given a variant name, the *Wrangelschrank*, because Count Wrangel, commander of the Swedish forces in the Thirty Years War, took it as booty. It was made at Augsburg in 1566 and differs a little from the usual pattern in that its length is covered by two hinged doors. They open to reveal small drawers ornamented in boxwood flanked by coupled alabaster columns. They pale into a partial insignificance against the main doors which are decorated with intarsia of scenes of Hieronymus Bosch complexity showing animals and ruins.

In 1567 Lorenz Stoer issued his *Geometria et Perspectiva* at Augsburg — a book of designs for inlay on furniture reflecting his interest in the ruins of antiquity. Hieronymus Cock issued his *Preacipua Romanae Antiquitatis Ruinarum Monimenta* at Antwerp in 1551 which included many views of ruins. The same

*Left: This cabinet was
acquired by the City of
Augsburg and presented to
Gustavus Adolphus of
Sweden in 1632. Cabinets
like this were meant to be a
repository of wonders and
a display of the art of
the metalworkers and the
cabinet-makers. Ivory
and semi-precious
medallions were set into
ebony or lacquer panels.
The inner structure
consists of drawers of
various sizes including
secret and swivel drawers.
Such cabinets were gifts
worthy of royal owners and
patrons and were the
speciality of the Augsburg
artisans. (Courtesy of
Uppsala University,
Sweden)*

Above: Presentation of the Pommerscher Kunstschrank. The cabinet in the painting was ordered in Augsburg in 1610 by Duke Philipp II von Pommera. It was finished by 1616 and presented to him in the following year. Regrettably, it was destroyed during the Second World War. (Staatliche Museen, Berlin)

preoccupation is found in France at this time in a suite of prints by Leonard Thiry published by Du Cerceau in 1550.

These cabinets came to a triumphal conclusion with a splendid series initiated by Philip Hainhofer, a diplomat-collector and owner of a successful art-export business who had been born at Augsburg in 1578. The *Pommersche Kunstschrank*, ordered in 1610 by Duke Philipp II von Pommera, was destroyed in the Second World War in Berlin. The *Florentiner Kunstschrank* was acquired in 1628 by Leopold, the Grand Duke of Austria, as a gift to the Grand Duke of Tuscany, and is now in the Palazzo Pitti in Florence. The *Kunstschrank* of Gustavus Adolphus was first in Hainhofer's own collection and was then acquired by the City of Augsburg as a gift to Gustavus Adolphus of Sweden in 1632 —it is now in Uppsala University. They were bright stars of achievement in an already dazzling firmament of accomplishment.

Both Augsburg and Nuremberg were renowned centres for the production of intricate gold and silver work in a high Mannerist style, and of complex clocks. In addition they gave attention to elaborate furniture in chiselled steel and some of the most splendid pieces were those given by the City itself as presents to other ruling bodies or influential individuals. In 1574 Thomas Rucker was commissioned to make a chair to present to the Emperor Rudolf II. After a hundred years in Prague it passed into Sweden and finally England, where it has remained. It has an elaborate four-tier top rail which illustrates the Babylonian, Persian, Greek and Roman

monarchies. The centre roundel depicts Nebuchadnezzar's dream.

Most German chairs were of course much less elaborate than these flamboyant pieces. The bench, popular in Gothic times, continued in use superseded by more convenient chairs with slightly raked backs, no armrests, and on occasion upholstered in the Italian manner. There was also a chair in common use of a decorated X-formation with a leather back and seat. It was a popular style, found in many countries throughout the Gothic and Renaissance period, but did not always fold as its earlier prototype, the folding-stool, did.

The start of the Thirty Years War in 1618, however, brought to a quick end the German supremacy in the creation of prestige furniture. A religious war, it was fought with great bitterness and had strong political and feudal overtones added to the struggle. Military violence was rife, and it embroiled most of the European monarchies before it came to an uneasy halt in 1648.

The main architectural styles current in Renaissance Europe did not penetrate the northern Scandinavian countries to any considerable degree. The main inspiration in Swedish architecture and decoration of the sixteenth century came from the Low Countries as the castles of Gripsholm, Uppsala and Kalmar show. It was a scene dominated by foreigners — German portrait painters worked in Denmark, and the court painter of the 1560s, Melchior Lorichs, had trained in Italy and was Mannerist in style. The decorative arts followed suit in their allegiance to Flanders, but were given some direct impetus by the great royal building patrons, Frederick II and Christian IV in Denmark and Eric XIV and John III in Sweden. But again it was Dutch, French and German architects who restored and extended old castles and built new ones and gave them furniture that came from workshops beyond the Alps. Even in Norway, which understood the uses of timber and had fashioned it in exemplary manner, the old Stave churches were not provided with furniture of quality or style.

We have also seen that the trophies of war carried back into Sweden were the great cabinets made at Augsburg. They spawned no copies and gave no inspiration to craftsmen mesmerized by intricacies they did not understand. The engravings of Hans Vredeman de Vries were, however, very influential in Sweden, as in Germany, England and the Netherlands, in showing what could be done.

The Low Countries

In 1508 the Flemish painter, Jan Gossaert, called Mabuse, left for Italy and on his return to Flanders introduced classical ideas of figure studies, poses and perspective into his painting. He was aided in the transfer of

Renaissance ideas on these subjects by the work of the designer Hans Vredeman de Vries (1527–1604), who had moved through Germany and the Low Countries living at various towns such as Antwerp and Hamburg. He was a prolific producer of series of prints which blended together his studies of Renaissance ornament, architecture, and gardens. They were published in numerous editions and had a considerable influence on architecture and decoration throughout northern Europe. In particular his *Differents pourtraicts de menuiserie* of about 1588 has designs for several sorts of furniture which joiners could show to undecided customers. It was a pattern-book of a most beguiling kind, ranging from stools, tables and buffets, to very elaborate beds, some with sphinx-like figures supporting fluted posts and canopies. His son Paul, born in Antwerp in 1567 — in a city which had become the principal centre of a Flemish school of painters won over to Italianate ideas — also produced designs suitable for use by furniture-makers. There is a mid-sixteenth century stone table at Lacock Abbey, Wiltshire, which bears a strong resemblance to one of his designs.

The work of the two de Vries, father and son, was widespread, and they poured forth engravings which joined those of many who were similarly talented. Two such were Cornelis Bos and, especially, Cornelis Floris. They published designs which incorporated the new type of interlacing strapwork which the Italians had taken into France when working for François I at Fontainebleau in the 1520s.

The important architectural treatise of Sebastiano Serlio, which spread knowledge of the orders of architecture throughout Renaissance Europe, was also given a Flemish translation in 1539. Serlio's engravings were those which in title-page formality could be enlarged into the three-dimensional form of furniture. They were also typical of those engravings which by their wide adoption rid the Low Countries and many other places of the last vestiges of Gothic furniture. The cupboard, always important in the Gothic period, took on several roles — of chest, of proud flamboyant statement, and of storage. Intricate carved figures adorned the door-panels and the best examples have caryatids which support, or appear to support, the richly decorated friezes. They were cabinets which followed the success of the trade-guilds in defining the respective roles of cabinet-maker and carver. The cabinet-maker made the carcase and the carver overlaid it with pierced ornament and showed his particular

Above: Frans Franken II's painting, The Living Room in the house of Peter Paul Rubens. While the chairs are shown as simple turned or pegged frames enhanced by leather backs and seats, the cupboard, with its canted pilasters and built-up stand at the back, is more Renaissance in feeling than the furniture of any Protestant country at this time. (Nationalmuseum, Stockholm)

Right: Fifteenth-century cabinet from Flanders. The mask faces, caryatid figures and Corinthian-capped pilasters show how architectural style affected furniture. The cabinet stands on a decorated plinth with ball feet at the front and plain ones at the rear so that it could be set against the wall. (Rijksmuseum, Amsterdam)

talent in the creation of the caryatid and other figures.

Like Augsburg in Germany, Antwerp became an important centre for production of fine cabinets. They were not in metal however, but were veneered and painted. They had the usual complicated, profuse and richly adorned sets of drawers in which gold coins, jewels, shells and other curiosities could be stored, or almost lost in interlocking labyrinths of secret drawers at the back of seemingly solid wood façades. Ebony was a wood which was extensively used for veneering these small drawers, and ebony cabinets were exported throughout Europe. Many of them were also painted with mythological scenes, or beloved stories from the Old and New Testaments. The most characteristic have tortoiseshell mounted against a reddish foil. This throws the tortoiseshell into sharp contrast, rendered even more striking by the black ebony veneers. The original stands have often been altered or replaced but usually consisted of eight tapered columns surmounting ball feet and a solid lower platform.

Ebony was also occasionally used for chairs, but walnut was more usual by the early seventeenth century. Some were upholstered or covered in leather, velvet or various cloths kept in position by large brass nails. An examination of Dutch portraits and genre paintings will show many detailed views of chairs, chests, screens and interior views. The sitters in Rembrandt portraits, for example, are frequently depicted on a form of folding-chair. The bed was also important and appears in many paintings, sometimes built into the corner of the room depicted. They are of a more human scale than any of those in the engravings of the de Vries and look as though they might have afforded a comfortable rest undisturbed by any architectural extravagances. They would appear soon enough at the introduction of the Baroque style into a Flanders which, as the centre of the Counter-Reformation, used all the devices of Catholic propaganda against the strongly entrenched Protestant reformists. Henri Pirenne has written that 'the entire society was worked on, and so to speak moulded, by religion'. The Jesuit movement introduced generations to Greek and Roman cultures and numbered amongst its ranks scholars, philosophers, painters, architects, and not least Peter Paul Rubens. With his vibrant sensibility and considerable skills Rubens was an able leader and exponent of all that was best in early seventeenth-century Flemish art. His great panels for the gallery of the Luxembourg palace in Paris, painted from 1622 to 1625, deal with the history of Marie de' Medici. They tell of reality and of myth and, above all, of a patronage to which all artists from lowly carpenter to skilled carver were indebted.

Spain and Portugal

The strongly Catholic country of Spain took the classical rigours of the Renaissance in a severe, reformist spirit. In its architecture it prepared itself by ridding itself of Gothic and in its material progress it could look to the first 50 years of the sixteenth century as witnessing the defeat of the Moors, the discovery of America and the conquest of Mexico and Peru. These were events which were to excite the volatile temperament of its people to abandon intellectual austerity and lead them towards the heady exuberance of Baroque. Spain concentrated its architectural effort in the building of the palace and monastery of the Escorial — at once a contradiction in its geometry and austerity to the richness which followed. It also had a long period of regal stability in the reigns of Charles V (1516–66) and Philip II (1566–98). This encouraged every kind of creative achievement, and in furniture the extensive use of walnut, chestnut, poplar, pine and orangewood gave exotic variants to what was common elsewhere in Europe. The Americas also had silver — particularly in Peru — and this was imported and used in its normal role and as a decorative addition to furniture.

In the Museo de Artes Decorativas in Madrid it is possible to see a wide range of furniture which displays the main woods, fabrics and decorative motifs. Tables and chairs were frequently hung with soft leather or fringed brocade studded with large brass nails. The chairs, called *sillónes de fraileros*, are the most typical of Spanish seat furniture, and were sometimes hinged to allow for folding and easy transportation. Most tables were covered with fringed 'table-cloths' and at a later stage were given filigree iron stretchers and ornate slender legs. Fabric also covered the four posts of the bed, the ornament being confined to the carved headboard.

The principal and richest piece of Spanish furniture, however, was the cabinet with a fall-front mounted on a stand. The vargueño, as it has been called since the nineteenth century, was usually placed on a stand (*pie de puente*) and was frequently decorated in the rich Plateresque style which resembled the grotesque ornament found on silver work. A superb vargueño in the Victoria and Albert Museum, London, is in the usual walnut with marquetry side panels, and the fall-front has carved boxwood reliefs mounted on a velvet ground, flanked by carved portrait heads. Other versions have *trompe l'oeil* landscapes, and some emulate the German Augsburg silver cabinets by having gilt-bronze plaques mounted in ebony.

In 1580 Philip II claimed the throne of Portugal and united the two Iberian kingdoms. During the seventeenth century its joiners, carpenters and turners created a national style of furniture-making which was outstanding in Europe for its use of extravagantly turned rosewood, imported from the Portuguese colony of Brazil. This was overlaid with pierced ornaments in gilt-brass. The great Benedictine and Cistercian abbeys in northern Portugal had long needed choir stalls, lecterns and monumental pieces of church furniture and many of these were garnished with gilt-brass. Both Spain and Portugal were obsessed with the search for precious metals in the New World, and these, together with brass, were then set over the walnut and local chestnut. During the second half of the sixteenth century Europe had been flooded with gold from the Americas. By the early seventeenth century this was no longer arriving and the colonial power of Portugal declined in the 1640s. Its furniture had long been influenced by trading contacts with the Orient and items appeared with lacquer and inlaid panels of ivory. Trade laid the basis, therefore, for the superb Baroque achievements in gilded and exotic woods which rivalled the finest in Europe.

England

By the time England's major writer and poet Geoffrey Chaucer died in 1400 the country had started the establishment of independence from French thought and contemporary European literature. The French had been setting the pace, too, in architecture with supreme achievements in the Gothic style, and Henry III's Westminster Abbey reflected this mood. But a growing disinterest in French ways led to the establishment of the Perpendicular style, a cheaper form of linear decoration in cut stone which appealed to generations who had been impoverished by war, the decline of agriculture and the ravages of the Black Death. Timber had always been abundant in England and the knowledge of working it had led to the creation of many fine roofs of hammer-beam type and also to the formation of strong guilds of joiners and of carpenters.

The hall of the great house was the hub of

Above: English armchair of about 1600, made of oak inlaid with various woods. The cresting and the brackets are carved with foliage. The legs and arm supports are fluted, the arms themselves being carved from a single piece of wood. (Victoria & Albert Museum, London)

Left: This early sixteenth-century English coffer has unusual horizontal linenfold panels, and is an example of the type of furniture made for small manor-houses or churches. (Courtesy of Leonard Lassalle, Tunbridge Wells)

the family's existence and was impressive in
its splendour. Hangings were rich and plentiful with the frequent use of covers and
cushions made in dyed wool. There were
heavy travelling chests — some in iron or
iron-bound wood. Benches, boards on trestles,
a dresser for the display of plate and great
chairs at the high table were surrounded by
ornate and abundant tapestries, illuminated
books and manuscripts on lecterns, and
musical instruments such as small organs and
virginals. The religious devotion of the time
found its expression not only in the building
of many private chapels and parish churches
but in their decoration. Apart from the splendid
roofs — particularly to be found in the counties
of Norfolk and Suffolk — choir stalls and
rood-screens were lavishly embellished. The
northern schools of woodcarvers who created
the choir stalls at Lincoln, Ripon, Beverley
and Chester were pre-eminent and their skill
was also extended to the misericord seats
with carvings of animals, foliage and domestic
scenes of amusing reality.

The evident skill depicted in the carving
of the misericords was not confined to church
furniture. In the earlier house a sombre
interior had been disguised by tapestry. The
rising middle class now felt a desire for
greater comfort and saw no reason why they
should not pursue it. They wanted more
furniture, better in construction by being
framed and panelled rather than of simple
design. At the beginning of Henry VII's
reign the simple chests and walls were
decorated with panelling of varying widths,
pattern and Renaissance detail — particularly
the Romayne style, where carved heads were
surrounded by a classical wreath. When
King's College Chapel at Cambridge was ready
to be equipped in the early sixteenth century,
the organ-screen (built in about 1532) was
carved in full-blooded Renaissance style. It
was a transitional point between mediaeval
and modern. The hall of the house was still
impressive but changes in hospitality, the
use of servants and estate management meant
that it declined in use. Other rooms became

more frequent and were defined by particular uses such as eating, relaxing and sleeping.

The most skilled furniture craftsman of this period of the early sixteenth century was the cofferer. The travelling coffer, usually of oak covered in leather, and tooled and gilt like an elaborate book-binding, was an important object for storage of papers, valuables and clothes. The early examples in iron had elaborate locking systems with inner and outer locks—a good example of 1427 is preserved at the Guildhall in London—and displayed an accomplished technique in their creation. There was still, however, a sharp demarcation between the oak furniture produced for church and small manor-house and the grander objects for the larger house in exotic woods such as ebony, holly and box.

The grand conception of Nonsuch Palace was planned in 1538 for Henry VIII by Nicholas Bellin of Modena, who acted as adviser to the chief officers of the King's Works. Bellin provided the link by which the Renaissance style, in all its jumble of Italian and French pattern, transferred to England. No effort was spared to make Nonsuch grand and enduring, though sadly it was pulled

down in the seventeenth century. A series of chests exists, heavily inlaid with designs representing formal architectural views—the so-called 'Nonsuch chests'. Recent research suggests, however, that this association was a nineteenth-century fantasy created because of a superficial resemblance of the marquetry panels to Henry VIII's palace. For the most part they represent contemporary buildings in the 'antique' style and were created by continental furniture craftsmen working in London in the late sixteenth century.

From this time the big houses of Elizabethan and Jacobean venturers incorporated not only Renaissance ideas of symmetry but also —as at Hatfield, Charlton and Bramshill— the well-proportioned loggias that suggested the white stucco and rich grotesque painting and furnishings of villas under a hot Italian sun. Furniture also started to incorporate within its repertory of decoration the interlaced strapwork that Rosso Fiorentino took as an idea from Italy to incorporate in his Gallery at Fontainebleau in 1535. Before long the Fleming, Cornelis Floris, was filling the pages of his pattern-books with it, and the Elizabethans prepared to abandon themselves

Above: The High Great Chamber of Hardwick Hall, Derbyshire. This house was built in 1597 for Elizabeth, Countess of Shrewsbury, 'Bess of Hardwick', to the designs of Robert Smythson. It typifies the emergence of the Renaissance in England. The marble chimney-piece is probably the work of Thomas Accres, a marble carver who also worked at Wollaton and the first Chatsworth. The details in the house are based on architectural pattern-books by Sebastiano Serlio and also reflect Flemish sources. (National Trust, Hardwick Hall, Derbyshire) to a riot of robust and vulgar styles. Before the Reformation in 1534, however, England had been able to boast few 'gorgeous, sumpteous, superfluous buildings' despite all the opportunities which the decoration and furnishing of such houses gave to artists intent on furthering their skills.

One of the best documented of the late Elizabethan houses is Hardwick Hall, Derbyshire, the creation of the much-married Elizabeth, Countess of Shrewsbury — 'Bess of Hardwick' — and her architect, Robert Smythson. The death of her husband in 1590 made Bess very rich and she started at once to build a new and grander house than the one a few hundred yards distant on which she had been lavishing her attention. Hardwick was built over seven years, Bess moving into it in October 1597, and the famous inventory of its contents, dated 1601, was published by The Furniture History Society in 1971. It shows the humble alongside the grander pieces such as the famous table, still in the High Great Chamber. This was made in 1568 upon the marriage of Bess's son, Henry Cavendish, with her step-daughter Grace Talbot. Her coat of arms impaled by Henry's appears amid strapwork ornament upon the walnut top which is also richly veneered with a profusion of coloured woods depicting musical instruments — viols, lutes, rebecs, flutes and sackbuts — an open music book, flowers, playing cards and a romantic legend.

The use of marble on furniture, while so well understood in Italy, was rare in England. Another inventory — that of 1590 of the possessions of John, Lord Lumley — shows, however, in rare illustrations in the inventory itself such a marble-topped table on six bulbous legs. None of these inventory pieces is known to survive but the tables are shown in the company of marble cisterns, fountains and lavabos, decorated with the Lumley arms and owing much in form to the drawings of Du Cerceau. Richly upholstered chairs were just as fashionable and the Lumley inventory shows that in the three residences listed there were '76 chares of clothe of gold, velvet and sylke'. The Great Chamber at Lumley Castle also contained two draw-leaf tables — a type which could be extended by leaves beneath the main top and which seems to have come into use in the 1550s.

These late Elizabethan inventories also contain references to the court cupboard, an open structure of three tiers which resembled those in France and the Low Countries. It was used for the display of plate and pewter and at a later stage, when enclosed, for the storage of these items and of food. Beds followed the Renaissance pattern of a richly carved tester being supported on a carved and inlaid headboard, frequently depicting bas-relief portraits. The posts, which first came into use about 1500, were usually turned or made up, in more elaborate examples, of combinations of joinery and ornament — carved lion supports and strapwork and arabesque scrolls in box and holly. There is a superb example of about 1605 at Berkeley Castle, Gloucestershire, which has small figures in the framing of the bedposts.

Below: This late sixteenth-century English chest has architectural arcading with pilasters and inlaid decoration. The Renaissance was imperfectly understood and much abused beyond the Alps, but this piece represents a simple attempt to master the ornamental intricacies. (National Trust, Hardwick Hall, Derbyshire)

The growth of trade which came about due to the efforts of the late Elizabethan merchant venturers encouraged an interest in the decoration of other countries and provided the means to indulge in copies. It also allowed for the occasional extravagance which can be found in the silver furniture at the great house at Knole, Kent, built for the Earl of Dorset about 1607. It was a period which recognized quality and even more acutely its absence. There was also an increasing use of walnut in less grand pieces than the silver pieces at Knole.

The early seventeenth century in England was characterized, however, by the influence of classical architecture. This was encouraged due to the travels of England's first strictly classical architect Inigo Jones, made in the entourage of Thomas Howard, second Earl of Arundel. The Earl became one of the greatest of English art collectors, was a leading figure in court circles and was intent on gathering works of art abroad. It gave Jones the opportunity to study Italian art and architecture for a second time — he had paid a previous visit to Italy in the last year of the sixteenth century. His return to England on both occasions gave encouragement to those intent on shaking off the rigours then imposed on interior design and furnishings. In 1615–16 Jones was appointed Surveyor of the King's Works, with all that meant in the supervision of work in the royal palaces. In the 10 years that followed his appointment he worked on

some 16 tasks for the King and Queen and other patrons of high rank. His approach was precise and moderate but the furniture in the interiors he created was, nevertheless, very elaborate.

The travels Jones and his contemporaries made accustomed English eyes to foreign decorative trends. Upholstery for the backs and seats of chairs came into widespread use in a growing search and demand for more comfort. At the same time there was much that was humble and practical. The university archives at Oxford contain hundreds of inventories of the 'goods and chattels' of 706

Top left: One of the 'Nonsuch' chests made in England about 1600. The front is divided into panels which are crudely inlaid. (National Trust, Montacute House, Somerset)

Above left: Early seventeenth-century English cupboard in carved and inlaid oak. (Temple Newsam House, Leeds) university members from 1568 to 1699. Those for the early seventeenth century show the ways in which various rooms were furnished. The main wood in use was oak, with occasional exceptions referring to walnut, elm, deal, cedar and the sweet chestnut which John Evelyn noted in his *Silva* was, next to oak, one of the woods 'most sought after by the Carpenter and Joyner'. There were many varieties of table, but most chairs were versions of extended stools with plenty of materials available, by the start of the Civil War, for their upholstery. Various leathers, Turkey work, baize and other fabrics

and rushes for wicker chairs have been listed. Couches, settles, close stools, beds, desks, chests and chests of drawers, cupboards and presses, boxes, screens, bookcases and candlestands are among the many items which furnished Oxford colleges. The greater items in gilt gesso were made in later years and belonged to those houses which Ben Jonson categorized in his poem *To Penshurst* — 'proud ambitious heaps and nothing else . . .'. The trauma of the Civil War and the death of Inigo Jones in 1652 sealed off the influences of the early years from those which followed the King's Restoration in 1660.

FORMAL SPLENDOUR
The Baroque age

Furniture is one of our most tangible links with the past, presenting us with direct visual evidence of a whole way of life centuries remote. Yet it can easily mislead. Without knowing from a whole range of other sources, from paintings and drawings, from contemporary literature and manuscripts, just how this furniture was placed and used, we could form the impression that these distant ancestors lived roughly in the same way as we do, that their tables, chairs and beds served just the same simple purpose as ours. Nothing could in fact be further from the truth, particularly with furniture of the Baroque period.

The Counter-Reformation, begun by the rigorous reforms of the Council of Trent in 1563, is always held to have precipitated the Baroque style, and there is no doubt that the arts were constantly employed to fulfil its primarily religious and political aims. Bernini's famous *St Teresa in Ecstasy* at Santa Maria della Vittoria in Rome, or Rubens' *Assumption of James I* on the ceiling of the Banqueting House, Whitehall, are unashamed propaganda, for Church and State respectively. Some of the most elaborate pieces of seventeenth-century furniture were made with the same obvious intention, like Prince Eugene's state bed at the Monastery of St Florian, borne by chained Turks to represent his relief of Vienna. The great beds

with their gilded balustrades, the canopies of state, the tiered buffets with their dazzling displays of plate, even the more utilitarian pieces, like the endless chairs and stools in regimented rows along the walls, served equally for propaganda, though in a less direct way. They were the necessary equipment for the ritual of a prince's life, the stage props (appropriately, since their design was so often derived from the theatre) for the daily performance of kingship.

The divine right of kings, that favourite theory of the Counter-Reformation, produced in seventeenth-century Europe one of the most rigidly structured, hieratic societies ever to exist. Louis XIV's self-identification with the sun-god Apollo brought the theory to its most advanced, quasi-religious stage. His *levée*, his audience, his meals (taken invariably in the public gaze), his various entertainments, and finally his *coucher*, became the secular offices of the day, at which the courtiers of Versailles officiated — in the same way as priests observed the daily offices of Terce and Nones, Mattins and Vespers.

The extremes of formality to which this led, not only in France but in every country open to French and Italian influences, reaching a climax in the small German courts of the early eighteenth century, must be clearly understood to realize how Baroque furniture came to be made. A state bed like those illustrated in the engravings of Daniel Marot is explicable only as a ceremonial object, an incredibly expensive but rarely used status symbol. The prince in his own palace, or the distinguished visitor to another's house, would be escorted by a large number of attendants and with great solemnity to his bedchamber, would be disrobed and put to bed. After the departure of the crowd, he would almost invariably retire to a smaller, warmer and far more comfortable dressing-room immediately behind the bedchamber. The balustrade served an even more cere-monial and less utilitarian role, separating those functionaries honoured enough to play an active part in the proceedings from those of lesser rank who merely observed from outside the bed alcove. The Duke of Portland as English ambassador to Louis XIV in 1698 was given the taper-stick to hold at one of the king's *couchers*, and this was considered a great honour since usually only Princes of the Blood were allowed inside the balustrade.

The Canopy of State, though comparatively few examples survive, was another key feature of the Baroque interior. The most likely explanation of its development is that it stems from the mediaeval practice of lords receiving requests, administering justice, and later even eating, from an armchair or throne on a raised dais with a canopy above. In time the

chair and canopy became in their own right symbols of state, to which obeisance had to be made whether they were occupied or not. Strict rules existed for the proportions of canopies proper to each rank: the backcloth of a king's canopy for instance reached the ground, while a duke's would be shorter and an earl's still less. Strict rules also existed for the use of quite ordinary chairs and stools. In general, armchairs (which seem to have derived from the traditional X-frame chairs of state, and placed under canopies from the sixteenth to the mid-seventeenth century) were reserved for sovereigns only at court, and nobles in their own houses; chairs with backs could be used only by the most privileged (usually members of the royal family); and at Versailles it was a much coveted honour to be able to use either the stool called the *tabouret*, or the *pliant*, an X-frame folding stool. Most people had to remain standing.

The placing of furniture in rooms was invariably formal, and usually followed the same pattern, adopted all over Europe. Chairs were placed very close to each other in straight lines along inside walls, while against the pier between the windows stood an almost inevitable set of matching furniture: a pier-glass with a table under it, flanked by a pair of candlestands or *guéridons*. Over and over again this arrangement can be found, executed in different techniques: from ebony Goanese sets of the 1650s, to Dutch and English floral marquetry of the 1680s, to Boulle and silver sets of the next decade and to gilt gesso versions of the early eighteenth century. Such was the rigidity of Baroque furniture arrangement that Louis XIV is said to have sharply rebuked one of his mistresses who had brought out a chair and left it in the middle of the room, thereby destroying its architecture. The almost complete absence of furniture in the centre of a Baroque interior is perhaps slightly misleading, for at any time chairs could be brought out from the wall by footmen and card-tables or eating-tables set up. These were, however, only temporary arrangements and the architectural character of the *chambre de parade* was at all other times preserved.

The use of allegory, that favourite Baroque device, became more and more standardized in the decoration of different rooms: staircases would be painted with Assemblies of the Gods, so that receptions of ambassadors or con-courses of courtiers should be appropriately mirrored by the divinities above; ante-chambers used for dining now might have Ganymede or Bacchus to inspire the company below to food and drink; bedchambers told the story of Psyche; and long galleries the Labours of Hercules. Furniture, made always for a particular place in a particular room,

Above: A great lady at her toilette, from an anonymous picture by a late seventeenth-century French artist. This crudely painted but charming evocation of contemporary life shows the typical arrangement of a Baroque state bedchamber: the bed itself stands in an alcove, with tall chairs, usually called backstools, ranged in straight lines against the walls on either side. (Musée des Beaux Arts, Rheims) was of course influenced by this iconographical plan. Tables used in eating-rooms began to be decorated with vine leaves, and chairs in bedrooms to be carved with cupids holding bows and arrows.

The sequence of rooms also followed a strict pattern in practically every Baroque house, from stuccoed palaces in Sicily to granite castles in Scotland. The progression from great staircase to guard, presence, withdrawing and bedchambers, with closets and 'cabinet' rooms beyond, became almost universal, even if certain rooms assumed greater importance in some countries than in others. At Versailles, for example, the sequence began from either side of the building converging on the King's bedchamber in the centre, while in Germany a gigantic staircase *(or Treppenhaus)* with an equally vast hall of assembly usually occupied the centre leading to suites of apartments either side.

In general, while the size of the rooms diminished during this progression, the decoration and the furniture became richer. Eventually those fortunate enough to have a private interview with the great person might be ushered through the state bedchamber to a room no more than nine or ten feet square, either hung with the most expensive Genoa velvet and with the choicest small pictures from the collection, or, as in Queen Mary's Water Gallery at Hampton Court, crammed with porcelain crowded onto the walls on tiny brackets—or laden with glass as at Frederik IV's castle of Rosenborg in Denmark. 'Cabinet' rooms like these, partly developed from the idea of the Renaissance princes' 'Wunderkabinetts', were also devised to give some privacy, impossible in the vast halls and galleries at the centre of the palace, permanently thronged with suitors. The clear distinction between state-rooms, used solely for great occasions and for public display, and private apartments, used for everday living, began to develop gradually during the Baroque period, though it did not reach its fullest expression until houses like Holkham and Kedleston, later in the eighteenth century, were built with entirely separate family wings. The Baroque 'cabinet' room or closet pointed the way to this solution however, and with its upholstered furniture pioneered a wholly new attempt at comfort, with 'sleeping chayres' (as they are described in English inventories) whose backs could be adjusted by means of ratchets, daybeds, wing chairs and 'squabs'—low, caned stools with small frames and enormous cushions. All these were of course supplied by upholsterers who, towards the end of the seventeenth century, began to supplant the carvers, up to that time easily the most important Baroque furniture-makers.

Left: The ante-chamber to the Queen's Bedchamber at Ham House, Surrey, furnished by the Duchess of Lauderdale in the 1670s. It exemplifies the passion for lacquer, part of the taste for the exotic which was so typical of the Baroque era. The artificially grained wainscoting, the damask and velvet wall-hangings, and the placing of the furniture around the walls are all as they would have been originally. (National Trust, Ham House, Surrey)

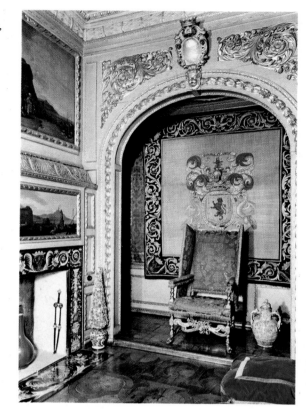

More important than this change, however, is the emergence during the Baroque period of a new phenomenon, that of the universal designer. The seeds of this idea, as with so many other components of the style, are to be found in early seventeenth-century Rome, with the total unity of Bernini's, Borromini's or da Cortona's church interiors. The extension of this practice to secular interiors quickly followed and spread north. As might be expected it received its strongest expression at Versailles where Charles Le Brun and Jean Bérain between them controlled absolutely, thanks to the ruthless order of Colbert's system, the appearance of every room. Their dictatorship in matters of design was helped by the strict guild system operating in France, which meant that an important piece of furniture might have to pass through the hands of five or six master-craftsmen working in different workshops at different techniques. Obviously the co-ordination of a *dessinateur* was essential to ensure harmony and unity in the final result.

In the hands of Bérain's most famous pupil, Daniel Marot, this treatment of whole rooms as a unity spread to Holland and England. The Adam brothers are often credited with being the first to design complete interiors 'in key', from plasterwork ceilings to carpets to sofas and tables and even door-knobs; in reality Marot was doing exactly the same 70 or 80 years earlier. His engraved designs cover every aspect of the decorative arts — patterns for silks, sedan chairs, clocks, beds, chairs, garden urns, painted ceilings — and his series of views of rooms show the care with which even the smallest piece of furniture had been designed and placed to achieve an effect of unity.

Unlike the spread of Renaissance ornament through Europe, which was a relatively uncomplicated northward movement, the Baroque is difficult to trace geographically. To follow its course country by country, as in the following pages, can therefore be misleading. While Italy, for instance, can be said to be the cradle of the Baroque, one of its most distinctive forms of furniture, the massive pietra-dura cabinet, was almost certainly derived from furniture made in Antwerp, Augsburg and Nuremberg. In other countries, such as Portugal and Holland, furniture design and technique was at least as much influenced by their contacts with the East, as with other parts of Europe. The discovery of new techniques in themselves gave certain places a virtual monopoly of certain pieces: the perfection of veneering made the Low Countries the home of floral marquetry from the early seventeenth century, while England after the Restoration was similarly the primary source of clocks. The Baroque was in fact a truly international style, not only because of the increase of imports and exports (velvet from Genoa, leather from Spain, marble from Livorno) but because the improvement of communications also brought increased mobility. In the past famous foreign artists had been summoned to distant courts — Torrigiani by Henry VII, Leonardo by François I — but from the middle of the seventeenth century more obscure sculptors, plasterers or furniture-makers began to move of their own accord to wherever the greatest demand for their services appeared to be. Louis XIV's expulsion of the Huguenots certainly played a large part in the diffusion of French Baroque forms to the rest of Europe, but it is interesting that a number of the best craftsmen who left France in the 1690s were in fact Catholics, forced to find employment elsewhere after the closure of the Gobelin factory and retrenchment at Versailles to pay for Louis' wars.

The inter-marrying of so many furniture-making, designing, carving or painting families also began to set up such a complicated international web of relationships that it is hard to disentangle influences and movements generally. It is typical for instance that the Flemish-born Pierre Golle, perhaps the most famous *marqueteur* in Paris before Boulle, should at the time of his death have owed money for glue and nails to a London cabinet-maker, John Johnson. Golle's brother Cornelius was another furniture-maker, practising in England, and both were brothers-in-law of Daniel Marot, William III's architect in The Hague. In turn Marot's own family included two engravers, four furniture-makers, five painters and a goldsmith, divided almost equally between France and Holland. Relationships such as these are typical, and should be a warning against seeing Baroque furniture simply in terms of national characteristics, distinct as these may seem initially.

Political and economic touchstones are rather safer. The Baroque has already been described as the style of absolutism, and in general the more despotic the system, the grander and more elaborate its setting. Florence under the later Medici and Venice under its oligarchy (a republic but scarcely a democracy), France under Louis XIV and the German courts after his death, reactionary and traditionalist, are the true homes of the Baroque. In England it was a court style abruptly halted after William III's failure to control Parliament and the advent of a limited monarchy in 1714. In the Low Countries, comparison between Rubens' house in Antwerp with its exuberant twisted columns and rich furniture, and the Town Hall in Amsterdam, altogether more restrained and classical, a monument to civic pride, leaves no doubt as to the political connotations of the style. It was no accident that the financial collapse in France after Louis XIV's death, and the more relaxed social atmosphere of the Régence, should have brought about the birth of a new and less rigid style, the Rococo.

Italy

Like so many useful words which have come to sum up a whole ideal, whether political or artistic, the Italian *barocco* began life as a term of abuse. Originally used by those still steeped in the order and balance of the early Renaissance to describe the tortured and grotesque, almost surrealist, exaggeration of Giulio Romano and his followers, we now think of the Baroque more as a synthesis of those two opposing attitudes — as seen in the work of Bernini and Cortona. Movement is still the key to their work (and even more to the work of Borromini), but it is balanced in the play of forces, in projection and recession, whether applied to a whole façade or to a mere confessional. The excitement is there, but it never oversteps the bounds of authority.

As an authoritarian, propagandist style the Baroque is often held to have been born at the Council of Trent in 1563. But although the new militant atmosphere of the Counter-Reformation undoubtedly affected painting and sculpture in the following generation, it was not until the early seventeenth century that this impetus began to reach the decorative arts. As always it was a case of supply and demand. Rome, which had remained weak and underpopulated ever since its sack by the French in 1520, was now once more the seat

of a powerful Papacy, entering perhaps the period of its greatest prosperity. Vast town-planning schemes and the rebuilding of innumerable *palazzi* resulted in a ferment of creative activity.

Utilitarian furniture for the private apartments of these great houses continued to be made extremely simply by carpenters or joiners and little effort was made, unlike in England and France later in the century, to make these pieces of any artistic value. For the state apartments, however, and in particular for the gallery which was where the best pictures were hung and where the artistic ambitions of the great Roman families were primarily displayed, huge console tables or cabinets were made by leading sculptors, fresh from carving statues for churches or fountains. A legacy of the Renaissance still

Above: The nuptial chamber in Villa La Rocca, Soragna, in northern Italy, decorated in about 1690. The ceremonial character of a Baroque state bedchamber is clear from this dazzling gilded room which is more like the chancel and high altar of a cathedral than a domestic interior. (Villa La Rocca, Soragna)

64

Above: This view of the nuptial chamber at La Rocca shows two large mirrors with frames decorated in blue verre eglomisée which come from Murano, the island in the Venetian lagoon famous for its glass-making. The gilt thrones and console tables, carved with a riotous assemblage of shells, foliage, birds and cupids, are in the manner of Brustolon and Corradini. (Villa La Rocca, Soragna)

very much alive in seventeenth-century Rome was the idea of the artist as an all-round craftsman, to whom painting a Crucifixion, carving a *Pietà*, designing a church or making a piece of furniture ought to come equally easily.

This influence of sculpture on Roman Baroque furniture was to be of paramount importance for the spread of the style all over Italy, and later in the century to the rest of Europe. Perhaps the best known piece of furniture ever made, Bernini's great Throne of St Peter, a giant's chair borne aloft on a swirl of clouds at the east end of the Apostle's own basilica, became a model for the huge gilded Baroque thrones which stood in the Audience Chambers of Roman princely families like the Pamphili or the Borghese. The console tables with thick tops of jasper

imported from Sicily, or of marble from elsewhere in Italy, were often supported by near life-size figures, like the famous Turkish captives at the Palazzo Colonna. A splendid pair of tables at the Palazzo Spada, made for Cardinal Bernadino Spada's new wing designed by Borromini in the 1640s, each have two great eagles supporting the slab on their heads and outstretched wings. Perhaps the ultimate in this totally representational approach to furniture was the state bed designed by Bernini's pupil J P Schor for the lying-in of the Princess Colonna in 1663. In the form of a huge shell, it was borne across windswept waves by four seahorses, while, above, a dozen or more putti held back gold brocade curtains.

In general, beds in Rome, and elsewhere in Italy, were not made with canopies until the late seventeenth century; their decoration was then confined to heavily carved posts at the four corners. If console tables with their thickly gilt sphinxes, tritons, putti or mermaids were the most ambitious pieces, a certain number of cabinets were also made. But these mostly date from after 1650 and were inspired by Florentine or northern precedents. One particularly fine example with ivory reliefs after famous paintings, designed by the architect Carlo Fontana and made between 1678 and 1680 by the brothers Domenico and Francesco Stainhart, is at the Palazzo Colonna.

In Venice, as much as in Rome, state-room furniture was almost entirely the province of the sculptor, and if anything the division was wider between simple functional pieces which filled the family apartments at the top of every palazzo, and the massive ornament-loaded furniture intended for the vast rooms of the *piano-nobile* looking over the Grand Canal. Longhi's genre scenes of Venetian life never show one of those armchairs carved all over with wriggling putti, or those overloaded tables, only the plainest leather-seated backstools and ungilded cabinets in the family apartments. Evidently, sumptuous furniture was not only made by sculptors but regarded in the same light as sculpture: strictly to look at, and not to use.

Undoubtedly the greatest Venetian furniture-maker of the seventeenth century was Andrea Brustolon. Born in Belluno in 1662 and employed first of all on carving crucifixes for local churches, he went to Venice and became at the age of 15 an assistant to the Genoese sculptor Filippo Parodi then working on the tomb of a Venetian patriarch, Francesco Morosini, for the church of San Nicolo da Tolentino. Contemporary documents tell us that Brustolon planned a visit to Rome, but not whether he actually went. His naturalistic and allegorical approach to furniture, however, may well be derived from Roman practice. Brustolon's fame rests on only one securely documented suite of furniture, the amazing chairs, side-table and candlestands made for Pietro Venier and now at the Ca' Rezzonico in Venice. On the basis of this, however, he has been credited with several other sets in the same style, amongst them one for the Correr family (now also in the Ca' Rezzonico) and one for the famous villa of the Pisani at Stra (now in the Quirinale Palace, Rome). The Correr chairs are if possible even less functional than the Venier suite. Their attenuated figures borne on a tidal wave of acanthus leaves must be some of the most beautiful and uncomfortable armrests ever devised. In 1699 Brustolon returned to his

Above: The Brustolon Room in the Palazzo Rezzonico, Venice, contains a famous suite of furniture made for a Venetian patrician, Pietro Venier, by Andrea Brustolon (1662–1732), the greatest Venetian sculptor-cum-cabinet-maker of the late seventeenth century. The vase stand on the left, made to hold three huge Oriental porcelain jars, incorporates the figures of Hercules, Cerberus, the Hydra and Classical river gods carved in boxwood. The guéridons are in the shape of negro captives with boxwood chains around their necks. (Ca' Rezzonico, Venice)

66

Right: A prie-dieu, veneered in ebony with pietra-dura mosaics and lapis lazuli columns. This piece, finished in 1687, is the work of the Grand Ducal workshops in Florence under the direction of Leonardo van der Vinne. The use of semi-precious hardstones is typically Florentine, though the openwork decoration round the central monogram of Christ is more unusual and demonstrates the northern influences of van der Vinne. (Palazzo Pitti, Florence)

here may even explain how candlestands came to be called 'guéridons', a word derived from a famous Moorish galley slave.

Above all, however, Venice was known for its glass. Since the late Middle Ages, the islands of Murano and Torcello in the Venetian lagoon had become centres of a glass-making industry unrivalled in Europe until Colbert's establishment of a factory in Paris in 1665, and the growth of England's Lambeth and Vauxhall works after 1700. Besides the large plates which were so much in demand, the Venetians developed for their own use elaborate glass sconces (wall lights) shaped like Baroque cartouches, and the enormous chandeliers still so much a feature of Venetian palaces, glowing with multi-coloured flowers and white opaque glass branches.

In many ways the development of Baroque furniture in Genoa followed a parallel path to Venice despite their distance from each other in geographical terms and their frequent conflict of mercantile interests. The system of oligarchic government in both meant that a certain number of immensely powerful families, some old, some *nouveau riche*, but all determined to outdo their rivals in ostentation and prestige, created a tremendous demand in architecture and the arts. In Genoa one particular street, the Strada Nuova (now Via Garibaldi) became, like the Grand Canal, lined with palaces jostling against each other

Below right: The Doge's throne, made in Venice about 1725, probably by Antonio Corradini. Corradini's work forms something of a bridge between the Baroque and the Rococo styles. The putti and mermaids riding horses are in the old allegorical tradition (referring to Venice's naval traditions), but the C- and S-scrolls which give movement to the whole composition point to a lighter and freer style in the years ahead. (Ca' Rezzonico, Venice)

native Belluno where he died in 1732, and where many of his furniture designs in this same extravagant style can still be found in the Museo Civico.

Brustolon's immediate successor as the leading furniture-maker in Venice seems to have been another sculptor, Antonio Corradini. The peculiarly Venetian use of natural woods in strong, contrasting colours was abandoned by him in favour of the more usual Baroque method of gilding, quicker and easier for the carver since it enabled soft woods like pear and lime to be used. A splendid throne by Corradini in the Ca' Rezzonico shows in its bold curves and scrolls how wood could be made to look as tractable and plastic as plaster. Another kind of furniture for which Venice became famous in the late seventeenth and early eighteenth centuries was lacquer, the technique of japanning having been learnt early on through Venice's trading contacts with the East. Green and gold lacquer, like the splendid set of furniture at the Palazzo Querini-Stampalia, became something of a speciality and continued to be made right through the Rococo period. Ebony blacka-moor candlestands were again a typically Venetian form, much sought after by foreign travellers and the epitome of the Venetians' love of carnival and fancy dress. Their origins on both sides. Their forbidding exteriors, immortalized by Rubens' celebrated engravings, concealed an explosion of gilding, mirrors and rich textiles within. Again like Venice, the initial impetus came from Rome: Filippo Parodi (1630–1702), perhaps the best-known Genoese carver of the late seventeenth century, worked in Bernini's studio from 1655 to 1661 and the three-dimensional nature of his furniture, and that of his son Domenico, is explained by the fact that both were primarily sculptors in marble. Domenico Parodi (1668–1740) was the maker of a combined pier-glass and table, now in the Palazzo Rosso, Genoa, which has claims to be one of the most megalomaniac pieces of furniture ever made. But another sculptor, Anton Maria Maragliano, was equally adept at monumental work of the same kind.

Genoa's major contribution to the Baroque interior was, however, the development of the richest furnishing materials to be obtained anywhere in Europe. Rich cut velvets in reds, greens and yellows, damasks woven for the first time in several colours, and silks either from Genoa itself or from Livorno, were exported to countries as far away as Scotland and Sweden. The availability of these materials with their huge bold patterns, for wall-hangings, for upholstering chairs and beds, for curtains or costume had an incalculable effect on all these branches of design from about 1680 onwards.

Turin in the seventeenth century had little separate identity from Genoa in the decorative arts. Still something of a backwater, its leading lights, like the Swiss-born Daniele Seiter, who is supposed to have designed much of the furniture in the Palazzo Reale as well as painting its ceilings, relied very much on Brustolon and Parodi models for the carved figures enmeshed in acanthus which support their tables. If there is a difference, it is a slightly tighter architectural control of the whole composition, perhaps influenced by French furniture of the same period. It was not until the arrival of Filippo Juvarra from Rome in 1715 that Turin became an important artistic centre in its own right. For the palace of Stupinigi built to his designs by Vittorio Amadeo II and begun in 1729, Juvarra realized many of the Baroque furniture designs he had incorporated in his earlier stage sets: pier-tables on piles of military trophies, enormous clocks flanked by sphinxes with butterflies' wings, or tripod stands culminating in three rams' masks—the last uncannily prophesying one of Adam's favourite ideas. The Roman inspiration for these pieces is clear but Juvarra brought to them a far more architectural discipline and concern for proportion than had hitherto been the case in furniture designed and made by sculptors. Juvarra's unmistakable architectural vocabulary, his canted corners with convex or concave curves and his partiality for ovals and ellipses, had a profound effect on Turinese furniture of the early eighteenth century. The tradition was continued in the outstanding marquetry furniture of Pietro Piffetti, despite the latter's fluent use of Rococo ornament to clothe what remained essentially Baroque forms.

Florence lies somewhat outside the mainstream of Italian Baroque furniture in the seventeenth century, largely because of its peculiarly different system of despotic government under the later Medici. The Grand Ducal workshops, first organized by Cosimo I in the galleries of the Uffizi early in the century, became the centre for the manufacture of *pietra dura* (literally 'hard-stone') inlay, an immensely time-consuming technique of marquetry using different coloured pieces of highly polished marble. The organization of the workshops is of the greatest interest, first because it shows how the most splendid pieces produced were the result of a co-operative effort by a whole range of different craftsmen, all paid by the Duke, and second because it was to be the model for the Gobelins as conceived by Louis XIV and realized by Colbert. At the head was always a renowned artist, architect or sculptor, upon whose initial sketches, and at whose orders, almost every work of art or piece of furniture was produced. Initially this director of the *Galleria* was Buontalenti, and after him respectively P M Baldi, G M Marini and G B Foggini. Under the director came the *capo-maestri* or heads of workshops, paid a fixed annual income, and under them the *cottimanti* or junior craftsmen, paid by the week: cabinet-makers, pietra-dura carvers (later removed to their own organization, the Opificio delle Pietre Dure, which still exists), as well as goldsmiths, casters, carvers and weavers.

The *stippone*, or great cabinet, which became the most characteristic product of the Florentine workshops, seems to have had a German derivation. Several Augsburg cabinets given to Cosimo I in the early years of the seventeenth century seem to have been imitated by the craftsmen in the Grand Ducal workshops, and under Ferdinand II, who reigned from 1621 to 1670, the characteristic combination of ebony, pietra dura and gilt bronze came to be developed. Ferdinand's own cabinet, which now stands in the Tribuna of the Uffizi, and a prie-dieu made for him now in the Museo degli Argenti, became the prototypes for pieces made well into the eighteenth century, so strong were the conservative traditions of the workshops.

An attachment to earlier models also explains how the *sgabelloni* and wooden stands for busts or vases originally designed by Buontalenti continued to be made up to the end of the seventeenth century. Some new types were evolved it is true, and the influence of Rome here was by no means negligible. Both Marini and Foggini came under the spell of Bernini: Foggini's showcase for the amber collection of Cosimo III recalls J P Schor's Colonna bed, while some side-tables supported by harpies and sirens, designed by Marini rather earlier, borrow an undoubtedly Roman theme, even if they are treated with a typically Florentine restraint and sense of architecture.

Pietra dura, although it remained the most famous, was by no means the only technique at which the Grand Duke's craftsmen excelled. Silver, and also steel, furniture was produced by the Galleria in some quantity. In about 1667 the arrival of an extremely accomplished Flemish or Dutch cabinet-maker, Leonardo van der Vinne, introduced the art of floral marquetry. Van der Vinne became in 1677 head cabinet-maker in the Ducal workshops, at a higher salary even than successful contemporary painters like Livio Melhus. A superb cabinet at the Pitti made by him about this date rests on a stand with ten blackamoor supports, and has four tables *en suite*, all inlaid with flowers in ivory as well as different woods.

The great strength of the Florentines was their lack of distinction between the major and the minor arts. G B Foggini as well as making designs for furniture personally executed silver statuettes and gilt-bronze ornaments for some pieces. Nor did the Grand Duke Ferdinando think it beneath his dignity to have Filippo Sangher, a lathe-turner and ivory worker by profession, as his 'uomo di fiducia', or right-hand man: both the Duke and his brother Gian Gastone practised ivory-turning themselves on occasion as a branch of science. Perhaps the peak of Florentine furniture-making was reached with the marvellous Elector Palatine's Cabinet, designed by Foggini, and made between 1707 and 1709, uniting all the skills then available in the Ducal workshops. Luckily for Florence it was later brought back to the city by the Elector's childless widow, along with an equally splendid prie-dieu made for her the previous year, 1706.

After this date, the quality of Florentine furniture design became somewhat stultified. Even the supremely inventive Foggini, designing a large table in 1716, could return for his model to a table-top (still in the Galleria Palatina) designed by Jacopo Ligozzi as early as 1649. The only breath of fresh air came from outside the Grand Ducal workshops, in the development of *scagliola*, the technique of painting on fine wet plaster, which was polished when dry. Enrico Hugford, a monk of English origin, is credited with the invention of this technique in Florence early in the eighteenth century, and another early practitioner was Piero Antonino Paolini, born in Lucca, the maker of a marvellous table dated 1732, now in the Museo degli Argenti. But scagliola only reached perfection later in the century, for instance in the superb work of Lamberto Gori; its flexibility and pastel colouring made it an ideal vehicle for Rococo ornament.

It is clear that the Baroque style lasted so long in Florence only because it was kept alive by the family piety of the last Medici and their reactionary policies. The religious mania of Cosimo III and his lugubrious daughter Anna Maria Luisa, the Electress Palatine, also played its part in seeing that sombre ebony and pietra dura continued to be made to the end of their lives — in marked contrast to what Louis XIV wished for in his last years '. . . de la jeunesse et de la gaité partout'.

France

The strong ties between France and the Protestant Netherlands, cemented by the struggle against Spain, and the equally strong ties between France and Florence, forged by two formidable Queens, Catherine and Marie de' Medici, were to have important results for the whole development of French furniture and decoration. During the gradual

recovery from the civil wars of the late sixteenth century, the nobility began to rebuild their houses in Paris, encouraged by Henri IV's example in embellishing the Louvre. The increased demand for furniture and works of art was met by a steady influx of foreign craftsmen, who settled generally in the area of the Faubourg Saint-Antoine. Here the strong mediaeval guild of joiners and furniture-makers could not enforce their monopoly as the land belonged to the nuns of Saint-Antoine and was therefore technically outside the bounds of the city. At first the majority of the immigrants were Flemish or Dutch, bringing with them new techniques of veneering and marquetry, but Germans and Italians also followed in the period after the accession of Henri IV, when France at last entered a period of security and prosperity.

From the first, leading furniture-makers benefited by the protection and encouragement of the King. In direct imitation of Cosimo I's Galleria in the Uffizi, Henri IV and Louis XIII housed craftsmen in workshops under the Grande Galerie of the Louvre, which linked the old palace with the Tuileries — amongst them Michel Campe, Pierre Boulle (father of the famous André-Charles), Jean Mace and Laurent Stabre. The period during and just after Mazarin's ascendancy was dominated by two great furniture-makers, one Flemish in origin, Pierre Golle (or Gole), the other Italian, Domenico Cucci. Golle's early furniture made in France consisted almost entirely of great cabinets, probably based on Augsburg and Antwerp models. These began as ebony pieces, usually with exquisitely carved scenes on the doors or the fronts of drawers giving an effect of polished black ivory. After about 1660, however, they became more and more richly inlaid with other materials, different coloured marbles, lapis and tortoiseshell. A technique in which Golle specialized still later was brass inlaid with pewter, which gave an effect of solid gold and

71

silver furniture, and in which his work prefigures and often equals the finest pieces by Boulle. Golle is also important for being one of the first to introduce the Baroque fashion for allegorical furniture to France: a Cabinet of the Liberal Arts, and a Cabinet of the Four Quarters of the World, both made by him for Cardinal Mazarin were the predecessors of Cucci's celebrated pair of cabinets representing Apollo and Diana, made for Louis XIV, or his even more famous 'War' and 'Peace' cabinets, showing the King as Mars and Marie Thérèse as Pallas Athene.

Cucci, born at Todi, though he probably worked in Florence in his youth, was summoned to France about the time of Mazarin's death in 1661, and was naturalized three years later, remaining a master-craftsman at the Gobelin factory until his death in about 1704. Cucci's cabinets are described in the early bills of the Garde-Meuble as being 'à la manière de Florence', many of them inlaid with 'commessi' (or incrustations) of semi-precious stones on a black marble background. The greatest innovation of his work was that it ignored the boundaries between the different crafts, combining always the most varied materials and techniques possible. Cucci is himself recorded as a sculptor, casting statuettes in silver or bronze for his own cabinets, as a marquetry-worker, laying a floor to a complicated design by Le Brun at Saint-Germain, as a bronzeur, making a casket for the King's jewels at the Tuileries, even as a musical instrument maker, supplying an organ-case, harpsichord and spinet for Louis XIV. Besides this, he had a team of mosaicists and lapidaries working under him, not to mention skilled gilders like La Baronnière. Cucci's master-pieces, such as the cabinets representing the Temples of Glory and Virtue made for the Galerie d'Apollon at the Louvre, must have been some of the most astonishing pieces of furniture ever made, a summation of Baroque craftsmanship. It is tragic to relate that so few of them still exist. A large number were in 1748 given by Louis XV to the Jardin Royal to be dismembered and their different stones kept as geological specimens, others were dispersed in a sale at the Louvre in 1751, and many more were destroyed in the Revolution. Almost the only evidence for what Cucci's furniture must have been like is provided by a pair of 'grandissimes cabinets' (as he himself would have described them) which miraculously survived the Revolution and are now in the collection of the Duke of Northumberland at Alnwick Castle.

Both Cucci and Golle were twin pillars of the Gobelins, the workshops founded in 1622 (in the former hôtel of the brothers Gobelin on the outskirts of Paris) in order to furnish the royal palaces. The 'Manufacture Royale

des Meubles de la Couronne', as it became in 1667, also had the wider aims of improving the standards of native craftsmanship in France, and stopping the demand for imports of luxury goods from abroad. Part of the great minister Colbert's far-reaching reforms, its foundation coincided with his strict regulations for the running of the Garde-Meuble, including the numbering of every piece of furniture, the taking of regular inventories and the indexing of accounts; this was swiftly followed by the establishment of carpet and tapestry manufactories at Aubusson and Beauvais, regular production of silk at Lyons and other textiles at Abbéville, Sedan and Carcassonne, of lace and embroidery at Alençon, Chantilly and Le Havre, and, above all, of large glass and mirror plates at the Royal factory of Saint-Gobain founded in 1665 under the direction of Noyen and Perotti (an immigrant from Altare). Saint-Gobain was soon producing larger sheets than those made in Venice, and the Galerie des Glaces at Versailles, made in 1678, is evidence both of its success and of a new aspect of Baroque taste, to reach a climax in the Spiegelkabinets of the German princely courts.

The hierarchical structure of the Gobelins was closely based on the Florentine Grand Ducal workshops, with the painter Charles

Above: The Grande Galerie at Versailles from an engraving by Sebastien Le Clerc. This shows the gallery in about 1685 with tables, tubs for orange-trees and chandeliers all made of silver, to the designs of Charles Le Brun. (Wallace Collection, London)

Right: One of a pair of cabinets made by Domenico Cucci in 1683, for the service of Louis XIV at Versailles, and perhaps the most splendid examples of the furniture made at the Gobelins to have survived. With their panels of pietra dura and central reliefs of inlaid stones, these pieces show how Cucci brought to France the techniques of the Florentine Grand Ducal workshops. (Collection of the Duke of Northumberland)

72

Le Brun as Director for the whole of the 20 years it operated at full strength. Craftsmen skilled enough to win a place in it were granted important privileges, such as immunity from the restrictions of the various guilds and free education for their children, as well as being highly paid. The list of its productions in this period makes extraordinary reading: brocades painted by Bonnemer, gigantic ormolu clocks, or whole balustrades, by Caffieri, and in particular the magnificent pieces of silver and gold furniture made by Du Tel, Loir and De Villers. Six silver guéridons, for instance, designed by Le Brun supported by sphinxes on great triangular bases, standing six feet high, *en suite* with three silver console tables and pier-glasses, give one some idea of the extraordinary splendour of Louis XIV's taste. The King personally supervised much of this work, insisting on seeing wax models for all the more important pieces.

Le Brun, the influential engraver Jean Lepautre, and Jean Bérain, who as director of the Menus-Plaisirs was second only to Le Brun in importance as an overall designer, used Baroque motifs within a more academic and classical framework than their Italian contemporaries. Their favourite forms of ornament — the arabesque and the lambrequin in particular — were derived from Raphael and the Renaissance, rather than from da Cortona and Bernini. In furniture, a similar, very much more static and balanced approach is noticeable in French as opposed to Italian pieces of the same date. Just as in Le Brun's frescoes, the heavily ornate borders of pier-glasses, consoles and cabinets are all-important, continuing and counteracting the movement of the figures within them. With André-Charles Boulle, the first native French cabinet-maker to achieve the importance of a Cucci or a Golle, the desire for symmetry reached almost tyrannical proportions. Boulle's pieces seem mostly to have been executed in the technique to which he gave his name, an intricate design of tortoiseshell and brass inlaid in ebony, and were often rendered in pairs of panels called *première-partie* and *contre-partie*, that is to say with the same design appearing on two matching pieces of furniture, once in brass on tortoise-shell and once (reversed) in tortoiseshell on brass.

Boulle's innovation lay not so much in his technique (Golle had after all been working in this vein much earlier), as in his development of new forms of furniture, widely spread through his engravings, published under the title *Nouveaux Desseins de Meubles*. Bureaux and commodes were the characteristic new forms, pioneered both by Boulle and by Aubertin Gaudron. In Italy such pieces would have been considered too utilitarian ever to

have been given a place in state apartments; but in the hands of Boulle (and Gaudron, who supplied two bureaux at Versailles for Madame de Maintenon) they became indispensable furnishings for the Cabinet. The commode likewise, rather like the bureau but with fewer (usually three) drawers extending the whole width of the piece, and often with a marble top, became an essential architectural feature of the state bedchamber, based in Boulle's case on classical and Italian Renaissance sarcophagi.

Mention of Gaudron raises the question of furniture-makers outside the Royal protection of the Gobelins or the Louvre workshops, and living usually in the Faubourg Saint-Antoine. Pieces made before the craftsman's stamp or

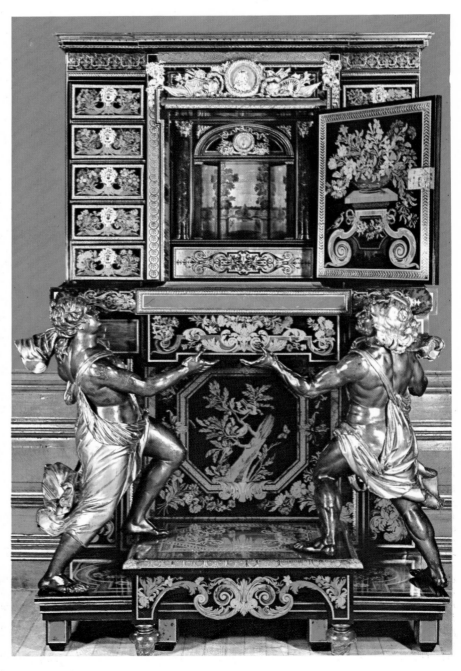

Below: Cabinet on stand, by tradition the gift of Louis XIV to Charles II. An outstanding example of the craftsmanship practised at the Gobelins, a piece such as this would probably have been made by a whole team of craftsmen working to an overall design, possibly by Le Brun himself. (Collection of the Duke of Buccleuch)

*Right: Armoire, of ebony
with tortoiseshell and brass
inlay, made about 1690,
possibly by André-Charles
Boulle himself to the
designs of Bérain. This is
one of the finest existing
early pieces using the
Boulle technique, and the
crossed L cypher
indicates that it was made
for the Royal service, even
if not for Louis XIV's
personal use. (Jones
Collection, Victoria &
Albert Museum, London)*

Left: One of a pair of
commodes by
André-Charles Boulle,
which are the only
securely documented
pieces of furniture by
Boulle. They were made
in 1708–9 for Louis XIV's
bedchamber at the Trianon.
The commode, which
became the commonest form
of carcase furniture in
France later in the
eighteenth century,
acquired its specific
character about this time
largely due to the work of
Boulle and Aubertin
Gaudron. This particular
example shows in its
overall shape the influence
of Roman sarcophagi. .
(Versailles)

estampille became compulsory under Louis
XV are virtually impossible to attribute to
particular Parisian makers. It can be said,
however, that the distinction first drawn at
this time, between *ébénistes,* or cabinet-
makers, on the one hand, and *menuisiers,*
generally chair-makers or joiners, on the
other, was a sign of increasing sophistication.
The Parisian ébénistes really came into their
own with the gradual cutting down of the
Gobelins after 1686, at the beginning of the
War of the League of Augsburg. Between 1689
and 1693 when the Royal workshops were
virtually closed down, an estimated 20 tons
of silver furniture was sent to be melted down.
While this was undoubtedly a body blow to
French prestige and to the country's hitherto
undoubted leadership of northern Europe in
artistic matters, it brought about changes in
style and technique which paved the way for
the Rococo. As precious and semi-precious
materials were no longer easily available an
effect of richness had to be obtained simply
by the use of contrasting woods, or by unadorned woodcarving. Aubertin Gaudron,
who had begun as an independent ébéniste
making more or less utilitarian pieces,
produced for instance an armoire for the
Antechamber at Marly in 1688, rivalling
Boulle in the complexity of its design, but
carried out entirely in wood-marquetry — of a
type which greatly influenced Huguenot
émigrés, and in particular the famous dynasty
of furniture-makers called Hache, of Grenoble.
The early eighteenth-century furniture
designs of Robert de Cotte and Claude Audran
III also show a new feeling for elegance.
Their gilt tables, relying on only one material
and one colour to make their effect, demanded
a simpler, more linear treatment.

A parallel development was the growing
importance of upholsterers, like Bon, Delobel
and Losné who, while their state beds do not
on the whole seem to have approached the
extravagance reached in Holland and England
under William of Orange, nevertheless

76

introduced the taste for brightly coloured furnishing textiles and in particular for more comfortable seat furniture. In part this also reflected a change in social convention. At the time of Louis XIV's death, 1,325 *tabourets* and *pliants* were recorded at Versailles, and these had been reserved only for high-ranking courtiers, others having to stand. The relaxation of these standards brought a demand for upholstered armchairs and day-beds which were invariably supplied by upholsterers rather than chair-makers. In time many of these upholsterers too became *marchands-merciers*, or middlemen, somewhere between interior decorators and dealers in furniture, taking a commission on the work of the *ébénistes* they ordered or sold.

But the most important change was in the atmosphere at Versailles itself, still the artistic centre of France. It was with the growing informality of Louis XIV's last years, due largely to the youthfulness and vivacity of the Duchess of Burgundy, that delicate colours began to take the place of pompous ornament, and flowers, trellis-work, arabesques and smiling masks to replace the heavy overblown allegories of the previous generation.

The Low Countries

At the opening of the seventeenth century Antwerp reached the peak of a period of extraordinary prosperity. Her international trading empire had not only given her greater material wealth than perhaps any other European city of the time, it had also given her artists and craftsmen the stimulus of constant contact with foreign designs, materials and techniques. While tapestries, leather wall-hangings and gold and silver work continued to be the most famous Flemish products, sent all over the continent, potters and furniture-makers alike started to imitate for the first time the goods brought back in increasing quantities from the East. New methods of veneering learnt from these

pieces facilitated very much more elaborate
and representational marquetry than had been
possible before, and also inspired the first
tentative efforts to make lacquer furniture in
the West. Italy too was a major source of
inspiration. Rubens' total of seven years
spent there, and Jacques Francart's Italophile
engravings were to have enormous influence
respectively in Antwerp and Brussels, where
the splendour of the Archduke Albert's court
was legendary. Rubens is known to have had
woodcarvers, as well as painters and sculptors
in marble, among his apprentices, and a
testimonial written by him on behalf of one
of these, Louis Faydherbe, still survives.

Views of interiors, like that of Rubens'
own drawing-room by Cornelis de Vos painted
in about 1622, show the extent of Antwerp's
opulence at this time: huge brass chandeliers
and andirons, green and gold stamped leather
on the walls, chairs with cushions embroidered
with flowers, mirrors and porcelain must
have given visiting English or Scandinavian
merchants the impression of an Aladdin's
cave. While techniques (like veneering, gilding
or silvering, and japanning) and materials
(such as tortoiseshell, ivory and marbles)
improved so rapidly, traditional sixteenth-
century and late mediaeval types of furniture
died hard. The two-stage court cupboard or
'buffet à deux corps' was still far the most
common piece of furniture, though enlivened
with auricular motifs or architectural decoration taken from pattern books. As late as 1694
the Antwerp Guild still insisted that presentation pieces, carved by apprentices as a
qualification for becoming master-craftsmen,
should be made in this antiquated form.

In part this conservatism can be explained by social practice: just as in the early sixteenth century, the exact status of a merchant was still determined by the quantity and quality of his plate, displayed on the buffet in his parlour, or stacked on tables in four or five tiers for special occasions. The other essential piece in any Dutch or Flemish household was the huge family cupboard so familiar from the pictures of Vermeer and de Hooch, where all the fine linen and other valuables were kept locked away — opened only by the key that hung from the waist of the 'huisvreouw'. These two, lumpy and unwieldy pieces, first of all received pattern-book decoration in the shape of arched panels, heavy cornices or twisted columns, and then later in the century became more Baroque with canted corners, shaped tops like the crestings of cabinets, and often three long drawers replacing the bottom cupboard. Cabinets, on carved stands, filled with a mass of tiny drawers for collections of coins or jewels, were popular from the late sixteenth century onwards, perhaps influenced originally by Augsburg models.

The closing of the Scheldt in 1609, as part of the truce between Spain and the Dutch, although it did not at once kill Antwerp, broke the almost total dominance it had previously enjoyed. Artistically as well as politically, Amsterdam began to develop its own identity, and after 1648 with the beginning of the work on Jacob van Campen's new Town Hall can be said to have seized the initiative. Dutch, as opposed to Flemish, Baroque was at first more sober and more classical, in keeping with its Protestant background and the comparative austerity of the Stadtholders'

court. The chief sculptor employed on the Town Hall was Artus Quellin whose father had been a sculptor in Antwerp and who had received his training there and in Rome. Quellin's garlands of fruit, flowers and sea-shells, strictly symmetrical and used with architectural effect, became a standard type of ornament for Dutch furniture up to about 1685. Mannerist ornament was by no means dead however. Crispin van den Passe's influential *Boutique Menuiserie*, published in Amsterdam in 1642, the first manual specifically dealing with furniture design since the engravings of De Vries 75 years earlier, still has motifs close to strapwork and extravagances worthy of Dietterlin; though it also shows simpler chairs, with straight backs, double stretchers and arms carved with dolphins, far more typical of the direction Dutch furniture was taking. The auricular style, that Mannerist (and highly mannered) form of ornament so called because its sinuous curving forms were supposed to resemble those of the human ear, had a final brief fling in Amsterdam in the work of John Lutma —though gradually it developed into the shallow scrolls seen on the front stretchers and backs of so many English and Dutch chairs of the 1660s and 1670s, described in early inventories as 'horsebone' decoration.

Marquetry, once again based on techniques developed in Antwerp, was the field in which Dutch cabinet-makers of the mid-seventeenth century excelled. Different woods, some imported from the East, some stained green, or purple, some spectacularly grained, were used, occasionally with the addition of ivory. Dirk van Rijswijk, working in Amsterdam, perfected a technique of inlaying mother-of-pearl in floral patterns on black marble, but others like Philip van Santwijk, at The Hague, concentrated on complicated geometrical patterns or still-life designs in more conventional woods of contrasting colour. The influence of contemporary Dutch flower-painting is clearer in the work of perhaps the finest Amsterdam cabinet-maker of his time, Jan van Mekeren. His cabinet doors inlaid with bouquets of flowers, spilling out of enormous vases, even on occasion show the butterflies, insects and drops of water on leaves beloved of artists like Rachel Ruysch and Jan van Huysum.

The Baroque arrangement of state apartments was slow to catch on in Holland, and it was indeed only with William of Orange's careful attempts to gain absolute rule, aided by powerful families like the Bentincks, Wassenaars and Pallandts, that French practice finally prevailed in the period after 1685. Until then the merchant-nobility, who almost invariably lived in town-houses (in marked contrast with the English system of country-seats) continued the demand for old-established national forms of furniture. Three or four amazingly elaborate dolls' houses of the 1670s and 1680s still miraculously survive to show how typically Dutch features of a previous generation, such as table-carpets, enormous branched chandeliers, chimney boards painted with still-lives or *trompes l'oeil*, or whole tiled walls, survived into the Baroque period. One particularly long-lived feature was the 'lit en housse', the type of bed common in Flanders and Holland since the late Middle Ages, with a simple square-domed tester suspended from the ceiling, and curtains at the corners pulled up and down by cords and pulleys. Seen in all the paintings of Ter Borch and van Steen, they achieved slightly later a more Baroque air by their upholstery of rich velvets with tassels and fringes, and by the addition of four large painted or gilded knobs, known as 'pommes' on top of their testers.

The Dutch merchant class also led the rest of Europe in their taste for oriental porcelain and furniture. Encouraged by the great

Left: Dutch lacquer cabinet, with door panels and drawers decorated with flower paintings, and the original carved and gilt stand. The Dutch love of flowers extended to furniture as much as to painting, and this type of decoration soon became as popular as the oriental scenes on earlier lacquer pieces. The stand is exceptionally richly carved with figures emerging from a background of thick acanthus foliage in the style of Quellin and Grinling Gibbons.

Above: Doll's House,
probably made in
Amsterdam about 1700.
Seemingly not intended
merely as toys, Dutch
dolls' houses of the late
seventeenth century are
often vivid records of
actual houses and their
contents, for which huge
amounts could be paid.
This particularly
splendid example is in
the original Boulle case.
(Rijksmuseum,
Amsterdam)

successes of the Dutch East India Company,
oriental customs as well as goods became all
the rage. By the middle of the seventeenth
century the tea-party had become firmly
established as a social convention, and all
the equipment necessary for it — the tea-table,
either a tambour or a tripod stand (preferably
lacquer but otherwise painted in imitation),
the little cabinet filled with caddies, the larger
cupboard to keep the precious porcelain cups
and rows of small pots — were eagerly sought
from Amsterdam cabinet-makers as well as
from the Company's own headquarters.

After about 1685, Holland came for the first
time under the dominant influence of France
in the decorative arts. That this was so was
largely the achievement of one man, Daniel
Marot, son of a famous French engraver,
Jean Marot, nephew of the cabinet-makers,
Pierre and Adrian Golle, and the chief pupil
of Bérain. As a Protestant, Marot was forced
to leave France at the Revocation of the Edict
of Nantes, and entering the service of William
of Orange soon became his *chef de dessein*,
acting in the same capacity as his master had
for Louis XIV. Marot's furniture designs in
general remained close to Bérain's but he
developed the French Baroque style in two
particular ways. Undoubtedly the major effect
of his style on furniture was to emphasize
the new dominance of the upholsterer, whose
state beds and wall-hangings of extraordinary
complexity, *en suite* with the covers of daybeds,
chairs and stools, matched the increasing

elaboration of costume at this period, the high lace headdresses (or *fantanges*) and the endless pleats and frills of bodices and skirts. Marot's other important innovation was the porcelain cabinet, a little room with thousands of cups, saucers, pots, or *blanc de chine* figures crammed onto brackets climbing the entire height of each wall, and on carved and gilt *étagères* in each corner. This new development in the Dutch craze for porcelain probably owed much to the personal taste of Mary II, who also ordered a series of superb Delft tiles to be made by the potter Adrianus Koeckz (to Marot's designs) for her dairy at Hampton Court. Marot's adaptation of French Baroque design to these new, and typically Dutch, requirements was to have a profound effect on the furnishing of German palaces in the following decades.

The editions of Daniel Marot's collected engravings published in Amsterdam in 1702 and 1712 rapidly spread his very individual style far beyond the immediate circle of his patrons. Their very universality must have made them essential equipment for every craftsman's workshop, and their effect on traditional forms of Dutch furniture was exceptionally long-lived. The large, usually green-painted, bench (or 'bank'), which was a standard piece of furniture in every Dutch hall, was soon covered with a profusion of carving — bulbous urns with stiff garlands and heavy symmetrical scrolls — in Marot's vocabulary; while long-case clocks (their mechanisms either from England or from Friesland, now fast becoming a clock-making centre) were given enormous, often top-heavy, marquetry or lacquer cases surmounted by gilded figures of Father Time or Mercury, flanked by trumpeting angels. A measure both of the power of Daniel Marot's influence, and also of the conservatism of the Dutch in the eighteenth century, is the fact that the cabriole leg, generally adopted in England by about 1710, hardly made an appearance in the Low Countries before the late 1730s.

England

Furniture-makers in England before the Civil War rather naturally lagged behind their counterparts in the richer, more cosmopolitan Low Countries and France. The more ambitious pieces, court-cupboards and chests, were usually inspired by Mannerist engraved ornament like the designs of Jean du Cerceau, Wendel Dietterlin or Martin de Vos. The equipment of court ceremonial was even more old-fashioned: the remarkable series of X-frame state chairs and stools at Knole, almost certainly made for James I and Anne of Denmark, or a chair and footstool made for Bishop Juxon of London about 1635 (now in the Victoria & Albert Museum) are, despite their superb upholstery, almost identical to

the chairs of state seen in the backgrounds of portraits by Eworth, and even Holbein, a century earlier. Inigo Jones' introduction of Italian taste to the court of Charles I seems to have had just as limited an effect on the furniture of the period as his brand of Palladian architecture had on contemporary English houses.

The experiences of so many Royalists, forced to travel abroad in the years before the Restoration, were of tremendous importance for the development of the decorative arts in England in the second half of the seventeenth century. The ebony cabinets inlaid with specimen marbles bought by John Evelyn in Florence are good examples of the more exotic taste acquired by educated Englishmen. Thomas Povey, another of these early

Above: A state bedchamber, from an engraving in Daniel Marot's Nouveau Livre d'Appartements, 1702. This shows one of the incredibly elaborate beds which, under Marot's influence, became popular in both Holland and England during the reign of William and Mary; it is of the so-called 'angel' tester type, dispensing altogether with end-posts. (Victoria & Albert Museum, London) cognoscenti and a friend of Pepys, bought an Indian tambour table, flanked by two Venetian candlestands in the shape of crouching blackamoors, for his parlour in London in the early 1670s, pieces which still look exotic today in the house built by his nephew, William Blathwayt, at Dyrham. Equally bizarre and fascinating to English eyes must have been the sets of carved ebony furniture from Goa, imported from the Indies after Charles II's marriage to Catharine of Braganza and its accompanying trade agreements between England and Portugal. Decorative pieces like these, but particularly lacquer from the East, were what English furniture-makers began to emulate after the Restoration.

The dominant influence in this period, up to about 1685, was Holland, whose East India Company was still the chief source of oriental imports for the whole of Europe. Oriental lacquer cabinets when they could be secured (usually at high prices) were given extremely elaborate stands and crestings by English makers after Dutch patterns. These, carved with swirling acanthus and gilt or silver gilt, set off the dark lacquer, and together with the porcelain grouped in masses above and below the cabinet created a sumptuous effect which was thought appropriate for objects of such comparative rarity. In time the cabinets themselves were imitated in England, and Stalker and Parker's *Treatise of Japanning* of 1688, the first English furniture-maker's pattern book, shows how popular lacquer had become by that date. Technically, English panels, made up into screens, chests, bureau-bookcases, mirrors, tables or pier-glasses, were initially crude. A naïve attempt at Chinese or Japanese landscapes often resulted in very English-looking ducks or swans, pursued by dragons with a marked resemblance to King Charles spaniels. Even where oriental lacquer or coromandel screens were cut up to make other kinds of furniture, no care was taken to ensure that the different scenes matched up, or even appeared the right way up. By the last years of the seventeenth and the early eighteenth centuries however, makers like Gerrit Jensen achieved extremely high standards—despite the fact that true shellac as used in the manufacture of oriental lacquer was still unobtainable in the West.

Until about 1685 most seat furniture was still produced by the joiner, although turned walnut rather than oak was now generally used for the legs, stretchers and arms. A more or less standard form of chair with caned back and seat, once more based on Dutch precedents, was developed, though makers like Thomas Roberts (who appears constantly in the Royal Wardrobe accounts) could vary the form by introducing elaborately carved aprons with 'horsebone' decoration, cupids

or garlands. These and the slightly later backstools, which had square upholstered backs, were ideal for the usual Baroque arrangement of chairs lined up against the walls, where their tall, narrow proportions gave them the appropriate look of guards on parade.

Another primarily Dutch influence was that of Grinling Gibbons, whose style of naturalistic carving, learnt from the Quellins and other carvers at work on the new Amsterdam Town Hall in the 1650s, inspired a whole generation of native English carvers. With England's economic recovery after the Civil War, the successful conclusion of the Dutch wars, and in particular with the Great Fire of 1666 which at one stroke necessitated the building and furnishing of thousands of

Above: Bow Window Room at Blenheim Palace, Oxfordshire. This room was designed by Sir John Vanbrugh as one of the family apartments for the First Duke of Marlborough. The capitals of the Corinthian columns are carved by Grinling Gibbons, whose work elsewhere at Blenheim is in stone and marble. (Blenheim Palace, Oxfordshire)

Above: Writing-desk of walnut, probably made in London about 1690. The type of marquetry known as 'seaweed', because of its intricate convoluted patterns, became very popular in England at the end of the seventeenth century. Its most famous exponent was the Flemish-born Gerrit Jensen, cabinet-maker to William and Mary. (Victoria & Albert Museum, London)

new houses and churches, London had suddenly become the centre of a thriving community of native craftsmen. It was to Gibbons' and the other Dutch immigrants' vocabulary of ripe fruit and flowers in full bloom, of dead game or fish, and plump cherubs chasing each other through luxuriant swirls of acanthus, that these craftsmen turned for inspiration. Mirror frames, the aprons of tables and the front stretchers of chairs all received this lavish Netherlandish Baroque treatment. Almost invariably these were executed in walnut, which had by now totally superseded oak as the staple furniture-making material being far easier to carve yet quite as strong as oak, and with attractive grain patterns and variations in colour that also made it ideal for marquetry.

One other important development under the last two Stuart kings was the great advance in the making of clocks and barometers, a field in which England's superiority was to last for well over a hundred years. Thanks largely to the scientific discoveries of Thomas Tompion, backed by founder members of the Royal Society like Wren and Hooke, English bracket and long-case clocks were soon *de rigueur* all over Europe. It still comes as a surprise to find the work of makers like Tompion and Quare in Venetian palaces, in Peter the Great's collection at the Hermitage in Leningrad, or in the opulent monasteries

Left: *Headboard of a crimson damask state bed supplied by the Huguenot upholsterer, Francis Lapiere, to the First Duke of Devonshire in 1692. Lapiere's amazingly ornate beds are extremely close to the designs of Daniel Marot. A comparatively large number of similar beds survive to show that, in one respect at least, England rivalled the rest of Europe in Baroque fantasy. (National Trust, Hardwick Hall, Derbyshire)*

of Coimbra and Oporto. Apart from the un-doubted mechanical excellence of these clocks their cases became more and more elaborate, japanned in green or scarlet with silver figures, inlaid with floral marquetry or in geometrical patterns with 'oysters' of olive-wood, mulberry, or stained burr-maple, and often with elaborate pierced crestings.

Walnut and japanned furniture of this sort continued to be made well into the eighteenth century, but the accession of William and Mary in 1689 undoubtedly brought new fashions and new influences to bear on English furniture-makers. Surprisingly, considering William's nationality and his life-long struggle against Louis XIV, the keynote of this period was French. Since the Revocation of the Edict of Nantes in 1685, Huguenot craftsmen, often trained in the Gobelin workshops, had poured into both England and Holland. One of the most influential of the émigrés was Daniel Marot, who, as has already been seen, became a kind of overall director of design to William III in Holland. Summoned to England by Queen Mary in 1694, Marot made at least three visits in the next ten years, and the close similarities between his engraved designs (published in a collected edition in 1702) and so many pieces of furniture produced in England during that decade show that he was at the centre of a circle of Anglo-French and Anglo-Dutch cabinet-makers, up-holsterers, carvers and gilders.

Undoubtedly the most important of the cabinet-makers was Gerrit Jensen, a Fleming by birth, and easily the most proficient

exponent of English marquetry in the manner of Boulle. As well as being from 1689 the principal supplier to the Royal Wardrobe of writing-desks, pier-glasses, stands and card-tables, his name also figures constantly in bills and receipts for other great private patrons. Jensen's work can be of 'seaweed' marquetry, in different woods of contrasting colours, of walnut inlaid with pewter, or of the usual 'Boulle' technique of brass on tortoiseshell. His designs for table-tops and the wide surrounds of cushion mirrors are sometimes close to the engraved ornament of Bérain, though they seldom include the latter's figurative content — monkeys, sphinxes and characters from the Commedia dell' Arte — relying more on involved geometrical patterns (almost filigree) to make their effect. In this he may have been influenced by contemporary metalwork pattern books such as Simon Gribelin's, primarily intended for the decoration of silver snuff-boxes. In the general design of his furniture, Jensen appears to have been strongly influenced by Daniel Marot; his tables and candlestands with caryatid supports, and his simple rectangular-shaped commodes of three drawers can be seen constantly in Marot's engravings. It is hard to believe that his masterpiece, the great writing-desk made for Queen Mary in 1693 and now at Kensington Palace, was not actually designed by the master, so novel is its form. Besides using Marot as her dessinateur-en-chef, Mary also patronized his cousin, the cabinet-maker Cornelius Golle (younger brother of the famous Parisian maker, Pierre Golle) who in 1692 made for her a table 'of dolphin fashion'.

In one respect England during this period surpassed all her European rivals in Baroque fantasy. While the normal mid-seventeenth century four-post state bedstead, with straight valances and with no carved or moulded decoration, continued to be used in France, in England Huguenot upholsterers like Francis Lapiere, Jean Casbert and Jean Poitevin, following the designs of (if not actually in contact with) Daniel Marot, developed an almost unbelievably ornate form of bed. Testers, backboards and bases were carved and pierced, and damask, trimmed with galloon and fringe, then applied to them; valances became gathered in impossible festoons, tied with silk cords and embellished with huge tassels; some, called angel beds or lits à la duchesse, dispensed with end-posts and had their testers suspended from the ceiling. Perhaps the most splendid example of all is the bed made for the Earl of Melville about 1690, now in London's Victoria & Albert Museum, but there are others which compare with the most extravagant of Marot's en-gravings, at Clandon, Warwick, Belvoir, Dyrham, Lyme and Knole. Beds such as these were intended to provide a climax to the Baroque progression of state apartments and it was for this reason that they became far and away the most important and expensive pieces of furniture in English houses. Invariably the upholsterer would also supply with them a set of seat furniture *en suite* to stand around the walls, probably consisting of two armchairs, six single chairs and two stools or 'squab frames' (low, caned frames on which were placed two large squashy cushions).

Another skill at which Huguenot craftsmen in England excelled was gilding. Men like René and Peter Cousin who undertook all the gilding work for Verrio's ceilings at Burghley, Paul Pettit, and the Pelletier family brought new techniques of water-gilding and burnishing over to England. Where the stands of early Restoration cabinets had been oil-gilt, leaving a thick coat which tended to obscure the crispness of the carving and give a somewhat dull matt finish, towards the end of the century the frames carved for Monnoyer flower-pieces, or for 'landskip glasses' placed over chimneys, glittered with a paler-coloured, but brighter gold leaf. Highlights were achieved in water-gilding by polishing the raised part of the decoration to an almost metallic sheen, leaving the background undisturbed. But even greater contrasts became possible with the introduction of gilt gesso, for which René Pelletier has been given the credit. This technique allowed for decoration to be stamped onto large gilded surfaces: coats of arms or monograms, arabesques after Bérain or purely geometrical patterns. Completely matt surfaces for backgrounds could also be obtained by stamping the gesso all over, while still wet, with a small round punch.

The climax of this technique can be seen in the work of John Gumley and James Moore, whose gilt gesso furniture was to replace almost entirely the marquetry furniture of Jensen and Golle in the second decade of the eighteenth century. This change of taste in the decorative arts reflects an even more momentous change in architecture: the rejection by Lord Burlington and Kent of the French Baroque in favour of Italian classicism. But whereas houses like Tottenham Park, Wanstead and Holkham returned to the Palladian villa ideal their contents continued to be unequivocally Baroque. Kent and Flitcroft were faced with something of a quandary, for the original furniture of Palladio's villas was not only sparse but also unacceptably simple for their Augustan interiors. When they did return to Italian models therefore, it was largely to Roman or Venetian Baroque precedents. The splendid gilt chest made for Sir James Bateman (probably by Gumley and Moore), now in the Victoria & Albert Museum, may be the nearest

Left: Centre table, probably designed by William Kent and originally at Wanstead House in Essex, one of the most influential English Palladian houses. The giant shell between the bracket-supports at each end, the lion's masks, garlands and generally over life-size proportions show Kent's debt to Italian Baroque furniture design. (Collection of the Duke of Devonshire)

Right: The green velvet bed at Houghton in Norfolk, the great house built by the first English Prime Minister, Sir Robert Walpole. Kent played a dominant part in the decoration of Houghton, and this bed was undoubtedly made to his designs. While the straight lines of the tester are what one might expect of his architectural, Palladian principles, the headboard with its giant double shell is more a backward glance to the Baroque state beds of Daniel Marot. (Collection of the Marquess of Cholmondeley)

an English cabinet-maker has ever come to the idea of an Italian *cassone*, but it is more reminiscent of a Bernini sarcophagus than of a simple walnut chest of Palladio's own day. Similarly the settees designed by Kent for the Double Cube Room at Wilton, where surrounded by the work of his beloved Inigo Jones he might have been expected to be at his most classical, rather recall the designs of Juvarra with their winged sphinxes and bottom-heavy proportions. Nor, with his paucity of Italian material to draw on, did Kent disdain to borrow from Daniel Marot. The candlestands, of which he was so fond, in the shape of caryatids on tapering pedestals (either cherubs or females with baskets on their heads), have almost exact parallels in Marot's engravings, despite the fact that he proudly called them 'terms' after the Italian *terme*.

In general, furniture of the Palladian period in England did, however, become gradually more architectural and less sculptural. The advent of mahogany may have been one reason, for its dark and beautifully grained surface demanded less ornamentation; the increasing availability of rich upholstery materials, cut velvets from Genoa, Chinese silks and 'bizarre' Spitalfields patterns was another, for these spoke for themselves and did not need immensely elaborate mouldings to set them off. Perhaps the last truly Baroque pieces of English furniture are the vast pier-glasses, made by the new glass manufactories first at Lambeth and then at Vauxhall. But it was the very heaviness and the ponderous

architecture of later Kentian mirrors with their pediments and egg-and-dart surrounds that eventually brought about the Rococo reaction. A world of frivolity, fantasy and lightness seemed to open up with the engravings of Gravelot and the furniture designs of Thomas Johnson.

Germany

Split into hundreds of small principalities, Catholic, Lutheran and Calvinist, constantly at loggerheads with one another, Germany cannot any more than Italy be said to have adopted a national Baroque style along the lines of Colbert's France. Each little state, open to different petty despots (enlightened or not), developed artistically along different lines. In general, however, it can be said that the full Baroque style came later to Germany than to most other European countries, that it achieved its most extravagant expression there, and that it was abandoned far less quickly, thanks largely to the innate conservatism of the German princes.

The great early centre of furniture-making was of course Augsburg, from whence magnificent cabinets and 'Prunkschreins' were exported all over Europe. The gold- and silversmiths, jewellers and sculptors who combined to produce these confections had a seminal influence on the development of Baroque furniture throughout Europe, first because they introduced the fashion for furniture made of precious metals, and second because they involved highly skilled craftsmen of every guild on the manufacture of pieces

ion in the Low Countries. The importance of Augsburg lay therefore in technique rather than design. The silver throne made by Abraham Drentwett for Queen Christina of Sweden in 1650, still in Stockholm, prefigured the silver furniture made a generation later for Louis XIV, while the sophisticated tools developed by Augsburg craftsmen, finer saws than had hitherto been made, or planes capable of producing wave-mouldings, were to have a profound effect on the development of Baroque furniture far beyond the Rhine.

The initial impulse towards sculptural furniture of flowing lines came, as might be

that would previously have been left to a single joiner or carver. On the other hand the forms (and often the decoration too) of Augsburg furniture before 1650 can hardly be called Baroque. The architecture of Ulrich Baumgartner's great cabinets, for instance, is more a development of the Renaissance altarpiece than a new departure in Baroque furniture. A marvellous octagonal table-top now at Dresden, inlaid with silver by another Augsburg craftsman, Theodosius Hasel, in 1636, also shows a devotion to flat Mannerist ornament that continued both at Augsburg and Nuremberg long after it had gone out of fash-expected, from Italy, and though after about 1690 French, and then English and Dutch, influences were also brought to bear on German furniture-makers, certain states, particularly in the south, remained loyal to bold Italianate forms. Several pietra-dura craftsmen had crossed the Alps by the 1650s, settling in Bohemia, Moravia and Würzburg. Salzburg and Vienna, where the Hapsburg court provided great demand, also received their complement of immigrant craftsmen, as did Bavaria where the Nymphenburg palace was begun in 1663 under the direction of the Italian architect, Barelli, later succeeded by

Viscardi. Two principalities in particular came under Florentine influence in the early eighteenth century through their rulers' connections by marriage with the Medici: the Palatinate, whose Electress Anna Maria Luisa was a sister of Gian Gastone, the last Grand Duke of Tuscany, and Baden-Baden, whose Margravine, Sibylla Augusta, was his sister-in-law. In both cases the Florentine techniques of pietra dura and scagliola were imitated by native German craftsmen, and at the Schloss Favorite at Baden there was a complete Florentine room with decorative panels inlaid in mother-of-pearl, agate, onyx

Far left: Interior with Musicians, by J H Schönfeldt. The gallery depicted here, with pictures hung in three or four tiers up to the ceiling, was a common feature of the palaces of German princelings in the mid-seventeenth century. Apart from the giant cabinet on the end wall, and the two large clocks on tables either side of the room, the furniture is comparatively sparse and formally arranged. The closeness with which the armchairs have been placed in serried ranks is a particularly Baroque feature. (Gemäldegalerie, Dresden)

Left: The family dining-room, Schloss Favorite, is particulary interesting for its evidence of direct Italian influence on the German Baroque. The walls here are of scagliola with painted decoration and the chairs with their tapering cartouche backs are also Italianate in form. (Schloss-Favorite, Baden-Baden)

91

and marble, and with imported Italian furniture. Just as Italianate in feeling was the famous bed at the monastery of St Florian, near Linz, made about the same time for Prince Eugene, by the Austrian carver Leonhard Sattler. With its chained Turkish captives groaning under the weight of the heavy frame, and with an ornate sculptural foot and headboard rather than a tester and posts, this owes more to Roman and Venetian models than to contemporary German fashion. One other Italian practice to have a long-lasting effect in Austria and Bavaria was the vogue for elaborate stucco covering the walls and ceilings of rooms. No less than 600 plasterers were, for instance, employed at one time at Wessobrunn. The furniture for these unsurpassed interiors, such as survive at Pommersfelden or the Residenz at Würzburg, was necessarily sparse, and also tended to be plain, perhaps purposely, so as not to rival the extraordinary movement and excitement all around.

In the new wave of prosperity that followed Prince Eugene's defeat of the Turks in 1683, however, new French influences can be detected in German furniture. The man more responsible for this than any other was the Elector Max II Emanuel of Bavaria, whose

exile first in Holland and then in France, between 1704 and 1707, and whose first-hand experience of Versailles, were to be crucial. The Elector not only brought French and Dutch artists and craftsmen back with him, but he also took Germans with him to France to be trained. The most influential of these was initially Josef Effner, who became a pupil of Boffrand, and who was able to put his French ideas into practice at Nymphenburg and Schleissheim after 1716. But even more important in the long run was to be one of Effner's draughtsmen, a Walloon who began as the Elector's personal dwarf before becoming a pupil of Blondel the younger — François Cuvilliés.

The most obvious result of French influence was the popularity of Boulle furniture. In response to Bavarian and other demands, Augsburg craftsmen like Johann George Escher soon mastered the technique and, indeed, in pieces like the fantastic red tortoiseshell cabinet in the Residenz at Munich made by Escher and Wolfauer for Max Emanuel's predecessor, the Elector Ferdinand Maria, in the 1680s, equalled the work of French contemporaries. Far the most famous exponent of this style however, was Johann Daniel Sommer, who trained in Paris before settling

Above: A pier-table and matching candlestands inlaid in the Boulle style with silver and tortoiseshell. This was made at Augsburg, between 1714 and 1716, by the silversmith Jeremias Jakob Aberell, probably in conjunction with the cabinet-maker, Heinrich Eichler. They demonstrate the strong French influence on German furniture in the early eighteenth century, which was especially encouraged by the Francophile Electors of Bavaria.

in the small town of Künzelsau in south Germany. Sommer's best pieces, such as a cabinet at Charlottenburg dated 1684, as well as being technically superb show a markedly individual style of design with freer arabesques and a less architectural framework than Gaudron or Boulle himself would have used. Two other notable German makers specializing in Boulle furniture in the early eighteenth century were Anton Lüchtenstein of Düsseldorf and Ferdinand Pflitzner, whose various Boulle cabinets and pier-glasses at Pommersfelden date from about 1720.

English and Dutch influences, especially in northern Germany, became more apparent after 1700, particularly in two fields, floral marquetry and lacquer. Unlike England itself where there was a break in the tradition of floral marquetry, in Germany the fashion continued throughout the eighteenth century, becoming more and more naturalistic with scenes and landscapes rendered in different woods, until with the work of Oeben and Roentgen it had a profound effect in turn on French furniture under Louis XVI. The outstanding lacquer worker of his time, not only in Germany but in Europe, was Gerhard Dagly, appointed in 1687 'Kammerkünstler' (or 'Directeur des Ornements') to Friedrich Wilhelm, the 'Great Elector' of Brandenburg,

and to his son, who in 1700 became King of Prussia. Dagly, who came from Spa, a small town just south of the German border long renowned for its production of japanned objects, appears only to have decorated furniture made by others, but his work, much of which still survives at Charlottenburg, is of extraordinary beauty, largely because of the white background (possibly intended to look like porcelain) which he regularly gave his 'oriental' scenes. His renown at the time can be judged from the fact that the Electress of Hanover, sending an English japanned clock-case to her Prussian son-in-law, should have remarked apologetically, 'Dagly makes much better ones'. Dagly's brother, Jacques, eventually went to live in Paris where he became a partner with Claude Audran and Pierre de Neufmaison in a venture to promote a new technique of lacquering, for which they sought a patent — another interesting sidelight on how France, having influenced, in turn learnt from German cabinet-makers. Dagly's most famous pupil, Martin Schnell, went to Dresden where he worked for Augustus the Strong.

Between about 1720 and 1750, when the freer, easier lines of the Rococo were already emerging in France and England, the Baroque style reached perhaps its European summit in the extravagance of German designers and furniture-makers. Two authors of pattern books published in Augsburg and Nuremberg between 1711 and 1724, Paul Decker and J J Schübler, must take much of the credit for this. Between them they elaborated the already fantastic engraved designs of Daniel Marot and made popular a style of almost unbelievable richness and complication. Schübler's *penchant* for mechanical devices (shown for instance in a design for a table incorporating a dumb-waiter and a fountain) illustrates a particular obsession of German cabinet-makers, again to reach fruition much later in the work of Oeben. Even more than this however, the Germans brought to their interpretation of the Baroque a taste for the bizarre and the exotic. One has only to think of Augustus the Strong's state bedchamber at Schloss Maitzburg near Dresden with wall- and bed-hangings made from the brightly coloured feathers of birds imported from Mexico, of the Porcelain Room at Charlottenburg (designed by Eosander von Goethe in 1710), its pale green walls barely visible under a mass of pink porcelain perched on carved gilt brackets and ledges stretching from floor to ceiling, or of Pflitzner's 'Spiegelkabinett' at Pommersfelden reflecting in a thousand tiny mirrors the very unecclesiastical behaviour of Archbishop von Schönborn, to realize that the late nineteenth-century castles of Ludwig the Mad were not the isolated whims of a lunatic, but the expression of a long-established German taste.

Scandinavia

It is questionable how far Danish and Swedish furniture of the late seventeenth and early eighteenth centuries can properly be called Baroque. As with the countries of the Iberian peninsula very few houses, apart from the royal palaces and the castles of occasional exceptionally powerful nobles, had any furniture with pretensions to artistic merit. Purely functional joiner's chairs and tables were otherwise the rule. Most of the more ambitious pieces in the royal collections came anyway from abroad: Frederick IV of Denmark's visit to Italy in 1709 for instance brought to Rosenborg not only a Florentine pietra-dura table designed by Foggini but also a whole room of Venetian glass, to add to the Augsburg silver furniture acquired by his predecessors. When an important item was commissioned from a native craftsman, it tended to be extremely old-fashioned in form, such as the anointment throne of narwhal tooth made by a carver called Bendix Grodtschilling for the coronation of Christian V in 1681, which actually appears to have a Romanesque derivation, with its arcaded base and back.

In general, however, it can be said that the traditional political alliances of the two countries reveal the dominant artistic influences on them. In the case of Denmark, friendship with England brought typically Restoration and William and Mary forms of chairs, after a time lag of some 20 or 30 years. A fine set of chairs, again at Rosenborg, documented as the work of Johan Weys in 1718, with ebonized 'horsebone' crestings to their backs, heavy front stretchers and curving arms and scroll legs, would not look out of place at Ham or Knole in England. On the other hand in the case of Sweden, used by Louis XIV and his successors as a 'buffer' to keep Russia out of Europe, one does not have to look far for French influence. The correspondence of the architect Nicodemus Tessin reveals the extraordinarily close cultural contacts between the two countries in the late seventeenth century. A great deal of French furniture was imported direct, such as the marvellous state bed given to an ambassador, Count Rielke, by Louis XIV, or the Parisian armchairs of the 1680s which can still be seen at the castle of Skokloster. Little is known of native Swedish craftsmen of this date, though they were evidently greatly influenced by these French models. One cabinet-maker whose name is known, and whose work seems to have been far superior in quality to most of his contemporaries', was Burchardt Precht, a carver of German origin working in Stockholm in the 1690s — the maker of an extremely accomplished pair of gilt guéridons in the form of angels with outspread wings, now in the Nordiska Museet. Precht, like Boulle, had a number of sons who continued to make furniture during the eighteenth century in the 'Tessin style' so successfully adopted by their father.

Spain and Portugal
The Pyrenees represented in the seventeenth century a far more formidable cultural barrier than the Alps. Spain and Portugal had until then drawn much of their artistic inspiration not from Europe at all, but from the Moors. Both were slow to adopt the forms and the decorative vocabulary of Baroque furniture normal elsewhere on the Continent, and indeed only began to do so after about 1680. In Spain the most common types of furniture continued to be movable, in marked contrast with the huge architectural pieces produced in Italy and France. *Vargueños*, square or rectangular chests with a fall-front concealing a mass of small drawers, were the staple product of Spanish cabinet-makers, usually with ornate iron handles at each side, with which they could be placed on simple, often folding, stands. The *papeleira*, another type of chest opening at the top and intended for the storage of papers, the trestle table with wrought-iron braces in the form of lyre or yoke-shaped scrolls, and the folding X-frame

chair or *sillón de cadera*, went on being made in the traditional forms throughout this century, testifying to the still nomadic existence of the Spanish nobility. The decoration of these pieces was also conservative, the Mudéjar, or Moorish style, lingered in the south, where furniture continued to be made with intricate geometrical patterns inlaid in ivory, metal and olive or cedarwood — the technique known in the Italian Renaissance as 'alla certosina' or 'damaschina', after its supposed origins in Damascus. Representational art, forbidden by Mohammedan law, became more popular in the north with the advent of the Churrigueresque style, named after the leading architect of the day, when areas of dense ornament, usually of figure-filled arcades, contrasted with totally plain, flat surroundings, on the fronts of cabinets as much as on the façades of churches. One important technical development was in bob-

Above: The saloon at Skokloster, Sweden, built in the late seventeenth century by a Swedish general, Count Wrangel. The Swedish debt to French Baroque design is demonstrated by the grisaille paintings on the ceiling, executed in 1674, which are based on engravings by Le Pautre; the carving of the chimney-piece and overmantel are also inspired by French pattern books, and the superb gilt armchairs were imported from Paris. (Skokloster Palace, Sweden) bin and spiral turning. Beds in particular, never as in the rest of Europe heavily curtained or with a tester (presumably because of the heat), relied for their effect on heavily carved backboards of pyramidal shape, carved as tiers of arcades with turned columns or spindles. Gilding, and also European Baroque forms like twisted columns, began to be used on later seventeenth-century vargueños, as on some unusually ornate examples in the Museo de Artes Decorativas at Madrid.

Seat furniture too, finally began to achieve a more European look through the use of turning. The X-frame chair developed first into the *sillón frailero*, a sturdy four-square armchair with straight back and arms and thick front stretcher, usually with very wide seats and backs of stamped leather, a type familiar from the portraits of Velásquez. While the simple overall shape of these chairs was largely maintained, spirally-turned legs and stretchers brought them gradually more into line with Louis XIII seat furniture, albeit long after the fashion had passed in France itself. The accession of a French king, Philip V, in 1700 brought more up-to-date Parisian fashions to furniture-makers round Madrid, but at the cost of that originality (in materials, techniques and design) which had hitherto been the hall-mark of Spanish furniture.

Portuguese furniture-makers were similarly at their most original between 1640 and 1700, after which date the fashions of London rather than Paris began to be imitated. The woods used by them were for a start strikingly different from the rest of Europe: chestnut had been and remained the most popular native wood, but Brazilian rosewood (*jacarandá* or *pau preto*), imported from her great colonial empire was increasingly used in Portugal, the first American tropical wood to be employed extensively by European cabinet-makers, at least a hundred years before the advent of mahogany in England.

Cupboards and vast chests of drawers in the sacristies of the great monastic churches were, to begin with, the only highly decorated pieces of furniture, often suggesting Spanish influence in their geometrical inlay. Two of the finest of all, at the abbey of Alcobaza (where the sacristy was described in the late eighteenth century by William Beckford as a room 'gorgeous and glistening, worthy of Versailles itself') are dated 1664 and seem to imitate in carved wood the geometric Moorish tiles of the period. The technique of parallel grooving, known as 'wave' or 'flame' pattern in northern Europe, became a favourite device in Portugal, where it was known as *tremido*. Sometimes, as on a wardrobe in the palace of the Dukes of Braganza at Guimaraés, the whole piece of furniture would be submerged in these heavy, but rippling, mouldings. Turning, too, was taken to new Baroque

heights in Portugal, where the profusion of easily worked imported rosewood enabled furniture-makers to indulge in virtuoso displays of discs, balls, reels and spiralling forms, giving a unique expression of rapid movement and revolving and exploding forms to large tables and cabinets, particularly in the region around Evora. Japanning also became popular, perhaps partly due to the influence of Stalker and Parker's treatise on the subject published in England in 1688.

In seat furniture, too, the early influence was Spanish, and leather, often stamped with coats of arms or floral designs and held in place by elaborate patterns of brass studs, remained the standard covering for seats and backs well into the eighteenth century. In about the 1680s, however, a new type of chair frame was evolved, the *cadeira de sola*, with turned (but not usually spiral) legs and arms,

Below: Ivory cabinet, the drawers inlaid with gold, silver and pearls, probably made in Portuguese Goa about 1670. Ultimately derived in form from the Augsburg cabinets popular all over Europe in the Baroque period, it is typical of much colonial furniture in its extraordinary mixture of precious materials with Buddhist and European decorative motifs.

a typically Baroque front stretcher of scrolls and a high, shaped back. In time these backs also acquired carved shells and garlands in the style of Daniel Marot, and also the so-called *pé de pincel* or 'paintbrush' foot, which was to be copied in England.

The cross-fertilization of ideas between England and Portugal is complicated. In the Restoration period, after Catherine of Braganza's marriage to Charles II, the turned ebony furniture imported by Portugal from her Indian colony, Goa, was much sought after in England, but, after the Queen's return to her native country in 1693 and the Methuen Treaty of 1703, Portugal owed much more to England. Regular cargoes from London to Lisbon and Oporto included, for instance, the scarlet and gold lacquer chairs of Giles Grendey, while native craftsmen emulated the Queen Anne style in their chairs with cabriole legs, splat backs, pad, slipper and claw-and-ball feet, the only difference being a more exaggerated curve of the back, and deeper aprons on both the chairs and tables.

Colonial Furniture

Indo-Portuguese furniture, made not only in Goa but in other trading posts along the west coast of India, and also the products of Portugal's South American colonies, deserve to be mentioned briefly as by-products of the Baroque. Although the forms they took were largely European, the materials and decorative patterns used were startlingly different. Teak, inlaid with ivory, ebony, bone and sometimes Brazilian woods in a mesh of small circles is sometimes reminiscent of the *certosina* inlay of the north Italian Renaissance, though it in fact derives from Mogul art. The caryatid figures supporting cabinets or chairs look from a distance like conventional Venetian negroes, but turn out at close range to be uncouth savages staring vacantly out of ivory eyes. Perhaps most beautiful of all was the furniture made in Goa entirely veneered in ivory, and decorated with incised lines in black. Pieces of this kind were coveted by European collectors throughout the eighteenth and well into the nineteenth century, despite the very rough finishing and naïve decoration they were so often given.

Furniture in seventeenth-century colonial America shows a familiar pattern of fashion following trade routes. Whereas in New York and New Jersey, the standard form continued to be the great Dutch cupboard, or 'kas', the New England seaports, Boston and Newport, produced joined pieces, such as chests of drawers and tallboys, of obviously English derivation. The Southern colonies had at this stage the closest links of all with England, and the ships which regularly brought tobacco and rice to London or Bristol returned with imported English furniture, thus delaying the establishment of an independent furniture-making tradition.

The time lag between English and American fashion is startlingly evident in the joined furniture of Massachusetts and Connecticut, which continued to be made until the 1700's on essentially Jacobean lines: court-cupboards, usually decorated with bobbin turning, or panelled chests, rarely ornamented and then only with stylized sunflower or geometrical motifs carved in shallow relief. It was only very gradually after that date that the more Baroque furniture of the William and Mary period in England came to be imitated. Sophisticated marquetry techniques even then did not catch on, and 'seaweed' patterns of the Gerrit Jensen type were usually imitated in painted decoration on a flat un-veneered surface. Japanning was practised in Boston, though again this amounted more to *trompe l'oeil* painting than to genuine lacquer. It also continued for a good 30 years after the fashion had died in England. Unmistakably 'Queen Anne' furniture, displaying not a hint of the

Right: Highboy by John Pimm, made in Boston, Massachusetts about 1745. Although by English standards a very old-fashioned piece, its lacquer decoration, with a background painted to look like tortoiseshell, is still of exceptional quality. (Henry Francis Du Pont Museum, Wintherthur)

Below: Early eighteenth-century revolving chair from Andra State, India, entirely veneered in ivory with incised black decoration. Like the furniture produced in Portuguese Goa, mainly for export to the home country, this shows how European forms were married to older native techniques. (Victoria & Albert Museum, London)

Rococo, like the famous Loring family chest by a Boston maker, John Pimm, was being made as late as the 1750s. High chests of drawers on stands (or 'highboys' as they were often called) became a favourite form in America and, far more than seat furniture, achieved a style quite distinct from their English models, lighter in proportion and with broken scroll pediments and finials giving them a livelier silhouette. The concave shell ornament in the centre of the apron, a feature possibly invented by the prolific maker, Job Townsend, of Newport, Rhode Island, is another distinctively American detail.

Chairs varied greatly from area to area, within different colonies, though most were closely based on English examples. Large upholstered wing armchairs from New Hampshire, ladderbacks from the Delaware river basin, and chairs with vase-shaped splat backs, a particular speciality of a maker called John Gaines from Portsmouth, New Hampshire, could easily be mistaken for provincial English furniture of a generation earlier. One new form developed in Connecticut, which seems to have had no true European counterpart, was the 'butterfly' table, so called because of the exotic curved shapes of the supports to its hinged flaps. Set against the inward slant of its legs, these gave a sense of Baroque movement to what was essentially a simple joiner's piece. As might be expected, more variety in the woods used was also a hall-mark of American colonial furniture: as well as walnut and mahogany, both adopted very early on, maple, fruitwood and gumwoods, and rarities such as 'butternut' (or white walnut) were available, and gave an interesting range of colours and finishes to pieces that might otherwise have seemed stereotyped.

After its settlement in 1682, Philadelphia swiftly became the cabinet-making centre of America, just as it became the second most important town in the English-speaking world. The earliest signed piece of Philadelphia furniture known to exist — a fall-front walnut secretaire at Williamsburg by Edward Evans, dated 1707 — would have done credit to a London firm like Coxed & Woster. In keeping with its grand Palladian buildings, more architectural forms of furniture began to be developed in Philadelphia in the 1720s and 1730s, usually based on English pattern books. The cabinet for an air pump, presented to the Library Company of Philadelphia by Governor John Penn in 1739, made by John Harrison, sums up this rather ponderous but impressive style with its huge fluted pilasters, Doric frieze and broken pediment. But if Philadelphia saw the last gasp of the international Baroque style in these cabinet-makers' work, it was also, as the centre of American fashion by 1760, to pioneer the late arrival of the Rococo.

THE LINE OF BEAUTY
The Rococo style

'Rococo' is applied to the style prevalent in the middle of the eighteenth century. It was first used as a term of abuse, by students of the painter J-L David in Paris. 'Pompadour, rococo' stood for everything that muscular neo-classicists disliked about the Louis Quinze period. The style was luxurious, aristocratic, sensuous, and, what was worse, frivolous. Above all, for the first time since the Renaissance, the designers had presumed to ignore the example of classical antiquity.

Today classicism is not the exclusive rule, and the Rococo period is rightly seen as one of the high points in European furniture. The style, originating in Paris, swept across Europe in a mood of relaxation. It was well suited to its period, which for the most part was a peaceful one. When, during the 1750s and 1760s, the neo-classical reaction set in, the Rococo style died quickest in England and France. In more conservative countries it lingered on, almost to the time of the French Revolution.

Rococo was an international style. At the courts of Europe, from Madrid to St Petersburg, rulers and princes decorated their palaces in the lively, glittering manner that was the eighteenth century's response to the Baroque splendours of Versailles. However, the original intention had not been to provide a setting for ceremony. Rococo grew up in Paris with the desire for an intimate, agreeable way of living. This led to the use of bright, cheerful colours, and to the invention of many new forms of furniture, most of which are still in use today. At the same time, the skills of the craftsmen improved, resulting in furniture of lighter construction and greater elegance.

Rococo was a style of interior decoration, and the part played by the architect-designer was of extreme importance. Carved pieces were made to fit in with the panelling, and never look quite the same when moved away from their original setting. The range of decorative detail was largely formulated by the designers. C- or S-scrolls developed from Baroque strapwork and arabesques. Acanthus foliage originated in the ancient scrolled *rinceau*, but took on an organic form as though freely growing. Other natural forms were used, such as palms, rushes and roses. The most characteristic motif was the *rocaille* (shell- or rock-work), which was crimped and indented, and bordered on one side by a curved moulding. Only highly skilled craftsmen could properly convey the Rococo sense of vitality and movement, and it is not surprising that in Germany and Italy many of the carvers were sculptors by training.

The Catholic courts and aristocrats of southern Europe were hedonist in their outlook, and their palaces were decorated and furnished with luxury. But the eighteenth

101

century was also a successful time for the bourgeoisie. Particularly in the Protestant north of Europe and in America, the merchants and traders, bureaucrats and city officials were becoming increasingly prosperous. They preferred practical and convenient furniture to an opulent display. Thus, two styles existed simultaneously. The division can be seen most clearly in Germany, where bourgeois furniture continued and developed within the established formulae, while princes and potentates followed or attempted to surpass the fashions of Paris.

France

On the death of Louis XIV in 1715 the tyranny of Versailles came to an end, and the aristocracy thankfully returned to Paris to pursue their own lives without risk of royal displeasure. French Rococo has often been associated with the extravagant behaviour of her society. Yet for all its privilege, arrogance and corruption, this society was one of extreme sophistication. Paris was the centre and model of European culture, and all other countries imitated her fashions in some degree. Though not exactly private, life in Paris became informal and intimate. Poise, wit, the art of conversation and the desire to please were cultivated to a level unknown elsewhere. Social life was largely dominated by women. The men were invariably agreeable to ladies,

and the ladies to each other. All this contributed to the *douceur de vivre* of the *ancien régime*, and to such manners the refined, jewel-like furniture seems a natural accompaniment.

The three styles or periods are Régence (till about 1730), Louis Quinze (from about 1730 to 1760), and transitional. Together, the dates cover most of Louis XV's reign, but the styles overlap to a surprising extent, and furniture can seldom be accurately dated without documentary evidence. Moreover, by the time of the King's death in 1774, the neo-classical style was firmly established.

Régence is named after the duc d'Orléans, regent to the infant Louis XV. From 1716, d'Orléans redecorated the Palais Royal with G-M Oppenordt (the son of a Dutch cabinet-maker) as his architect-designer. Although many elements of Rococo can be detected before 1716 — as, for example, in the delicate scrolls and arabesques of Bérain, or the grotesques and fantasy figures of Watteau — it was at the Palais Royal and other Parisian houses that the style lost the restraints of classicism. Oppenordt and others designed furniture such as side-tables, sofas and chairs. These carved pieces were probably made by the same craftsmen who worked on the panelling of the rooms for which they were intended. The designs can be florid and heavily loaded with detail.

Above: This room in the Château de Champs was panelled in the early eighteenth century, but when Madame de Pompadour acquired the Château in 1757, she employed the painter Cristophe Huet to paint it in the chinoiserie style. The fantasy landscapes and figures have little to do with true Chinese painting, but are derived from the exotic decorative style of Watteau. They are not unlike the chinoiserie tapestries designed by the painter Boucher and made at the Beauvais factory. The furniture here is in the Régence style, rather heavier than that of the following Louis Quinze period. The seat furniture is covered with Beauvais tapestry of exotic landscapes with birds and animals.

About 1718, the armrests of chairs were set back a little to allow room for panniered skirts, and the backs of chairs were lowered lest they interfere with the elaborate coiffures of the time. As for veneered furniture, a cheerful tone had been set when Boulle used kingwood about 1711, rather than the sombre ebony, tortoiseshell and brass. The typical Régence commode, known as *à tombeau*, is a solid piece with three drawers and short feet. It seems to have been made as late as the 1740s. The ormolu mounts slowly took on a Rococo vigour as acanthus and scrolls became lively, and stern classical masks gave way to more graceful forms. The influence of Watteau can be seen in the affected twisting of ormolu heads placed at the corners of tables and commodes.

During the Louis Quinze period, increased lightness of form and decoration resulted in a simplification of outline and detail. Many new types of furniture appeared, and there were fresh techniques in cabinet-making. The best known of the designers were Pineau and Meissonnier. Nicholas Pineau (1684–1754) returned from Russia in 1727. Besides designs for panelled rooms, there survive a number of his drawings for chairs. He carried the unclassical manner of Oppenordt a stage further, introducing asymmetrical scrollwork and rocaille. This, however, was more evident in the work of J-A Meissonnier (1695–1750),

originally a goldsmith in Turin, whose metalwork includes the famous and immensely influential candlesticks which were engraved in 1728. Meissonnier designed rooms and furniture, using shell- and rock-work combined with forms such as carved rocks, water and foliage. This lively asymmetrical style was known as the *goût pittoresque*. All the decoration of a room, with its gilded carving and brightly coloured upholstery, was to be reflected back and forth 'as by magic' in the great looking-glasses let into the panelling. The Rococo of Meissonnier was influential abroad, but in France it was short-lived as Parisians soon turned to a more restrained style.

The typical Louis Quinze commode was of bombé shape, with two drawers, its graceful outlines melting together in continuous curves. The mosaic-like parquetry of kingwood, purplewood or rosewood was carefully matched and gave subtle reflections with changing lights. By 1740 there was a revival of marquetry, with delicate flower stems and scrolled borders, inlaid in contrasting woods. These developed into the lavish marquetry of the 1750s, where realistic bunches of flowers were inlaid in numerous different woods, stained, etched and scorched to give detail and chiaroscuro. They could be in bright colours, but much of this work has now faded.

Right: Made in about 1730 by Charles Cressent, this magnificent commode is in the late Régence style. Cressent, one of the finest cabinet-makers of Paris, had originally been trained as a sculptor, and this accounts for the high quality of the ormolu figures. The ormolu work is set off by the sparkling background of kingwood parquetry. (National Trust, Waddesdon Manor, Buckinghamshire)

completed nine years later by Riesener, is a hybrid piece. The curves of the bodywork are straighter, while the lower part remains true Rococo. At the same time, classical or architectural details were beginning to appear in the ormolu work. The transitional period delighted in marquetry, but turned to classical landscapes or perspectives, urns and other utensils. Cube parquetry is a feature of the transitional period.

The forms or types of furniture became very numerous after the 1730s, and are best referred to by their French names, partly because these are in use by writers and auction houses today, and partly because there is often no proper English equivalent. Even in the eighteenth century, some of the names were already in dispute, and since then many more have been invented. Guild regulations divided the furniture craft between *menuiserie* (joinery and chair-making) and *ébénisterie* (cabinet-work and veneering), and by legislation of 1744 and 1751 makers were obliged to sign their works with an approved stamp. The considerable number of pieces that are unsigned were, presumably, made either by those who were protected by royal patronage, or who lived in areas outside the jurisdiction of the city. From 1745 to 1749, ormolu and all metalwork containing copper had to be stamped with a small mark of a crowned 'C', but this proved impossible to enforce, and the order was repealed.

Above: Known as a voyeuse, this chair, a variant of the bergère or enclosed armchair, has a flat back, surmounted by a rail for a person to lean on from behind, in order to join in conversation or watch a card game. This one was made in about 1760 by J-B Tilliard. (Musée des Arts Décoratifs, Paris)

Right: A commode with two cupboard doors rather than two drawers was known as a commode à vantaux, and was imitated in England, around 1770, by Chippendale and other London makers. This elegant example by Pierre Migeon is veneered with tulipwood, with contrasting scrolls of purplewood. (Musée des Arts Décoratifs, Paris)

The *corporation des menuisiers-ébénistes* included not only the two principal crafts but all related trades. Strict regulations ordered that the menuisier could only make the frame of the chair, which then had to go to the carver, the gilder or painter, and the upholsterer. Similarly, by law the ébéniste could only make the case and marquetry of a commode or other piece. Ormolu was a different trade, and so was painting and lacquer work. Tiresome as the guild regulations may seem, they produced specialists in all the crafts whose skills have probably never been equalled. Among the enormous number of furniture-makers, perhaps the most famous are Charles Cressent, who worked for d'Orléans; Jean-François Oeben, a German by birth, who was in Paris by 1749 and is associated with a number of new forms and marquetry styles; and Bernard Vanrisamburgh.

The sinuous forms of menuiserie are typified by the superb chairs that envelop the sitter in curves well adapted to the shape of the body. Stretchers connecting the legs of the chair could be dispensed with by about 1725. 'Architectural' chairs, made to stand against the panelling, were of the type known as *à la reine* with flat backs. Smaller movable chairs 'for convenience' included the *fauteuil en cabriolet* with a curved back, and the chair without arms *(siège)*. Louis Quinze chairs were imitated in all European countries.

Other forms of chair had special purposes. The *bergère* was the most comfortable: this had an upholstered back which sometimes had wings at each side, and arms reaching the seat which was fitted with a thick down cushion. The *voyeuse* had a padded rail across the back so that a second party could lean over it to watch a card game. The desk chair *(fauteuil de bureau)* was normally caned and cushioned, and the seat lozenge-shaped, coming forward to a central leg. This was more comfortable for those seated for long periods at a desk. The two forms of stool, the *tabouret* and the folding *pliant* were still made, but now seemed rather formal in this period of relaxed manners.

The different forms of sofa included the *canapé*, made to match the 'architectural chairs', and less formal types: the *marquise*, made for two sitters only; the *ottomane*, with curved ends; and the *veilleuse*, often made in pairs, with one high and one low end for lying upon at full length. The *chaise longue* was rather wide, with a raised end, upholstered or caned, and the *duchesse* was narrower, with one high and one low end.

There were two principal types of bed. The *lit à la française* generally had a headboard

Above: This small type of chaise longue, known as a veilleuse, made for a lady's boudoir, epitomizes the relaxed luxury of Parisian private life. The veilleuse, made for reclining, was a sofa with one high and one low end. This example is unusual in its curved ends. The thick down cushion makes it extremely comfortable, while the frame is delicately carved with flowerheads in the style typical of the Louis Quinze chairmakers. It is signed by J-B Tilliard, a famous menuisier who made chairs for the King, and dates from the 1750s. (Victoria & Albert Museum, London)

Right: An historic painting, entitled Tea in the English Style with the Princesse de Conti in the Salon of the Four Mirrors at the Temple, Paris, by Michel Olivier (1712–1784), which shows Mozart aged eight during his first visit to Paris in 1766. He is playing on a plain walnut harpsichord before a party at the Princesse de Conti's apartment. The decoration of the rooms is rather plain and old-fashioned, but typical features of the French interior are the enormous looking-glasses set in the panelling, the candle brackets, the portraits framed over the doors and the French draw-curtains. The furniture includes tea-tables and painted chairs covered with needlework. Serving and dining-tables were generally of plain deal, to be covered with damask cloths, and were brought in for occasions such as these. (Louvre, Paris)

and a footboard as well as four posts and a canopy. If the canopy was suspended from the ceiling, the bed was *à la duchesse*. But beds without canopies were also made to fit into alcoves, which were then curtained all round. The second type of bed was the *lit à la polonaise*. Here the small, oval canopy covered only about a third of the bed surface, and was supported by curved iron rods that were concealed by the curtains.

Side-tables were very elegant. In spite of their apparent delicacy, they were strong enough to support their marble tops without shaking. The console table was attached to the wall and had only two legs that curved inwards towards the feet, and were often joined by a richly carved 'nut'. Side-tables, like most 'architectural furniture', were made to match the panelling both in carving and decoration. Other forms of furniture were made by menuisiers, especially wardrobes. But the best writing-tables, dressing-tables, and buffets belonged to the cabinet-maker's art, and when they were joiners' pieces they tended to look provincial.

The art of ébénisterie lay principally in setting veneer or marquetry onto curved surfaces. All the Rococo details which in menuiserie were carved in solid wood were here applied in ormolu. The commode was always a luxurious piece, and is one of the most typical forms of the period. The top was invariably of coloured marble, generally quarried in the south of France. By 1750, small commodes were popular. The rather rare *commode en console* stood on two legs only, with its back fixed to the wall. A *commode à vantaux* had two doors in front, enclosing shelves or drawers. Buffets, or low wardrobes, were rather similar but slightly taller, and had the cumbersome name of *meuble à hauteur d'appui*, or *meuble d'appui*. Pairs of small commodes with shaped fronts (*encoignures*) were made to fit into corners, and matched other cabinet-work in the room. They often

had shelves above for porcelain, but these have only rarely survived, and their existing marble tops are generally replacements.

The *bureau-plat* or flat writing-table was a large functional piece that always remained popular. The rectangular top became serpentine, recessed at the centre of each side. Smaller *bureaux-plats* were made from about 1740, sometimes with extension slides at either end. The *bureau Mazarin* or kneehole writing-table survived only in the provinces. Meanwhile, fresh forms were developed. The English bureau, with a sloping front that could be locked up, is a rare instance of the French borrowing a foreign form, and was known as a *bureau en pente* or *bureau de dame*. It evolved by about 1760 into the cylinder writing-table. The upright secretaire (*secrétaire à abattant* or *en armoire*) made its appearance before 1750 and became very popular later in the century.

The fashionable way of life called for numerous kinds of small tables in the ladies' private apartments. They were called *tables ambulantes*, and often included differently fitted drawers, so that a single table could be used for needlework, writing, reading, taking private meals, or dressing. The *table à écrire* was a miniature bureau-plat, with a front or

Above: the bureau plat, made throughout the eighteenth century, was a writing-table of a strong and masculine character. This example, made by Charles Cressent in the late 1720s, still retains the rectangular top and sturdy legs of the Louis Quatorze period, which after 1730 developed into more supple curves. The grain of the kingwood and tulipwood veneer runs in different directions, giving subtle reflections of the light. The vivacity and freedom of the scrolling leaves, and the slightly affected female busts at the corners show the informality of the later Régence style. (Louvre, Paris)

Right: An exceptionally fine example of the drop-front secretaire (sécrétaire à abattant) by J-F Dubut, which became increasingly popular in Paris after 1750. Just four feet (over one metre) high, it is designed for a lady's use. The floral marquetry at the sides is inlaid on a tulipwood and purplewood ground. The Chinese lacquer panels, taken off imported screens, is skilfully laid down on the curved surfaces, and the bold ormolu mounts emphasize the luxurious quality of the piece. (Metropolitan Museum of Art, New York)

side drawer fitted for pens, ink and paper. One type of table, perhaps invented by Oeben, had a top made to slide back to reveal a drawer fitted with a looking-glass, reading-stand or compartments. The French aristocracy were compulsive gamblers and ordered a large number of games tables. Madame de Pompadour had six of these in her salon at Meudon.

Dressing-room furniture tended to be more functional, but could be equally decorative. The *coiffeuse* had a central hinged mirror, flanked by two flaps underneath which were compartments for scent bottles. Bedside-tables contained small cupboards with marble shelves to hold a chamber pot, and occasionally a drawer below containing the *chaise percée*. Candlestands with tray tops, known as *guéridons*, tended to be rather wide and low, and were also useful as coffee- or worktables.

French provincial furniture was of two kinds. Important towns like Dijon, Lyons and Bordeaux had their own guilds and craftsmen who more or less followed Paris fashions to supply their merchants and officials. Such work is sometimes signed. A provincial origin of a commode may be indicated by its carcase being of pine rather than of oak, or by its general lack of finesse. True regional styles, however, are of greater interest and can have undoubted charm. Such country furniture features in paintings by Chardin and Greuze. It was made for country aristocrats and the bourgeoisie as well as for the better-off peasants. Provincial Rococo can be handsome and distinctive, but is hard to date. The style reached Brittany and Gascony later, and it survived in many districts into and beyond the nineteenth century.

Over the whole country, the basic forms did not vary much. In contrast with the increasing sophistication of Paris, provincial furniture kept alive many outmoded pieces: kneehole writing-desks, buffets, dough bins and food cupboards. Ladderback chairs with rush seats, and simple tables with curved legs seem almost timeless in their style. The show-pieces were cupboards, often in two parts, and the panelling, with chanelled and scrolled mouldings, and carved flowers either in high or low relief, can be very fine. The woods used varied slightly with the resources of each district. The best and most expensive were oak and walnut, with boxwood for turned chair legs. Other native woods such as cherry, chestnut, elm, beech, ash and poplar were less expensive.

Each region had its own traditions. Flemish influence can be seen in the north-east, while the furniture of Picardy tends to have little carving. In Normandy, fine cupboards were made in great quantity, and are hard to distinguish from those of Paris. In Brittany, where a middle class hardly existed, there was

a marked reluctance to accept Rococo decoration, and many pieces were ornamented with geometrical rather than scrolling or naturalistic patterns. A feature of Breton interiors is the use of dressers with open shelves to hold pottery. In order to exclude draughts, Breton beds were enclosed by panelling so as almost to become closets. Gascony was also conservative and kept to Louis Treize styles for a long while. In the south-east, the country styles of Burgundy were more sophisticated and bourgeois in character, while in Provence they became almost luxurious. Provençal cupboards are often swelled or even bombé, and the influence of Piedmont is obvious in the shapes of chests of drawers and their richly carved decoration.

The French provincial style extended to the Canadian colonies, centred at Quebec. Furniture was well proportioned, but sparing in its carved decoration, and the wood generally used was pine. Finer work with carving, and the use of walnut, cherry and maple, was reserved for church furnishings.

Above: Chardin's painting, Saying Grace, of about 1740 shows a simple interior typical of the French lower bourgeoisie. Of the provincial forms shown here, the high-back chairs derive from Louis Quatorze types, while the rush-seat chair and the buffet are forms which were still being made in the twentieth century. (Louvre, Paris)

Above: The tapestry room in the Hôtel d'Ansembourg, Liège, was completed during the early 1740s. The stucco ceiling, which has allegorical scenes concerned with music, was made by Italian craftsmen, and the walls are hung with Audenarde tapestries of country scenes. The dado panelling, of carved oak, and the marble chimney-piece are in the French style, and are similar to the designs of Pineau, Blondel and others. The chairs were made at Malmédy, near Liège. The magnificent conference table is made of oak, and has panels of marquetry, worked chiefly in native woods: ash, sycamore and cherry. The top is fitted with drawers, and has six rising bookrests.

Liège was the centre of a wealthy bishopric situated between Flanders and Germany. Although part of the Holy Roman Empire, its furniture is not typical of the German style. Some of the forms and all the decoration came from France, but the result is too fine to be classed as French provincial. The industries of Liège had been stimulated by the wars of Louis XIV, and the Walloon population included many brilliant craftsmen. The houses built by the 1730s include the Château de Seraing for the Prince-Bishop, and the Hôtel d'Ansembourg for the banker Michel Willems. The craft guilds flourished, but very little furniture is actually signed.

The principal wood was oak, carefully chosen for its fine quality, close grain, and consistent, delicate sheen. Some pieces were partly gilded and painted, but bronze and ormolu were sparingly used. The most typical pieces are the great oak cupboards and buffets in one or two parts, tall clocks, commodes with four equal drawers and short feet, writing-tables, bureaux, and glazed cabinets and bookshelves. The delicate carving, always carried out in solid wood, resembles that on French wall panelling. Furniture outlines were simple, and the effect, unlike that of Dutch or German furniture, was never bulky or ungainly. Chairs were either in the French style and caned, or in the Germanic-Dutch tradition with back splats and loose seats. These were often of walnut, ash or elm. For simple furniture, pine and beech were also used.

Italy

Italy took up the Rococo spirit comparatively early, for a definite relaxation of style can be detected around 1700. Many features of the mature Rococo, as for instance those in Meissonnier's engravings of the thirties, originated in Italy — whether in the sixteenth-century grottoes decorated with rocks and shells, in the architecture of Borromini, or in late seventeenth-century carving, where scrolling strapwork has a surprising freedom and movement. Some late seventeenth-century sculptors, notably Filippo Parodi in Genoa, had already abandoned the seriousness of the Baroque for grace and gaiety. In the early eighteenth century, the Venetian painters like Ricci, Pellegrini and Guardi established the bright, fanciful fresco style that culminated in the work of Tiepolo. Many of these artists travelled all over Europe, and their painted ceilings and walls brought Italian light and air to northern palaces.

Thus, there is no clear division in Italy between Baroque and Rococo. The furniture is often hard to date, and in the absence of documented works, Italian furniture must be judged chiefly by its style. The general picture is one of regional characteristics modified by the various influences coming from France, Germany, and, occasionally, England, while Spanish influence can be seen in the south and Sicily.

Eighteenth-century Italy consisted of a number of separate states. In the kingdoms of Piedmont and Naples, palaces were built to rival the splendour of Versailles. In the Papal States, noble families contrived to redecorate their palaces with ceremonial splendour, even though many of their fortunes were now diminishing. Genoa and Venice were republics where there was a great demand for furniture from the nobility and successful merchants, and on the whole it is these two districts that have left us with the most distinctive variations of the Rococo style. In spite of so many regional differences, certain features developed over most of the peninsula, and make it possible to speak of 'Italian Rococo'.

Certain traditions of craftsmanship were continued. The most important was the skill of Italy's carvers. This was put to its greatest use in the churches, as in the gilded organ-cases, altar furnishings and sumptuous confessionals. The line dividing carvers and sculptors can be very thin, and Venetian and Genoese side-tables often abound with putti and nymphs or with groups of Chinese figures. At first, tables were heavily loaded with carving. Later they became extremely delicate, often appearing too fragile to support their marble tops. Luxurious mirror frames were made to hang over them, as were characteristic small looking-glasses with cartouche frames —wider at the top than at the bottom. Not much use was made of ormolu, Rococo borders and crestings on cupboards and commodes being ordinarily of carved and gilded wood.

Another traditional Italian material was marble. White or grey marble from Carrara was inexhaustible; Sicilian marble, streaked with salmon and green, was quarried principally for Naples. The famous coloured marbles, however, were taken from the ruins of classical buildings, and they too seemed to be in endless supply. *Verde antico*, yellow Siena, *cipollino*, porphyry, Egyptian alabaster and many others were all worked into table-tops. The Italian carved side-tables that are often seen in English country-houses may well have been bought for the sake of their marble tops.

Marquetry, or *intarsia*, had first been

developed in fifteenth-century Italy. Though it was now executed more extensively in France and Germany, Milanese marquetry was very delicate, showing panels of *galant* or *Commedia dell' Arte* figures in shaped Rococo borders. Natural woods rather than stained ones were used, often with ivory for the flesh parts.

Although the shaped or bombé commode originated in France, the Italian versions are instantly recognizable, whether in the exaggerated Venetian or the simpler Genoese forms. Their bodies tend to be large, the legs to be extremely thin. Chests of drawers were sometimes veneered, but by the 1750s they were often japanned or painted with flowers against white or pale grounds. The outward appearance has great charm, and conceals the case work where, by French or English standards, the joinery can be shockingly bad. In painted furniture, japan *(lacca)* at first imitated Chinese lacquer, but this gave way to a more European style decorated with flowers on a light ground. Venetian lacca was rather thickly applied, but elsewhere, as in Genoa and the South, for instance, it could be so thin as almost to show the wood underneath. This tends to add to its charm. A less expensive kind of decoration was used, especially in the Venice district, known as *lacca povera*, in which small coloured engravings of pastoral or stage scenes, or topographical views were cut out and stuck on to the furniture, the remainder being painted and gilded, and the whole varnished over.

Some types of furniture are particularly Italian in form. Prie-dieus were made in great numbers, and the more elaborate were fitted into chapels and oratories while simpler pieces were used in bedrooms. The *trespolo*, much favoured in Venice, was a light, simple stand for a candle or dressing-glass. As regards seat furniture, the Italian chair of the Louis Quinze type generally has rather wide mouldings with concave chanellings, and the upholstered back and seat may be removable. Generally, the Italian version of the French chair lacks its comfort; the lines tend to be upright and its appearance hard. A north Italian form of the sofa is that known as *a ventaglio* or 'fan-shaped', in which the arms incline outwards at an angle of 45 degrees.

German influence was strongest in Lombardy and Venice, but it can be found as far south as Naples. The elaborate bureau-cabinet, known as a *trumeau,* with an elaborately shaped lower part and an arched and crested upper part, shows how northern forms that were never popular in France were common in Italy. Sometimes these bureaux are plain and rectangular, following English types. English influence is also found in chairs of the Queen Anne pattern.

Furniture for private rooms could be quite simple, and was either painted or made of walnut or cherry. The different forms were not nearly so numerous as in France, and they consisted chiefly of chairs, tables, chests of drawers large and small, and cupboards, often made in two parts. In general, physical comfort was not well catered for.

As for the different states, the various

114

Right: The Chinese Room in the Palace at Turin was designed by Filippo Juvarra, the architect to the King of Piedmont, and carried out from 1735 to 1738. The state rooms in the Turin palaces have a formal character very different from the intimacy of contemporary French interiors. Chinese lacquer was removed from imported screens, and set in Rococo borders of carved and gilded wood. The furniture was made for the room about 1740, and is based on French models. There are ten folding stools, two sofas and four side-tables. (Palazzo Reale, Turin)

regional styles can often, though not always, be recognized. The northern states were more active in making fine furniture than those of the centre and south. Lombardy, with Milan as the centre, was subject to Austria from 1717, and here German influence seems to have been strongest. Milanese furniture tends to be severe in outline and precise in workmanship. The typical piece was the bureau, or bureau-cabinet, generally veneered with figured walnut, or inlaid with marquetry scenes in discreetly contrasting woods. Milan, however, could match the height of Rococo opulence, as can be seen in the gallery of the Palazzo Clerici, designed during the 1740s, with its mirrored walls, gilded tables and sofas matching the panelling, and a superb ceiling painted by Tiepolo.

Piedmont was an independent kingdom of increasing power and influence. The Duke Vittorio Amadeo II assumed the title of King in 1713, and embarked on an ambitious programme of building churches and palaces with Filippo Juvarra as his architect. The poet Thomas Gray described the Royal Palace of Turin as 'the very quintessence of gilding and looking glass, inlaid floors, carved panels, and painting wherever they could stick a brush'. The Castello di Stupinigi, built from 1739 just outside Turin, has an even more grandiose interior with a great deal of chinoiserie decoration. Juvarra's panelling was richer than anything in Paris, and the gilded carving is equally inventive in chairs and side-tables, though not, curiously enough, in commodes. Juvarra seems to have designed much of the furniture himself, and used the best craftsmen he could find. Luigi Prinotto made splendid marquetry furniture during the 1720s, but was overshadowed by Pietro Piffetti, who was brought from Rome. Piffetti's furniture is among the most highly ornamented in Europe, with astonishing marquetry worked in all manner of rare woods, ivory, mother-of-pearl and silver. Some of it incorporated sculptured ormolu mounts made by Ladatte from Paris, while on other pieces the sculptured ornaments are of gilded wood. Apart from the great cabinets, tables and prie-dieus that are to be seen in the palace, Piffetti made simpler pieces, such as a card-table with *trompe l'oeil* inlay simulating playing cards. A feature of the Piedmontese bureau or cabinet in two parts is that the upper part is often raised up to stand on separate feet.

Furniture from republican Genoa was considerably simpler than that from the court of Turin, and its decoration was seldom excessive. Bombé chests of drawers tended to be large but well balanced, and were often painted with flowers in a pattern covering the whole front. The painting can be so thin as almost to show the wood underneath. Bureau-cabinets were always popular. Kingwood was used for veneer, and the characteristic Genoese parquetry has 'oyster' pieces of kingwood or olivewood combined in pairs to make a heart-shaped pattern. Genoese seat furniture was restrained, and close to French models. Ornamental side-tables were finely carved, and the sculptural tradition of Parodi continued with his son Domenico and other notable sculptors in wood.

The style of Venice is the most easily recognizable in Italy. The gilded tables, chairs and thrones made by the sculptor Antonio Corradini for the Ca' Rezzonico are really Baroque pieces designed in a playful mood, made to impress rather than to be used. More typical are the mid-century commodes, often made in sets, with exaggerated bombé shapes and carved, gilded borders. Chairs would still be large, with high backs when made for galleries or salons, or small and comfortable for private rooms; they were often made of walnut with open backs and seat-rails carved with interlaced mouldings. The general effect of these pieces is one of continual movement, as though reflected across rippling water, or in a distorting mirror. The Venetians loved colour, whether in damasks and silks, or in their brilliant lacca. Venetian looking-glasses, large and small, were often engraved with Commedia dell' Arte figures in patterned borders. Glass made at Murano was exported all over Europe.

In central Italy, great silk and textile works continued to flourish at Lucca, and Lucchese beds were designed principally to show off their hangings. Florentine Rococo tends to be rather florid and formal, but is hard to assess properly because the Medici patronage ceased altogether with the death of Giovanni Gastone in 1737, and much court furniture was sent to Vienna or sold. The Florentine production of *pietre dure* for table-tops and cabinet panels continued, though the designs were not so splendid as formerly. As this was so expensive, the cheaper technique of *scagliola*, which was decorated with sprays of flowers and classical landscape scenes, continued in the hands of Lamberto Gori, the pupil of Father Hugford. Such table-tops were often bought by English tourists, but they are easily damaged and not many survive today. In Rome, the nobility liked formal magnificence in their state-rooms. The best known of the Roman galleries is in

the Palazzo Doria Pamphili, redesigned after 1734, with its gilded tables and chairs covered in Genoese velvet that can seldom if ever have been used. Other families who had their palaces redecorated included the Barberini, Borghese and Chigi.

Southern Italy became independent of Hapsburg rule in 1734. The Bourbon king, Charles III, set up tapestry, porcelain and bronze works at Naples, all of which contributed to the decoration of his palaces in Naples and at Caserta. Neapolitan furniture, however, tends to be heavy in style, and northern Italians think ill of its proportions. The parquetry, in walnut, kingwood or other closely matching materials, is often centred by a flowerhead or eight-pointed star, within rope-twist or chequered borders. Sicilian furniture is full of gaiety, making use of silvering rather than gilding, and of flowers painted against light blue grounds. Much of it has a pleasant naïvety resulting from folk traditions or Spanish influence. Raised details on chests of drawers and other pieces were often applied in composition *(pastiglia)*.

Spain and Portugal

The demand for furniture by the hereditary nobility of Spain was not great. English travellers in the 1670s noticed the contrast between the vast size of their palaces and their scanty old-fashioned furnishings. At the same time, silk and velvet hangings were rich, and the eighteenth century produced a number of carved and gilded looking-glasses with tables to stand underneath. The carving on Spanish woodwork, though in the Rococo style, lacked the vitality of the French and Italian spirit. The Spanish were a conservative race, and even the tools used by the craftsmen were old-fashioned. Oak and walnut were becoming expensive, and painted furniture of soft wood was a cheaper substitute.

The old types of chair persisted, and they were often covered with tooled leather held in place by brass nailing. On the whole, the English forms were interpreted better than the French, and much English furniture was imported through Galicia or from Menorca. A different form of chair developed, with rush seating, turned uprights and carved ladder-back rails. These might appear somewhat rustic, but they were placed in noblemen's houses, and were often painted and gilded.

King Charles III, however, was a Bourbon descended from Louis XIV, and he had already been king of Naples for 25 years. He established royal furniture workshops on the lines of the Gobelins in Paris, and moved the Naples porcelain factory to El Buen Retiro. The furnishing of the palace in Madrid was directed by the Neapolitan Matteo Gasparini. The throne-room has vast looking-glasses and side-tables attributed to Ventura Rodriguez,

117

and a large carved and gilded throne. Many of the chairs designed by Gasparini were not carved, but veneered with kingwood or marquetry.

In general, the furniture of Portugal was more distinguished than that of Spain. Portugal became prosperous under King John V in the first half of the eighteenth century, and the disaster of the Lisbon earthquake in 1755 must at least have stimulated the demand for furniture as the city was rebuilt. The Portuguese style shows unmistakable English influences, and there were, in fact, many resident English families conducting the wine trade who imported English furniture. Chairs show both early Georgian and 'Chippendale' characteristics, and were finely made with crisp, lively sprays of acanthus carving on the backs and cabriole legs. Portuguese tables, bureaux and commodes were made in practical, well-balanced shapes, and their joinery was good. Much of this furniture was made in a variety of rosewood imported from the Brazilian colonies.

Germany

German furniture presents a very diverse picture, which is almost as baffling as the country's political condition. In the eighteenth century, Germany consisted of over 600 different states, loosely bound together as the Holy Roman Empire. Neglecting the tiny dominions of the knights, they group roughly into temporal principalities, ecclesiastical principalities, and free cities. If, broadly speaking, Rococo furniture can be divided between localized bourgeois styles and the international court style originating in Paris, this division is nowhere better seen than in Germany. The city merchants of the north were predominantly Protestant, and their furniture generally continued in the traditions already established by their guilds. At the courts, on the other hand, each prince, whether powerful or poor, endeavoured to rival the grandeur of Versailles and to surpass his neighbour. Palaces were built as emblems of state, and German Rococo decoration symbolizes grandeur and influence rather than informality. The southern courts were mostly Catholic, and at times interior decoration seems to have been limited neither by financial considerations nor by the nature of the materials used. The extreme of the European Rococo style came with the Bavarian churches, where the Catholic religion itself turned into a fantasy of extraordinary proportions.

The princes enjoyed chinoiserie, and Chinese rooms were constructed to display lacquered walls and collections of oriental porcelain. Chinese pleasure-houses in the parks, such as the Tea House at Potsdam, Schloss Pillnitz near Dresden, and the Pagodaburg at Nymphenburg, were for courtly diversions. Their furniture, including chairs, tea-tables and stands to display porcelain, might be either gilded, or japanned in the Chinese manner. Among the decorative arts, porcelain seems to express the epitome of

Left: Known today as the Gasparini Room, this was originally the Dressing Room of King Charles III. When Charles became King of Spain in 1759, he completed the interior of the Palace in Madrid regardless of expense, bringing painters (including Tiepolo and Mengs) and craftsmen from Italy. Mathias Gasparini was Neapolitan, and designed this room and the seat furniture. The elaborate stucco ceiling is complemented by the inlaid floor and embroidered silk wall-hangings. The chairs have something in common with German work, not only in their bulbous shapes, but in the unusual way the frames are veneered rather than carved. (Palacio Real, Madrid)

Right: One of the most famous of the Rococo commodes that were made for the Elector of Bavaria. It was made by Johann Adam Pichler in 1761, possibly to designs by Cuvilliés, and continues the delicate, pleasing style that he had established at the Munich Court 30 years before. The details show subtle refinements of the French Rococo style, and are of carved and gilded wood. In Paris they would have been of ormolu. (Residenzmuseum, Munich)

the German Rococo spirit, and by the end of this period many courts had established their own factories in rivalry to that at Meissen in Saxony. Exquisite porcelain figures were arranged in specially designed rooms with brackets built into the panelling. Their grace and sparkle, and the gilded furniture was reflected by the mirrored walls to make a glittering effect that could hardly be matched elsewhere in Europe.

At the beginning of the century, court architecture and decoration had been predominantly Italian, but from 1720, native designers were sent to study in Paris. Early Rococo furniture, therefore, was based on the *goût pittoresque* of Blondel, Pineau and Meissonnier, but in the important states regional variations quickly developed under the influence of court artists, sculptors and craftsmen. Among the great centres were Munich, Würzburg, Bayreuth and Bamberg, while further north, Saxony and, later, Prussia were very active. The Hapsburg court at Vienna, however, was an exception. It relied chiefly on Italian or French furniture and craftsmen. When a national Austrian style emerged after 1750, it was a predominantly middle-class one.

The most delicate of German Rococo developed in Bavaria, where the Elector Max Emanuel had his Residenz or city palace in Munich, and his Schloss Nymphenburg just outside the city. The character of Bavarian Rococo was established early by the architect Joseph Effner and the designer Cuvilliés, whose traditions were continued later by the carvers J A Pilcher and J M Schmidt. François Cuvilliés, Flemish by birth, began his royal service as the court dwarf, but his talents were recognized by the Elector, who sent him to study under Blondel in Paris from 1720 to 1724. His most famous interiors are those of the Reichenzimmer in Munich, and the Amalienburg pavilion at Nymphenburg. Cuvilliés was the most advanced of the German Rococo designers, and delighted in the French style while relaxing its disciplines. Cuvilliés' designs were reproduced in engraving, and had a great influence in France and England as well as in Germany.

Of the southern courts, one of the wealthiest was that of the Prince-Bishop Lothar Franz von Schönborn at Würzburg. His Residenz was begun in 1719 by the architect Balthasar Neumann, and during the 1750s Tiepolo went there to paint the magnificent ceilings. Much of the furniture was designed by the court sculptor Franz Anton von Schlott, and was made by a number of outstanding craftsmen. The carved furniture of Würzburg includes some of the most richly ornamented in Germany. Ansbach and Bayreuth, though Protestant courts, also have splendid interiors in their palaces, while at Bamberg the carved

furniture shows the influence of the sculptor Ferdinand Dietz.

German cabinet work, with elaborate veneers of walnut and mahogany, could be very fine, particularly at Würzburg and Bamberg. Bureaux and cabinets from Bamberg were made in surprising shapes, which could be either reticent and suave, or rather bulky and obtrusive. At Bayreuth, the Spindler brothers created a masterpiece in the marquetry room at the Schloss Fantasie (now removed to Munich), where the walls are inlaid with landscapes and classical ruins,

Below: This Prussian corner cupboard, probably made by Johann August Nahl in 1750, is veneered with cedar, and the gilded ornaments are of carved wood and ormolu. (Schloss Charlottenburg, Berlin)

and chests of drawers were made to match. During the 1750s there was a revival of landscapes and perspectives worked in marquetry, recalling the old fashion of the Renaissance. Worked as panels in the decoration of cupboards and bureaux, they looked more than ever like stage settings, peopled by actors with faces and hands picked out in ivory. Further north, marquetry designs tended to be stiff and old-fashioned, often keeping to the late Baroque formula of scrolling arabesques, and incorporating brass in the outmoded French style of Boulle.

Saxony kept closer to traditional forms than the southern courts. Typical of Dresden furniture are the bureau-cabinets and cupboards, made in two parts and fitted with mirrored doors above. Underneath their judicious Rococo decoration, they are basically solid pieces with well-defined outlines, and their restraint is said to show English influence. Japanning in the oriental style was practised by Martin Schnell from 1710, and was continued by other makers after his death in 1749. Seat furniture for the Elector's court tended to be heavily carved, as though to continue the ponderous magnificence of the Zwinger Palace, begun in 1713. Saxony suffered during the Seven Years War (1756–63), and orders for court furniture were greatly reduced.

Rococo came late to Prussia, for King Frederick William had little time or taste for the arts. Frederick the Great, who succeeded him in 1740, immediately embarked on a great building programme, which began with a new wing containing the Golden Gallery at Charlottenburg, Berlin and the Stadtschloss, or town palace, in Potsdam (now demolished). In 1745 he began his famous summer retreat, Sanssouci at Potsdam. Until 1746 his architect was Georg von Knobelsdorff, who established the rather aggressive character of 'Friderican Rococo'. When, 20 years later, the vast new palace at Potsdam was built to celebrate Frederick's victories, so conservative were the artistic tastes of the King that the style of interior decoration had hardly advanced at all.

Of Knobelsdorff's craftsmen, the carver Johann August Nahl was pre-eminent. He carried out stuccowork and panelling, and designed chairs and side-tables with bold projecting curves and florid carved details. In 1746, Knobelsdorff was succeeded by the Hoppenhaupt brothers, whose chairs, tables, commodes and looking-glasses, though bulbous and angular in design, are always

Above left: This chair was made for Frederick the Great in about 1765, probably to the designs of J C Hoppenhaupt. It is of walnut and upholstered with pale blue and silver damask. (Schloss Charlottenburg, Berlin)

Above right: Sanssouci was completed in 1747 as the summer retreat of Frederick the Great of Prussia. The Concert Room shows Knobelsdorff's decorative style at its best. (Sanssouci, Potsdam)

well balanced. A softer note was provided by the cabinet-work of Melchior Kambli, who arrived as a sculptor in 1746, and the Spindler brothers who came from Bayreuth in 1764. Kambli designed magnificent ormolu mounts for his commodes, which were often veneered with cedar or tortoiseshell. The cabinet-work of the Spindlers is among the highest achievements of German Rococo. The richly designed marquetry was carried out in coloured woods, with mother-of-pearl, silver and ivory.

The free cities of the north had maintained their independence through the now defunct Hanseatic League. Mainz, on the Rhine, was a free city, but it also had a Catholic episcopal court, and court influences can be detected in its marquetry and carved ornament. The Mainz craftsmen were famous for their veneered cupboards and cabinets, which were inventive in design and superb in their workmanship. Frankfurt, though not far from Mainz, was Protestant and notably conservative in spirit. The typical Frankfurt cupboard was solid and simple in shape, and it was only during the 1750s that it developed bombé or more fanciful outlines.

Throughout the north of Germany, furniture supplied to the middle classes of the cities was for use rather than for show, and cupboards, cabinets and tables tended to remain within the traditional Baroque formulae. Large surfaces lent themselves to veneers of native woods, principally walnut, oak, elm and ash, which were laid in panels of geometrical and scrolled parquetry within broad borders. The wardrobes, now commonly made in two parts, show a certain Dutch or English influence. The bureau-cabinet, also made in two parts, was another Anglo-Dutch form which became very popular throughout Germany. North Italian bureaux were clearly made in imitation of these. The curved surfaces of the lower part of a bureau were very varied in their bombé and swollen shapes. In the north, these were sometimes grossly exaggerated, and remarkable pieces were made in Schleswig-Holstein and even in Denmark. Chairs generally followed the Dutch or English style, with hooped backs and splats, often with caned seats. After the 1750s a simplified form of the English 'Chippendale' chair was made. Hanover, allied to the English crown, was probably the principal source of English influence.

One craftsman, Abraham Roentgen, deserves a special mention as he combined several national styles and achieved an international reputation. After working in England for eight years, and also in Holland, in about 1750 he opened his workshop at Neuwied on the Rhine. Sometimes he made use of English furniture forms, and he excelled at marquetry and mechanical fittings. He is also known to have made chairs

Left: This bureau-cabinet, perhaps made by Johann Raab in about 1765, shows how Rococo decoration could be applied to the rather bulky case furniture that was made in Franconia and the cities of North Germany. The walnut veneer combines diamond parquetry with interlaced scrolls.

Right: This painting, The Family of Count Vries, by J V Tischbein, shows ordinary furniture in use, and the style of the hoop-back chairs and the tea-table is clearly based on the Anglo-Dutch tradition. (Kunstmuseum der Stadt, Düsseldorf)

Below: The card-table was made in about 1755 by Abraham Roentgen. It is of cherrywood, and the top has brass inlay in the German manner. The top leaf opens to form a card-table with counter-wells, and with the second leaf open it becomes a writing-table. (Victoria & Albert Museum, London)

based on the Louis Quinze style, not carved but veneered and inlaid. This technique derived from Holland, and was widely practised during the revival of Rococo in the nineteenth century. From 1761, Roentgen was assisted by his son David, whose work was to become even more important.

Poland and Russia

Rococo in eastern Europe was not in the main of German origin, even though Poland was ruled until 1764 by the Electors of Saxony, who brought their own architects and craftsmen. The carvers, joiners and turners on Polish estates were highly skilled, but the traditional Baroque forms were only slowly displaced. Polish culture had strong links with Paris, and French furniture was imported by wealthy aristocrats. Some of Meissonnier's most elaborate designs of the 1730s, which we know of only through his engravings, were for the rooms and furniture of Polish diplomats.

In Russia, too, furniture was imported, chiefly from Paris. But the skill of Russian carvers was very great, and they had no difficulty in executing the Rococo designs. Russian Rococo reflects chiefly the ambitions of its four empresses, who reigned almost continuously from 1724. The extravagant Empress Elizabeth (1742–62) successfully achieved the westernization of the arts that had begun under Peter the Great. She established manufactories of silks and fabrics, jewellery, porcelain and metalwork. All these decorative arts were predominantly French in character.

The early Rococo style was established by Frenchmen, including Pineau who worked at

Peterhof until 1727. His carved work was a sumptuous version of the French Régence. During the 1740s, the St Petersburg palaces were in the brilliant hands of Bartolommeo Rastrelli, the son of Peter the Great's principal sculptor, who had studied in Italy and France. He built or enlarged the Winter Palace, Peterhof and Tsarskoe Selo, and designed much of the furniture. Not a great deal of his Rococo is now to be seen, because some was replaced during the neo-classical period, and a great deal was destroyed during the Second World War.

Antonio Rinaldi came to Russia from Italy in 1752, and was employed by Catherine the Great who did not care for Rastrelli. Rinaldi's superb work can be seen at Oranienbaum (literally, the 'Orange Tree'), near Leningrad, and combines vigour and fluidity with a fine sense of colour. Katalnaya Gorka, a pleasure-lodge at Oranienbaum, is markedly Rococo within, and the furniture is characterized by its slender scrolled outlines. The most exciting example of Rinaldi's work is, perhaps, the Chinese Palace, which draws on both chinoiserie and European styles. Exotic motifs were used boldly, and the furniture, though basically European in form, makes use of Chinese frets and characters.

Denmark and Sweden

At this time, Sweden was an independent kingdom, though of less influence than formerly, and Denmark and Norway were united under the Danish crown. The long-standing trade with England in timber and iron ore helped to establish English influences in furniture simultaneously with the more enduring Dutch and German influences.

The early eighteenth-century chair with a hooped back and broad splat persisted to about 1760. English chairs were so popular in Denmark that in 1747 an order was made forbidding their importation. The Danes appreciated the economical lines of English furniture, however, and by the 1760s a light form of chair based on the 'Chippendale' type was made. Other imitations of simple English forms included clocks and bureau-cabinets. Mahogany was expensive, and walnut was more generally used, or pine which was painted or japanned. A delicate marquetry in stained woods can sometimes be found.

The guilds in both Denmark and Sweden were organized on German lines, and the traditional craftsman's piece, the cupboard, can be very similar to those from Germany. The north German commode or bureau with a bulbous, swollen front was made in Copenhagen. Sweden developed a distinct type of three-drawer commode, with pronounced bombé curves, a rather narrow top and base, and projecting feet. The drawers were separated by concave mouldings, the

Left: This bureau-cabinet shows how, in Denmark, the German style could reach the limits of extravagance. It was made for the Danish King by C F Lehmann in 1755, and is one of the most elaborate pieces of its type. The complexity of the commode base is matched by the exuberance of the Rococo carving in the cresting. The veneer and parquetry are principally of kingwood, and the corner panels are of bone and ivory on metal. The gilded mounts are partly of gilt-bronze, and partly of carved wood. (Rosenborg Castle, Copenhagen)

Above right: This Danish commode, made by C J Preisler in the early 1740s, is a courtly, luxurious piece. The restrained outline is broken by the arching mouldings on the front, which continue the curve of the feet. Many Danish furniture-makers were sent by the court to study their craft in Germany, and this piece shows more German than French characteristics. (Rosenborg Castle, Copenhagen)

Below right: Furniture in Sweden made in the international Rococo style, such as this table, indicated royal patronage. Like all European rulers, the King of Sweden wished to keep abreast of the latest Rococo fashions, and the court architect, Carl Harleman made several visits to Paris, where he studied under Vassé. The table, made in about 1750, is of carved and gilded wood, but the well-defined curves and solid construction give it more German character than French. (Royal Palace, Stockholm)

parquetry was in geometrical mosaic, and the ormolu rather sparingly applied.

French furniture was imported for the courts, and served as models for the royal palaces. Unfortunately, the palace of Christiansborg in Copenhagen was destroyed in a fire in 1794. In Stockholm the new palace was completed in the middle of the eighteenth century. Much of its furniture was designed by the architect, Harleman, and craftsmen were sent to study in Paris. Many pieces look very French, combining Parisian techniques with an admirable restraint in their design.

Holland

Dutch Rococo was not stimulated by the court, but was absorbed into traditional bourgeois forms. Chairs generally kept to the old-fashioned Anglo-Dutch forms with hooped backs and cabriole legs. Meanwhile, small pieces of furniture such as tea-tables and chests of drawers could be fine and well-proportioned.

The various forms of cupboard, whether wardrobes, bureau-cabinets or glazed display-cases, could be enormously wide. They were generally made in two parts, the lower

Below: Two-part cabinets were the show-pieces of eighteenth-century Dutch rooms. The commode base is of the Dutch bombé shape (the curves not being fully three-dimensional). The upper part has looking-glass painted with exotic water birds and plants, and just behind the Rococo carvings of the arched cornice there are five platforms for pottery or porcelain vases. The cabinet is veneered with burr-walnut, crossbanded with rosewood, and there are small marquetry panels of flowers. This fine piece shows the continuity of the best Dutch traditions. (Rijksmuseum, Amsterdam)

section being shaped in bulky curves. In the upper part, the panels or glazing bars were outlined by scrolling mouldings with carved Rococo leaves, and the arched cornices often had platforms for Delft or Chinese vases. Holland retained the claw-and-ball foot long after it had gone out of fashion in England, and on these cupboards it occurs in a massive form. The most pleasing veneer was of burr-walnut, but mahogany was also used. A marquetry tradition continued, but compared to the splendid work of about 1700 it became uninventive—though still distinctive—working flowersprays into the surfaces with tedious repetition.

It cannot be maintained that mid-eighteenth century Dutch furniture has a high place in European design. Perhaps their own traditions failed to develop because of the popularity of English and French furniture, and in 1771 all such imports had to be prohibited. Meanwhile, French chairs and commodes were imitated. A Dutch commode might easily be mistaken for French provincial work, but the marquetry

generally lacks vigour, and the ormolu mounts seem mechanical and repetitive.

England

By the mid-eighteenth century, the character of English furniture had become quite distinct from the rest of Europe. The standard of joiners' and cabinet-makers' work, which was already high in Queen Anne's reign, improved steadily, and the general excellence of London furniture was second only to that of France. This might not be expected from the *laissez-faire* state of the country. But if there were no guilds or central authorities to supervise the level of craftsmanship, the standards exacted by patrons and the competitive spirit among the makers themselves served equally well.

The established traditions made for logical construction, simplicity of outline, and classical ornament. When Rococo decoration came in, it was as though by the 'back door', and was not imposed by the taste of the court or the aristocracy. 'French' ornament, however, steadily increased in popularity from about 1740 until after 1760, and it could be lavish. Sometimes, as in the familiar 'Chippendale' dining-chairs, it was judiciously applied to the English style; at other times it seems uneasy, disjointed or even superfluous. The chinoiserie and 'gothick' variations were very popular as novelties. Since straight lines were much used in these styles, their ornaments could be more easily adapted to the English tradition than convoluting scrollwork. Furniture in the Chinese taste was more plentiful in England than in any other country. The eighteenth-century gothick style was almost totally confined to England.

Rococo in Europe was a courtly style. But in England the court had scarcely any power or prestige, and exercised almost no influence on the arts. Even George III, who was interested, never directed their course. The landed aristocracy, who governed the country, were predominantly Whigs whose wealth lay in their property. In both their town- and country-houses, they required comfort and convenience as well as a degree of splendour. Materially, England was now prospering as never before. With the growth of banking and colonial trade, merchant families could build and furnish houses as lavishly as any aristocrat.

The habits of society were not to change much until the Industrial Revolution. In contrast to France, English society was not noticeably dominated by women. Furniture remained masculine and functional, designed for its usefulness rather than for a luxurious indolence. On the other hand, through 'Beau' Nash's example at Bath, manners were more gentle, and the greater consideration given to women is reflected in their drawing- and dressing-rooms, which during the 1750s were decorated with gay fabrics and chintzes and Chinese wallpapers, and furnished with such pieces as china cabinets and small tables for use at tea gatherings.

The English attitude towards France, her traditional enemy, was somewhat equivocal. France was ruled despotically by king and church. Politically she supported the outlawed Stuarts, and economically she threatened colonial trade. These dangers were resolved by wars in 1745 and 1763 respectively. Meanwhile, certain cultivated Englishmen such as the Earl of Chesterfield mixed freely in Parisian society. French Rococo was taken up at first by those opposed to the Whig establishment, including the Tory aristocracy, the entourage of Frederick, Prince of Wales, and many London craftsmen who favoured the style as a welcome release from the tyranny of Palladianism.

There was no Baroque tradition in England comparable to the courtly styles of Europe. When Rococo appeared, it was a decorative novelty, not a logical development of what already existed. Rococo design was taught in London at the Academy of St Martin's Lane, which was founded by Hogarth. It came chiefly through H-F Gravelot, a French painter who came to England in 1732 and taught drawing and design at Hogarth's Academy. Rococo ornaments first appeared in engraving and silver work, and then, most suitably, on a large scale in the buildings at Vauxhall

Pleasure Gardens. It was probably at Vauxhall, too, that chinoiserie was first presented to the pleasure-seeking public.

Designs for furniture in the Rococo style can be seen in the engravings of an Italian, Gaetano Brunetti, published in 1736 and in those of some architects such as William Jones, who published a series in 1739. The details were handled with greater ease during the next decade. Rococo furniture was not normally designed by architects; rather, the style was left in the hands of the craftsmen, many of whom learned the important art of drawing at St Martin's Lane. English Rococo up to 1760 is often called the 'St Martin's Lane style'.

The best of the designers was undoubtedly the carver Matthias Lock. His drawings and engravings for looking-glasses and side-tables from 1740 show delight in the elaborate unclassical Rococo formula. In designs by Lock and others, one can see a progressive refinement and order of ornament, and by 1754, when Thomas Chippendale published his great folio volume, *The Gentleman and Cabinet-Maker's Director*, the style was fully mature. The book contained 161 plates illustrating nearly every type of furniture, and a third edition with 200 plates was published in 1762. It seems that he employed Lock and others as designers and engravers, but Chippendale's own contribution is likely to have been great, and he claimed to have

Above: Bed made for the Duke of Beaufort in about 1752 by the Linnells in the early chinoiserie style. It is japanned in red and green and gilded. (Victoria & Albert Museum, London)

Right: One of John Linnell's many designs for rooms. The decoration was to be carried out in pine. (Victoria & Albert Museum, London)

invented and drawn a number of the pieces himself.

The long and distinguished list of subscribers to Chippendale's first edition is astonishing, and it was highly influential both in England and abroad. Some of the designs are plain and traditional, while others are of the wildest Rococo fantasy. Yet hardly a single piece of existing furniture made before 1764 can be attributed to him with certainty. All over the world, his name typifies the mature English Rococo style; yet his work after 1764, in a neo-classical idiom, was to be, if anything, finer.

None of the rival publications provoked by the *Director* approaches it in its comprehensiveness, and few do so in the quality of design and engraving. Ince and Mayhew's *Universal System of Household Furniture* (published in parts from 1759 to 1762) tells us more about their very reputable firm than about furniture styles. Robert Manwaring's

book of chairs (1765) was used in America, but appeared too late to influence the Rococo style in England. On the other hand, Thomas Johnson's designs for *girandoles* (published in 1755) and for other carvers' pieces—looking-glasses, side-tables and candlestands—(published between 1756 and 1761) are rather more elaborate than those in the *Director*. They include carved figures, both European and Chinese, and animal scenes from Barlow's engravings for Aesop's Fables. The girandoles are perhaps Johnson's best inventions, creating little worlds of their own, with rocky landscapes, mills and temples. The Rococo framing is quite asymmetrical, but exquisitely balanced. The designs may have been criticized as being too difficult, for in his second work he asserted that 'they may all be performed by a Master of his Art . . . I am well satisfied they can be executed by myself.' There are examples in existence which have been taken from Johnson's engravings, but we do not know if they were carved by him. William Linnell and John, probably his nephew, worked in London's fashionable Berkeley Square. They made excellent Rococo looking-glasses and chairs. John Linnell is known to have studied drawing in St Martin's Lane, and his very personal style is well known from the large number of his drawings which survive.

Since furniture was rarely signed, and few makers' labels have survived, we know very little about the craftsmen themselves. There were, however, an enormous number of them and the most distinguished, including Chippendale, William Vile—famous for the furniture he made for Queen Charlotte—and John Cobb, William Hallett, John Channon and Samuel Norman lived in or close to St Martin's Lane. Furniture-making included a number of different trades: the cabinet-maker, joiner (including specialized branches for chair and picture frames), carver, gilder and glass-grinder all made their contributions. Upholstery was carried out by the 'upholder', who also supplied curtains, carpets and wallpaper. A capable upholder supervised the entire business, and we may assume that Chippendale, Linnell and Norman acted as such. The work was often contracted out, however, to smaller specialist firms.

William Linnell, it seems, made the famous Chinese bed for Badminton in about 1754. Furniture in the Chinese taste had become the craze by the early 1750s in England. A room where tea is taken suggests oriental treatment, and cabinet-makers enthusiastically followed the fashion. The 'Barbarous gaudy *goût* of the Chinese', of which Mrs Montagu complained in 1749, included some japanned work copying imported screens and cabinets, while mahogany pieces of all kinds became Chinese by the inclusion of the oriental fret or paling, a temple roof, or a canopy. China cabinets naturally figured in such work, but so little attempt was made to understand true Chinese style that chinoiserie could be combined with Rococo or even classical details in a single piece.

English chinoiserie is seen at its best in carved looking-glasses. Pine could be carved into fragments of landscape, with Chinese peasants stepping delicately across palings, rocks, water and vegetation. The details that had originated in oriental lacquer and wallpaper underwent a transformation: peonies and bamboos became roses, acanthus or palms; dragons became cranes (ho-ho birds), dogs or other animals. Such exotic fantasies were essentially Rococo in spirit, and they quickly lapsed with the rise of Neo-classicism, to return with George IV's romantic work at Brighton Pavilion.

The gothick taste, which had appeared during the 1730s, was more enduring. The dream here concerned England's mediaeval past, and, when taken up by Horace Walpole and others, was allied to a kind of dilettante archaeology. Gothick was more masculine in character than chinoiserie, and well suited to a library. Chippendale illustrated gothick bookcases,

writing-tables, sideboards, hall-chairs, and a bed, but did not show the style in commodes or china cabinets, even though these occasionally were made. Furniture was gothick in detail rather than in form, with pointed arches, quatrefoil panels, balustrading and pinnacles. The resulting furniture bears no resemblance to the true mediaeval style in its construction or form.

English Rococo, then, presented a choice of the French, Chinese or gothick styles. But traditional or classical structure and proportions formed the basis of them all, and the amount of decoration could be varied according to the taste of the maker. Up to the 1760s, construction grew steadily lighter, and the ornaments more refined. The most obvious characteristic of mid-Georgian furniture is the universal use of mahogany, an expensive material imported from San Domingo or Cuba, which was strong and tough, and lent itself to fine and lively carving. It could also be cut into wide sheets of veneer, either with a fine grain or, when cut from a root or fork, figured with a curl or flame. Walnut furniture was still made, but chiefly for bedrooms. Virginia walnut, imported from the American colonies, was sometimes used, as its grain is close and hard, resembling mahogany, and it was often stained red. Other materials included gilded pine for carved pieces (looking-glasses, side-tables and wall brackets), and japanned or painted furniture was used in Chinese rooms.

The different types of furniture were, with a few additions, much as before. Beds were of the four-poster variety with cornices often of carved mahogany. Bulky clothes-presses could be monumental when made with serpentine or bombé lower sections and carved corners and panels. Dressing-tables with fitted drawers were illustrated by Chippendale in plain styles as well as in the extremes of French Rococo. Dressing-cabinets, with bookcases above, look much like writing-cabinets, and served both purposes. In the dining-room, oval gate-leg tables tended to be made square in order to fit together more easily. Neither the dining-table nor the sideboard, as we know them, had developed as yet, and sideboard tables, though finely ornamented, seldom had drawers.

In the library, the pedestal writing-table became a piece of some magnificence, and there are famous examples by Vile and Chippendale. The bureau-bookcase had either mirrored or panelled doors above, or glazing bars carved delicately with Rococo or gothick details. During the 1750s a characteristic version developed with a diagonal pattern, which eventually took on the standard 13-panel formula. Many long bookshelves were made with glazed doors above and a projecting central part, surmounted by a broken pediment into which a plaster bust could be placed. In state-rooms and drawing-rooms there were gilded mirrors, side-tables, and candlestands which varied from simple rectangular shapes to the most elaborate fashions. The small and functional Pembroke table, named after the Countess of Pembroke, appeared by 1760, and was generally rather plain. The circular tripod table with a pie-crust top could be richly carved, and was accompanied by various forms of tea-table, including the rectangular type with a pierced gallery, raised on four elegant cabriole or columned legs, and kettle-stands — small tripod tables now erroneously called 'wine-tables' — which also could be of great delicacy. Other pieces for use in ladies' rooms included display-cabinets and hanging shelves for showing china.

Dining-chairs are, perhaps, the pieces that are most characteristic of the period. The type most conveniently described as 'Chippendale' has its top-rail shaped like a bow, forming sharp angles at the ends, and the delicate tracery of the back splat requires the strength of mahogany. This form developed by about

Below: This combined dressing- and writing-table is almost unique in English furniture for the profusion of its gilt-bronze Rococo mounts and the complicated swellings and recessions of the bodywork. It is attributed to John Channon, who worked in St Martin's Lane specializing in furniture inlaid with brass, and was made during the 1740s. There is obvious German influence in both the shape and ornamentation, but the interpretation of Rococo design has become rather confused. Note the inclusion of dolphins at the bottom centre. The pair to this table exists, and originally the two were designed to stand back-to-back when required to form a library table. (Victoria & Albert Museum, London)

Right: Probably made by William Vile of St Martin's Lane, London, who worked for Queen Charlotte after 1760, this bookcase shows the English tradition at its best. The classical form is a development from the Palladian style of William Kent, and the ornament, though chiefly classical, is carved with all the delicacy of the Rococo period. At this time mahogany was the wood used for most fine furniture. The flat surfaces are covered with veneers that show a curl, or 'flame' figure, and the carved work, the mouldings and frets, are glued over this. The platform at the centre of the pediment would have contained a bronzed plaster bust of a writer or philosopher. (Victoria & Albert Museum, London)

1750, and was imitated particularly in Scandinavia and America. Chippendale illustrated a large number of them, saying that more or less carving could be applied at will. The backs have occasional hints of gothick arches. Alternatively, the backs and arms might be formed of Chinese frets. The legs could be straight, with carved or applied frets (especially suitable for Chinese or gothick patterns), or cabriole, carved with acanthus leaves and cartouches. Although the claw-and-ball foot survived into the 1750s, Chippendale only illustrated the more fashionable rocaille or French scrolled types. Upholstered armchairs with cartouche-shaped backs were of the French form, but when made in England they tended to look disjointed and stocky. Sofas, too, made either of mahogany or gilded pine, were frequently made in the French style, and the tradition of forming the back of a settee out of several chair-backs persisted.

Commode chests of drawers, in imitation of the French, appeared by about 1750. They were made of mahogany with bold scrolling outlines, which in France would have been applied in ormolu, and their Rococo handles of gilt-bronze could be large and showy or small and delicate. Many of these commodes are rather ungainly, and demonstrate how England often failed to understand the principles of French Rococo construction. A revival of marquetry had begun by 1760, probably through the elaborate work of

Above: Solid mahogany armchair which closely follows a design dated 1759 in the Director for a 'French chair'. 'French' referred to the comfortable upholstery of back, seat and arms, and to the Rococo-style carving. (Victoria & Albert Museum, London)

Right: Pierre Langlois made this marquetry commode in England in about 1760. The carcase is made of pine in the English tradition (whereas the best French case-work was of oak), but a marble top to a commode is unusual in England. (Victoria & Albert Museum, London)

Pierre Langlois. His commodes are ostentatious show-pieces, making great use of ormolu in the French manner although tending to be rather heavy whan applied to the feet. One of his typical designs in marquetry included stems of flowers tied together by ribbons. English commodes, whether made by Langlois or others, almost invariably have their tops of mahogany or marquetry veneer, and rarely of marble as was used in France.

The neo-classical revival of the 1760s caused Rococo decoration to die even more suddenly than it had begun. The traditional logic of English furniture moved by degrees into the style of the 1780s known as 'Hepplewhite', and the only legacy of the Rococo period was the serpentine or bombé outline that can be found on chests of drawers and Pembroke tables up to the 1790s. However, an imitation of the Louis Quinze chair in its most economical form seems only to have been made right at the end of the Rococo period, and it still goes by the anomalous name of 'French Hepplewhite'.

The quality of provincial furniture varied enormously. At its best it was equal to London work. When furniture was made of native woods such as walnut, yew, fruitwoods or oak, it had a provincial appearance, and is generally known as country-made, even though it was often made in cities. A dresser made of oak may be quite in the style of about 1710, with simple cabriole legs and panelled doors; yet a later date is betrayed by the mahogany crossbanding around the drawer fronts. Dressers, for displaying pottery and china, were the show-pieces in the country, and other forms tended to be simple. The bureau was a popular country piece right through the eighteenth century. Chairs and tripod tables were made in great numbers, often in mahogany, and were simplifications of London types.

Windsor chairs were a distinct regional type, and had been made in large numbers in Buckinghamshire since the early eighteenth century. It is not uncommon to find the legs and rails of ash, the seat of elm, and the hooped rail over the top to be of yew; but more ambitious pieces could be carried out completely in mahogany. The back splat might be shaped and pierced, showing a distant relationship with London chairs, and gothick examples are known, standing on cabriole rather than turned legs.

America
Although the English government did their utmost to prevent it, the American colonies became so prosperous during the eighteenth century that they were able to defy the taxes,

133

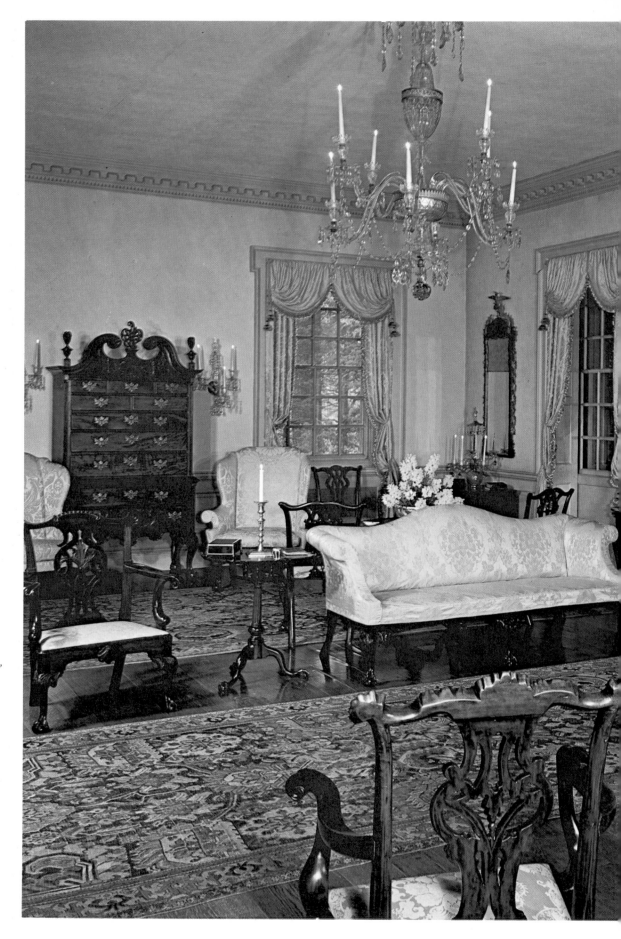

Right: This is a room from the country-house built for a wealthy Philadelphia merchant, Edward Stiles, in 1762. The furniture, all of mahogany, shows both the sophistication of the Philadelphia 'Chippendale' style, and its close relationship to English models, though mostly it dates from the 1770s when this style was no longer practised in England. Note the luxurious and rare pair of sofas, the carved chairs in the style of Benjamin Randolph, and the mahogany and gilt looking-glass. The high chest of drawers, however, is a specifically Philadelphian piece, and was made by Michael Gratz in 1769. (The Henry Francis Dupont Winterthur Museum)

openly to rebel, and to have their independence recognized in 1783. But English traditions survived in American culture, and their Rococo furniture was based on that of London. Sometimes an American chair or table can hardly be distinguished from an English one.

The 'Chippendale' period in America runs from the 1760s almost until the end of the century. In a country so large, where communications were difficult, innovations were naturally late in appearing. Rococo ornament was known for a long time in Philadelphia as 'the new French style', despite the fact that it came from England where by then it was far from new. The Chippendale style reached America in three ways. Immigrants occasionally included a cabinet-maker such as Thomas Affleck, who arrived in Philadelphia in 1763. Secondly, English furniture was imported, though in diminishing quantities as the century progressed. Third and most important were the pattern books, including Chippendale's *Director* (1754 and 1762) and the rival publications by Manwaring, and Ince and Mayhew. American Rococo carving often has a two-dimensional quality that suggests its having been copied from an engraving.

Colonial houses were neat buildings of brick and wood, combining the traditional Wren proportions with Palladian decorative features. The rooms were not large, and furniture tended to be narrow and taller than English works. The proportions were lean but crisp and stylish, and the top of a chair, settee or high chest was emphasized by shapely curves and finials. Although furniture from Philadelphia or Boston has style and beauty, and often a certain magnificence, it was practical and seldom luxurious. There were not a great number of forms. 'Chippendale' chairs were plentiful, as were upholstered settees, card-tables, and tea-tables, either of the round snap-top form with a bird-cage, or the rectangular tray top variety. Pembroke tables made their appearance rather late. There were firescreens, mirrors and tall clocks. The show-pieces were chests, high or low, and bureau-cabinets. Beds tended to be simple, with posts and draped testers, and low chests or kneehole writing-tables, when placed in bedrooms, served as dressing-tables.

The furniture industry was a thriving one. Just before American Independence, there were about 150 cabinet-makers, chair-makers and carvers working in Boston alone, and over 50 in Newport, Rhode Island. But apart from furniture and silver, no decorative craft was as yet properly developed, and all glass, bronze and brass, wallpapers and many fabrics had to be imported.

The American colonies, spread along 1,200 miles of coastline, may be divided conveniently into three areas. The South did not lead fashion at this time, and not much is known of the makers, although Thomas Elfe of Charleston had a large workshop. His account books show that he used the blind fret around his chests and bookcases. Many of the Southern craftsmen were, apparently, slaves. More than once there were complaints by white migrants against the employment of cheap labour.

In the middle region, Philadelphia was undoubtedly the most advanced and prolific centre. The makers included Affleck, Folwell, Savery, Gillingham and Shoemaker, whose trade labels occasionally appear on their works. Benjamin Randolph is probably the most famous, and his elaborate trade card was engraved in the style of St Martin's Lane. Philadelphia furniture could be very ornate, and looking-glasses, though not so large as English ones, could be almost as decorative. Tripod tea-tables with pie-crust trays, and card-tables with sharp angles and serpentine sides showed subtle variations of English types. Thomas Affleck is known for straight, solid 'Marlborough' legs, often with a blocked foot.

The cabriole leg with a claw-and-ball foot, though by now outmoded in England, remained popular. Dining- or side-chairs generally had cabriole legs, and the carved backs were based directly on English patterns, complete with gothick arches or Rococo carving. Among the popular types of chair was the ladderback with wavy pierced rails. While the chairs made in New York up to the end of the century were rather heavy in comparison with those of Philadelphia, New York card-tables generally are crisper and more stylish in their sheer, serpentine lines. The most famous Philadelphia piece was the high chest, now known as a highboy. Although it was the show-piece, and stood in the principal parlour, it appears generally to have been filled with family clothes.

Furniture was made in great quantity in the North, and was often traded for corn and tobacco grown in the South. New England furniture was less florid than that of Philadelphia, as though reflecting the puritan tradition. It also tended to retain the old Queen Anne styles, as for instance in dining-chairs with their hoop backs with shaped splats, and their cabriole legs with webbed feet. At Newport, Rhode Island, the furniture trade was dominated by the related families of Townsend and Goddard. The most recognizable feature of New England furniture, the blocked or 'swelled' style, is first known in a secretary desk signed by John Coit Jnr of Boston, but was most developed in Newport. The blocking, carved out of solid wood, resulted in raised or sunken panels with smoothed corners, and their heads were often given shell ornaments with the radials slightly curved at the perimeters. In Boston, the blocked style generally occurs only on the lower part of a piece of furniture. The style travelled inland to New Hampshire where it can be seen in a rather less sophisticated form, and seems to be somehow related to north German work.

High chests were made in New England, but the more common show-piece was a two-part bureau or cabinet, raised on elegantly moulded bracket feet, or on sturdy claw-and-ball feet. Boston chests often had a swollen or bombé shape, which is generally associated with the name of John Coggswell. The bombé outline, though occasionally found in English furniture, probably reached America from Holland.

Small but interesting regional differences can be seen in claw-and-ball feet. In Philadelphia they were elegantly shaped, with the balls rather flattened. In New York they tended to be more sturdy, the back talon and lower leg being in the same upright line. The Boston form was quite distinct, and the side talons inclined sharply backwards giving an animated, nervous effect. At Newport, R.I., the claws were often undercut to show daylight between the talons and the ball.

The finest wood for furniture was mahogany, which came from the West Indies in most of the varieties that were used in England. However, it never quite displaced black walnut, which grew all along the Eastern seaboard and especially in Virginia. Other

native woods were used, particularly in the north, such as maple, with a curly or bird's-eye grain, which was suitable for veneers, and cherry, which was popular especially in New Haven. Solid work or drawer linings might be of maple, cherry, tulip tree (a variety of poplar), white cedar, birch or pine. Other indigenous woods suitable for work in the country style

or on Windsor chairs included ash, chestnut and oak. Although regional traditions certainly existed, such as the use of oak for fine carcase work at Newport, these were seldom hard or fast, and one should not be dogmatic about defining local styles, the more so as both craftsmen and completed furniture tended to travel up and down the Eastern seaboard.

While fashionable Rococo styles adorned the houses of successful merchants, country furniture in established traditions continued to be made. The comfortable Windsor chairs and settees, often with a high arched back or shaped top-rail, were popular at all levels from the early eighteenth century through the nineteenth. In Pennsylvania there were a large number of German settlers who made their own furniture in what is now often known as the Swiss style. The chairs have block seats, splayed spindle legs, and carved backs made from single pieces of wood. These, and marriage chests, which were often painted, show a continuation of local traditions that derived from mediaeval and Renaissance Europe.

PURITY OF FORM
The neo-classical reaction

The neo-classical revival developed in the mid-eighteenth century and it was widely established throughout Europe by the 1770s. Like the Rococo which preceded it, it became an international style, although allowing less leeway for varying interpretation from country to country. Different national styles were united in the study of the same sources in Italy, Greece and Egypt, and, as a result, they inevitably developed along similar lines. Much emphasis, moreover, was laid on adherence to classical principles and this became more marked, as the movement gained momentum. A studied eclecticism was adopted after 1800 — leading to a more archaeological approach and creating even closer stylistic links between countries.

The ferment of intellectual ideas in late eighteenth-century Europe led to a stringent reassessment and questioning of many existing traditions. Numerous political, as well as artistic, changes took place in a striving toward an apparently attainable perfection. There was an accent on modernity, on sweeping innovation in an age of progress, yet classical antiquity was nonetheless still studied for guidance and inspiration. Winckelmann wrote: 'There is only one way for the moderns, to become great, perhaps unequalled: by imitating the ancients.' He drew careful distinction between imitation and mere copying, suggesting that classicism should be

studied for its regenerative powers, and allowing for a romantic interpretation of the style.

In this world of high ideals and moral improvement, the frivolous Rococo would indeed appear decadent, and the reaction against it would become fierce, especially in France, the country of its origin. Abbé Le Blanc protested against it in his *Lettre d'un Français* of 1745, addressed to the Comte de Caylus, and Nicholas Cochin levelled another attack in the *Mercure de France* in 1754. But despite these publications, the Rococo lingered on for a number of years, especially at the conservative French Court, and Baron Grimm's remark of 1763 that 'tout à Paris est à la Grecque' may be taken with a pinch of salt at that early stage.

Paris was undoubtedly the most important centre for the promotion of the neo-classical revival, and among the many books produced there, the *Recueil d'Antiquités* by the Comte de Caylus was probably the most influential. Appearing from 1752 onwards, it illustrated his own collection of antiquities, making classical ornament familiar and laying the basis for the Louis Seize style. It also foreshadowed an important trend in stressing the simplicity of Greek classicism, which many would soon hold superior to that of Rome.

Another French writer of the day, the Abbé Laugier, supported this view in his *Essai sur*

139

l'Architecture of 1753, in which he presented a rationalist view of classicism and urged a return to primitive purity. 'Architecture' he wrote, 'owes all that is precious and solid to the Greeks alone.' It is not surprising that the first major work on Greek monuments — *Les Ruines des plus beaux monuments de la Grèce* by LeRoy — should have been published in Paris in 1758. This work had been preceded by the more intensive researches of two Englishmen, James Stuart and Nicholas Revett. They had visited Athens as early as 1751, and must take the credit for first showing an interest in Greece, even if their *Antiquities of Athens* did not appear until 1762.

In Germany, too, an interest in Greece developed through the writings of Johann Joachim Winckelmann, who was based in Rome as secretary to Cardinal Albani, but whose books were published at home. His *Reflections on the Imitation of Greek Art in Painting and Sculpture* of 1755 and his magnum opus *The History of Ancient Art* published nine years later, present a poetic account of Greek art, even though the moving descriptions of various masterpieces are more inspiring than instructive. In the words of Goethe, himself a vital force in German Neo-classicism, 'we learn nothing by reading Winckelmann, but we *become* something'.

The emphasis on Greece in preference to Rome not unnaturally sparked off a reaction within Italy, which was led by G B Piranesi.

He produced a splendid series of etched views of Roman remains to demonstrate, most effectively, the magnificence of Roman architecture. With their dramatic lighting and gargantuan representation of scale, these popular etchings played a part in the development of a Romantic brand of classicism within Europe. They served their purpose well, although visitors such as Goethe and Flaxman, familiar with Piranesi before visiting Rome, expressed disappointment with the tameness of reality when they arrived there.

Despite the swing towards Greece, Rome still exerted considerable influence during the late eighteenth century and remained the cosmopolitan centre of neo-classical Europe and the goal of both English and German Grand Tourists. Studies of the famous sites and collections were now reinforced by the discoveries at fresh excavations, such as that at Tivoli with which Piranesi was personally involved and which produced such important finds as the Warwick Vase.

With the Roman monuments recorded, distant sites were being explored: Palmyra and Baalbek were to become the subject of two books by Robert Wood in 1753 and 1757, while the young Robert Adam chose Diocletian's Palace at Spalatro in Dalmatia for his first book in 1764. Pompeii and Herculaneum in the south of Italy were much studied for they provided a wealth of evidence about Roman domestic architecture. Excavated in 1738 and

1748 respectively, at the instigation of the king of Naples, these two cities had survived miraculously intact under the laval dust of Vesuvius since the first century AD and thus provided a unique opportunity to study the interior decoration and furnishings of the Romans. There was, however, some confusion as to dating, and imitations of the decorations there were often mistakenly called 'Etruscan'.

Actual pieces of furniture were unearthed at these sites, but surprisingly, they were seldom reproduced accurately during the eighteenth century. Neo-classical furniture consisted at first of simple geometrical outlines, devised to carry the all-important classical ornament, and, with a few exceptions such as the tripod stand, the form of ancient furniture was rarely copied before the nineteenth century.

The ornament was derived mainly from Rome, at the outset, as illustrated in the new books. The Renaissance, especially the painted grotesques of Raphael at the Vatican, provided another source which was important to such designers as Adam in England and Clérisseau in France. Individual countries harked back to their own earlier classical revivals too; a nostalgia for the Grand Siècle of Louis XIV is thus noticeable in early French neo-classical pieces. But soon the heavy classical forms

t: Mahogany
hair based on the
an curule form. This
ical of the later work
orges Jacob, with its
sweeping, simple lines
olain mahogany finish.
y well be after a
n by Percier and
aine. The back has
me time been
lstered, but it now
a splat in the form of a
ical incense-burner.
ée des Arts
ratifs, Paris)

would lighten, and the 1770s and 1780s saw an increasing delicacy and refinement in furniture.

After 1800, however, a marked reaction set in, with a craving for exactitude as the inevitable fruit of further researches. Vase paintings and bas-reliefs were closely studied for the clues they might provide as to antique furniture shapes, and many pieces were based on marble prototypes. Now the lessons of Pompeii and Herculaneum proved invaluable, and Greece was used as a source of ideas rather more than before, despite Napoleon's preference for the grandiose decoration of Rome.

Napoleon and his favourite designers, Percier and Fontaine, clearly played on Roman ideas for their associational value. The triumphal arches and classical temples of Paris were created with propagandist intentions, the French Empire being inevitably associated with that of Rome. This style was widely disseminated throughout Europe by Napoleon's campaigns, which also led to the development of an Egyptian revival after Napoleon had organized a programme of excavation in Egypt during his Nile campaign.

Egyptian antiquities, of which there were a number in Rome, had excited interest in the eighteenth century, and various advanced pieces of furniture with hieroglyphic ornament bear witness to a certain knowledge of Egyptian design. But this fashion was to accelerate after the publication of Baron Denon's *Voyages dans la Basse et Haute Egypte* in 1802 with Napoleon's encouragement, and thereafter Egypt joined Greece and Rome as a major inspiration.

The accurate character of this second phase of the neo-classical revival — which even affected fashions of dress — led to a decline in originality in due course, as the fervour of the revolutionary eighteenth century waned. The endlessly repeated classical forms became monotonous and Neo-classicism had subsided into a bland, even superficial, decorative style by the middle of the nineteenth century.

France

The decorative motifs of the classical revival in France, as everywhere, had their origins in antiquity, but the shape and proportions of the furniture were purely eighteenth century. It was not until the very end of the eighteenth century that furniture and decoration took on a purer classical form. The immediate inspiration for the revival is now difficult to trace. To a certain extent it was a return to the Renaissance, and also to the more severe, more classical Baroque of the time of Louis XIV, and, at first, there were affinities with the work of the Palladian designers in England.

The Rococo movement in France had powerful opponents from its start. Voltaire pilloried it in *Le Temple du Goût* in 1733, and the architect, Soufflot, in 1741, decreed that all right-minded people should look down on these frivolous products. Soufflot was later to accompany the Marquis de Marigny, in effect France's future Minister of Culture, on his tour of Italy during the years 1749 to 1751 — an important journey in the evolution of French taste.

The French Academy had a school in Rome, at the Palazzo Mancini, where, throughout the late 1730s and 1740s, French artists of outstanding talent were sent to further their studies. All these French artists met, at some time or another, the leading light of the Italian classical revival, Piranesi, and all were influenced by his work. Le Geay, for example, returned to Paris in 1742 from Rome with a widely publicized folio of work, and Saly, in 1746, published engravings of his designs for vases based on antique originals.

1745, Madame de Pompadour became the
ial mistress of Louis XV, and by 1749 was
ing plans for her brother, the Marquis
Marigny, to become the Director-General
he Arts. Accordingly she sent him on an
nsive tour of Italy. His travelling com-
ions became whole-hearted supporters of
classical movement, but Marigny seems
to have been quite so certain about the
ection of classical art at this stage and he
not completely won over until the 1760s.
rchitecturally the Rococo movement had
had a tremendous impact. From the out-
buildings, especially public buildings and
rches, were still classical, although the
of columns, colonnades, pediments, and
the other classical devices had become
ceably lighter and fresher as the eight-
h century advanced. The interiors of
ses at this time, especially the grand ones,
a sequence of rooms, used for entertaining,
it was usually only in the private apart-
ts of the house where high fashion was
wed full rein, and therefore many rooms in
s were still being decorated in the middle
ie eighteenth century in a classical vein,
being a survival from the Baroque age
er than a revival of any antique style.
ie only type of furniture from the Louis
period which was admired throughout
eighteenth century was that decorated
the Boulle technique. These were usually
e sombre pieces of case furniture veneered
ony, and with marquetry of brass and
iseshell, richly mounted in ormolu. The
test exponent of this technique was
ré-Charles Boulle, hence its name. Boulle
elf died in 1732, but his workshops con-
d under the direction of his son. Several
iet-makers, trained in these workshops,
ched out on their own, notably Etienne
sseur, who became an independent
iet-maker in 1760, and continued to work
e same style and technique so favoured
uis XIV. Furniture by Boulle was already
rly sought after and collected by the mid-
f the eighteenth century. Ange-Laurent
e de Jully, a man of taste and a collector,
l Louis-Joseph Le Lorrain, who had been
me in the 1740s, to design a suite of furni-
for him in the Boulle tradition, consisting
ureau-plat, a cartonnier, a cabinet and a
. This Lorrain did, and the furniture,
of which is now in the Musée Condé at
tilly, was finished in the mid-1750s, and
arded as the earliest neo-classical furni-
in France. Its ponderous architectural
and the technique used—ebony veneer
l with brass and richly mounted in ormolu
ertainly reminiscent of the furniture of
e, though the overall effect is very differ-
t was regarded as ultra-modern by Lalive
lly's contemporaries, though reactions
were mixed, some, like the Comte de

Caylus, having nothing but praise for it, and
others, such as the designer and engraver,
Cochin, being distinctly against it. The furniture was designed to stand in Lalive's *Cabinet
Flamand*, decorated in the classical manner
by the architect Barreau de Chefdeville, and
it was after this that the taste for works *à la
Grecque* or in the *goût grec* began to spread.
These became catchphrases of the time, and
anything remotely fashionable or in the new
classical vein was immediately described as
à la Grecque, regardless of the source of
inspiration. The maker of Lalive's suite is
not known, though the mounts were executed
by the *bronzeur*, Philippe Caffieri. These
pieces were in no way attempts to reproduce
classical Roman or Greek furniture, the appearance of which was known to Lalive and
Le Lorrain from contemporary publications.
The furniture was something entirely new, and
caused a sensation in Paris, where it seems to
have been known by virtually everybody, as
there are many contemporary references to
the suite, and even advertisements for bureaux
in the style of that of Monsieur Lalive, suggesting that everyone would know what style
that was.

Oeben was another important maker of the
transitional period from Rococo to Neo-
classicism, and the early neo-classic period.
Most of his later work, though less heavily
architectural in appearance than Lalive's
furniture, is in the new style; both he and
Garnier, however, show their lack of architectural training by certain obvious mistakes
such as including an even number of flutes in
a pilaster. Floral marquetry, having returned

143

to fashion in the late 1740s, was still popular, and Oeben, like many of his contemporaries German by birth, was one of its greatest exponents. Each of his flowers was usually identifiable, and most were probably copied from contemporary engravings. It was Oeben who started work on the *Bureau de Roi*, ordered for Louis XV in 1760, but he died in 1763 when the desk was still unfinished, and it was completed by his journeyman, Jean-Henri Riesener. Though the basic shape is still bombé and typically Rococo, much of the decoration is pure classical, and shows that, by the 1760s, the classical revival had gained quite a hold. Moreover, the desk was being constructed to stand in a room at Versailles with Rococo *boiserie* and furniture. Oeben's widow carried on her husband's workshop and used his stamp on pieces of furniture. In 1767 she married Jean-Henri Riesener, the most talented of her husband's journeymen, and thereafter Riesener used his own stamp on everything that was produced by the workshop.

The new rectilinear forms were obviously far more suitable for some pieces of furniture than others. *Secrétaires à abattant,* long-case or pedestal clocks and bureaux-plats were soon being constructed in an entirely classical fashion, but commodes were made well into the 1770s partially retaining the bombé shape of the Rococo, and still supported on cabriole

legs, as were smaller movable pieces of furniture, such as work- and writing-tables. Possibly it was felt that a totally classical interior, composed of heavy rectilinear furniture, would be too overpowering, and the necessity was still felt for the softening effect of curved forms. Work by most of the leading cabinet-makers at this time, such as Vanrisamburgh, Joubert and Riesener, all show this tendency to have classical mounts and sometimes marquetry on a commode with cabriole legs.

In 1769 François-Joseph Bélanger executed for Marie-Antoinette a design for a jewel cabinet. In form it resembled the cabinets on stands of the seventeenth century, having a pair of doors enclosing numerous small drawers, and supported on eight legs. This was the first piece of furniture with straight legs to be provided for a member of the royal family, and was quite different to the furniture of the mid-century.

In the early 1770s the Prince de Condé carried out radical redecorations in the Palais Bourbon, and the few pieces which are known to have been executed for him by Leleu at this time are in a totally classical style, though there are few, if any, datable examples extant. With chairs more than with veneered furniture, designers and makers clung tenaciously to the old lines, and chairs with voluted arm supports and cabriole legs were still being constructed in the 1780s.

Right: Jewel-cabinet presented to Marie-Antoinette by the City of Paris in 1787 and made by Jean-Ferdinand Schwerdfeger. The form of the piece is seventeenth-century, but the decoration is eighteenth-century. The mounts are probably by Thomire, one of the most famous bronze-workers of the day. The central bronze medallion symbolizes the arts, and the caryatid figures represent the four seasons. (Château de Versailles)

Below left: Writing-table made by Jean-François Leleu, possibly for Mme Victoire, Louis XVI's aunt. This is one of the few existing pieces which bears a resemblance to the more elaborate designs of De Wailly with its unusually convoluted legs. The maker's mark appears on the top of one of the drawer-fronts which is unusual in the eighteenth century, the most usual place being on the back or underneath.

An interesting connection between France and England at this time is provided in the work of Gravelot, who had lived for some time in England where it is known from contemporary references that he did designs for cabinet-makers and upholsterers. The content of these designs is unknown but at the time when they were done, about 1740, the Palladian style still held sway in England, and he would certainly have been conversant with it. By the 1760s Gravelot was back in France and was doing designs for ornament in the field of carpets and tapestries for the Savonnerie and Gobelins workshops. His familiarity, while in England, with the Palladian style must have made it easier for him to work in the vernacular of the classical revival.

By the middle and late 1760s the Marquis de Marigny was ordering furniture for his own use in the new style, though we can only judge this loosely from contemporary descriptions, as there is no visual record of the pieces he ordered. The Duc de Choiseul, France's first minister, also ordered pieces in what was to become known as the Louis Seize style. In

*: The Duc de Choiseul's
:hamber painted by
is-Nicolas van
renberghe, about 1770,
mounted on a gold
f-box. There is a
ical secrétaire à
tant and a matching
-cabinet; the picture
es and the overmantel
ll neo-classical, but
hairs, firescreen and
re in the Rococo
. (Louvre, Paris)*

*right: Chair bearing
ker's stamp of
Delanois, one of the
st chair-makers of
ly neo-classical
. The carving was
l out by Joseph-
s Guichard.*

*Console table in
-mounted kingwood,
ed in 1781 by
er for Marie-
ette's private study
sailles. The table
the plain veneers
became popular in
0s. The ormolu-
on the table are
larly fine, and
rate cornflowers,
Antoinette's
tes.*

the late 1760s, Delanois supplied furniture to Madame du Barry—208 pieces in all, both for her apartments at Versailles and for her Pavilion at Louveciennes. Most of this furniture is now either no longer identifiable, or no longer in existence, but some of the chairs do exist, and these favour the new classical style, and, from descriptions, so did most of her other furniture.

There existed in Paris at this time a ready-made market of furniture and objects in the establishments of the *marchands-merciers* and the *marchands-tapissiers*. The marchand-mercier was a middleman between the craftsman and buyers, and the best of them had shops in the Faubourg St Honoré. Lazare Duvaux, one of the most famous, died in 1758—too early to have much effect on the decline in the taste for the Rococo. Simon-Philippe Poirier, however, does seem to have played a part. Already in the early 1760s he had in his stock several pieces of furniture and ormolu in the 'Greek' style, and persuaded several influential people into buying them. Poirier specialized in furniture set with porcelain plaques from the

Sèvres factory, and the carcases were often made by the ébéniste Martin Carlin. He usually made several pieces to the same design, and there are several versions of a ladies' writing-table which seems to have been a speciality of his—set with rectangular flower-painted Sèvres porcelain plaques, but still raised on elegant cabriole legs, a bow to convention. In 1777 Poirier's firm was taken over by his erstwhile partner, Dominique Daguerre, and its success continued.

The marchands-tapissiers specialized in seat furniture, beds, mirrors, and draperies of all kinds. At a time when rooms were usually decorated throughout in a co-ordinated style these entrepreneurs were of some importance, and many *menuisiers*, Louis Delanois for instance, sold more furniture to the marchands-tapissiers than to private clients. The marchands-tapissiers were actually craftsmen, most of them being upholsterers in their own right, and often had their workshops away from the smarter areas of Paris.

Many of the greater ébénistes of the latter half of the eighteenth century were German by birth. Oeben had secured royal patronage, thus also securing his position in Paris. Riesener, also a German, born in Gladbeck in 1734, took over Oeben's workshop, and, on the accession of Louis XVI to the throne in 1774, succeeded the aged Gilles Joubert as *ébéniste ordinaire du Roi*. His work for the Crown was ornate, full use being made of ormolu and marquetry, and his earlier pieces are heavy in appearance, typified by the commode, now at Chantilly, supplied in 1775 for the King's bedroom at Versailles. He also supplied a charming mechanical table to stand beside the Queen's bed. Made in collaboration with the mechanic, Merklein, this piece was constructed to answer all the Queen's needs. It was a dressing-table, writing-table, breakfast-table, and reading-table all in one. In the 1780s Riesener's elaborate pieces became too expensive for the royal family who were deep in debt, and many commissions went to the ébénistes, Stockel and Beneman. Riesener simplified much of his work, still retaining his individual style, and some of his later pieces, in plain, beautifully grained mahogany, free from marquetry and with simple ormolu mouldings, are among his most charming creations. He lived until 1806, working until 1801, but his major work after the collapse of the monarchy was to replace the royal arms and insignia on pieces of royal furniture with something which would be less offensive to the new order.

Another German working in Paris at this time was Adam Weisweiler, received as a *maître ébéniste* in 1778. Unlike Riesener, who seems to have designed his own furniture, Weisweiler worked almost exclusively for the marchand-mercier, Daguerre, who must have

147

Left: A cabinet and chest-of-drawers surmounted by a clock, veneered in tulipwood and lavishly mounted with ormolu and Sèvres porcelain plaques. Thirty of the plaques have the Sèvres date-letter N for 1766. This piece shows signs of having been altered at some time, and it is probable that it was made by either Martin Carlin or J-F Leleu. (Wallace Collection, London)

Right: A Japanese lacquer secrétaire en pente, made by Martin Carlin. Carlin made high quality furniture, particularly for the marchands-merciers Poirier and his successor Daguerre, who had a virtual monopoly on the importation of oriental lacquer into France, as well as on porcelain plaques from the Sèvres factory. This is one of the few sloping-front desks made in the late eighteenth century, as by then the bureau à cylindre had become fashionable.

finished work, one just had to close the cylinder front to hide them from view. Commodes and corner cupboards *(encoignures)* were still as popular, and the *console desserte*, a type of sideboard with open shelves, made its first appearance. The more informal way of life favoured by Louis XV for his subjects was continued under Louis XVI, and many small movable tables for all sorts of uses were still popular. Reading-tables, writing-tables, worktables, *rafraichissoirs* — a kind of table with apertures in the top for ice-buckets for wine, *tables de chevet* — tables with a shelf and sometimes a drawer to stand beside the bed, *tables en commode* — small tables with two or three drawers in the frieze — were all still made in large quantities to satisfy the old aristocracy and the new rich.

In Paris and in the grander homes outside Paris, these pieces were nearly always veneered and often decorated with marquetry, sometimes, although rarely, with *vernis martin*, a kind of elaborate painting process built up in layers to imitate lacquer, invented and patented by the four Martin brothers. In the provinces, however, and in the not so rich bourgeois homes pieces were often made in solid wood, and were, of necessity, of much simpler form than the grander pieces they were imitating. Often the wood was simply polished and sometimes painted to match the decoration of the room for which it was intended. The Rococo style continued longer in the provinces and became more attenuated and elegant as the Louis Seize style spread. The charm of these provincial pieces is undeniable, and they are much sought after today.

ated to him how the pieces he made should :, and probably provided him with designs. creations are elegant and sometimes al-t jewel-like. His richer pieces make use èvres porcelain, on which Daguerre had a ual monopoly, oriental lacquer, and some-es *pietra-dura* panels, usually taken from nteenth-century cabinets which had been ken up. His plainer pieces are often in ogany with simple ormolu mounts, though is finer works the mounts are often by the ous *ciseleur-doreur*, Gouthière. Certain orative features are typical of Weisweiler's k, for instance interlaced stretchers, and ie or top-shaped feet.

artin Carlin was another German work-in Paris who preferred to work for the chands-merciers. His most famous pieces those studded with porcelain plaques, olied to him by Poirier, and later, by his essor, Daguerre. He also worked for nault, known to have supplied him with uer panels for furniture for the Château ellevue, where the aunts of Louis XVI had r home.

ery few new pieces of furniture made their earance in the latter part of the eighteenth tury. The secrétaire à abattant, the upper of which falls forward to form a writing ace and to reveal drawers and pigeon-s, became much more popular because it up so much less space than a writing-e. Riesener made several fine and orately decorated examples for the royal ily. The cylinder bureau *(bureau à cylindre)* became more widely used in preference he writing-table as, instead of clearing 's private papers away each time one

Left: Secrétaire à abattant in lacquer and ebony, made by Jean-Henri Riesener. The plaque of the sacrifice to love and the mounts in the form of cornflowers appear on several pieces supplied by Riesener to Marie-Antoinette.

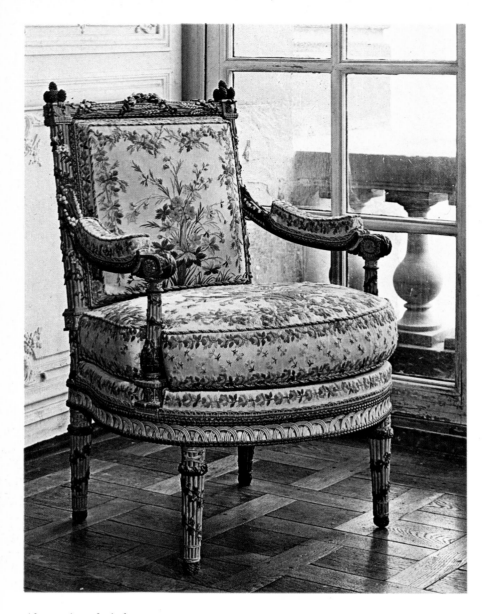

As was the custom earlier in the century there were still two types of chair in the late eighteenth century — the *sièges meublants*, which always stood against the wall, and the *sièges courants*, which were disposed about the centre of the room and could be moved about at will. The frames were, as earlier, of carved wood, either gilded, painted, or polished, the latter technique becoming noticeably more popular in grander establishments towards the end of the eighteenth century. The materials used to cover seat furniture were the same as earlier — damask, velvet, silk, brocade, printed cotton, embroidered silk, tapestry and needlework, with leather usually used for desk chairs.

Settees became more elaborate, and each variation had a different name. The reasons for these names, and the variations to which they referred are now difficult to trace. One does not know how a *sultane* differed from an *ottomane,* or a *turquoise,* and what the distinctive feature was of a *paphose.* Stools were still of the same basic types as before; the *tabouret,* the *pliant* and the *banquette.*

Beds were usually of carved wood, either painted or gilded, and with a canopy. They were nearly always placed with one long side against the wall, and the canopy was supported either by carved columns (*lit à colonnes*), metal supports hidden by the bed hangings (*lit à la polonaise*), or it was attached to the wall or ceiling behind or above the bed (*lit à la duchesse*).

The construction of furniture in France at this time, below the top level of craftsmanship, was not of the finest quality, and the parts that were not seen by the eye were often very badly finished indeed. Veneered pieces of furniture had carcases of oak or pinewood, and there appear to have been well over 50

Above: Armchair by Georges Jacob, made for Marie-Antoinette in 1787. The frame was carved by Triquet and Rode and painted by Chaillot de Prusse. (Château de Versailles)

Right: Commode made for Louis XVI's bedchamber at the Château de St Cloud, by Guillaume Beneman. The frieze has ormolu mounts symbolizing royalty — coronets, lilies, cockerels, and the crossed L's.

erent types of wood, some native, some
tic, in use for marquetry work.

lost chairs were constructed from beech-
od or walnut, but fruitwoods and pinewood
e sometimes used, and veneered seat
iiture was sometimes made, though rarely.
er in the century chairs were made in
nogany à l'anglaise.

eorges Jacob, perhaps the most famous
ir-maker of the time, became a maître
uisier in 1765, and by the 1780s had
iblished himself as one of the leading
ir-makers of Paris. He made pieces not
/ for the haute monde of Paris, but for
uential clients abroad, such as the Duke
Zweibrücken-Birkenfeld, for whom he
le a famous bed, now in the Residenz-
eum, Munich, which caused quite a stir
n it first appeared. He also made seat
iiture for George IV of England and the
e of Bedford, via the marchand-mercier,
uerre, who was busy supplying pieces for
Carlton House and Woburn Abbey.

acques-Louis David, the painter, com-
sioned Jacob to make the furniture for his
lio to his own designs. These pieces,
ct copies of antique originals, were the
of their kind, and were in the style now
)ciated with the French Empire. Hitherto
small decorative pieces, such as pedestals
uthéniennes, had been modelled at all
ely on Greek or Roman prototypes. At
it the same time he made some chairs after
gns by the painter, Hubert Robert, in what
known as the Etruscan style, for Marie-
oinette's dairy at Rambouillet. These
e only Etruscan in that some of the
)rative motifs had been found on pots,
)ably of Greek origin, dug up in Etruria.
ter the chaos of the Revolution in France,
advent of Napoleon brought, if not peace,
east a measure of order. Following their
)eror's example, the new rich were able
irn their attentions to patronage of the
There was a strong inclination towards
r and less fussy forms, and also a con-
ation of the trend towards antiquity,
uraged by the Emperor with his strong
iration for the art of Imperial Rome.
ady in the 1780s certain architects,
bly Charles-Louis Clérisseau, Jean-
osthène Dugourc and François-Joseph
nger were designing interiors in the
)esque' or 'grotesque' style, culled from
quity, which was favoured under the
ctory and Consulate (1795–1804). At the
nning of the nineteenth century, a distinct
rn to the classical forms in all their
ty became apparent. In 1798 Louis-Martin
hault designed some bedroom furniture
he renowned lady of fashion, Juliette
imier, and in 1801 Percier and Fontaine,
nost important designers of the Empire
)d, published the first of their Recueil de

Décorations Intérieures. Other publications
which strongly influenced taste and design
at this time were Plans, coupes et élévations
des plus belles maisons et des hôtels construits
à Paris et dans les environs by the architect
J C Krafft and the engraver N Ransonnette,
1802, Nouveau Recueil en divers genres
d'ornements et autres objects propres à la
décoration by Charles Normand, 1803, and
Fragmens d'architecture, sculpture, et peinture
dans le style antique by P N Beauvallet, 1804.

The painters of the day also dabbled in
furniture design. As we have seen, Robert had
provided chairs for Marie-Antoinette, and
David, having designed his own studio
furnishings, later designed furniture for the
Emperor's rooms at the Tuileries, while
Prud'hon designed a dressing-table for the
Empress Marie-Louise and the cradle for the
King of Rome. An important publication of
the time was the periodical Collection des
Meubles et Objets de Goût, the management of

Above: In this painting,
La Consolation de
l'Absence, the room is
furnished entirely in the
neo-classical style. The
table is painted, probably
in the technique known
as vernis martin which
imitated oriental lacquer,
and behind it is a fire-
screen. The mirror, console
table, chair and cartel
clock are all in the full
late eighteenth-century
Louis Seize style. (Musée
Cognacq-Jay, Paris)

which was in the hands of Pierre de la Mésangère. What it was that prompted a former professor of philosophy to take over the running of a magazine must remain a mystery, but its importance was that it was seen by a large section of the public, to whom it showed the latest fashions in furnishings, and it was also seen by all the cabinet-makers who could then tell what the buying public would ask for, and have it ready for them.

The bible of designers of this time was the *Recueil de Décorations Intérieures* by Percier and Fontaine, containing 72 engraved plates, some showing designs which had already been executed. Charles Percier and Pierre-François-Léonard Fontaine met first at the studio of Peyre le Jeune, Inspector of the Royal Buildings. They met again when they were both in Italy, and in 1798 published their first work together, *Recueil des palais, maisons et autres édifices modernes dessinés à Rome*.

It was probably Georges Jacob who secured for the two architects their first official commission which was to design the furnishings of the Salle de Convention at the Tuileries in 1793. During the Consulate they were kept busy working on the restoration and redecoration of the old royal palaces, stripped by the revolutionaries, and which Napoleon now wanted to use. They worked at the Tuileries, the Elysée Palace, Saint-Cloud, the Grand Trianon, Compiègne, Rambouillet and Fontainebleau, and they also worked for the Empress Josephine at her country-house, Malmaison. In 1804 Percier and Fontaine designed the coronation throne for Napoleon who, in 1805, in recognition of their services, gave them the title of Architects of the Louvre and Tuileries. In 1811 they became members of the Institut de France.

Their influence was strong throughout Europe, where their *Recueil de décorations* was widely read and followed, and spread to Russia, where Czar Alexander commissioned a series of water-colours with accompanying notes of the interiors and furnishings of the Tuileries.

The great arbiter of Imperial taste was Dominique Vivant, Baron Denon, the director of the Musée Napoléon, who supervised everything made in the *ateliers* of the artists and craftsmen working for the court; everything had to be given his approval. He had begun his career in the household of Madame de Pompadour, looking after her collection of engraved stones, and was sent as secretary to the French embassy in Naples. There he assembled a fine collection of vases, later acquired by Louis XVI for the Sèvres porcelain factory. In 1802 he was made Director of the Musée Napoléon and Master of the Mint, and advised the government in all artistic matters, busying himself with the smallest details of the furnishings, and sometimes even submitting designs himself.

Denon is most famous for his publication *Voyage dans la Basse et Haute Egypte*, a series of drawings done by him while following Napoleon's armies. He sketched many of the temples along the Nile, and architectural details as well, and the album of these achieved international fame, being published in

gland, Germany and Italy by 1808. Cabinet-
kers used many of the motifs he had
tched on furniture and in decoration, and
re was a new wave of popularity for *le*
t d'Egypte. Denon commissioned Jacob-
smalter, the most famous furniture-maker
he period, and Biennais, a goldsmith and
letime furniture-maker, to supply furnish-
s, using details from his drawings, amongst
ich were a bed decorated with Egyptian
ires, and a medal-cabinet based on a portico
the ancient city of Apollinopolis Parva.
h Thomas Hope and George Smith, two
portant contemporary English designers,
nowledged their debt to Denon in their
igns for rooms in the Egyptian taste.
acob-Desmalter was the son of Georges
ob and was christened François-Honoré-

Georges Jacob — he took the name Desmalter from a family property. He received the best training possible in his father's workshop, which he took over on his father's retirement and ran until 1825. As we have seen, Georges Jacob already in the eighteenth century was an ardent exponent of what was to become the Empire style and his son must have been conversant with this at an early age. In 1798 Jacob-Desmalter married the daughter of Martin-Eloy Lignereux, the successor of the marchand-mercier, Daguerre, and an early exponent of the Egyptian taste.

Among his first commissions after his father's retirement was the re-furbishment of the house for General Bonaparte and his new wife, Josephine, and the execution to designs by Berthault of the bedroom furniture of Madame Recamier, which included a boat-shaped bed with swan's head scroll ends — an early example of a style of bed which became universally popular in the Empire period. Percier and Fontaine commissioned Jacob-Desmalter to carry out many of their designs for Napoleon, at Malmaison, the Tuileries and other former royal palaces. By 1807 Jacob-Desmalter had a sizable and successful firm. He employed about 350 workmen, and his annual output was worth 700,000 francs, one-third of which was for export. Despite his success he went bankrupt in 1813, owing to the tardiness of many of his clients in paying their bills and the slump in commerce caused

Above: Bathroom at the Château de Malmaison. The dressing-table is in burr-elm with ormolu mounts. Pieces like this with the mirror and table joined as one piece of furniture only became popular in the early nineteenth century. The wash-basin and stand is based on an antique incense burner. (Château de Malmaison)

Right: A bed designed by Baudry, known as a lit bateau, or boat-bed, because of its shape. It is also sometimes known as a lit en courbeille (basket-bed). The simplicity and flow of this piece is typical of Empire furniture, as is the use of indigenous woods, rather than the exotic imported woods such as mahogany which were difficult to obtain because of the trade embargo brought about by the Napoleonic Wars. (Musée des Arts Décoratifs, Paris)

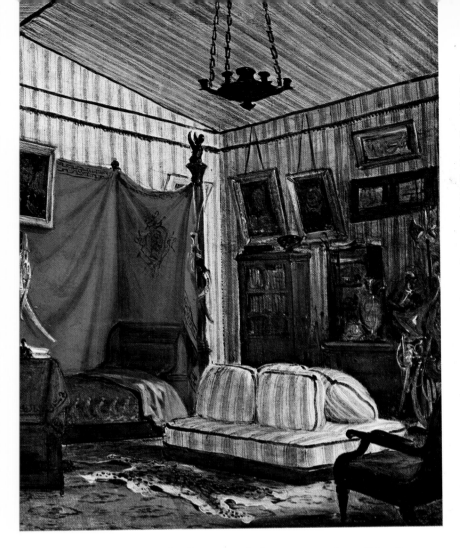

by Napoleon's later campaigns. The firm was soon running successfully again, though on a smaller scale, and when Jacob-Desmalter died in 1841 it was continued by his son.

There were other dynasties of cabinet-makers working under the Empire — the Bellangés, the Lemarchands and the Mansions were three of the most famous — but competition was much stronger now, since the Assembly had abolished the guilds in 1791. Increased industrialization caused more furniture of mediocre quality to be made, and the Continental blockade, started in 1806, made it increasingly difficult for cabinet-makers to import exotic woods or to export their finished wares to England.

Martin-Guillaume Biennais was one of the foremost makers and suppliers of the period. He came from Normandy, but settled in Paris in about 1790. He was appointed goldsmith to Napoleon and on his trade cards he described himself as a dealer in fancy goods, furniture, and fans, with a depot for display of his wares. His furniture was often to designs by Percier and Fontaine, and Denon, and his famous workshops, Au Singe Violet — 'at the sign of the purple monkey' — were in the fashionable Rue St Honoré.

Many cabinet-makers continued to stamp their goods with their names and sometimes even their addresses as well, such as Biennais, though the necessity to do this had been removed with the dissolution of the guilds.

Napoleon went to great lengths to encourage the arts, and was much more than just a patron. He considered that luxury was a necessary adjunct to a healthy economy. He and Josephine visited the Gobelin and Sèvres factories, amongst others, and visited the leading cabinet-makers in their *ateliers*, as well as inviting many of them as dinner-guests. He was as much concerned with building the prestige of these establishments and the quality of their products as Louis XIV had been, and he also took a tremendous and almost finicky interest in the furnishing of his own living quarters. Despite the new accent on comfort and informality, strict protocol was still observed on public occasions, and the Empress and the Emperor's mother were the only people allowed to use an arm-chair in his presence — all others, including members of the Imperial family, used ordinary chairs or stools.

Although the style and decoration of furniture changed radically in the early nineteenth century, the only new type to make its appearance was the cheval-glass, sometimes called a *psyché*. This was a full-length mirror, pivoted between upright supports.

The exotic woods, particularly mahogany, satinwood and rosewood, were popular at the beginning of the Empire period, but the European blockade made these scarce, and native woods, such as maple, beech, walnut, oak and fruitwoods, were used much more. With the new fashion for large expanses of wood, the more highly grained examples became popular, such as amboyna and thuya, the attractive burr being obtained from the part of the tree close to the root.

After 1815 the quality and craftsmanship declined, and furniture became plainer and heavier. Louis XVIII's reign saw a revival of the Louis Seize style, and the Empire style lingered on in a watered-down plainer version through the reigns of Charles X and Louis-Philippe.

England
The 1750s saw the English Rococo at its height and, at the same time, the stirrings of the successive Neo-classicism all over Europe. In 1754, the very year of Chippendale's important *Director,* the young Scottish architect, Robert Adam, was embarking on the four-year Italian trip which would prepare him for a highly successful career as a classical architect. Within a few years he would have pioneered a revival, which would undermine the short-lived Rococo that preceded it and would lead to a clarification and discipline of design.

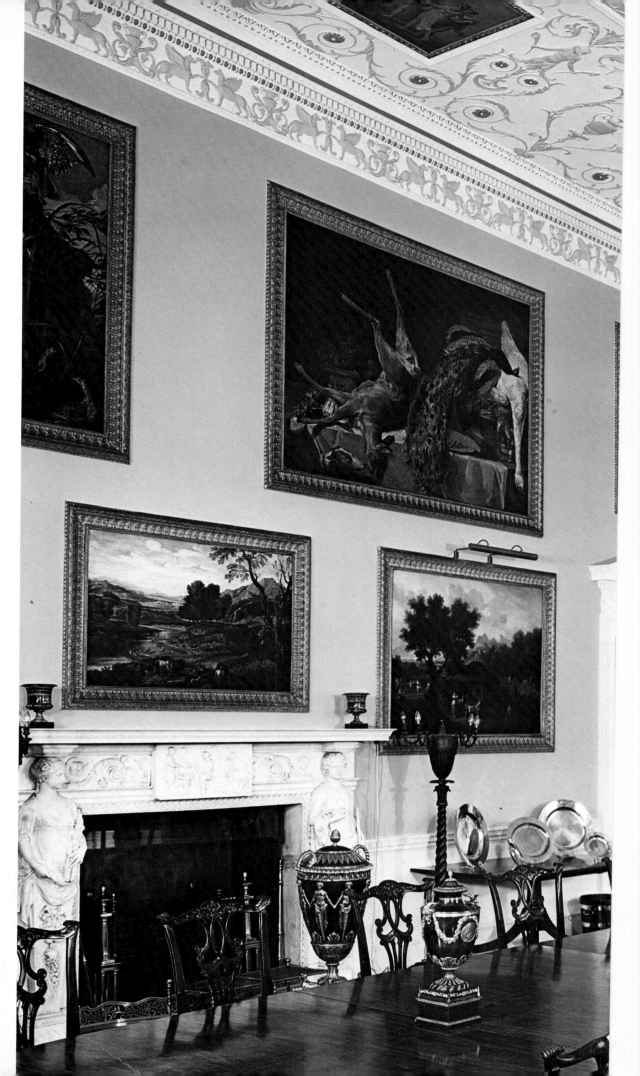

Right: The Dining-Room at Kedleston designed by Robert Adam in about 1761. The large scale of the neo-classical plaster-work decoration is typical of this early phase in Adam's career. With its inset paintings and neo-classical furniture, this room was evidently meant to present a unified whole, the sideboard apse forming the focal point, especially when the central floor space was cleared between meals. The complex sideboard group, on which the family plate was to be displayed in the traditional manner, may well have been inspired by James Stuart, and the vast jasper wine-cooler certainly belongs to Stuart's work in the house. (Kedleston Hall, Derby)

Although the Rococo years had been extremely productive as far as interior decoration and the decorative arts were concerned, the style was not necessarily universally followed. For those who disliked the wild extravaganzas of Rococo a conservative Palladian style was still employed into the mid-eighteenth century, and, certainly, Palladian principles still held good for external architecture.

With this continuing tradition of Italian inspiration — reinforced throughout the century by the Grand Tour — it was perhaps easier for the English to slip comfortably into the neo-classical revival than it was for their European contemporaries. The Rococo had been a fleeting fashion, and now, with Roman classicism stressed once more, architects and designers could develop effortlessly from a sound Palladian foundation. They were, after all, in many cases studying the same Roman sources as their Palladian predecessors; it was merely the interpretation that was to change in the late eighteenth century. It is not surprising, therefore, to find certain basic similarities between the interiors of William Kent and Robert Adam, or between those tentative experiments towards neo-classical furniture of the 1760s and the pieces of 20 or 30 years earlier.

The Palladians, with their sound knowledge of important centres like Rome, were less adventurous than their successors, who now scoured Europe for uncharted sites. Hence the influential trips made by Dawkins and Wood to Palmyra and Baalbeck in the 1750s, and hence Adam's choice of Spalatro for the subject of his book. These studies, opening up new fields, would lead to a more serious imitation of classicism than that of the Burlington circle earlier in the century.

The most important work to be produced was undoubtedly Stuart and Revett's *Antiquities of Athens* of 1762, which with LeRoy's less extensive survey would ultimately lead to the new Greek revival. James Stuart, the more important architect of the two, put some of his Greek studies into practice on his return to England in 1755, but, unfortunately, he rarely carried out large-scale commissions, and was soon eclipsed by Robert Adam. His surviving decorations within Spencer House,

Above: Design for the Painted Room at Spencer House of about 1759 by James Stuart. This sketch is for one of the earliest neo-classical interiors in England. Much of the ornament is drawn from ancient Rome, while Raphael's sixteenth-century 'grotesque' decorations at the Vatican are another source of inspiration. The rectilinear furniture is far in advance of its time, the ormolu tripod being based on a Greek design, although the lion, crouching beneath the table-top, is reminiscent of Palladian furniture earlier in the century. (The British Museum, London)

James, remind us of his importance,
...ever, as the first great neo-classical
...gner in England.

...urprisingly the Painted Room at Spencer
...se, with its rinceaux, swags of corn
...ks, sphinxes, vases and classical figures,
...ore reminiscent of Rome — which Stuart
... also visited — than of Greece. But Greek
...nents were introduced into the furniture
...igned by Stuart for this setting. Great
...ged lions, drawn from the Temple of
...icrates in Athens, were incorporated, for
...mple, into the sides of the splendid carved
... gilded sofas, which survive with their
...ching set of chairs at Kenwood House
...ay. The side-table included in Stuart's
...tch of 1759 centred on another crouching
...1, to relieve no doubt the severity of this
...anced neo-classical piece with its fluted
...ze and tapering, square-section legs.

...he small ormolu tripod, visible in the
...tch, was based on another Athenian
...nument, the Lantern of Demosthenes, and
...ame a popular form in the late eighteenth
...tury. Although shown equipped with
...nches, for use as a candelabrum, it could
...ily be adapted for incense-burning, which
... become fashionable. Candelabra to this
...ign were supplied to Lord Spencer in about
...9, with tall, painted and gilded *torchère*
...nds which were appropriately carved with
...ffins symbolizing fire. These are early
...mples of the type of torchère which Adam
...rroneously credited with introducing into
...gland.

...dam dismissed the decorations of Spencer
...use as 'pitifulissimo', and went on to
...cribe Stuart's work for Lord Scarsdale as
...ill done that [it] moves to pity rather than
...tempt'. However, he evidently learnt a lot
...m Stuart, and admitted later, in mellower
...od, that he had 'contributed greatly to-
...rds introducing the true style of antique
...oration'.

...o doubt he benefited from the chance to
...dy Stuart's technique at Kedleston, Derby-
...re, when he succeeded him there in 1761.
...e severely classical sideboard group, al-
...ough finally carried out under Adam's
...ection, seems to belong to Stuart's inspira-
...n and to be in advance of Adam's neo-
...ssical development at that date.

...he Kedleston dining-room, with its shallow
...sterwork decorations and inset paintings,
...ves as a reminder of the style of architecture
...h which Adam built up his reputation on
... return in 1758? He completed Kedleston
...ich had been begun by James Paine, and,
...eed, many of his other early commissions
...re also for the completion or remodelling
...existing buildings. Adam quickly proved
...nself to be extremely adept at coping with
...oblems of 'conversion', as, for instance, at
...on, where he tackled the task of classicizing

a monotonous, long, low, Jacobean gallery
with very successful results.

Enlivening rooms with apses and columnar
screens, he transposed on to walls and ceilings
the repertoire of ornament he had learnt in
Rome. Piranesi had claimed that he had 'more
genius for the true and noble architecture than
any Englishman ever was in Italy'. This
sound understanding of the antique, combined
with a knowledge of the sixteenth-century
vividly painted motifs of the Raphael School
known as 'grotteschi', led to a balanced and
confident arrangement of classical decoration.
Sphinxes, griffins, caryatids, rams' heads,
vases, tripods, classical shields were arrayed
time and again amidst acanthus leaf scrolls,
anthemions, palmettes, swags of ribbon or
chains of corn-husks in ever changing combinations. Contained within squares, rectangles, semicircles or the popular oval, the
stuccowork would frequently centre on inset
medallions, painted with suitably classical
subjects. At first used on a bold scale, these
antique patterns were to dwindle to a great
delicacy and over-refinement toward the end
of Adam's life.

*Above: Armchair designed
by Adam in 1764 and made
by Thomas Chippendale.
Despite neo-classical
sphinxes, anthemions and
acanthus-leaf scrolls,
Rococo and Palladian
elements linger on in this
early Adam chair design,
which bears little relation
to his later, more delicate
work. When, in 1765, it was
delivered as one of a set of
eight such chairs,
Chippendale charged the
high price of £160 for the
set.(Victoria & Albert
Museum, London)*

159

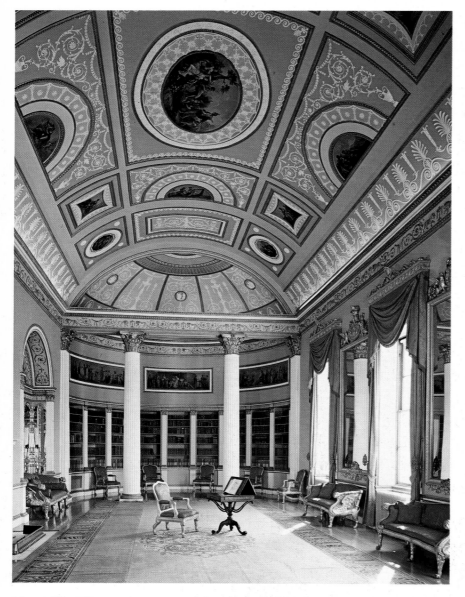

but by the late 1760s he had developed a more suitable rectilinear style.

The mid-1760s were to see the return of the rectangular side-table, equipped with a top of marble, *scagliola*, or marquetried wood. Classical motifs decorated the carved and gilded or painted frieze, and the legs, which were generally arranged in pairs, were of tapering square-section or slender, baluster form. In the semicircular tables, which were soon to emerge as an alternative, decorative stretchers might also be included.

Side-tables — especially if intended for the pier between windows — would frequently be surmounted by a mirror in a rectangular or oval frame. The decorative crestings on mirrors and girandoles were reduced in scale as the 1770s advanced and a round-topped tripartite 'Venetian window' design developed during that decade.

Although the repertoire of classical ornament was adapted to a variety of uses, the lyre being a favourite device for the chair-back for instance, surprisingly few pieces of classical form were made. It would be some years before the recent discoveries at Herculaneum and Pompeii would bear fruit. Only in the urn-on-pedestal and torchère-stand were these archaeological tendencies foreshadowed, and both these forms had already appeared in Stuart's designs, before Adam's rise to fame.

The vases-on-pedestals which now flanked the sideboard-table were an elegant adjunct to the dining-room. Resembling the splendid marble urns sought by many a Grand Tourist on his travels, they served a practical purpose as well as a decorative one. The vase might be used as a knife-box, or provide a water-container. The pedestals, lined with tin and equipped with charcoal-burners, became useful plate-warmers — or else, to the horrified amazement of visiting foreigners, one pedestal was often found to contain a chamber-pot.

Tripod torchères, supplied in sets or pairs, for the support of candelabra and incense-burners, were based upon classical altars. Although Stuart had used this design as early as 1759, it seems that their great popularity in the 1770s was largely due to the French fashion for athéniennes.

French Neo-classicism made a great impact on the English now that the Seven Years' War had drawn to a close. Ideas were freely exchanged between the countries, and French goods — including furniture — were supplied to English clients. A number of Adam's patrons bought elegant tapestry hangings and matching upholstery sets from the Gobelins factory in Paris, and the furniture supplied to rooms of this type accorded closely with contemporary French taste. In chair design the similarities are particularly marked as with the oval-backed form popular on both

Above: The Library at Kenwood House, designed by Robert Adam in 1767. This barrel-vaulted library with its apsidal ends and columnar screens was intended, as Adam explained, 'for receiving company', and was accordingly impressive. The carved and gilded pelmet-boards, and the pier-glasses with their neo-classical crestings are original furnishings. The mahogany reading-desk is Rococo in design, but the set of chairs and sofas, although at first glance seeming to belong to the Palladian era, were in fact inspired by Greek sources.

Adam intended his rooms to present a unified and harmonious aspect, with all components interrelating in the French manner. To this end, he designed floor-coverings to echo ceiling patterns, and even provided designs for such small details as the handles and keyhole escutcheons of the doors. Naturally enough, he would wish to supervise the furnishings of his interiors as well, and fortunately, through the survival of many of his drawings in Sir John Soane's collection, this aspect of Adam's work is very well documented.

Although Adam's first recorded furniture design is for a chair in the 'gothick' taste which was executed for Alnwick Castle in Northumberland, his pieces generally draw their ornament from Ancient Rome. Apparently rejecting the uncompromising severity of Stuart, Adam at first translates his classical patterns on to bulky forms, reminiscent of Palladian and Rococo fashions,

Left: Marquetry commode and torchère-stands by John Cobb, made in about 1771. The inspiration for this bombé commode comes from the Louis Quinze style in France although the deeper shape and marquetried top are typically English features. Despite the Rococo outline of the piece, its marquetry decoration is in the neo-classical taste and includes vases of flowers and swags of corn-husks. The unusual bombé pedestals were probably intended as torchère-stands, but within ten years white marble urns had been fixed to them. The set of furniture is completed by a pier-glass designed by Adam in 1772. (Corsham Court, Wiltshire)

sides of the Channel. Sofas followed French trends as well. The 'confidante' — with angle seats at either end — became so popular that in 1788 the firm of Hepplewhite considered an elegant drawing-room 'scarce complete' without one.

The commode played an important role in fashionable interiors of the late eighteenth century. It was generally veneered with a light coloured wood such as satinwood, according with the pale clear colours of the rooms better than mahogany, which tended to be relegated to the hall and dining-room. Classical patterns were introduced through marquetry — revived now in England as in France — and ormulu mounts were used in the French manner.

In the 1760s there was a belated vogue for bombé Louis Quinze commode forms, mounted with meagre Rococo mounts and decorated with the Adam repertoire of ornament. Pierre Langlois, a French-trained ébéniste practising in London, produced much work in this manner. Tailoring his French style to suit his English clientele, he reduced his mounting, generally employed marquetry in place of the marble tops used in Paris, and adopted the low form of commode — sometimes cupboarded — which the English preferred. John Cobb, formerly a partner of the Royal cabinet-

maker William Vile, and described by one of his contemporaries as the 'proudest man in England', also produced work of this incongruous Rococo-classical character.

The 1770s saw a growing preference for commodes of rectangular or semicircular shape. Sometimes these centred on delicate panel 'pictures' in the manner of Angelica Kauffman, which were carried out in a wide range of exotic woods and inset into the furniture in similar fashion to the Sèvres plaques of contemporary France. No doubt, these ambitious schemes were the work of specialist *marqueteurs*, and Fuhrlohg, a Swedish ébéniste who worked in London, is known to have produced some of the finest examples.

Many of the firms associated with the Rococo style through their publications distinguished themselves in the succeeding style. Ince and Mayhew were working in a sophisticated neo-classical manner at Croome Court within a few years of their *Universal System* and some of Chippendale's finest executed work is in the Adam taste. The rosewood- and mahogany-mounted sideboard group, the marquetried library desk, fall-front secretaire and dressing-commode delivered to Harewood in the early 1770s are generally considered to be amongst the most

Above: Japanned bedroom commode made for Harewood House, probably by Thomas Chippendale in about 1771. Several of the Harewood bedrooms were hung with India paper and appropriately furnished with japanned pieces. A combination of chinoiserie and neo-classical patterns was common at this time, and corn-husks, paterae and palmettes frame the oriental scenes on this example.

splendid pieces of furniture ever produced in Britain. They too, especially the secretaire, show a clear debt to France which Chippendale had visited in 1768.

The Harewood furniture, made for a house in which Adam and Chippendale were working simultaneously, was long assumed to have been made to designs by the architect. It is now realized that Chippendale—who was, after all, a competent and fashion-conscious designer—most probably designed the pieces himself. Adam, with his busy architectural career, can scarcely have had time to design all the furnishings in every house upon which he worked. No doubt he delegated work to other designers, or else his patrons consulted cabinet-makers independently. A firm of Chippendale's standing could be relied upon to marry up furniture with its setting, without the guidance of the architect.

A similar situation arose on several occasions between Robert Adam and the cabinet-maker, John Linnell, who had inherited his father's thriving business in 1763. Architect and furniture designer first collaborated at Kedleston, where Linnell's famous mermen sofa in 1762 still echoes the free-flowing Rococo, absorbed during his studies at the St Martin's Lane Academy. By the mid-1770s, when Linnell designed and made some of the furnishings for Osterley, he had developed a more classical style, which harmonized admirably with Adam's interiors.

Chinoiserie, like gothick, had certainly not died out with the advent of Neo-classicism, and japanned furniture was frequently provided for the bedroom, which, in the late eighteenth century, might still be hung with painted Chinese wallpaper. Two black and gold japanned commodes remain at Osterley today, while a green and gold colour scheme was preferred for the famous Chippendale bedroom suite of 1771 at Nostell Priory in Yorkshire. Mrs David Garrick planned her green and white bedroom furnishings round a present of Indian chintz in 1772, and Thomas Chippendale carried these out for her in the flat paintwork that was now preferred to the raised designs in imitation of relief lacquer.

Although Mrs Garrick's bedroom was in the Chinese taste, the bed itself was decorated with Adamesque motifs. Overall neo-classical painting was often done, in a variety of pale colours, although the 1770s saw the vogue for 'Etruscan' rooms, with striking Pompeian decorations in black, white and terracotta and furniture painted to match. An alternative to marquetry, it was not until the last decade of the eighteenth century that painting over veneers became standard practice.

Adam was the only late eighteenth-century English architect to publish any neo-classical furniture designs and he only included a few in his *Works of Architecture* of 1773. But he was by no means unique in his interest in furniture, and it was quite customary for eighteenth-century architects to suggest furnishings for interiors, and even, on occasion, to provide silver designs.

The sketches by Sir William Chambers, Adam's rival, reveal an early appreciation of French Neo-classicism, with which Chambers had come into contact when studying in Blondel's Ecole des Arts in 1750, and through subsequent friendships with students at the French Academy in Rome. He appears to have been in close contact later with the Swedish contingent in London — he had himself been brought up in Sweden — and probably supplied them with designs.

James Wyatt returned to London from Italy in 1768 to find 'the public taste corrupted by the Adams' and complained that he was thus obliged to comply with it. Nonetheless, gaining widespread fame with his Pantheon in London's Oxford Street he went on to design a number of neo-classical houses and their furnishings, which were often painted to harmonize closely with the wall and ceiling decoration. James Paine, Thomas Leverton and Joseph Bonomi are among other architects known to have designed furniture for their interiors.

The 1750s had seen a spate of pattern books, which had helped to accelerate the widespread adoption of the Rococo, but there was to be a marked dearth of corresponding books in the neo-classical movement. In John Soane's words, 'Manufacturers of every kind felt as it were the electric power of this Revolution in

Art', long before the major publications of the late 1780s.

Matthias Lock had produced some neo-classical pier-frame designs in 1769, Darly included one or two pieces of furniture in his *Ornamental Architect* of 1770, and a few impractical designs in the Piranesi style appeared in the *Builder's Magazine* from 1774 to 1778. But there was no book on the scale of Chippendale's *Director* before George Hepplewhite's *Cabinet-maker and Upholsterer's Guide* of 1788, and even then this posthumous publication tended to reflect the general taste of the decade rather than to propagate new ideas. Some of the designs for bedroom furniture hark back to Chippendale's plates, and a number of pieces illustrated were in the bowed serpentine curves of the 1760s. The cabriole leg is included in numerous designs.

The objects stated in Hepplewhite's preface —'to unite elegance and utility' and to avoid 'articles whose recommendation was mere novelty'—were fully realized, however, in a comprehensive range of practical pieces, intended to be of use to foreigners as well as 'our own countrymen and artisans whose distance from the metropolis makes even an imperfect or superficial knowledge of its improvement acquired with much trouble and expense'. Copious imitations both in England and abroad provide evidence enough of the success of the *Guide* which went into a second edition in 1789 and a third in 1794.

Thomas Sheraton wrote in a spirit of rivalry 'this work has already caught the decline, and perhaps, in a little time will suddenly die in the disorder'. His jibes, especially at the out-moded curves of Hepplewhite's chairs, were answered by the revisions in the 1794 edition, rectangular-backed chair designs of the Shera-ton type replacing some of the more curvi-linear designs of the first two issues.

Hepplewhite did much to popularize the shield-back, which, with oval and heart-shapes, was to be copiously used for chairs in the 1790s. His chair-backs were often decorated with neo-classical motifs of a less intricate nature than Adam's. The carved swag of material and Prince of Wales' triple feathers were favourite patterns. Simplified Adam-esque ornaments were likewise included in the radiating marquetry designs for side-tables and for the popular Pembroke tables which had evolved from the hinged breakfast table of the mid-century. Some useful mech-anical pieces included a neat tambour-fronted desk in the French manner, and practical storage space was provided in the compact deep-drawered sideboard, which now formed an alternative to the sideboard group with flanking pedestal cupboards.

Similar cabinet-furniture was illustrated in Thomas Shearer's smaller trade catalogue,

The Cabinet-Maker's London Book of Prices,
also of 1788. Sheraton wrote that Shearer's
designs were 'more fashionable and useful . . .
in proportion to their number' than Hepplewhite's, although they tend to have been
overshadowed by the greater fame of the
Guide. As the title suggests, the book throws
an interesting light on costs.

Little is known of the working life of Thomas
Shearer and although Hepplewhite himself
was a practising cabinet-maker, no furniture
actually made by him has yet been authenti-
cated. Hepplewhite is known to have worked
with the firm of Gillow, which was based
in Lancaster, opening a showroom in London
in 1760. Although they did not produce
a pattern book, the style of the firm can
easily be assessed from the surviving cost-
book sketches and through their practice,
later on, of stamping their furniture.

Seddon & Company were great rivals of
Gillow's in the late eighteenth century.
Something of their importance can be gauged
from the 1786 account of their workshop by
Sophie von la Roche, which provides in-
cidentally an interesting picture of the range
of products within a fashionable cabinet-
maker's of the day. Mr Seddon, she wrote,
'employs four hundred apprentices on any
work connected with the making of household
furniture — joiners, carvers, gilders, mirror-
workers, upholsterers, girdlers — who mould
the bronze into graceful patterns — and lock-
smiths. All these are housed in a building with
six wings. In the basement mirrors are cast
and cut. Some other department contains
nothing but chairs, sofas, and stools of every
description . . . while others are occupied by
writing-tables, cupboards, chests-of-drawers,
charmingly-fashioned desks, chests both large
and small, work- and toilet-tables in all manner
of wood and patterns . . . chintz, silk, and

wool materials for curtains and bedcovers,
hangings in every possible material; carpets
and stair-carpets to order; in short anything
one might desire to furnish a house . . .'

The 1790s were to see an increasing severity
in the interpretation of classicism, which was
reflected in the 113 plates of Thomas Sheraton's *Cabinet-Maker and Upholsterer's Draw-
ing-Book* published between 1791 and 1794.
The first two parts of this publication were
given over to geometry and perspective and
to drawing instruction which Sheraton practised professionally, the third being 'intended
to exhibit the present taste in furniture, and
at the same time, to give the workmen some
assistance in the manufacturing of it'.

Although Sheraton had apparently trained
as a cabinet-maker, he had clearly abandoned
the craft by now, for he supplied the names and
addresses of various firms where his pieces
could be ordered, and he even implied that he
had gleaned his ideas from associates in the
trade. In describing his Harlequin Pembroke
Table he wrote: 'In this I assume very little
originality or merit . . . except what is due in
the manner of shewing and describing the
mechanism of it; the rest is due to a friend,
from whom I received my first ideas of it.'

Although the categories of furniture illustrated correspond inevitably with those in
Hepplewhite's *Guide,* the pieces are rather
different in character. Flowing serpentine
curves are replaced by rectangular forms —
although some bizarre banana and kidney
shapes are suggested — and elaborate classical marquetry patterns give way to geometrical banded borders and bold oval and
lozenge insets in contrasting woods.

A vertical emphasis is lent to chests of
drawers and commodes by the inclusion of
slender colonette uprights which break into
the frieze area. In chair designs, the front leg

*Above: Sofa design by
Thomas Sheraton, 1805.
The decoration on the back
is borrowed from Greek
architecture and the
cylindrical ends are
probably adaptations from
antique furniture. Many
of Sheraton's later designs
include sculptural animal
forms, such as these gilded
lion's masks. The swagging
across the front of the sofa
is an unusual feature
which may relate to the
brief, late eighteenth-
century fashion for
swagged drapes beneath
the seat-rail.*

*Above right: Design for a
sideboard from Thomas
Shearer's London Book of
Prices of 1788. Both
Hepplewhite and Shearer
illustrated these new
deep-drawered pieces
which were produced in
the 1780s as an alternative
to the sideboard group
with pedestals.*

*Right: Library desk
made by Thomas
Chippendale the Younger
in about 1804. With its
monumental simplicity
and sculptural decorations,
this desk is an early
example of fully-fledged
Regency design. The
Egyptian figures illustrate
a new interest in the art
of Ancient Egypt. (National
Trust, Stourhead House,
Wiltshire)*

bonheur-du-jours and fall-front secretaires are clearly based on French ideas, even if they were intended to be carried out in less lavish materials.

The French influence — so constant in late eighteenth-century English furniture — had been reinforced for Sheraton by a visit to Carlton House, the London residence of the francophile Prince of Wales. Sheraton included a general sketch of the dining-room, and more detailed views of the Chinese drawing-room with its French pieces, probably supplied by the marchand-merčier Daguerre, who had opened a depot in London.

On this visit he was clearly struck by the sparing quality of the designs of Henry Holland, the architect in charge. Holland, whose 'august simplicity' was now widely preferred to the fripperies of Robert Adam, had started work on Carlton House in 1783, going on three years later to build the Prince of Wales' first Marine Pavilion at Brighton. He worked for several members of the Prince's political circle, including Lords Palmerston and Spencer and Mr Samuel Whitbread of Southill.

Like Adam he strove to create a sense of unity within his interiors, designing furniture as an extension of his clear-cut economical

soars upwards into the chair-arm support in an unbroken line. These features — and the spinning-top feet admired by Sheraton — relate to contemporary French fashions, and the work of such furniture-makers as Carlin, Weisweiler and Jacob. The commodes with curving open shelves at the sides, the delicate style of architecture. Holland made constant use of rectilinear forms, and enclosed large-scale classical motifs within clearly defined outlines with bold colour contrasts. The recessed colonettes and concave quadrants of his boxy commodes reveal an understanding of up to date French design, and an admiration for the archaeological *style étrusque* in France led him to anticipate Regency development.

The severe classicism of David is echoed in the set of chairs which Holland designed for Southill in about 1796. Here already are the sabre-legs and bolt-head ornaments associated with the second, nineteenth-century phase of neo-classicism. They were probably carried out by the firm of Marsh & Tatham, who had worked extensively for the Prince of Wales.

Charles Heathcote Tatham (1772–1842), the brother of one of the cabinet-making partners, was a pupil of Holland, who sent him to Rome in 1794. Over the next three years, Tatham built up a collection of classical fragments for his master, and, more importantly, supplied him with sketches of Graeco-Roman ornament, which Holland incorporated into his designs. Among these was the monopodium which soon became widely used as a sculptural support in England. Tatham eventually published his researches in 1799 in his *Etchings of Ancient Ornamental Architecture drawn from the Originals in Rome and Other Parts of Italy*, which led to his being credited with the rise of the 'Anglo-Greek Style' in Joseph Gwilt's *Dictionary of Architecture* of 1842.

The sculptural forms suggested by Tatham play an important role in the more accurate Neo-classicism of the 1800s, when much of the furniture takes on the appearance of carved stone. No longer content with the mere adaptation of classical ornament, designers now sought to recreate the furniture of antiquity. Bas-reliefs and vase paintings were studied for guidance, and Pompeii and Herculaneum naturally provided a fount of ideas. The classical daybed, X-frame stool, deep-yoked klismos chair and tripod monopodia table or stand came into popular use. There was an emphasis on monumentality, in contrast to the fragile femininity of the 1790s, and dark colours — mahogany, rosewood, ebonizing and bronzing — were used in preference to the pale gold of satinwood.

Rome was no longer the chief source of inspiration. In the 1790s Tatham had already noted that the Grecian taste was gaining ground, and now the purity of Greek classicism was held by many to be superior to the ornamental Roman style.

Tatham had foreshadowed another shift in taste when he illustrated some of the Egyptian antiquities in Rome, in his correspondence with Holland, although this was of course

given tremendous impetus by Napoleon's Nile Campaign and the subsequent publications of Baron Denon. Canopic jars, scarabs, lotus leaves, winged discs of the sun, and the jackal and hawk-headed figures of Egyptian mythology were rapidly seized upon by the furniture designers. The tapering outline, based on the famous Pylon gateway, was widely popularized and the swathed and headdressed figure of the mummy-case was translated into side-terminals for bookcases, commodes and desks, like that supplied to Stourhead by Thomas Chippendale the Younger in about 1805. Mary Russell Mitford writes in *Our Village* of a library 'all covered with hieroglyphics and swarming with furniture crocodiles and sphinxes' — incongruous features that were to become commonplace in English settings.

The first designer to publish Egyptian motifs alongside Greek and Roman in furniture was Thomas Sheraton, whose *Cabinet Dictionary* of 1803 was followed by *The Cabinet-Maker, Upholsterer and General Artist's Encyclopaedia*, still incomplete at the author's death in 1806. Sheraton was living in considerable penury at the end of his life and his incipient insanity has been read into

Below: Armchair dating from about 1803, designed by Thomas Hope, and decorated in black and gold to relieve the pale yellow and bluish green of the Egyptian Room in his Duchess Street mansion. The winged sun-god, Ra, appears on the seat rail and the cow, symbol of the goddess Hathor, on the back. Seated figures of Egyptian priests form the arm supports and the back is surmounted by miniature canopic jars – all motifs taken from first hand knowledge of Egyptian decoration. (National Trust, Buscot Park, Berkshire)

Left: Sketch of the Flaxman Room, Duchess Street, designed by Hope in about 1800. Decorated to enshrine the sculpture of Cephalus and Aurora which was commissioned from his friend, Flaxman, in 1790, this room embodies Hope's principle of 'symbolical and narrative ornament' which made a great impact on the character of nineteenth-century design. The X-frame chairs and accompanying footstools, monopodia and caryatid-supported table plinths are close to classical originals, and 'reflect the growing archaeological interest of the 1800s. The dramatic combination of hangings and mirror, to reflect the sculpture from different angles, illustrates the romantic vein in Hope's neo-classicism.

 these wild impractical designs so far removed in character from those of the *Drawing Book*. But, in the ghoulish animal forms which lend a nightmare quality to many of the pieces, Sheraton had already sensed the sculptural emphasis of the high Regency, and he illustrated such advanced pieces as the classical chaise longue.

He had possibly been inspired by the furnishings of Thomas Hope's famous house in Duchess Street, which, acquired in 1799, was completed around 1804. The house could be viewed by appointment, and imitations of its contents had already 'started up in every corner of the capital' by 1807 when Hope published views of it in his *Household Furniture and Decoration*.

The house had been planned to enshrine the great classical collection of its dilettante owner, built up on his travels in Europe, Asia and Africa, and each room had decoration carefully selected to create an appropriate setting for its treasures. In the Flaxman Room with its sculpture of Cephalus and Aurora, for example, the entire programme of decoration centred upon 'these personages and the face of nature at the moment . . . the goddess of the morn is supposed to announce approaching day . . . The bird consecrated to night perches on the pillars of the black marble chimney-piece, whose broad frieze is studded with golden stars. The sides of the room display, in satin curtains, draped in ample folds over panels of looking-glass, and edged with black velvet, the fiery hue which fringes the clouds just before sunrise . . . The broad band which girds the top of the room contains medallions of the ruddy goddess and of the Phrygian

Above: Gothic design for a
state bed designed by
George Smith in 1807. The
'gothick' style had never
completely died out in the
late eighteenth century.
This design employs an
elaborate Perpendicular
Gothic, a style which
gradually gave way to an
Early English revival as
the century advanced.

youth, inter-mixed with the instruments and
the emblems of the chase, his favourite
amusement. Figures of the youthful hours,
adorned with wreaths of foliage adorn part of
the furniture, which is chiefly gilt in order to
give relief to the azure and black and the
orange compartments of the curtains.'

This description gives some idea of the
brilliance of colouring used throughout the
interiors which included an Indian gallery
and an Egyptian room described by West-
macott as Hope's 'little Canopus'.

In the cold linear engravings, Hope outlines
an orderly arrangement of carved and sabre-
legged chairs, X-frame stools and chimera-
ended banquettes, of caryatid or monopodia
tables, tripod torchères, shield-shaped wall-
sconces and spirit-lamp chandeliers. One may
agree with George Dance's comment that it
'excited no feelings of comfort as a dwelling'
despite the warmth of colour.

Hope also included large-scale furniture
designs in the antique manner, alongside his

general views. Several of the pieces from
which these designs were taken still survive —
despite the later demolition of Duchess Street
and the Deepdene, Hope's country-house.
Boldly carved and painted or gilded, they
bear some resemblance to the furniture of
Napoleon's designer, Charles Percier, whom
Hope knew.

Hope's pedantic designs were of prime importance but there was probably more direct
imitation of those of George Smith. Smith's
Collection of Designs for Household Furniture
and Interior Decoration came out in 1808,
drawing heavily on Hope's inspiration but
diluting and coarsening the classicism to
such an extent that his proud claim of 'the
most flattering testimonials from Mr Thomas
Hope' is difficult to believe. If less scholarly,
however, his comprehensive range of designs
was infinitely more practical.

Although classicism predominated in the
early nineteenth century, other Romantic
revivals existed alongside. Amongst the 158
plates of Smith's book several are 'after the
Gothic or old English fashion and according
to the costume of China'. Perpendicular
Gothic forms lived on, now given a heavier
treatment than during the mid-eighteenth
century, as the designs of A C Pugin show.

Chinoiserie had become fashionable once
more through the Prince of Wales' use of it at
Carlton House, and later for the Brighton
Pavilion. Lacquer and japanning were popular, as were Chinese-inspired designs used in
painting and the now fashionable penwork.
With the importation of Chinese furniture,
bamboo became the rage and was pain-
stakingly copied in European woods.

In the 1820s a Rococo revival emerged, no
doubt as a result of mid-eighteenth century
French furniture flooding the market in the
years after the Revolution. Louis Seize cabinet
forms continued to be reproduced, and a fashion for Boulle led to the metal and shell
marquetry of Le Gaigneur and Bullock and
to the widespread vogue for brass inlay in
mahogany or rosewood.

Mounting was copiously used now, and
metal grilles set in commode doors. Galleries
ran round shelves on desks and cupboards
were frequently inset with mirror glass which
played an important part in the Regency
interior. The convex mirror in a circular
frame topped with eagles or dolphins was a
regular feature.

Many new pieces of furniture made their
appearance during these years: the what-not,
the davenport, the circular bookcase, the
sofa-table, which, with its end-flaps, was a
useful accessory to the sofa or chaise longue.
A spate of tables, large and small, but usually
at this date on heavy bases, bears witness to
the more informal room arrangement now
favoured. 'I think', wrote Fanny Burney in

[rig]ht: The Saloon of the [Bri]ghton Pavilion by [Na]sh, redecorated in a [sum]ptuous version of [chi]noiserie by Robert [Jon]es and John Nash [dur]ing the remodelling of [the] house. The new Indian [the]me of the exterior was [car]ried into the 'Mughal' [for]ms of the mirror frames [and] pelmet-boards, and [Ind]ian and Chinese motifs [we]re combined in a set of [iv]ory-painted and gilded [cab]inets which are still in [posi]tion today. Not all the [fur]niture was Eastern [how]ever, and this water-[col]our shows a row of [neo]-classical, sabre-legged [cha]irs arranged before the [win]dows, and gives a [spl]endid idea of the heavy [dra]peries and swagging [the]n in vogue. The [cus]hioned banquettes and [the] central pouf are a [rem]inder of the luxuriance [of R]egency upholstery. [(Ro]yal Pavilion, Brighton)

[Be]low right: The narrow [sof]a-table, with hinged [end]-flaps came into fashion [at] the turn of the century [as] an elongated version of [the] more compact Pembroke [tab]le. With the centrally [pos]itioned sofa or chaise-[lon]gue, within the new [inf]ormal room arrangement [of] the 1800s, this piece was [a n]ecessary and attractive [add]ition to the drawing-[roo]m. This example of [abo]ut 1810 is made of [ros]ewood and is inlaid [wi]th brass, in imitation of [Bo]ulle marquetry. The [bro]nzed lion's masks and [pa]w feet and the lion-and-[rin]g handles are typical [Re]gency features.

1801, 'no room looks really comfortable, or even quite furnished without two tables — one to keep the wall and take upon itself the dignity of a little tidyness, the other to stand here there and everywhere, and hold letters . . .' At last the rigidity of eighteenth-century rooms had given way to a cosy clutter which in turn would soon lead to crowded interiors. Already in the pattern books of George Smith, the heavily fringed and tasselled window-draperies of the Victorian era were being shown.

The term 'Regency' is used as a label for a style which far exceeded the political limits of the period of George III's reign from 1811 to 1820, extending over the first 30 years of the nineteenth century. Associated with classicism, the style also encompassed various other undercurrents as we have seen, which were later embodied within the Victorian mélange of styles. Classicism did not die out as the nineteenth century progressed, but already in the design books of Richard Brown, Henry Whitaker and Peter and Michelangelo Nicholson in the 1820s and in the instalments of Ackerman's *Repository*, a coarseness crept in which diminished the power of both the elegance of Adam and the archaeological exactitude of Hope.

Germany

German furniture design in the latter part of the eighteenth century was dominated by the work of David Roentgen, the only German designer at this time to have any international influence. In 1769 he organized a very successful sale of furniture by lottery in Hamburg, and, in 1772, on his father's retirement, came into full control of the Neuwied workshop. David Roentgen quickly realized that he would have to widen his horizons if he wished to continue making high quality furniture, and in 1774 he visited Paris. In 1779 he went back to Paris with several loads of the best furniture made at Neuwied, and set up a depot there. His success was astounding and he was soon making furniture for the royal family. He was appointed *ébéniste-mécanicien du Roi et de la Reine* and, during the 1780s, was paid more by them than Riesener, the

Left: Writing-table by David Roentgen, the most celebrated and successful ébéniste of the late eighteenth century. This is typical of Roentgen's plainer work, being beautifully made and finished in fine quality, well-figured wood, and discreetly mounted in ormolu. The drawers and cupboards have elaborate mechanical fittings, a feature of much of Roentgen's work. (Bavarian National Museum, Munich) official Royal ébéniste. The Paris guild of menuisiers and ébénistes, jealous of his success, forced him to join them and he became a maître ébéniste.

In 1783 Roentgen made the first of several visits to St Petersburg where he had an introduction to the Empress Catherine the Great, who, in 1785, wrote to Baron Friedrich Melchior Von Grimm 'David Roentgen and his two hundred cases have arrived safely and at the right moment to satisfy my gluttony'. Several pieces he supplied to her are still in the Winter Palace in Leningrad.

Roentgen also travelled around Holland, Italy and parts of his native Germany, but the French Revolution robbed him of his French clientele, his Paris depot was confiscated and his Neuwied factory was destroyed by Republican troops, and, despite being appointed Court furnisher to the erratic Frederick-William II of Prussia, he was ruined.

Roentgen's success had been spectacular, and he had been paid unprecedented sums by Louis XVI and Catherine the Great for his more elaborate pieces, the mechanisms of which were made with the help of Peter Kintzing. Roentgen's furniture was always flawlessly executed, as beautifully finished inside as out, and the style and quality of his marquetry, sometimes floral, sometimes pictorial and often to the designs of Januarius

Zick, was unsurpassed by any of his contemporaries. He retired to Berlin after the Revolution, but returned to Neuwied in 1802 to try to re-establish his workshop. He was unsuccessful in this, and died when travelling in 1807.

Apart from the work of Roentgen, the new classical style took a long time to find favour in Germany, and the Court furnishers in Potsdam and Berlin were still working in the full Rococo style well into the 1770s. The first neo-classical designs for furniture were not published in Germany until about 1780 by Franz Heissig of Augsburg. In Weimar the *Journal des Luxus und der Moden*, established in 1787, finally published designs for fully classical furniture based on English and French prototypes. In Austria also it was not until the 1780s that furniture became less florid, with the influence of English designs becoming clearly discernible.

What has come to be known as the Louis Seize style was never favoured to the same extent in Germany as elsewhere, and, by the time it had found a hold in Germany, the Empire style was spreading quickly from France, and soon superseded the clumsy adaptations of Louis Seize furniture. The severe lines of the Empire style and the use of dark woods, usually mahogany, and the more exact knowledge of antique forms appealed to German taste.

173

During the reign of Jerome Bonaparte in Westphalia a French architect and pupil of Percier, Grandjean de Montigny, re-furnished the castle at Kassel and the Palace known as Wilhelmshöhe, then temporarily known as Napoleonshöhe. Some of the furniture for these magnificent rooms was commissioned from Jacob-Desmalter and other pieces, in much the same style, were made by the native craftsman, Friedrich Wichmann.

In Bavaria, the Empire style was most popular at Munich and Würzburg. On the eve of the Battle of Jena in 1806, Napoleon occupied the new apartments in the Empire style in the Baroque Residenz at Würzburg. Much of the early nineteenth-century furniture in the Residenz was copied directly from French originals and supplied by Johann Valentin Raab.

In Prussia King Frederick-William III openly embraced the French style and had the designs of La Mésangère's publications slavishly copied. In Austria, M Seuffert, Elias Weinspach, Thomas Hoss, and J W Sohn were all working in the French Empire style, with a leaning towards the new Biedermeier style, soon to become so popular. At the same time, Johann Haertl of Vienna started to make his ingenious secretaires shaped like lyres or drums.

This grander type of Empire furniture was soon found to be too expensive and out of keeping with the new Germany, impoverished by warfare, and the simpler Biedermeier furniture quickly found favour with the middle classes. Based on the classical style, it was simple and functional, and the darker heavier mahogany was often replaced by the lighter coloured elmwood or fruitwoods. The accent

was on comfort and simplicity, and interiors were less formal.

With the plainer interiors came a stress on the importance of seat furniture, and pieces that were decorative rather than functional disappeared. Most rooms had a large comfortable sofa, probably with a table in front of it, and a suite of chairs grouped around it. There would often be a worktable or two for the ladies of the house, a mirror on the walls, and cabinets for writing and the display of china.

Vienna was a great centre of middle-class affluence and housed a number of cabinet-makers. The most famous of these was Josef Danhauser who ran a factory from 1804 until his death in 1830.

In Berlin Karl Friedrich Schinkel, with his work for the Prussian royal palaces, introduced a new Neo-classicism to the German states. Born in Neurippen in 1781, he began to study architecture under Friedrich Gilly at the age of 17 and later at the Berlin Academy. In the early 1800s he travelled around Europe, but by 1809 he had returned to Berlin and was considered important enough to design furniture for Queen Luise's rooms in the Charlottenburg Palace. His most famous work was as an architect, but his furniture, ultra-modern in its day, foreshadowed the Biedermeier style and, less immediately, much Art Deco furniture of the 1920s. His furniture was strikingly simple in design and had neither the fussy prettiness that epitomized the English Regency, nor the uncomfortable correctness of Thomas Hope's classicism. It was distinctive and functional, but sneered at by contemporary designers in France and England, who often sacrificed comfort and elegance to achieve archaeological correctness.

Another architect, Leo von Klenze, also
designed furniture. Working in Munich, he
was influenced by Percier and Fontaine, and
his designs made full use of motifs and forms
taken from Greek architecture and decoration. His most famous patron was Ludwig II
of Bavaria, who shared his enthusiasm for
antiquity, and he was appointed Supervisor
of Court Buildings, and later head of the
building Authorities of Bavaria.

The Empire and Biedermeier styles continued in Germany well into the mid-part of
the nineteenth century, though by then they
had become very heavy and ponderous and
ran concurrently with the newer historic
styles.

Russian furniture in the late eighteenth
century and early nineteenth century had
been a compromise between the contemporary
English and French styles, but, by 1815, the
strongest influence came from Germany, and
much Russian furniture of this time, if it is
not known to be Russian, is described as
German Biedermeier.

Johan Hartwig Ernst Bernstorff, whose r[...]
dence in Copenhagen was being redecora[...]
in the semi-classical transitional Louis Qui[...]
Louis Seize style. Jardin's first commissio[...]
Denmark was the dining-room in the pala[...]
the Lord High Steward, Count Moltke[...]
Amalienborg. In 1759 and 1762 he worke[...]
another Moltke house, Marienlyst, much [...]
which was rebuilt and redecorated in [...]
classical taste after Jardin's designs. In [...]
he was appointed Surveyor of the Ki[...]
Works and his first royal commission wa[...]
replan the park at Fredensborg and redeco[...]
Count Moltke's apartments. In the winte[...]
1762 Jardin went back to Paris, and, on retu[...]
ing to Scandinavia, redecorated the Banq[...]
ing Hall at Christiansborg in preparation [...]
the wedding of the future King Christian [...]
He continued to carry out royal commissi[...]
in the Louis Seize style until his dismissa[...]
1770.

Jardin's position as Court architect [...]
taken by his pupil, Caspar Frederik Harsd[...]
who continued carrying out royal co[...]
sions, including some painted mirrors, de[...]
ated *en arabesque* at Frederiksberg. He u[...]
the full repertoire of classical decora[...]
including fasces, laurel wreaths, cornuc[...]
and portrait medallions and executed w[...]
for many private clients, including Coun[...]
Moltke.

In 1754 the name of Joseph Christian L[...]
first appears in the royal accounts for pro[...]
ing furniture, and, by 1790, he was the C[...]
decorator and furniture designer. Work[...]
with Harsdorff he carried out much import[...]
work, including the suites at Christiansb[...]
for Crown Prince Frederik and Prin[...]
Marie, and rooms at the Amalienborg. [...]
also carried out various commissions [...]
Norway, and, at the beginning of the n[...]
teenth century, moved to Lubeck where [...]
died in 1827. Jardin and Harsdorff had b[...]
been strongly influenced by the French [...]
classical style, while Lillie was influenced [...]
English as well as French taste. Two ot[...]
designers of some importance at this tim[...]
Denmark were G E Rosenborg (designer [...]
the Royal Furniture Emporium from 177[...]
1781) whose designs Harsdorff someti[...]
used, and Nicolai Abildgaard, who carried [...]
many interiors in the same manner as Li[...]

The most important Swedish cabinet-mak[...]
of the late eighteenth century were [...]
doubtedly Georg Haupt and Christop[...]
Fuhrlohg, both of whom worked in Fra[...]
and England, Fuhrlohg remaining in Engla[...]
Both showed strong European influence [...]
their magnificent marquetry furniture. Ge[...]
Haupt, born in Stockholm, was apprenti[...]
in 1754 to Johan Konrad Eckstein. He bec[...]
a journeyman in 1759, and left the next y[...]
with Christopher Fuhrlohg to study cabi[...]
making in Germany, Amsterdam and Pa[...]

*Above: Reception-room at
Haga Slot, Sweden,
designed by Louis-Adrien
Masreliez. The chairs,
based on the ancient
klismos and known as
senator chairs in Sweden,
are the work of Erik
Öhrmark and were carved
by Jean-Baptiste
Masreliez, the designer's
brother. The side-table at
the back, known as a
console-desserte, is typically
French in form. (Haga
Slot Pavilion, Stockholm)*

Most Polish furniture of the late eighteenth
and early nineteenth centuries derives from
the French Directory and Empire styles. With
the work of the brothers Friedrich and Johann
Daniel Heurich and the 'Simmler furniture',
the influence of the German Biedermeier style
is much more apparent, though often linked
to the Polish love of carved decoration.

Scandinavia and the Low Countries

The new classical taste came to both Sweden
and Denmark at quite an early date — the
Swedish country-house, Akerö, had a classical room designed by a French architect in
1754. In 1755 Nicolas-Henri Jardin, the French
architect, was invited to Copenhagen by
Frederick V's Minister for Foreign Affairs,

aupt lived and worked in London from 1768
 1769, and returned to Sweden in 1770 to
ke up his appointment as *ébéniste du roi*
d to submit his masterpiece to the Guild. He
mained in Sweden as head of a large work-
op until his death in 1784, and produced
rniture in a transitional and later a full
o-classic style, strongly influenced by the
chniques of Oeben and Riesener.

During the latter part of the eighteenth
ntury, the Scandinavian countries had
joyed almost total non-involvement in the
ropean conflicts, but the rise to power of
apoleon and the ensuing wars began to
fect them, their trade being severely dimin-
hed by the English blockade of Continental
rts. Denmark's fleet and parts of Copen-
gen were destroyed by the British, who were
raid their alliance with Russia might change
 an alliance with France and by 1813 the
nish government was bankrupt. The more
rcumspect Swedes made no pacts, and kept
eir neutrality, and, despite having invited
e of Napoleon's marshals to become Crown
ince, eventually sided with England.

In the middle and late eighteenth century
glish influence had been strong on func-
nal middle-class Scandinavian furniture,
t Scandinavia was isolated by the war in
e early nineteenth century. English and
ench forms came to Scandinavia via
rmany which was the strongest influence
 this time, and there emerged a simple
pire style, partly necessitated by the
onomic situation. This first appeared in
nmark, and soon spread throughout
andinavia and with it, because of the
ficulty in obtaining mahogany, came a
ing for the paler native woods such as
ch, ash and maple.

The classical revival survived in Denmark
most until 1850, under the influence of
stav Friedrich Hetsch, who had studied
der Percier in Paris, and still favoured the
ench Empire style. He was Professor at the
ademy and a leading decorator and designer
o wielded great influence. In Sweden the
pire style gave way much more quickly to
 revival styles which reached their peak in
 middle and latter part of the century.

nglish and French furniture enjoyed such
ularity in eighteenth-century Holland that
1771 the Amsterdam guild forbade the im-
tation of furniture made outside the
herlands, and all furniture had to be
nded with the mark of the Amsterdam
eph's Guild, the letters J G flanking the
s of Amsterdam.

rench furniture was popular, and was much
ied by contemporary Dutch makers, such
Andries Bongen, and the ban on imports
ouraged the Dutch makers to improve and
eriment with the new classical style. The
ner pieces were made in mahogany, and

Left: One of a pair of Swedish secretaires made for Princess Sophia Albertina by Georg Haupt, who studied cabinet-making in Sweden, as well as in Germany, France and England. The marquetry and mounts on this secretaire, based on French originals, are typical of much of Haupt's work. (Tullgarn Palace, Stockholm)

Below: Opflagtafel or Dutch serving-table. This kind of serving table was made only in the Netherlands. The overall shape with chamfered corners and short square tapering legs is typically Dutch. (Rijksmuseum, Amsterdam)

curves were more or less eliminated. The more elaborate pieces were made in exotic woods, often satinwood, and were usually inset with panels of either floral marquetry or oriental lacquer.

The shape of the furniture at this time in Holland was based on English or French originals, though the resulting pieces, often with canted corners, bands of inlay and tapering legs or feet, are closer to Italian models.

In 1808 King Louis-Napoleon gave orders for the Town Hall in Amsterdam to be converted into a royal palace, and refurnished by Dutch craftsmen. The most important of these was Carel Breytsspraak, who provided furniture in the French Empire style, using plain mahogany veneers and simple shapes, often with classical ormolu mounts. The seat furniture was mostly provided by the upholsterer, Joseph Cuel.

The inspiration for most early nineteenth-century Dutch furniture came from France in the form of Percier and Fontaine's *Recueil de décorations intérieures* — and even more obviously La Mésangère's *Meubles et objets de goût*.

After 1815 the Royal Palace in the Hague was partly redecorated at the behest of King William I. The style was noticeably Napoleonic in its splendour, with large suites of gilt-wood chairs. One of the most important suppliers was G Nordanus, who worked in mahogany often incorporating panels of floral marquetry in his work.

The classical style persisted in the Netherlands well into the second quarter of the century, becoming noticeably simpler and closer to the German Biedermeier style. This well-proportioned functional furniture, often made in lighter native woods, such as ash or maple, was eventually ousted by the emergent revival styles, soon to become so popular.

Italy

Despite the researches in Greece and the criticism levelled at the 'debased' classicism of Rome, Italy still remained the centre of Neo-classicism in the mid-eighteenth century. Rome attracted a great number of foreigners, and, within her cosmopolitan itinerant society, the foundations of the neo-classical revival were laid.

That they were laid by foreigners has already been stressed; indeed, it could have been argued that eighteenth-century Italy contributed virtually nothing to the initiation of the movement, were it not for Piranesi, whose romantic vision of the splendours of Rome redressed the balance in the Graeco-Roman controversy, and served as a major catalyst in the international advance of neo-classical architecture.

Born in Treviso in 1720, Giovanni Battista Piranesi had studied architecture and theatri-

cal design in Venice, before visiting Rome in 1740, where he decided to settle permanently five years later. Having studied etching under Giuseppe Vasi, he produced his *Prima Parte dell' Architettura e Prospettiva* in 1743, with its theatrical visions of reconstructed ancient Rome and its evocative views of ruins.

Over the next 33 years, Piranesi was to etch more than 1,000 plates, which would do much to aggrandize his adopted city and fire the imagination of architects all over Europe. The views shown in his dramatic *Vedute di Roma* were far removed from the standard topographical views of the day, and, if exaggerated and distorted, were, in Robert Adam's words, designed to 'inspire and instil invention'. Piranesi's major four-volume *Antichità Romane* of 1756 did indeed leave a marked impression on the French students of the Academy in Rome, and on visiting English architects such as Adam.

The more controversial character of Piranesi's work in the 1760s was due to his

Above: Design for clocks, vases and table by Giovanni Battista Piranesi, 1769. The crowded mixture of classical motifs is less an attempt to recreate antique forms than a means of producing original outlines. Although the large cartel clock was executed, it is doubtful whether many of his eccentric, unbalanced designs — which almost evoke Rococo — were actually carried out.

involvement in the dispute over Greece and Rome. As champion of Roman supremacy, he produced *Della Magnificenza ed Architettura dei Romani* in 1761 — in which he also praised the Etruscans — which led to a dialogue with the Greek protagonist, Mariette. At first dry and rationalistic, he abandoned this approach in *Parere sull' Architettura* of 1765 to urge a free adaptation of classical elements, which would also be applied to his furniture designs.

In the meantime, Piranesi was working for Carlo Rezzonico, Pope Clement XIII. For Clement's nephew, the Cardinal Giovanni Battista Rezzonico, Piranesi executed his only building, the church of the Knights of Malta in Rome, Santa Maria del Priorato, and decorated an apartment in the Palazzo Quirinale. Some of the designs for the apartment were included in *Diverse Maniere d'Adornare i Camini* of 1769, a folio largely given over to fireplace designs which show 'what an able architect may make of the ancient monuments by properly adapting them to our manners and customs'. Half a dozen furniture plates were also included, which, like Piranesi's other unpublished furniture designs, bear little relation to classical Rome as far as form is concerned but are loaded with Roman, Etruscan and Egyptian ornament. Winged chimeras, sphinxes, vases, masks and caryatids crowd the sedan chair, commode, side-tables and outsize clocks in Piranesi's illustrations, and are outlined with a metallic precision reminiscent of the bronze furniture excavated at Pompeii in the succeeding years. Piranesi's *Parere* motto 'They scorn my novelty, I, their timidity' seems appropriate to these fantastic, exaggerated essays, which, with their sweeping sarcophagus curves, veer, at times, close to the dying Rococo.

Piranesi later published a book devoted to *Vasi, Candelabri e Cippi*, and already in 1769 he revealed a sound knowledge of the classical vase in his urn designs, which he incorporated into his furniture plates. This is, no doubt, the result of his studies as a restorer and agent in the sale of antiquities.

His influence was to be far-reaching, and especially important for the English development, even if later generations came to disapprove of his tendency, in Tatham's words, to 'sacrifice accuracy to what he conceived the richer productions of a more fertile and exuberant mind'.

Piranesi had illustrated Egyptian motifs in his etchings and he used the Egyptian style for his Caffè Inglese decorations of 1765. Mengs was simultaneously executing Egyptian paintings in the Vatican, and some late eighteenth-century Roman furniture carries decoration drawn from the Egyptian antiquities in Rome, thus anticipating the French 'goût Egyptien' by several decades. For instance, in the 1777 Pécheux portrait of that great blue-stocking, the Marchesa Gentili Boccapaduli, a table with hieroglyphic ornaments and Egyptian caryatid legs is clearly visible in the background. But this is surprisingly advanced taste for the 1770s, a decade which saw, on the whole, a mingling of Rococo and classical elements all over Italy. In certain centres, such as Venice, Neo-classicism had barely taken root.

The sculptural tradition of Italian furniture lent many neo-classical pieces a positively Baroque appearance, as with the massive bronze table, for example, made for the Vatican in 1789 which has been described as perhaps the finest piece of furniture produced in late eighteenth-century Rome. Its Herculean supports were modelled by Vincenzo Pacetti and cast by Giuseppe Valadier, and the gilt-bronze reliefs and inscriptions of the frieze inset commemorate the important events of the pontificate of Pius VI. The Egyptian granite top was cut from a block discovered in the wall of the Pantheon of Agrippa during the 1740s; thus the table provides a marriage between genuine antiquity and the Romantic evocation of the classical world.

The Italian intarsia tradition carried on also into the late eighteenth century. Marquetried furniture in the neo-classical taste was made in Rome, most notably by Rosario Palermo, but Milan is generally recognized as the most important centre for this technique. Although a number of cabinet-makers practised it in Milan, they tend to be eclipsed by Giuseppe Maggiolini, who became official *intarsiatore* to the Archduke Ferdinand, Governor-General of Milan. Maggiolini's work is well documented, both through his signed works and through the careful records of G A Mezzanzanica whose father had worked with him.

Born at Parabiago near Milan, Maggiolini had been trained nearby and moved to Milan in 1771. With archducal patronage, he quickly established a great reputation and could command the highest prices. He produced rectilinear furniture in the Louis Seize manner, without, however, the rich mounting favoured by the French. His severe tables and commodes were decorated with profile heads in roundels, military trophies, and ivy tendrils in different woods. Some of the more ambitious marquetry designs were provided by the Milanese painters, Andrea Appiani and Giuseppe Levati. He disapproved of the use of ivory or stained woods, and in 1765 had woods of 86 different

180

Far left: Mechanical desk by Giovanni Socchi, made in about 1810. Socchi made several versions of this ingenious desk, which when closed forms a compact oval table. Mechanical furniture had been very popular in late eighteenth-century France and Germany, but this piece is more ambitious than most French examples.

Left: Writing-cabinet by Giuseppe Maria Bonzanigo, made in 1775. This sculptural piece is one of the best known works by the famous Turin wood-carver, Bonzanigo. Although Louis Seize in inspiration, the carved carcase is typically Italian in its cluttered elaboration. It was made for Vittorio Amadeo III to whom Bonzanigo was appointed Court woodcarver in 1787. (Palace of Stupinigi, Turin)

181

colours in his workshop, which gives some idea of the subtle colour variations in the intricate neo-classical panels.

With the French invasion and subsequent expulsion of the Austrians, Maggiolini worked under the new Napoleonic viceroy, Eugène Beauharnais, although he does not appear to have adapted to the Empire style before his death in 1814.

Ignazio and Luigi Revelli worked in a similar vein in Turin, where there was also a close stylistic link with France, even if the Louis Seize themes were treated with a free exuberance when executed here. Giuseppe Maria Bonzanigo, who worked for the Court in Turin from 1773, was famous for his exquisite carving, which led to a Court appointment as woodcarver to Vittorio Amadeo III in 1787.

Born at Asti, Bonzanigo came of a family of woodcarvers who specialized in organ-cases. He produced a wide range of furniture, with delicate deep-cut carving, which was, however, often too small in scale for the piece it adorned. For this reason A L Millin commented in 1811 that his pieces showed 'more dexterity than taste'. His fragile swags of flowers have the appearance of meticulously carved ivory, and, not surprisingly, 1803 saw Bonzanigo attempting to set up a gallery and workshop 'to perfect the art of carving in wood and ivory'.

After the French occupation of Piedmont in 1796, Bonzanigo turned increasingly toward portrait sculpture, carrying on his carving in the Louis Seize style after the restoration of the monarchy. He, like Maggiolini, seems to have made few concessions to the heavier Empire style of classicism then in vogue.

Although French fashions were reflected in the commode and chair designs of Italy, English pattern books also played their part in the absence of Italian equivalents. Simplified versions of Chippendale, Hepplewhite and Sheraton chairs are to be seen throughout Italy as a reflection of this English influence. It was French taste, however, that predominated in the early nineteenth century, with the establishment of the Bonapartes as rulers of the different states of Italy. There was little opportunity for private patronage now, but the Napoleonic taste was stamped on Italy so effectively by the members of his family that the Italians continued to imitate it for many years to come, long after the liberation.

The Bonapartes had little faith in Italian craftsmanship, a sentiment that was shared by much of Europe. In 1805, the German dramatist, Kotzebue described the furniture at the Villa Borghese, the Roman house of Napoleon's sister, Pauline, as 'magnificent and tasteful for which circumstances a visitor immediately guesses that it is not an Italian lady who rules here'. They imported most of their furnishings from Paris, although they sometimes made a public-spirited endeavour to promote local industry: for example, Elisa Baciocchi, another Bonaparte sister, commissioned pietra-dura table-tops for the Pitti palace in Florence and helped the Opificio there to flourish once again. She also trained Italian craftsmen in the French manner, and set up a *manufacture royale* under the direction of a Parisian ébéniste named Youf. At first, their activities were concentrated in her principality of Lucca where she was redecorating the Palazzo Signoria, but when in 1809 Florence was annexed to Lucca she turned her attention to furnishing the Pitti, where a number of her pieces survive.

Some of them were made by Giovanni Socchi, who had already worked for her in Lucca. He supplied the unusual drum-shaped commodes

Left: Stool designed by Pelagio Palagi in about 1836. Palagi's Palazzo Reale furniture of the 1830s combines the controlled classicism of the French Empire style which was still popular in Italy with the natural flowing exuberance of Italian furniture. (Palazzo Reale, Turin)

with gilt-wood mounts and marble tops, which stand in the Sala dei Tamburi, and he made a series of ingenious mechanical desks, shaped like oval tables, which, when fully opened, reveal a chair and desk with sliding top and rising pigeon-hole section. Although these pieces are unlike any documented French work, their inspiration clearly stems from Paris, and we know that some Italian cabinet-makers were using imported French mounts at this time, as well as studying imported pieces of furniture.

The same process was carried on, albeit in a shorter space of time, by Elisa's sister, Caroline Murat, in Naples. The heavier Neo-classicism was more readily accepted there, however, for quite an archaeological tradition had already been established in Neapolitan furniture in the late eighteenth century; fragments found in the excavations at Pompeii and Herculaneum had often been incorporated into court pieces, in the same way that sections of the local lava were inset decoratively.

Extensive redecoration in the French taste was carried out under the new régime, which

Above: The Throne-Room
at La Granja. Situated
near the Escorial, this
palace was built during
the eighteenth century.
The carved and gilded
throne combines Rococo
curves with an early
neo-classical medallion-
framed head. The other
mahogany and gilt
furnishings reflect the
Spanish Empire style of
the early nineteenth
century when French
influence far outlived the
Napoleonic occupation.
(La Granja, Spain)

greatly pleased the Bourbons when they eventually returned. 'If only we had been away for another ten years' one of the princes is said to have remarked as he looked at one of the altered palaces. Far from defacing the Napoleonic emblems, the restored monarchs of Italy chose to continue the style of their conqueror after 1815. Eagles, caryatids and lions' masks found their place in a style of debased classicism, which long remained in currency. The 1830s were to see a gradual increase in the inevitable carving which had been suppressed during the severe classicism of the Empire years. This is reflected in the florid style of an Anglo-Italian furniture-maker called Peters, who worked in Piedmont, and in the work of the influential Pelagio Palagi (1775–1860), who designed the interiors of the Royal palace in Turin for Carlo Alberto from 1832, employing Empire and Baroque elements in his showy 'palace' furniture. As Director of the School of Ornamental Design in the Accademia Albertina in Turin, Director of the Academy in Rome, professor of the Milan Academy, and a member of the Academy

of St Luke, Palagi's ideas were widely imitated. But although remembered for his neo-classical work, Palagi chose to decorate the royal summer palace of Racconigi in the Gothic taste, a reminder of the stylistic choice that confronted architects all over Europe as the nineteenth century advanced.

Spain and Portugal

The same development from light and graceful Neo-classicism in the eighteenth century to the ponderous Napoleonic style of the 1800s took place in both Spain and Portugal.

In Spain the French influence, strong through the Bourbon link, led to a popularity for chairs in the Louis Quinze manner at least until the 1770s. French fashions for veneered furniture tended, however, to come indirectly, via Naples. Charles III had ruled there before he came to Spain, and it was from Naples that he brought Gasparini, who became director of the Manufactura Real in 1768. Thereafter many advances were made in Spanish techniques as well as in fashions.

Gasparini was largely responsible for the

importance of the commode, which now tended to replace the *vargueño* as a show-piece. At first of flowing Régence form, it took on a more severe rectangular outline in the 1770s. Pompeian painting, mirror insets, Wedgwood or Buen Retiro porcelain plaques, or white marble inlays were used, but many commodes were decorated with elaborate *trompe l'oeil* marquetry worked in the Italian manner.

English pattern books were to lead to elongated versions of Chippendale and Sheraton chairs, although the English influence was more marked in Portugal on the whole, where it coexisted with French and Dutch tendencies. The Portuguese commode, like the Spanish in shape, differed in decoration, being marble-topped, and marquetried with simpler geometrical patterns, with enamelled handles in the Dutch style. In the late eighteenth century semicircular commodes on tall, tapering legs were also popular.

Although Portugal and Spain both fell prey to the Empire style, English Regency influences were apparent at the time of the liberation in 1811 of Portugal, whereas the the Spaniards clung to the French style until about 1830. Heavy mahogany furniture with coarse carving and mounting in the classical taste continued to be in vogue until the Gothic and neo-Baroque revivals.

America

The advent of Neo-classicism in America dates historically from the time that the 13 colonies emerged as an independent nation. The small writing-box, now in the Smithsonian Institute, on which Thomas Jefferson set out the Declaration of Independence in 1776 was one of the first pieces to give an intimation of what was to come. Made by Benjamin Randolph with a simple line inlay it was a harbinger of what was to become known as the Federal Style. American cabinet-makers were quick to take advantage of the growth and expansion brought about by the new peace and the advance of trade and commerce.

By 1788, the date of the adoption of the Federal Constitution, Chippendale furniture was out of style in England, but still the fount of fashion as far as America was concerned. In the same year Hepplewhite's *The Cabinet-Maker and Upholsterer's Guide* and *The London Cabinet-Maker's Book of Prices* were published, and shortly afterwards Sheraton brought out his book of designs. These were widely used in America as the basic material for cabinet-makers who gave the pieces their individual and regional interpretation.

The apprenticeship system in America was strictly adhered to, and supervised not only by the guild concerned but also by the local civil authority. In 1660 in Boston the period of apprenticeship in a trade was laid down by law to be seven years, but in the eighteenth century, especially in the later years, the period of apprenticeship became progressively shorter as the demand for furniture, and thereby journeymen to fulfil this demand, increased. Repairs were a major part of the business of any cabinet-maker in the eighteenth and nineteenth centuries; for instance Samuel Ashton of Philadelphia made 120 new pieces of furniture in the year 1801, and repaired 70 old pieces. In the smaller cities one cabinet-maker would undertake to make and finish all kinds of furniture, while in the more important centres work was carried out by several different specialists. These were very similar to the divisions in Paris at the time, and consisted mainly of cabinet-makers, chair-makers, inlay-makers, carvers and gilders, turners and upholsterers. Usually these people all had separate establishments though sometimes they worked under one roof; the best instance of this being the workshop of Duncan Phyfe, who had a virtual factory employing over 100 men. Because there were no separate guilds to supervise the different branches, as was the case in Paris, one man was often capable of carrying out several or all of these jobs, though the increased demand for furniture, and the new fields of expansion in the late eighteenth century tended to encourage people to specialize. The setting up of larger workshops in the more important centres, such as those of Thomas Affleck, Benjamin Randolph, Thomas Tuffts and William Savery in Philadelphia, the Burlings in New York and the Townsends and Goddards in Newport, Rhode Island, also tended to encourage the journeymen and apprentices to specialize in one branch of their work.

Men became apprenticed at about the age of 15, and were usually journeymen by the age of 21. They would then work for many different establishments for the next few years, until they had enough money and experience to set up either in a business of their own or in partnership with another cabinet-maker or upholsterer, at which time they would take on apprentices of their own. In a large city the cabinet-maker would purchase his inlays ready-made from a

185

specialist such as Thomas Barrett of Baltimore, who sold panels of inlay, veneers of satinwood and purplewood, window cornices, brass and iron rods for stairs and blinds, hair seating, gold leaf, composition, glass-paper and mahogany knife-cases, much of which was imported.

Cabinet-makers living near the coast or a waterway would use mahogany as their principal wood though inland the native walnut was more widely used as mahogany was difficult to come by, and cherry wood was used extensively, though especially in Connecticut. The carcase of the furniture was constructed in soft wood, usually a variety of pine. Haircloth was the most popular material for upholstery, and leather was often used, dyed to suit the client's taste. Horsehair, being hard-wearing and durable, was popular, and the grander house had silk and wool velvet, often imported from Europe. Printed cottons were used to make covers.

An important insight into the lives and work of the cabinet-makers is given by the price-books. These set out suggested prices for particular items of furniture and wages for journeymen, and also gave engraved designs for furniture. These price-books and the restrictions they imposed eventually led to great strikes in Philadelphia in 1796 and

New York in 1802, which were eventually resolved by the employers agreeing to a 50 per cent advance on the current stated prices in the London price-books.

Samuel McIntire, born in Salem, Massachusetts in 1757, was an architect and furniture-maker, most famed for his carved decoration, which he often added to pieces of furniture made by other craftsmen, as well as carrying out the carved details for the rather simple houses he designed. This mixture of accomplishments was the norm rather than an exception in America.

Duncan Phyfe, considered by many as the greatest of all American cabinet-makers, began a new tradition in the field of furniture manufacture in America. Born in Scotland, his family emigrated to America in the early 1750s when he must have been 15 or 16 years of age. They settled in Albany, and his father started work as a cabinet-maker. By the early 1790s, Duncan had gone to New York and changed the spelling of his name from Fife to Phyfe. By 1815 he owned three adjoining houses which were his workshops, warehouse and showroom. His designs for furniture never

Above left: Commode by Thomas Seymour of Boston, made in the early nineteenth century. This piece is again based on English originals. The radiating pattern on the top is inlaid, but the shell half-medallion at the back is painted. (Museum of Fine Arts, Boston)

strayed far from those in Sheraton's design books, and in the early nineteenth century he faced stiff competition from immigrant French craftsmen working in the fashionable Napoleonic style, such as Charles-Honoré Lannuier and G J Lapierre.

Lannuier arrived in New York in 1803 and set up business working in what came to be known as the American Empire style, based on the French Directory and Napoleonic styles. His pieces were more elaborate than other New York contemporary work and made use of gilt-metal mounts imported from France.

European styles now reached America much sooner than in the eighteenth century because of improved communications. George Smith's *Cabinet-maker and Upholsterer's Guide* had tremendous influence after its publication in 1828, as did the French Restoration style, giving rise to heavy, late classical pieces either in plain wood or sometimes stencilled with classical fruit or floral decoration. The leading manufacturer of this plainer furniture was Joseph Meeks and Son, and this soon developed into the heavy, early Victorian style.

THE MACHINE AGE
The nineteenth century

A number of new factors radically affected the development of furniture design during the nineteenth century, and these make a study of this period unusually complicated. It is therefore necessary, before embarking on any kind of historical survey, to try to isolate new influences and to see how they changed the progress of taste throughout the Western world.

The major social change was the growing ascendancy of the middle classes, and it is not unreasonable to suggest that they, or their values, completely dominated aesthetic development from the early 1800s to 1914.

Before the nineteenth century, artistic innovations were usually initiated through the agency of either a feudal or a monarchical-aristocratic *élite*, and the end-products of the attitudes that such groups normally display are very different from those which result from the values of a bourgeoisie. The traditional assurance of inherited continuity in an aristocratic society gives to its members a sense of stability, and this in its turn produces an emotional climate that can accept change, progress or innovation. The members of such a group, surrounded by all the advantages of stability, have the self-confidence which is needed to promote a developing culture. While traditional continuity is maintained, there is time, and room, for experiment. The middle classes, on the other hand, have little of this sort of self-confidence. Rising bourgeois societies are not usually artistically creative, and their uncertainty pushes them constantly to copy their 'betters', and to seek reassurance in the well-tried and the familiar. The desire to make every object seem better and more valuable (which we find evidenced throughout the nineteenth century) expresses such aspirations with poignant clarity, and it is thus easy to explain why during the nineteenth century, soft wood was grained to simulate hardwood, cast-iron was painted to imitate bronze, wallpaper was printed to look like silk or velvet, plaster was marble-ized, stucco was colour-washed in stone tints and houses were paired to look twice as large.

The life-style of a middle-class reflects its members' middle-of-the-road social and financial status, as they conform anxiously to their particular nostalgic ideal. On the other hand, as the members usually make up the major part of the mercantile community, they will also wish to obtain best value for money, and to avoid aristocratic frivolity and monarchical extravagance. Austerity has little attraction for the bourgeoisie, and solidity, conformism and comfort are the qualities that are most appreciated.

The universal 'embourgeoisement' of society took place in every western country and at most social levels during the nineteenth

189

century, and whilst the poorer sections of the community aspired to all the benefits of middle-class life, the breakdown of the old hierarchical systems led the monarchs and the old aristocrats to modify their attitudes to agree more closely with those of the new middle classes. An English politician remarked of Queen Victoria, 'If I want to know what the middle classes are thinking, I ask the Queen.'

It is within this context, therefore, that we can begin to understand the numerous 'revived' styles that were popular throughout the century, and to appreciate how each of them fulfilled a particular aspect of the bourgeois desire for reassurance through familiarity. At the same time, elaboration of workmanship and apparent costliness were essential elements in the display which a primarily materialistic society demanded.

Another vital influence on the development of the domestic arts during the nineteenth century was that of a rapidly expanding technology. Not only did mechanical methods of production allow for the manufacture of vastly increased amounts of furniture, but it also provided the means of reproducing cheaply and easily the elaboration of workmanship that had hitherto been available only to a privileged few. The inevitable loss

Above: The novelist Charles Reade in his London study, painted by C Mercier in the 1860s. This shows an 'Elizabethan' chair (in fact it resembled a Charles II piece), a bobbin-turned occasional table at which Reade is writing, and a standard kitchen chair of a type that persisted unchanged for some 40 years, on which Reade is seated. (National Portrait Gallery, London) of artistic spontaneity caused by the erosion of craft techniques was easily overlooked by a market which was dominated by a desire for richness, novelty and value for money. Technological processes were also directly responsible for radically changing the appearance of furniture, and, for example, the invention of the coil-spring, the perfection of methods of laminating and shaping timber and the introduction of metal parts all permitted the production of pieces in new forms, and with new functions.

Technology changed the very quality of life itself throughout the nineteenth century, not only by facilitating the introduction of devices which immensely increased the comfort and hygiene of seating and sleeping furniture, but by bringing about the development of efficient lighting systems, drainage and sanitary appliances, cooking stoves and heating arrangements. It must be accepted,

too, that in certain ways technology retarded progress; the pollution and squalor that accompanied industrialization led many advanced thinkers to retreat into a dream limbo, based on a past when life was supposed to have been simple and happy, and to attempt to revive historic styles and ways of life to accord with their vision.

There were various further influences on the development of furniture in the nineteenth century which had not previously been felt, but it will suffice to mention three of the most important. One was the role played by the collectors of antique furniture. Here was a type of person who seems not to have existed

before the nineteenth century, for although 'Cabinets of Curiosities' and collections of relics had been put together by rich men throughout Europe since the early Renaissance, it was not until the early 1800s that collectors began to acquire pieces of old furniture and to introduce them into their houses for everyday use. Three key figures stand out — the first is King George IV, who bought seventeenth- and eighteenth-century furniture from France at the time of the Revolution, thereby not only setting a fashion that has persisted up till the present time, but also becoming a major promoter of the 'neo-Louis' styles. The second figure is the Empress Eugénie of France, whose fascination with Marie-Antoinette led her to seek out and replace in the royal apartments any pieces of eighteenth-century furniture that had not been sold by the revolutionaries. She also put in hand the redecoration of several of the imperial palaces in a revived Louis Seize style and commissioned pieces of new furniture to complete the ensembles. The third person is, of course, William Morris, whose passion for old craftsmanship and admiration for pre-industrial ways of production led him to surround himself with objects from the past. Although in many ways we might consider him as a progressive, who was outside the middle-of-the-road course of majority taste, he was certainly influential over a large number of people connected with the arts, and a whole generation of collectors in the last third of the nineteenth century followed where Morris and his circle had shown the way.

Loosely connected to the idea of collecting, another impetus relates to the rise of nationalism that affected the worldwide political scene toward the end of the century. The Franco-Prussian war, the unification of Germany and of Italy and the American Civil War were all in their way responsible in each of these countries for stimulating a search for national identity, and this in its turn brought about a new enthusiasm for what were believed to be 'national' styles. Colonial furniture in America, furniture in eighteenth-century England, Renaissance and even Biedermeier furniture in Germany all became the objects of nationalistic pride, and in the absence of sufficient original pieces to meet the new demand, they were copied in large quantities, but with more conscious accuracy than had ever been the practice in the earlier part of the century.

The third significant influence which must be accepted is that of increasing female emancipation. In England and in America this culminated in the achievement of women's suffrage immediately after the First World War, but the changing status of women was an important issue all through the nineteenth

Above Right: The nineteenth century concern with enhancing apparent value extended to objects which hardly required this attention. In the early 1800s, Baxendale & Company, a firm of Birmingham ironmongers and suppliers of plumbers' ware, offered a range of cast-iron baths which were stencilled with patterns that suggested fresco painting, or grained to simulate wood.

century, and was inevitably reflected in the appearance of the home.

It is noticeable that throughout the century there was a constant breaking-down of formality in the arrangement of furniture; whereas in an eighteenth-century house it was lined up round the walls, and individual pieces were brought out for use and then replaced, by the beginning of the nineteenth century chairs, sofas and tables were placed permanently in the centre of the floor. By the end of the century the rooms over which the lady of the house exerted her dominance (the drawing-room, the boudoir, the bedroom) were often cluttered to such an extent that it was difficult to walk without collision.

Dr Siegfried Giedion describes this phenomenon as 'the devaluation of space', and relates it closely to the devaluation of aesthetic symbols which he traces to the French Empire. He also admits, however, that the romantic lounging attitudes that it became fashionable for women to adopt in the early 1800s required large pieces of comfortable and conveniently placed furniture to support them, and that the encroachment of the furniture into the centre of the room

expresses the breakdown of formality which accompanied the rise of the middle classes and the gradual disappearance of an aristocratic society. The busy emerging bourgeoisie and its ladies had little time for the kind of etiquette prevalent in eighteenth-century France, where much of the seat furniture was not even meant to be sat on.

The gradual breakdown of the old formality took place in many ways, and many of them can be directly attributed to feminine attitudes; the introduction of flowers and plants into living-rooms, the proliferation of small objects and ornaments, the increasing attention which was paid to physical comfort and *bien-être*, all confirm the tendency for the women of the family to take over more and more of the decisions relating to the household. Towards the end of the century much of the output of the new, popular periodicals contained endless information about how to make feminine surroundings more 'dainty', 'pretty' or 'cosy', in a manner that was obviously intended to appeal to a specifically female readership.

Before looking in detail at the various furniture styles which were popular between

Above: The Waterloo Gallery at Apsley House in London was added onto the existing building for the Duke of Wellington in 1828, and the architect was Benjamin Dean Wyatt. It was intended to provide an appropriate setting for the annual Waterloo Banquet, and the decoration seems to be one of the earliest examples of 'neo-Louis' in Europe, although the furniture was still in the current 'fat-classical' style. (Wellington Museum, London)

192

the early 1800s and the Great War of 1914, it is also essential to realize that, unlike previous centuries, nineteenth-century taste did not follow a development of continuous progression. The introduction of a style did not immediately cause all those that had previously existed to become unfashionable, and practically all the major nineteenth-century stylistic expressions co-existed to a greater or lesser degree throughout the hundred years.

It became customary early in the century to furnish the different rooms in prosperous households in different styles, each of which was considered to be appropriate to their function. Thus a large house decorated and furnished in, say, 1865, might have a neo-Rococo drawing-room, an Elizabethan dining-room, a Gothic library, a Moorish billiard-room. The bedrooms might have 'fat-classical' pieces while the boudoir could be neo-Louis Seize. This practice makes the precise dating of much nineteenth-century furniture extremely difficult, particularly that which was made in styles such as neo-Rococo or 'fat-classical', since they retained their popularity for almost the whole of the century. Furniture catalogues of the early 1900s still offered pieces, especially those intended for bedrooms or the less showy rooms, in styles which had first originated in the 1840s.

The enormous increase in the number of people who made up the buying public during the nineteenth century meant that taste operated over a wider variety of social levels than ever before. The new rich were no longer

necessarily progressive, the progressives were often not rich. This overlapping and confusion has tempted many historians to simplify their task by concentrating on the 'advanced' designs, and to leave the vast bulk of nineteenth-century production largely undocumented.

The intricacies of the Arts and Crafts movement or the wilder fantasies of Art Nouveau have been examined in detail, whilst the 'middle-of-the-road' expressions of middle-class taste have been contemptuously ignored. Whether or not such expressions appeal to us is largely irrelevant; they are a major part of the stuff of history, and it is proposed in this chapter to try and chart the course of 'middling' taste in furniture from around 1830 until 1914.

The Louis styles

Of the many revived styles which were popular during the nineteenth century, the interpretations of the French styles of the seventeenth and eighteenth centuries survived the longest. Indeed if one were to look for the 'real' nineteenth-century style, the Louis revivals could lay the most convincing claim.

Examples of one or another of the Louis styles appeared in every country in the civilized world from the 1820s to the 1900s, although the neo-Rococo enjoyed the greatest popularity in furniture. Curiously, there is strong evidence that the idea of reproducing the grandeur that surrounded the French monarchy originated in England rather than in France.

The interiors at Lancaster House in London that the architect Benjamin Dean Wyatt designed from 1825 to 1826, the Waterloo Gallery that he designed for the Duke of Wellington at Apsley House in 1828 'in brilliant mimicry of Oppenordt, Boffrand and Verberckt', and the state reception room at Windsor that Sir Jeffry Wyatville built for George IV in the late 1820s, were all of them well in advance of any similar revivals in the country of their origin. These interiors, with their strongly monarchical associations, must have concisely expressed the mood of the establishment at this time, when many people hoped to return to the old ways, as they had been before the French Revolution and the wars with Napoleon.

The furniture trade did not catch up with the new fashion for some ten years however, and these rooms were all furnished with pieces in the prevailing 'fat-classical' style, although in the case of the royal palace they were so enriched as to be hardly describable as classical at all. George Smith, in his *Cabinet-Maker and Upholsterer's Guide* of 1826, showed a design for decoration of 'The Age of Louis XIV', together with several suggestions for curtains, but there was no

Right: By the end of the first quarter of the nineteenth century there was a very evident growing interest in the styles of the French seventeenth and eighteenth centuries. George Smith's book of patterns entitled The Cabinet-Maker and Upholsterer's Guide, published in 1826 in London, contained several suggestions for decoration and curtains in the Louis styles. This one was described as being in the manner used in France during the lifetime of Louis XIV'. The book showed no complementary furniture however.

furniture to match, and he no doubt intended that the movable pieces should be in the 'fat-classical' style. Indeed, in the 1830s a modified type of 'fat-classical' began to appear, which had leafy naturalistic carving and was described as 'Louis Quatorze'. By the mid-forties however, neo-Rococo furniture was being made by virtually every firm in the country, although it is often difficult to identify the manufacturers as few of them signed or labelled their productions.

William Smee & Sons showed typical mid-nineteenth century Rococo chairs with sprung, deep-buttoned upholstery in their catalogue of 1840 (described as 'superior lounge chairs'), and Miles & Edwards, who were in business at 134 Oxford Street, London between 1822 and 1846 also made pieces in the neo-Rococo style. It is interesting that this firm would also undertake any sort of work in the home, apart from the supply of furniture, and we may cite this organization as typifying a tendency, which began at the start of the nineteenth century, for furniture and upholstery firms to take over many of the functions which had previously been the province of architects.

The increasingly numerous well-to-do families who were setting up house in the new suburbs were hardly likely to consult a first-rank designer for advice, yet they all wished for a background which was showy, durable, respectable and not too startlingly unusual. The neo-Rococo style filled all these requirements admirably, but it remained very much a 'decorator's style', never much favoured by architects or progressive designers. The curving shapes of the furniture, with its scrolls and volutes, provided a luxurious product which could nonetheless be executed by indifferent craftsmen, and it also lent itself successfully to machine production and the mechanical carving techniques which were being developed to answer the demands of the expanding markets.

It was during the 1840s and 50s that two developments occurred which were to set the character of so much mid-nineteenth century furniture, especially pieces made in the neo-Rococo style. The first was the appearance, round about 1850, of the 'balloon-back' chair, in which the back uprights were merged into the top-rail in one continuous curve. This design was obviously based on the French Louis Quinze panel-back side-chair, but the upholstery and filling in the back were omitted, and the general form was much more flowing than that of the French original. Some of these chairs had turned front legs and a more solid frame for use in the dining-room, but the most typical examples were the cabriole-legged drawing-room chairs, which usually formed part of a suite.

The other particular mid-nineteenth century development was the introduction of coil-springing and deep-buttoning, and these not only revolutionized the comfort of seat furniture but also produced a new shape of chair.

Patents for coil-springs had first been taken out in England in the 1820s, but by the 1840s and 1850s their use was universal in chairs that were meant for comfort. The typical comfortable mid-century chair either had a show-wood frame with neo-Rococo detail, or was completely overstuffed with the form being derived entirely from the presence of the coil-springing. This was usually combined with deep-buttoned upholstery, the use of which one writer has tried to ascribe to psychological forces, comparing the button with the navel, which he suggests is the emotional centre of a bourgeois and domestic society! Be that as it may, deep-buttoning was also a clever commercial device for using up the short-staple cotton and wool combings which are the by-products of mechanical spinning, and it served to hold in position the large quantities of filling required in overstuffed sprung furniture.

Neo-Rococo furniture was designed for use in every room, but its principal popularity was in the drawing-room or the boudoir, where feminine influence was strongest. The style was infinitely adaptable however, and was used for carcase furniture as well as for chairs. (The term 'carcase' furniture applies to any pieces that are basically a shell such as wardrobes, commodes and chests of drawers.) It was also very popular for a type of fully gilded console table with marble top, and for overmantel glasses, and the ornament in the cheaper versions was often executed in plaster composition on wire armatures.

By the mid-1860s neo-Rococo had begun to go out of fashion, to be superseded by a more rectilinear and more controlled Louis style with much closer affinities to Louis Seize, but although popular enthusiasm for it diminished over the last thirty years of the century, neo-Rococo never disappeared completely.

Towards the end of the century the demand seems to have split two ways, and the typical mid-Victorian 'free-Rococo' vanished somewhere in between. At the upper end of the market, a knowledgeable clientele was requiring really good copies of eighteenth-century French furniture which could be mixed indistinguishably into collections of genuine pieces. Indeed some of the furniture made by firms like Gillows in the early 1900s was of such quality and so close to the models that, at a distance of 70 years, it now requires an expert to say whether or not they are genuine eighteenth-century pieces.

Many great collections of French seventeenth- and eighteenth-century furniture

were assembled during the latter part of the nineteenth century; Baron Ferdinand de Rothschild used his to furnish the great house that he had built at Waddesdon near Aylesbury in the late 1880s. Even as far back as the mid-1850s, Lord Hertford found nothing strange in commissioning a copy of the famous eighteenth-century 'bureau du roi', to place among his collection of original French furniture. He paid Pierre Dasson, the Parisian furniture-maker, the huge sum of £3,600.

At the lower end of the furniture market the trend towards fussiness and spindliness, which became very pronounced in the 1890s and early 1900s, had the effect of making the end-products barely recognizable as having any relation at all to eighteenth-century France.

In the early years of the twentieth century many firms making lower priced furniture had given up describing their wares with any degree of precision, and any piece with 'frenchified' cabriole legs, curving shapes or a Rococo fret was just called 'Louis', or merely 'fancy' if the French connection seemed too tenuous. Much of this furniture was constructed in a very dark mahogany with a highly polished surface, which gave it even less of a French look.

The Edwardian period did, nonetheless, witness a considerable revival of interest in Louis Quinze and Louis Seize, and many decorating firms made a renewed speciality of such interiors and furniture for wealthy houses. The styles also enjoyed a considerable success in the commercial world, one of the most famous examples being the interiors of the Ritz Hotel in London, completed in 1906.

Far left: Baron Ferdinand de Rothschild furnished the Grey Drawing Room of Waddesdon Manor with French Rococo pieces in 1889, but the ensemble retains an indefinable late nineteenth-century atmosphere. (National Trust, Waddesdon Manor, Buckinghamshire)

Left: One of the neo-Rococo pieces designed by Philip Hardwick for the drawing room at Goldsmiths' Hall in London, on which he was working in 1834. (Goldsmiths' Hall, London)

197

At this time every store had to have its
'French Dress Department', and every Grand
Hotel or Atlantic liner its 'French Grill Room'
or 'Trianon Bar'.

The neo-Louis Seize manner always found
much more favour with the top-class furniture
manufacturers than the Rococo, and pieces
in this style were made throughout the 1860s
and 70s by Wright & Mansfield, Johnstone &
Jeanes, Holland & Sons, Gillows, and Jackson
& Graham, although these last two had
shown lavish examples of neo-Rococo furniture
at the Great Exhibition of 1851. Whilst the
firm of Gillows, which was originally founded
in 1695, is perhaps the most famous of all
English furniture manufacturing firms,
Holland & Sons enjoyed a very high reputation
throughout the nineteenth century, but more
especially for the 'fat-classical' pieces that
they supplied to the great new clubhouses,
and to some of the royal palaces.

France was somewhat behind England in
taking up the neo-Louis styles, although the
brilliant Aimé Chénavard made designs for
neo-Rococo chairs in 1835, and some manufacturers' catalogues even showed details in
this style as early as 1830.

It was not really until the beginning of the
Second Empire in 1851 that the neo-Louis
styles made much impact on French taste.
In fact, as soon as the Prince-President
Louis-Napoleon Bonaparte became Emperor,
he embarked on a series of official building
projects and public works which were specifically designed to promote the new régime and
to remind Frenchmen of their glorious past.

French official architecture, decoration and
furnishing were launched immediately into a
full-scale neo-Louis revival, and the emphasis
in furniture was towards Louis Quinze and
Louis Seize. Neo-Rococo furniture was made
for the new Louvre, the palace of Chantilly,
and for the theatre and some of the private
apartments at Fontainebleau, but the Empress
Eugénie's enthusiasm for Marie-Antoinette
led her to order the redecoration of the
apartments at her favourite château at St
Cloud in a neo-Louis Seize style. The existing
interiors were gone over and 'heightened',
and although a great deal of coil-sprung
seating furniture was introduced, much of
the remainder was genuine eighteenth-
century. New pieces were added in a
'matching' style however, (later to be known
as 'Louis Seize Impératrice'), and full rein
was allowed for the current desire for rich
display. Indeed it even came to be considered
permissible to add extra decoration and
enrichments to historic pieces in order to
make them as acceptable as the new ones.

Pictures of the St Cloud interiors also
show what might be described as the second
phase of the 'devaluation of space', if we
accept that the first phase merely entailed

moving furniture away from the walls; for, by the late 1850s and during the 1860s, basic furnishings were being supplemented by a whole series of new pieces which were introduced extraneously. Most of these were usually given one of the prevailingly popular Louis styles, since their market was essentially middle-class, and they were intended for the rooms where such styles were most likely to have been adopted. Occasional tables, 'whatnots' and étagères, stools, poufs, fireside chairs, worktables for embroidery and sewing, screens—the list is endless, and the general effect relates directly to the visual breakdown of formality, where this had traditionally been expressed by symmetry and balance. It is very tempting to interpret the whole tendency as a manifestation of extending feminine influence, especially in France where women's social position had always been stronger than in other European countries.

Round about the middle of the century the 'Chiavari' chair, or 'chaise volante' (literally, 'flying' chair) first appeared, and these seats were made in lightweight woods so that they could easily be moved by a guest who wanted to move from group to group. They became very popular in drawing-rooms and libraries, where the user himself might need to move his seat frequently. The increasing practice of fitting castors to chairs and tables also added to the mobility of furniture, and showed

a definite intention to break away from static arrangements. So great did the clutter and mobility eventually become in many of the rooms in the Imperial Palaces that the duc de Morny remarked that one had to move about with as much caution as a ship avoiding shoals of rocks!

Numerous important Paris furniture-makers worked in the various Louis styles during the Second Empire; L A A Beurdeley, A G Fourdinois, Henri Dasson, G Grohé, L E Lemarchand were some of the most famous, and many of them supplied the palaces. The firm of Krieger, who began production in 1847 and continued until the 1930s, and Sormani (also in business by 1847 and continuing until 1934) both enjoyed a reputation for high-quality production, but Jeanselme probably had the highest prestige.

In 1847 J P F Jeanselme took over the famous company of Jacob and became one of the leading makers of fine furniture in France. The various partnerships and amalgamations of the Jeanselme family are rather difficult to sort out, but the firm produced a steady output from 1824 until the 1930s, although their greatest fame seems to have been under Napoleon III.

After the doldrums of the 1830s and 1840s, the French furniture industry moved back into an international position during the fifties and sixties. At the Great Exhibition of

Above: The Empress Eugénie's enthusiasm for Marie Antoinette initiated a change in taste towards a neo-Louis Seize style, and in 1863 J B Fortuné de Fournier portrayed this in a series of watercolours showing the interiors of Eugénie's favourite palace at St Cloud. In the Empress' bedroom, two original eighteenth-century pieces by Guillaume Beneman (first intended for use as sideboards) are shown in an interior largely furnished with typical mid-nineteenth century over-stuffed and deep-buttoned easy chairs. The ensemble is dominated by a huge four-poster bed of a type unknown in the eighteenth century, and in the style which came to be known as 'Louis Seize Impératrice'. (Château de Compiègne)

1851, French furniture had already carried off several major awards, and Queen Victoria bought various pieces from leading Paris manufacturers when she visited the Imperial family in 1855.

The defeat of the French armies by the Prussians in 1870, and the ensuing unrest, administered a severe setback to every part of French industry, but by about 1876 it was well on the way to complete recovery, a fact which was triumphantly underlined by the Paris International Exhibition of 1878.

The neo-Louis styles, with their unfortunate associations, underwent a temporary lapse from public favour, although they never completely fell from fashion. The firm of Beurdeley, which had always been famous for its furniture in the Rococo style, did not close down until 1895, but its later productions showed the tendency towards elongation and fragility that characterized contemporary work throughout the world. Henri Dasson did not die until 1896, but although he was capable of copying original pieces to a high degree of accuracy, many of his 'free' interpretations from the 1880s showed the typical spindly elongation of the time. The firm of Zweiner, also producing fine furniture in the neo-Rococo manner, was principally active between 1880 and 1895, but it seems evident that much of the traditional French fondness for curved forms (which is so

brilliantly expressed in the Rococo) had been diverted towards the sinuous shapes of 'Art Nouveau' by the turn of the century.

As a final pointer to the persistence of neo-Rococo taste however, we may note that even the London firm of Maple, which opened a branch in Paris in 1896, was still offering the French public a large range of 'Meubles Louis XV et Louis XVI' in their catalogues up until the First World War, and even after.

Most other European countries took up the neo-Louis styles as enthusiastically as England and France, although, of the German-speaking nations, Austria was the first to do so. The mid-eighteenth century traditions had never wholly died in conservative Vienna in spite of the revolutionary pressures of the first quarter of the century, and the haute bourgeoisie and the Court eagerly accepted a fashion which suggested a monarchical tradition so clearly.

The neo-classical severity of Austrian Biedermeier had been becoming more and more softened throughout the 1830s, and by the mid-1840s neo-Rococo was firmly established. The firm of Karl Leistler received praise for their furniture at the Great Exhibition of 1851 in London (amongst which were some chairs of extremely curvaceous form), but they had already supplied a large number of neo-Rococo pieces from 1842 onwards for the Palais Liechtenstein in

Vienna, together with the Thonet company. Heinrich Dubell, another noted Viennese furniture-maker, provided tables and desks for the re-furnishing of the Hofburg in 1853, and, unlike England and France where neo-Rococo was often confined to certain specific rooms, the Hofburg seems to have been completely done in this style. Even Michael Thonet, famous for his invention of bentwood furniture, made numerous pieces in the most lavish neo-Rococo style in the late 1840s and early 1850s, and it must be admitted that the celebrated bentwood itself has a strong affinity with neo-Rococo in its curved forms and convoluted, interlaced structure. As late as 1902 the architect Otto Hofer was designing neo-Rococo chairs for the Vienna State Archive, and we may take the continued popularity of bentwood throughout the second half of the nineteenth century and on into the twentieth as an indication of the deep affection that Rococo enjoyed in western Europe.

The other German-speaking countries were slightly slower to take up neo-Louis, probably due to the continued influence of the two great exponents of Neo-classicism, the architects Karl Friedrich Schinkel in Prussia, and Leo von Klenze in Bavaria, both of whom remained staunch upholders of Neo-classicism throughout their working lives. Neo-Louis came a little sooner to Prussia than to Bavaria, but by the late 1850s and during the 1860s neo-Rococo enjoyed as much popularity in Germany as elsewhere in the world, and much of the output came from Mainz in the Grand Duchy of Hessen. This was one of the most important centres of the German furniture trade throughout the entire nineteenth century, and a large export trade to foreign countries was conducted from there.

The most famous manufacturer in Mainz was Anton Bembé, who not only made furniture which reflected the various changes in fashion in Germany throughout most of the century, but also provided designs for decoration and hangings and for complete rooms. The firm was already making pieces in the neo-Rococo style by the early 1840s, and continued to do so during the 1850s and 60s.

Another famous Mainz firm, that of Wilhelm Kimbel, was promoting neo-Rococo even earlier than Bembé, and from 1835 onwards Kimbel produced three famous pattern books in numerous instalments containing many designs in this style. Anthony Kimbel, a member of the same family, set up in business in New York, thereby extending German influence far beyond the usual range of export markets.

Although the popularity of the neo-Louis styles, as in most other European countries, tended to slacken after 1870, it received the most unexpected renewal under the influence of King Ludwig II of Bavaria, whose increas-ing eccentricity drove him to commission several extraordinary architectural extrava-ganzas. The king's disenchantment with the nineteenth-century world bred in his mind an obsessive worship of the absolutism of the French seventeenth- and eighteenth-century monarchy, and this, combined with his desire for solitude, was the reason for the building of two country retreats in a romanticized French style.

Schloss Linderhof, built between 1870 and 1886 to the designs of Georg Dollmann, looks to our eyes rather as though the Petit Trianon had been redesigned by Charles Garnier, the architect of the Paris Opera. On the other hand, at Schloss Herrenchiemsee, which was constructed between 1878 and 1886, Dollmann reproduced accurately many features of the palace of Versailles.

Each of these buildings required suitable furniture, and this was provided in a style of luscious excess which matches exactly the exaggeration of the architecture. Seat furniture, tables, beds, desks, a pianola-organ, were all designed in a riotous elaboration of neo-Rococo. At Linderhof the principal supplier seems to have been the Munich firm of Anton Possenbacher, working to designs by Adolf Seder, and delivery took place during the mid-1870s. At Herrenchiemsee most of the furniture was designed by Julius Hofmann — helped by Adolf Seder — who worked under Dollmann and succeeded him as architect to the building in 1884. Delivery continued during the 1880s until work was stopped in 1886 when the king was confined for insanity, but it is certain that Ludwig's commissions greatly encouraged craftsmanship of every order among the fine-art manufacturers in Bavaria at this time. It is tragic that he bank-rupted himself and the country in the process.

It is certain that no comparable neo-Rococo furniture was made, either before or since, but it must be admitted that German Rococo furniture always had a certain measure of excess, which may be appreciated by comparing the productions of Nahl, Spindler or Kambly with those of, say, Cressent, Oeben or Tilliard. The vogue for neo-Rococo continued until the end of the nineteenth century in Germany, and on into the twentieth, becoming in the process almost a revival of a revival; as late as 1898 the firm of Julius Zweiner was supplying rich Rococo bedroom furniture for the Royal Palace in Berlin, whilst at the lower end of the market A & L Streitenfeld were offering thin neo-Rococo in their collection of *Reiche und Elegante Sitzmöbel* published in Berlin by C Claeson.

Trends in Scandinavia and Russia followed those in Germany very closely, and neo-classical enjoyed a long spell of popularity in these countries, but by the 1850s and 1860s

neo-Louis was firmly established. During the 1840s Russian furniture, whilst it still retained the basic neo-classical forms, had become considerably softened by the introduction of naturalistic carved foliage and curving leg shapes, and by the late 1840s neo-Rococo was already popular.

It is probable that the architect A I Stackenschneider designed a set of neo-Rococo furniture for the Pink Drawing Room at the Winter Palace in St Petersburg on which he was working in 1846 and 1847. He certainly provided designs for the furniture in the Gilt Drawing Room in 1850, and this suite was executed by Vasily Bobkov who, with Peter Gambs and Andrey Tour, was one of the leading furniture-makers in St Petersburg.

In 1894, Robert Melzer designed a complete neo-Rococo scheme for the Private Dining Room in the Winter Palace, and the white-painted furniture was made by Friedrich Melzer. This displayed none of the improper elongation and spindliness that was so prevalent at the end of the century, and possibly the Czar and his family were sufficiently discerning to demand a fairly accurate and convincing product.

Italy was the most important of the Latin countries in matters of design during the nineteenth century, and supported her own Louis revival in spite of the long-lasting Napoleonic influences in favour of Neo-classicism.

As we have seen in the previous chapter, Filippo Pelagio Palagi (1775–1860), a designer of great importance, continued to work in the neo-classical style until the middle 1840s, and, had it not been for the sequence of political events which overtook the whole country between 1849 and 1860, its popularity might have continued much longer.

It seems very likely that the neo-Rococo style was adopted by the new régimes, and by the progressive forces that were working towards the eventual unification of Italy that took place in 1861. Count Camillo Cavour, for example, one of the principal politicians who brought about unification, is shown in an engraving of 1861 standing in his study in Turin, surrounded by neo-Rococo furniture and decoration.

Italian furniture-designers had in fact been flirting for a long time before the mid-century with ideas that were far from strictly neo-classical. Giuseppe Borsato re-published his *Opera Ornamentali* in Milan in 1831, and, unlike the 1822 edition, it contained a number of suggestions for furniture in eclectic and Gothic styles. Giuseppe Cima's *L'Addobatore Moderno* however, published in Milan round about 1840, showed a whole series of furniture designs in the most fully developed neo-Rococo style, and such influences soon began to be reflected in production. Another work

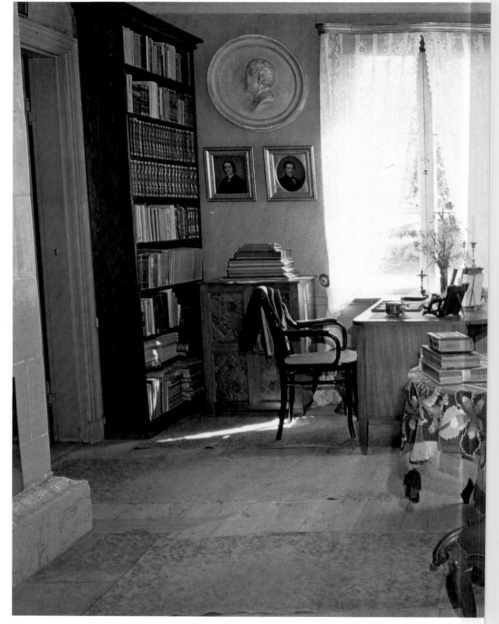

showing a large amount of neo-Rococo designs was *L'Artista Italiano*, published in 1854, which had contributions from, among others, C Invernizzi and A Sidoli. The architect Alessandro Sidoli was a prolific producer of engraved designs, and even after his death some of his proposals in a type of revived Louis Quatorze were shown in *L'Arte Illustrata* published in Turin in 1870.

The firm of Ferdinando Pogliani in Milan made a great deal of neo-Rococo furniture during the 1850s, and gave it an Italian flavour all its own. Curving backs were often combined with straight square legs in the seat furniture, and many of the carcase pieces and desks showed a curious amalgam of Renaissance elements. Most of their furniture was beautifully inlaid and decorated with veneers of contrasting woods, and turned finials and

Above: The universal popularity of neo-Rococo was reflected in the furnishings of the study of Arthur Hazelius, one of the founders of Stockholm's Nordiska Museet, in 1870. The balloon-back chairs, the Rococo sofa, the scroll-legged table, might have come from any mid-century bourgeois interior. (Nordiska Museet, Stockholm)

Above right: Count Camillo Cavour, one of the leading figures in Italy's unification, was frequently depicted in neo-Rococo surroundings, and it is possible that the style was considered to suggest a forward-looking attitude, in contrast to the associations of Neo-classicism with the old Italian monarchies. (Musei Civici, Brescia)

open frets were also used to achieve the desired richness. Pogliani's work received special praise at the Vienna Exhibition of 1865, together with that of Ferri and Bertolazzi of Siena, Frullini of Florence and Pazzi of Rome.

Neo-Rococo appears, nevertheless, to have had a relatively short life in Italy, and it may always have seemed a rather foreign importation. After the Risorgimento had become an established political fact, middle-class taste tended to turn towards styles that suggested the great periods of Italian history, and away from the frivolity of Rococo.

The style remained popular in certain Italian circles however, especially those dominated by the Italian royalty and aristocracy. The salon in the apartments occupied by Queen Margherita in the Palazzo Pitti in Florence had already been completely redecorated and furnished in a rather Bavarian Rococo style in 1860, and when the state-rooms in the Quirinale Palace in Rome were re-furbished for King Umberto in the last years of the century some rooms were given a complete neo-Rococo scheme. The villa Pignatelli in Naples, originally built in 1829, was completely redecorated in neo-Rococo when that family acquired it just before the end of the century, and in this case the furniture, whilst following the original French and Italian models fairly closely, included many pieces which were unknown in the eighteenth century.

America's contribution to neo-Louis was perhaps the most interesting of any in the world, and the American furniture industry developed the forms to a much greater degree than was customary in Europe, making use of technology in ways that were relatively unknown in other countries.

The neo-classical style remained popular for building until well into the 1860s (although by about 1855 it was permissible to vary this by the introduction of other building styles), but furniture in the more rigid classical manner was being rapidly abandoned in favour of neo-Rococo by the early 1850s.

Neo-Rococo furniture of a fairly standard type was available from a number of American firms by the mid-century, of which a typical parlour set was that provided by Elijah Galusha of Troy in 1853 for the Robert Milligan House at Saratoga Springs, and which is now at the Brooklyn Museum.

The unique development of American neo-Rococo furniture resides in the work of John Henry Belter (1804–63), who perfected revolutionary techniques for laminating timber

Right: Many firms copied Belter's technique and style with varying degrees of success. Prudent Mallard, who worked in New Orleans at almost the same time as Belter, produced large pieces of high quality, such as this bed in a New Orleans bedroom, 'suited to the cavernous splendour of ante-bellum mansions'. (The American Museum in Britain, Bath)

which allowed the formation of sweeping curved shapes, which in their turn could be elaborately carved. Belter's furniture was usually executed in rosewood, and he was able to achieve a remarkable degree of strength. The firm that he founded in New York in 1844 enjoyed a great success producing parlour and bedroom suites, and chairs and tables, and many other firms imitated his designs. Prudent Mallard and François Seignoret in New Orleans, Ignatius Lutz of Philadelphia, Charles A Baudouine, Alexander Roux and even the Meeks Company all made similar elaborate pieces during the 1850s, but none of them seems to have achieved the technical virtuosity of Belter. Baudouine was said to have pirated Belter's patent, and indeed whilst the Belter firm went bankrupt in 1867, Baudouine prospered.

The American Civil War (1861–65) brought radical changes to the American furniture industry, and many of the smaller firms were forced to close for financial reasons. The form taken by the eventual economic recovery completely revolutionized the industry, and mechanical processes overtook many of the traditional skills of the craftsmen.

By the 1870s manufacturers in the Mid-West

had virtually eliminated the smaller East Coast firms, and Grand Rapids, Michigan, and Cincinnati, Ohio, had become the centres of production for the middle-of-the-market trade, supplying their goods from highly mechanized factories to the whole of the American continent. New York still remained the centre of the upper end of the market however, and it is noticeable that taste had begun to turn away from excesses of neo-Rococo by the mid-1860s (much as it did in Britain) and a much more rectilinear and restrained style with strong affinities with the Louis Seize style became popular. Ebonizing, emphasized with ormolu mouldings and gilt-incised lines, was used on many pieces, and foremost in this quality field was the firm of Léon Marcotte.

By the mid-1860s the company had become New York's leading decorators, and although they also made furniture in the neo-Renaissance manner, the output of neo-Louis Seize continued well into the 1870s. Several other firms worked in this style — Thomas Brooks

and Herter Bros in New York, Jelliff of Newark and Henkels of Philadelphia — and its popularity continued until the early twentieth century, although, as the nineteenth century grew to a close, the pieces were made to look progressively more like the original prototype and less of an interpretation.

On both sides of the Atlantic, the market seems to have divided, the higher end demanding copies of convincing accuracy, whilst the lower was flooded with spindly pieces on which any addition of swirling fret would label them 'Louis Quinze'.

In the 1890s the Kimbel company of New York and the Brooks Household Art Company of Ohio were turning out neo-Rococo furniture that bore a close resemblance to the original article, and a growing market was developing in the importation of copies from France, where they tended to be made with even greater accuracy. Some were obviously intended for sale to the gullible as genuine antiques, to satisfy the growing snob appeal of collecting.

It will be seen from this brief survey that the neo-Louis styles were universal throughout the Western world during the nineteenth and early twentieth centuries. There was a vigorous interchange of import and export between countries which served to disseminate new fashions and their regional variations. Furthermore there was a constantly growing market during the nineteenth century for furniture and decorative items in the new colonies that were being opened up in every remote corner of the globe.

Many London firms, right from the beginning of the century, concentrated specifically on colonial markets, and, within the limitations imposed by the necessity of using the furniture both on board ship and of it being easy to stow, metropolitan fashions were adhered to as closely as possible. Special suites of parlour furniture and dining-chairs in the neo-Rococo style were made in London for export to Australia and New Zealand from the 1850s to the 1870s and although they were provided with easily removable arms and legs, they were very like the London models.

Other contemporary styles

It is, as has already been mentioned, a particularly confusing aspect of nineteenth-century furniture history that numerous styles enjoyed popularity at the same time, and that various different styles might be considered appropriate to express different functions within the same building. Whilst the neo-Louis styles were generally the most persistent throughout the last two-thirds of the century, several others were held in almost equal esteem.

Whilst it was usual to adopt a neo-Rococo or neo-Louis Seize style in the rooms over which the women of the family had most influence, from as early as the 1820s it was also believed that the masculine preserves of the household should be treated rather differently. Gothic or Renaissance were often adopted for the library, study or dining-room, and neo-classical also continued to be favoured in these rooms for many years — and even, sometimes, for the drawing-room, boudoir and bedrooms as well. Indeed a kind of 'utility classical' of almost indeterminate date survived in the humbler rooms of most domestic establishments right up to the end of the century, and even into the twentieth. In order to identify the most important styles

Left: The furniture made in New York by John Henry Belter's firm between 1844 and 1867 is perhaps the most interesting variant of the neo-Rococo style. Whilst the pieces are loosely based on Louis Quinze models, the shaped, laminated backs, the deeply pierced naturalistic carving and the exaggerated proportions are all characteristic of the nineteenth century. (The American Museum in Britain, Bath) contemporary with the neo-Louis, we may perhaps divide the main ones under the four headings of 'fat-classical', neo-Gothic, Elizabethan and technological.

Fat-classical Furniture that is still basically neo-classical in form and inspiration, but which has been 'fattened' by an increasing amount of rich, carved ornament, often of naturalistic form, and by the adoption of a more flowing form than was normal in strictly neo-classical pieces, is termed 'fat-classical'; almost invariably such furniture, however elaborate, had turned legs.

The type appeared in England early in the nineteenth century, and in 1812 Morel & Hughes supplied suites of the richest kind for the Prince Regent at Carlton House. Similar seat furniture, all with beautiful matt and burnished gilt show-wood, was made by Morel & Seddon for Windsor Castle in 1828.

All the important furniture-makers used this style, and it may be studied in all its rich diversity in pattern books like George Smith's *Cabinet-Maker and Upholsterer's Guide* of 1826, or *The Practical Cabinet-Maker* by Peter and Michael Angelo Nicholson of the same date. Its popularity lasted until at least the 1860s, and fine examples were provided for the new London clubhouses during the 1840s and 1850s, notably those made by Holland & Sons for the Reform Club in 1838. Indeed this style, in simplified form with very little ornament, became classic for furniture in rooms where no display was deemed necessary, and catalogues of the early 1900s still offered timeless, rectangular, functional carcase pieces of the sort that first appeared in the 1850s.

The equivalent in French furniture was remarkably similar, and the enriched Empire style of the Restoration and Louis-Philippe gave way to straightforward functional pieces, usually in fine 'plum-pudding' mahogany like the English counterpart, with little carved enrichment and no metal mounts. French pieces often had slightly more panelling and raised beading than was to be found in English examples, and sometimes the top of a wardrobe or the side of a bed would be given a small sweep which had something of a neo-Louis suggestion. These pieces were nearly always made anonymously, especially in the 1860s and 1870s, as they were seldom intended for display. Similar furniture may be found in Germany, although there appears to have been a stronger tendency for the German-speaking countries to adopt the 'romantic' styles.

In Italy, furniture with fattened Empire forms was produced from the 1830s onwards, and the panelled components, the absence of metal ornaments, the 'fat' carving and the fine, opened veneers, were all used in a manner that followed contemporary European practice very closely. Paolino Moselini of Cremona enjoyed a reputation for the quality of his furniture in the 'fat-classical' style in the 1830s and 40s, and much of it was decorated with subtle, contrasting inlays. Giuseppe Cairoli and Speluzzi of Milan were two other firms who made this type of furniture in the 1850s and 1860s, and an Englishman named Peters, who had a factory in Genoa, made pieces that were almost indistinguishable from English productions. Undoubtedly the most remarkable Italian 'fat-classical' furniture, however, was designed by Pelagio Palagi for King Carlo Alberto at the Royal Palace in Turin. Some of the beautiful neo-Etruscan furniture that Palagi designed for the King's palace at Raconigi was exhibited at the Great Exhibition in 1851, and was judged to be '. . . deserving of a place in the palace of any sovereign'.

America's 'fat-classical' furniture was of a rather simple kind, which reflected the country's relatively undeveloped economic state in the 1830s and 1840s. It is clearly

Below: An Aristocrat's Breakfast, painted by P A Fedotov in 1849, shows a room which is completely furnished with 'fat-classical' pieces that might have been made 20 years earlier — the only concession to modernity being the over-stuffed easy-chair. (Tretyakov Gallery, Moscow)

exemplified in the early output of the firm of Joseph Meeks & Sons of New York and there were many references to the French Louis-Philippe style in their production. The use of the newly invented steam sawing machinery to cut large, flat members, which were covered with mahogany veneer, enabled a fairly showy product to be made without resort to too much carved work.

Duncan Phyfe, who is usually associated with the late eighteenth-century style, turned out a considerable amount of 'fat-classical' furniture, and in 1840 an English immigrant working in Baltimore, named John Hall, published a pattern book called *The Cabinet Maker's Assistant*. It contained 198 plates showing suggestions for pieces in the simplified French form, and it provided a whole repertoire of massive but practical furniture. Some American late-Empire furniture was decorated with designs which were stencilled onto the flat surfaces in a gold-dust mixture, and this seems to be a uniquely American practice. The 'fat-classical' style hardly survived the 1840s in the United States, and the growing fashion for neo-Louis was adopted in a much more wholesale manner than was customary in most European countries; the survival of the earlier style in the humbler rooms was therefore rather more rare.

The 'fat-classical' style was very popular in Russia, and some of the furniture produced by Andrey Tour in the 1840s was very similar to contemporary English pieces. Peter Gambs executed a magnificent set of full-gilt furniture for the Winter Palace in St Petersburg in 1830 to the designs of Montferrand, but the most outstanding suite was made by Andrey Tour from 1850 to 1852 to the designs of Leo von Klenze. It was intended for the Hermitage Museum, and it was remarkably like the furnishings provided in London for Carlton House 40 years earlier.

Neo-Gothic This furniture seems to have originated in England as a direct descendant of the pieces that were made for the dilettante collectors of the eighteenth century, who required furnishings for the romantic fantasy dwellings that they had had built.

King George IV gave encouragement to yet another branch of artistic creation, in his decision that a number of the interiors that were being re-furbished at Windsor Castle should be decorated and furnished in the neo-Gothic style. His architect, Sir Jeffry Wyatville, was able to make use of the unusual talents of a young designer named Augustus Welby Northmore Pugin (1812–52) to help him in a style in which he lacked confidence.

Pugin was a key nineteenth-century figure, and although he practised as an architect, his flair for publicity gave him great influence over the taste of his contemporaries. His passionate religious faith led him to believe that Gothic architecture was the only true style, and he expressed his views in forceful and highly controversial writings.

Although he was only 15 at the time of his commission at Windsor, Pugin made numerous designs for decoration and furniture during 1827 and 1828, working directly for Morel & Seddon, who eventually were to supply the furniture. All of it displayed a remarkable, precocious talent, and a certain frivolity that had great charm, but Pugin was later to express extreme dissatisfaction with his early work. Whilst it is possible to attribute some of the design faults to Pugin's youth and inexperience, the chairs, side-tables, sideboards and stools that he produced merely underline his basic difficulty in creating furniture in a Gothic style, since there was no precedent which allowed sufficient sophistication to appeal to early nineteenth-century taste.

Such mediaeval furniture as still existed looked extremely crude to nineteenth-century eyes, and so all early neo-Gothic pieces made

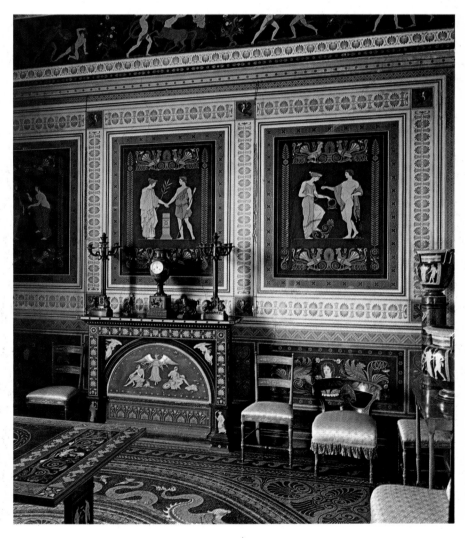

Below: Pelagio Palagi and Carlo Bellosio carried out alterations to the Castello di Raconigi near Turin in 1834, and a rich, late neo-classical style was maintained throughout. The Etruscan Room served as a dining-room, and the chairs were awarded special praise when they were exhibited in London in 1851. (Castello Reale di Raconigi, Turin)

use of purely architectural details and ornaments, which were grafted, more or less successfully, onto the basic functional furniture shapes. Although Pugin's later designs (for instance the many pieces that he produced from 1844 onwards for the new Houses of Parliament in London) displayed much more understanding of mediaeval precedent, the original difficulty still persisted, and he was driven to such anomalies as the use of linenfold panelling to decorate the doors of writing-desks, or ogee — S-shaped — arches to brace the legs of tables. Pugin was, nonetheless, an exceptional designer, and most commercial neo-Gothic furniture remained unashamedly impure in its detail. It was not until much later in the century, under the influence of Bruce Talbert and Charles Eastlake that neo-mediaeval began to lose its fancy-dress look, and came to look much less 'neo-Gothic' in the process. This trend really formed part of the Arts and Crafts movement however, and is covered in the following chapter. The kind of honest, basic furniture proposed in Talbert's *Examples of Ancient and Modern Furniture* (1876) or Eastlake's *Hints on Household Taste* (1868) never appealed very strongly to the middle-of-the-road market.

Most countries produced neo-Gothic furniture at some period during the nineteenth century, although its popularity had generally waned to a very large degree by the 1870s. The style had a long life in the German-speaking countries of central Europe, where it had become romantically fashionable to build country houses in mediaeval style, or

Above left: The exaggerated quality of most neo-Gothic French furniture is certainly apparent in this chair 'à la cathédrale' of about 1840. (Musée des Arts Décoratifs, Paris)

Left: One of the hundreds of neo-Gothic pieces that A W N Pugin designed between 1844 and 1852 for the new Houses of Parliament in London, providing a remarkable testimony to his ability. (Victoria & Albert Museum, London)

to emphasize the Middle Ages in houses that already existed. Designs for neo-Gothic furniture had appeared in Germany as far back as the end of the eighteenth century, and they were put out from all the main centres of the German furniture trade during the 1830s and 1840s. Kimbel of Mainz made neo-Gothic furniture, as did the Leistler firm in Vienna, and this company submitted an enormous Gothic bookcase to the Great Exhibition of 1851. The Rhine castle of Stolzenfels was restored, and filled with neo-Gothic furniture, some designed by Franz Xavier Fortner in 1842, some by Johann Wilhelm Vetter in 1844. Fortner also designed furniture for Schloss Hohenschwangau in 1835. Schloss Sychrov near Prague was given an incredible neo-Gothic interior, which, although designed by Josef Pruvot in 1847, was not actually completed until 1862.

After 1880 German taste turned much more to the Renaissance, and the solemn Gothic furnishings that were made to the designs of Julius Hofmann and Peter Herwegen for King Ludwig of Bavaria at Neuschwanstein in 1883 were no longer very much in accord with contemporary German interest.

France had but a brief flirtation with 'faux gothique' or 'stile cathédrale', and this mostly took place between 1830 and 1850. Aimé Chénavard made designs for Gothic furniture and decoration round about 1830, and Pierre-Antoine Bellangé, the influential Empire furniture-maker, had made Gothic furniture for Count Esterházy as early as 1811. But in most cases French neo-Gothic merely consisted of the addition of a few vaguely Gothic shapes in shallow mouldings onto pieces of basically late-Empire form; the furniture designed by Eugène-Emmanuel Viollet-le-Duc (1814–79) for Roquetaillade in the 1860s, or for the reconstructed interiors at Pierrefonds was far too archaeological for the average French market.

In Italy, however, quite a considerable fashion developed for neo-Gothic furniture, and this is somewhat surprising in that the true mediaeval Gothic only touched the edge of the mainstream of Italian architecture. In about 1850, Alessandro Sidoli published a number of engravings of neo-Gothic furniture and decoration, but as far back as 1818 the versatile Palagi had worked in this style at the Tempietto of the Villa Tittoni at Desio, and various Gothic architectural designs had been published by L F Basoli in 1826. Many houses in the Gothic style did not have special furniture, and the extraordinary painted interior of the Villa Amalia at Erba, completed in 1843 to the designs of the painter A Scrosati, seems to have been mainly furnished with neo-Renaissance (or 'Dantesque') pieces, as was the equally incredible castle at Carimate. The architect Celeste Chierichetti of Milan did, however, design neo-Gothic furniture for the interiors of the Villa Litta at Vedano in the 1850s, but it is noticeable that it was round Trieste (ruled by Austria until 1919) and the parts of northern Italy which came under Germanic influence that the neo-Gothic style was most popular.

Neo-Gothic furniture was made sporadically in Italy right through the century however, but towards the closing years such pieces were designed much more consciously to look like original mediaeval ones. At the Turin Exhibition of 1898, the Carlo Zen firm showed several Gothic items which were relatively close copies, including a carved and canopied throne, but these were accompanied by other pieces in the Moorish style and even some Empire Revival chairs.

A certain amount of neo-Gothic furniture was made in America, imitating the European fashion, but the style had no particularly strong emotional connection with America's past, in the way that it was felt to have in some parts of Europe. Many of the important furniture-makers turned out pieces in the neo-Gothic style during the 1830s and 1840s however — notably Joseph Meeks of New

York, John Jelliff of Newark and Richard Byrnes—but most of their productions were either merely standard plain neo-classical carcase pieces with a little 'blind' Gothic ornament tacked onto them, or wildly spiky fragile examples of fret-cutting, especially in chair-backs; even at the time these were recognized as being totally impractical.

The Elizabethan style 'Elizabethan' is a term that was particularly favoured in England during the first half of the nineteenth century, and it tended to be used fairly indiscriminately to describe any furniture which was neither classical nor Gothic. Many pieces in this loosely-named style had strong Renaissance affinities, since the Elizabethan period itself adopted many details of Continental Renaissance art, but free use was also made of the seventeenth-century Jacobean and Caroline motifs, especially bobbin or corkscrew-turned legs and stretchers. It was a style which was particularly popular for the re-furnishing of existing historic houses, and was also used for dining-rooms, libraries, halls, and in fact for all the rooms which were considered to have formal functions.

In England, the Elizabethan style was the precursor of the neo-Renaissance style which in its turn eventually became one of the most popular furnishing types during the second half of the nineteenth century. All the architects who favoured the Old-English fashions wished to use furniture that could be considered appropriate to their buildings; furthermore the large legacy of dwellings throughout England which dated from the fifteenth to the seventeenth centuries evoked an immediate response amongst the early nineteenth-century middle classes who wanted instant ancestry to bolster their social position.

Most leading furniture firms promoted one version or another of the Elizabethan or Old English style, and there are numerous designs by Gillows dating from the 1840s. Shaw's *Specimens of Ancient Furniture*, published in 1836 and Robert Bridgen's *Furniture with Candelabra and Interior Decoration* of 1838, were two influential works which contained many plates that were widely copied.

The architect Anthony Salvin made a speciality of the design of 'Olde Englyshe' furniture for many of his houses, and both at Mamhead in Devonshire and at Scotney Castle in Kent there were fine bedroom suites

Left: The furniture that Carl Leistler of Vienna showed at the Great Exhibition of 1851 in London received considerable acclaim. This great bookcase, in which elaboration of workmanship was pushed to its ultimate, was described at the time as doing 'infinite credit to those who have produced it'.

Right: Although the first part of Lyndhurst near Tarrytown was designed by Alexander Jackson Davis in 1841, the dining-room was not added by him until the mid 1860s. The furniture, which also dates from that time, makes an interesting comparison with the pieces that Davis produced 22 years earlier, and clearly shows how much more heavy and 'serious' the Gothic Revival had become, although the same inappropriate use was still made of architectural elements. (Lyndhurst, Tarrytown, New York)

Right: The architect Anthony Salvin made a speciality of houses in the Elizabethan or Jacobean styles, together with appropriate furniture. This bed, for which the design drawing still exists, was based on Jacobean models. (Private collection)

and other neo-Elizabethan or neo-Caroline pieces dating from the 1840s. By the late 1860s, the so-called Elizabethan style was beginning to merge into the neo-Renaissance style, which eventually superseded it in the 1870s.

Technological advances The development of technology precipitated many important changes during the whole of the nineteenth century, and technological processes were applied to many aspects of furniture manufacture. Experiments were constantly being made with new materials, sometimes purely in order to provide novelty, and these were not always a success. Into this category must be placed the macabre chairs made of horn and antlers, which were made in England, Germany and America in the middle years of the century, or the chairs and tables made of coal, which created a mild sensation in the 1850s.

Papier-mâché furniture was perhaps the most appealing of all the oddities. It was first made in England, from about 1830 but became popular all over the world. Papier mâché-panels, combined with wood framework and supports, were used as chair-backs, table-

213

tops, and as decorative elements on carcase furniture. The papier mâché itself was usually japanned in black, and this was in turn decorated with mother-of-pearl inlay, naturalistic paintings of flowers or scenes, and stencilled patterns of gilding. Jennens & Bettridge of Birmingham was the principal firm which turned out these decorative objects, and they were in business from 1816 till 1864, although some other firms continued working until the early twentieth century. The style was usually some form of neo-Rococo, since this allowed full expression to the curvaceous shapes into which papier mâché could be moulded. Complete sets of furniture were

rare, but occasional chairs in varying degrees of elaboration, side-cabinets, light tip-top tables, firescreens, desk-sets, were all introduced into fashionable homes to help give that air of variety, contrast and novelty which was considered to be so appealing.

The main technological innovation that took place during the nineteenth century was, of course, the introduction of metal parts where only wood had previously been used. The invention of the coil-spring and its effect on the appearance of comfortable seat furniture has already been noted, but metal came to be employed in many ways that had hitherto been unknown. Furniture made completely

Left: Thomas Willment
('Heraldic Artist by
appointment to King
George IV) assisted with
the extensions to Charlecote
Park, the Elizabethan
home of the Lucy family,
from 1829 to 1834. The 24
oak chairs in the dining-
room, upholstered in
scarlet Utrecht velvet, were
delivered in 1837; although
they were described as
Elizabethan, they were
actually a very close
imitation of chairs of the
time of Charles II, some
150 years later. The
remarkable sideboard was
made by J M Willcox of
Warwick in 1858; Thomas
H Kendall, his assistant
and successor, produced
'Elizabethan' furniture
until the early 1860s.
(National Trust, Charlecote
Park, Warwickshire)

Right: Furniture which
incorporated papier-mâché
parts was very popular
during the middle years
of the nineteenth century.
The papier-mâché sheets
were usually japanned
black in imitation of
Oriental lacquer, and
decorated with mother-of-
pearl inlay, gilt stencilling
and naturalistic paintings
of flowers or views. The
style was usually the
currently popular neo-
rococo, and this allowed
full expression for the
curving forms into which
the material could be
shaped. Many English
firms made these products,
and Birmingham was the
centre of the trade.

of metal (usually cast-iron) first became commonplace in the 1840s, and was mostly produced in the expanding metal manufacturing
centres of the English Midlands. Before this,
most metal furniture had been made of
wrought iron, and out of doors, where such
pieces had their principal use, it required
constant painting to prevent rapid deteriora-
tion through rusting. Cast-iron, sometimes
combined with wood-slat seats or marble
table-tops, became very popular for garden
furniture, or for furniture which was likely
to be subjected to hard usage (in pubs or

cafés), and many delightful designs were
invented. The Coalbrookdale Company made
the famous 'fern' seats from 1858 onwards,
and hall-stands, umbrella-stands, 'door
porters', fenders and flower-pot stands were
all popular. In accordance with the nineteenth-
century taste for a 'valuable' appearance,
these objects were painted to simulate either
brown or patinated green bronze.

A great amount of cast-iron furniture was
exported from Britain in the middle years of
the century, but most countries soon developed
their own centres of production. M Dupont of

Paris exhibited a cast- and wrought-iron bed and a child's cot at the Great Exhibition of 1851, and the bed had sheet-iron ends and a side formed by a cast-iron panel ornamented with naturalistic foliage and hunting scenes in relief. Peyton & Harlow of London exhibited iron bedsteads, one of them with a beautiful domed canopy frame rising to a cast-iron corona. Tomás de Megne of Madrid also exhibited an iron bed, with cast ornament in relief. Cast-iron, combined with iron rod, was used extensively in the production of beds from the 1830s, for metal beds afforded a most welcome alternative to the wooden beds of the time, so many of which were infested with vermin, even in rich households. The cold strength of iron must have provided a miraculous release from the massive wooden bed of nineteenth-century legend, with its thick dusty hangings, oppressively hot feather mattress and lurking bed-bugs.

By the 1870s beds were being made of brass which looked much more light and cheerful than black-painted iron, and which would permit a higher standard of ornamental work. The complete tester had almost disappeared by the second half of the century, and even the half-tester had been replaced by small hinged side-screens, over which a little thin material or muslin could be draped.

Left: The American public were among the first to be interested in 'patent' furniture that was designed specifically for comfort, and this chair, made by the American Chair Company of New York, was shown at the Great Exhibition of 1851. The supporting 'C' springs also allowed the chair to revolve, and the Art Journal Illustrated Catalogue stated 'we have never tested a more easy and commodious article of household furniture'.

In England it was the Arts and Crafts Movement, especially as expressed in the productions of Liberty's and Heal's, that brought wooden beds back to popularity after their eclipse during the last 30 years of the nineteenth century, although brass still remained popular into the next century. The later brass bedsteads were without any particular style and with virtually no ornament. They were often made of square brass tubing which relied merely on a small curved sweep or turned finial for decoration. The first brass beds of the 1860s, on the other hand, were formed out of circular tubes of varying sizes, and enriched with castings, plaques of mother-of-pearl and massive knops in order to achieve as rich an effect as possible.

Cast-iron furniture, especially the outdoor type, was also made in the United States during most of the century, and many patterns continued to be marketed for over 50 years. A set of cast-iron garden seats with members romantically shaped to imitate twigs and rustic logs was advertised by the Boston Ornamental Iron Works in 1857, and the identical pattern was being sold in the 1890s. Many firms made cast-iron furniture in America, based in Cleveland, Boston and New York, and the styles moved from rustic and neo-Rococo through Gothic to neo-Renaissance, although the most consistently favoured always incorporated a sort of naturalism, made up of elements of realistic plant forms, presumably as this was felt to fit in best with the usual open-air use.

There were, however, two particular areas where America specialized in 'technological'

furniture: firstly in that which had particular provision for comfort; secondly in mechanical pieces which were transformable in some form or other. These two furniture types are closely related, and it is tempting to see American interest as connected at least partly, with that country's early development of long-distance rail travel. Trains which could be lived in for several days and nights required kinds of space-saving devices which were unknown even on ships, together with provisions for extra comfort in adjustable and well-sprung seating. The general American travelling public was able to become familiar with these advances rather before they had become usual in Europe, largely due to the considerably more democratized nature of the country's social structure.

In England, and in Europe generally, most mechanical and 'patent' furniture was intended for the use of invalids, and much American 'comfortable' furniture was of a kind which had little parallel in Europe.

Numerous devices were invented for 'digestive' chairs, smokers' chairs, adjustable chairs and rocking-chairs, and most of them made use of metal springs, ratchets, levers, cast-iron bases or revolving supports. The railway connection is obvious, and many of the later pieces might have come straight out of a contemporary Pullman Drawing-Room Car. By the very end of the century, however, American enthusiasm for gadget furniture seems to have waned, and the market gradually faded.

The second uniquely American development in furniture design was that of transformable

Below: Metal beds first appeared in about the middle of the nineteenth century, and provided a welcome hygienic alternative to traditional wooden beds which were often vermin-infested, even in rich households. The introduction of the use of brass members allowed a high degree of ornamentation, combined with a glittering surface quality, and metal beds remained popular until well into the twentieth century.

pieces. In the small flats in the rapidly expanding cities that were the homes of so much of the American population during the second half of the nineteenth century, devices with space-saving properties became necessary; the typical 'dumb-bell'-shape apartment house plan, which was common building practice at this time, shows vividly the cramped layouts which gave rise to the development of dual-purpose furniture. (Whilst the population of London multiplied by four during the nineteenth century, that of New York multiplied by 80!)

The item upon which most ingenuity was expended was the bed, and although sleeping-frames which folded, either vertically or horizontally, into a cupboard had been known

in Europe since the mid-eighteenth century, no country ever took the practice of bizarre fantasy further than America. The most extraordinary device was that which allowed a bed to be given the appearance of a piano when not in use, and perhaps in this we can see the ultimate in the expression of nineteenth-century middle-class pretension — the suggestive bed was finally transformed into the appearance of the very object which came to symbolize most of the aspirations of the growing bourgeoisie. The fact that this piano could not be played was probably largely irrelevant.

Experiments also took place in the use of certain organic materials for the manufacture of furniture. Cane, rattan and wicker were all used with varying degrees of success, and rattan and wicker were to achieve results which expressed engaging fantasy. Some-

times the materials were imported from their country of origin to the industrialized countries to be made up, sometimes the pieces would be made up near their source and exported complete. The usual basis was a wood frame over which the material would be formed in various shapes, and rattan furniture became very popular in conservatories and winter gardens, from about 1850. Towards the end of the century the ever-increasing number of unrelated elements in the middle-class drawing-room was further swelled by the introduction of basket chairs, with chintz covers and backrests. They undoubtedly helped to promote the feeling of cosiness and informality which expressed the increasing influence of women over every aspect of life in the developed countries, and in America in 1886 it was stated that a few such pieces were 'indispensable in modern apartments'.

Above left: Chairs and tables made of cane, rattan and wicker were first made round about 1850, and enjoyed a considerable vogue for furnishing conservatories and winter gardens.

Above: The interior of the Café Griensteidl in Vienna, painted by Rudolf Vokel in 1890, includes typical Thonet bentwood chairs in the surroundings for which they were admirably suited. (Städtische Museen, Vienna)

Probably the most famous technological furniture of the nineteenth century, and certainly that which had the longest life, was the bentwood furniture developed by a German named Michael Thonet. Thonet first started a small factory for making conventional furniture at Boppard, on the Rhine, and in 1830 he began experimenting with methods of economizing on labour and materials. He tried to make use of the techniques of bending veneers, already well known to the Biedermeier furniture-makers, and also to develop this practice further by gluing various parts together with their grain running in different directions so that curved shapes could be held in tension. Thonet's early productions were not particularly successful, but he was able to interest Prince Metternich in the ideas, and he moved to Vienna under the Prince's protection in 1842.

Thonet set up a factory in Vienna in 1849, and by this time he had given up his experiments with shaped, laminated sections, and was concentrating on bending solid wood. At the Great Exhibition of 1851 he showed pieces made of solid, bent rosewood, which were the precursors of the famous bentwood furniture which the Thonet factories were turning out in huge quantities by the 1860s, making use of mass-production and industrial techniques.

The opening-up of the United States in the second half of the century, together with the development of the colonial countries, provided a huge market for furniture which was cheap, strong, light and easily transported, and Thonet's bentwood pieces fulfilled all these requirements. Furthermore, the pieces themselves, (mainly chairs — including the famous 'American' rocker — but also tables, stools, hat-stands, sofas, and even artists' easels) all displayed a delightful, inventive elegance. The snaky convolutions of the

Right: This advertisement by Thonet Brothers, issued in 1862, gives an indication of the variety of the firm's products that could be manufactured from the same basic components.

circular sections—and their relation to neo-Rococo must not be overlooked—exerted an appeal to the eye which, combined with qualities of strength and durability, have ensured the popularity of this furniture up to our own time. It was Thonet, not the idealist William Morris, who created something approaching the 'decorative, noble, popular art' which Morris hoped to produce.

The remarkable success of bentwood seems to lie in its classless simplicity, which found acceptance at every social level. Thonet products could be seen at the end of the century in middle-class English drawing-rooms, in popular Viennese restaurants and cafés, in Australian mining towns and in American hotels.

Thonet's company remained very flexible in its commercial attitude, and a certain number of pieces were made in the early 1900s which had specificaly neo-Louis details, and which became popular for use in the ladies' departments of big stores and in exclusive tea-rooms.

Neo-Renaissance

By the late 1860s and early 70s the fashion for the neo-Louis styles had been caught up, if not overtaken by that for the neo-Renaissance in most countries of the western world. The style varied considerably in interpretation from one country to another, but certain characteristics and details were common to all. It was generally based on the use of ornament derived from the sixteenth and seventeenth centuries, but this allowed for a considerable amount of variation in different countries. Furniture now exhibited a rectangular outline unlike the neo-Rococo, together with massive forms ornamented with areas of rich carving, turnery, or contrasting inlays. Few pieces, if any, were painted, and the obvious intention was always towards a weighty and impressive richness.

The possibility of national variations, which could express through slightly different detail the past of the country of origin, may well have been one of the reasons for its rise to popularity, and it could be used to help satisfy the trend towards nationalism which marked the progress of taste, as the nineteenth century moved into its final third. The striving for national identity which accompanied the struggle for unification in Italy and Germany was one of the influences which had an important bearing on the course of late nineteenth-century middle-class preferences.

Britain was of course not subject to the strong emotional impulses that the style evoked in some other countries, and the English variant was somewhat less 'serious'. It is perhaps best known as 'Free-Renaissance', since few pieces followed the originals very closely; it has also been called, rather contemptuously, 'the bracket-and-overmantel style', and this does suggest the marked tendency towards spindly fussiness that characterized much English furniture towards the end of the century.

Many architects designed furniture in the Free-Renaissance manner, including Robert

Left: Maple & Company of Tottenham Court Road, London, issued this advertisement in the Graphic in 1880. The firm conducted a middle-of-the-market trade for many years, and the goods that they offered are typical of bourgeois English taste of the time.

Right: All levels of the British market offered neo-Renaissance furniture towards the end of the century, and even catalogues of low-price ranges often contained suggestions for complete furnishing schemes. It is evident that the general effect was obtained by the use of a great deal of crude mechanical carving, which was applied fairly indiscriminately to pieces of fundamentally simple construction.

Right: The American neo-Renaissance style could be extremely impressive when used for a whole scheme of decoration. The members of the Hatch family were painted in the library of their Park Avenue mansion in New York by Eastman Johnson in 1871, and the richness of the interior was as closely portrayed by the artist as the likenesses of the sitters. (Metropolitan Museum of Art, New York)

Edis and T E Collcutt, and many of the plates of Edis' influential *Decoration and Furniture of Town Houses*, first published in 1881, showed not only furniture in this style, but also fireplace surrounds, overmantels, fixed cupboards and panelling. Indeed it is difficult to draw the line between good Free-Renaissance furniture and that which was designed by other important figures who were more closely tied to the Arts and Crafts Movement than to the popular market.

The influence of two Arts and Crafts architects, Eastlake and Talbert, can be traced in the development of the English Free-Renaissance style, although their work was much more consciously mediaeval in the manner of William Morris, and showed links with the neo-Elizabethan of the first half of the century. Charles Eastlake gave his name to a whole style of furniture in America, through the publication of his *Hints on Household Taste* in 1868, which found an eager public on both sides of the Atlantic. In fact, the American interpretation of the East-lake style was much closer to the designs of Bruce Talbert, whose *Gothic Forms Applied to Furniture* (1867) and *Examples of Ancient and Modern Furniture* (1876) contained designs of a less austere kind than Eastlake's, and suggested a logical development of the work of Pugin.

Furniture firms at all levels of the market made pieces in the Free-Renaissance style, and in the upper bracket, Gillows, Collinson & Lock and C & W Trapnell consistently maintained a high level of quality. Panels incorporating carving or inlays based on north Italian ornament of the sixteenth century, designs based on Flemish strapwork or François I or Henri II ornament were freely used, and all of them were drawn together within a framework of rectangular and architectural character. The interior of Scott's new St Pancras Hotel in London was furnished in the richest neo-Renaissance manner by Gillows in the early 1870s, and this type of decoration came to supersede Gothic or Elizabethan for dining-rooms and libraries. Edis even recommended neo-Renaissance for drawing-rooms and bedrooms.

Although the better firms maintained their quality output as the end of the century approached, the cheaper and more commercial furniture-makers steadily bastardized the neo-Renaissance style. Papers like the *Furniture Gazette*, and the trade catalogues of the 1880s and 1890s, offered pieces that were becoming increasingly fussy in design and flimsy in construction. Carcase furniture took on a profusion of shelves and brackets, often supported on small turnery, and panels of bevelled glass or mirror, together with elaborate inlays of contrasting woods. All these features were included to give an effect of elaboration

223

on pieces whose basic form was thin and unsatisfactory. Some makers turned to a more specifically reproduction style, and catalogues at the turn of the century carried ranges made in oak, which was given a dark, fumed finish, and elaborate carvings and strip ornament.

An interesting variant of neo-Renaissance was the furniture which emanated from the United States. This had a much looser relationship with the style of origin than its European counterparts, and seems to us, therefore, to belong much more truly to the nineteenth century, as well as being strongly American.

Gaining popularity rapidly after the end of the Civil War in 1865, furniture in the American neo-Renaissance style exactly matched the attitudes of that period of commercial expansion and development which extended over the next decade. Massive, rich, rectangular, this furniture was decorated with projected panels of contrasting veneers, gilded incised linear patterns, and a profusion of turned ornamental knobs. Rosewood, burr-walnut, ebonizing, gilding, porcelain plaques and ormolu mounts might all be combined on one of the more costly examples, to produce an effect of magnificent opulence, which was often carried through the decoration of the whole house. Such interiors became the visible expression of men who had 'arrived', and they must have reflected exactly the ideals of railway magnates, expanding frontiers, industrialization and progress.

Most of the New York furniture-makers worked in this style, and Alexander Roux ('ever the tasteful proponent of the latest style') made a great amount of Renaissance revival furniture. Leon Marcotte made typical pieces during the 1860s and 1870s, together with others that were much closer to the original European models. John Jelliff of Newark, and Thomas Brooks & Company of Brooklyn were also known for their fine pieces, but it was the highly mechanized Grand Rapids firms that usually produced this essentially middle-market style.

The Berkey & Gay firm of Grand Rapids, and Mitchell & Rammelsberg of Cincinnati virtually dominated the furniture section of the Philadelphia Centennial Exhibition of 1876 with huge Renaissance revival pieces. These firms, together with the Phoenix Furniture Company, and Nelson Matters & Company, of Grand Rapids, took over a large part of the middle and lower ends of the market with products that ranged from near exhibition standard down to the humblest three-part bedroom suite for the newly-married small-time farmer.

By about 1880, however, the popularity of Renaissance revival was beginning to wane, and one of the reasons was undoubtedly the

Left: The American neo-Renaissance style took a somewhat different course from the European equivalent, in that the pieces displayed even less similarity to genuine Renaissance models. Indeed, in this rosewood cabinet made by Alexander Roux of New York in 1866, a highly eclectic collection of ornaments has been grafted rather arbitrarily onto the basically monumental neo-Renaissance form. (Metropolitan Museum of Art, New York)

poor-quality bastardized versions that were manufactured in huge quantities by the less reputable Grand Rapids factories. Furthermore, a new generation of the buying public was growing up in the United States by the last two decades of the century, and its members had not the same inclination for the ostentation and massive display that their parents required to demonstrate the position they held in society.

The development of the neo-Renaissance style divided in the late 1870s. On the one hand, there was the appearance of a sophisticated simplicity which tended to eliminate much of the lavish applied ornament, whilst retaining the rectangularity and the incised linear decoration. On the other hand, a slightly self-conscious trend led towards 'honesty' and 'reform' which in turn encouraged a renewed interest in the more rugged woods, like oak, and oiled rather than french-polished finishes. Both these trends came to be known as the Eastlake style, although the products were

as much akin to those proposed by Bruce Talbert as by Eastlake himself.

One of the principal firms which made the more sophisticated type was Herter Bros, of New York, and much of their output had a great deal in common with the 'Art furniture' being made in England at about the same time. Great use was made of ebonizing, which was enlivened by stencilled gilt designs and inlays with a distinctly Japanese flavour. But these beautiful, bland pieces were never intended for a mass market, nor could such quality be produced in sufficient quantity.

The simpler aspects of the so-called Eastlake style were more in line with developing popular taste, and Kimbel & Cabus of New York, and Mitchell & Rammelsberg specialized in this furniture during the late 1870s and the 1880s. An important influence on the continuance and development of the Eastlake style's concern with 'honesty' was the work of the architect H H Richardson; his brilliant ideas on decoration had a great impact, and his pieces

225

often relied on the use of local woods, which might carry some judiciously disposed carving, but no applied ornament. Although Richardson died in 1886, a talented band of contemporaries carried on his theories in Chicago and on the Pacific Coast during the remaining years of the century, and could be said to have been achieving a truly national furniture style.

The development of neo-Renaissance furniture in the countries of the European mainland proceeded in a much less unconventional manner than in the United States. The style followed fairly closely such models as were felt to be appropriate from the historical furniture of each country, and there was little attempt at any departure from precedent.

In Germany and Italy, a return to what was dimly seen as the 'glorious past' had a considerable appeal in the upsurge of nationalism which took place in each of these countries at the time of their unification — which in both cases was during the 1860s and 1870s; the neo-Renaissance style appeared to be exactly what was required to provide an acceptable background. In Germany the final effect suggests a kind of Wagnerian late Middle Ages, whilst in Italy it is the world of Dante or the Medicis.

In Germany and Austria, neo-Renaissance furniture had first appeared in the 1840s, and a number of the highly praised pieces that Carl Leistler sent from Vienna to the Great Exhibition of 1851 were quite distinctly neo-Renaissance in character. In the 1870s and 1880s, the style was eagerly adopted by the increasingly prosperous German bourgeoisie, and the dark, elaborate character to which it lent itself so easily became completely associated with German late nineteenth-century middle-class life.

During the latter half of the 1870s, and throughout the 1880s and 1890s, neo-Renaissance remained popular all over the German-speaking countries. Most of the new official buildings were decorated in the style, and the interiors of the Reichstag in Berlin, designed by Paul Wallot in 1884, but not completed until 1894 with furnishings from the Munich firm of Pössenbacher, were totally given over to neo-Renaissance. Hugo Stamman and Gustav Zinnow designed interiors and furniture for the new Hamburg Town Hall in 1897 in the neo-Renaissance style, and Karl Köchlin provided interiors in 1884 for Heinrich von Ferstel's new neo-Renaissance Vienna University.

Many architects designed neo-Renaissance furniture all over Germany, such as Gustav Kachel of Karlsruhe, Hans Grisebach of Berlin, Rudolf Feldscharek and Alexander Wielemans von Monteforte of Vienna and the Munich architect George Hauberisser, who also worked in a rather Puginesque Gothic at the new Munich Town Hall in the early 1880s.

Middle-class demand continued to be served by firms like Bembé of Mainz, who not only made furniture but also designed complete interiors like the one published in *Building*, the English magazine, in 1883.

Neo-Renaissance furniture was made throughout Germany and Austria by such firms as Würfel or Franz Michel of Vienna, the Pallenbergs in Cologne, Philipp Niederhöfer of Frankfurt, Ziegler & Weber of Karlsruhe or George Schölte of Stuttgart.

Napoleon III's revivalistic ventures in French official building involved the use of the neo-Renaissance style, based on the architecture of the time of François I or Henri II, and appropriate pieces were required to furnish both new work and restorations.

The palaces with original Renaissance interiors were in a number of cases refurnished, notably the palace of Fontainebleau. Massive neo-Renaissance pieces were provided by Guillaume Grohé in 1860, typical of which was a magnificent set of chairs enriched with fine carving, which were made to designs by Ruprich-Robert. Even before this, in 1856, Grohé had executed the cradle, designed by Froment-Meurice, that the city of Paris had presented to Napoleon and Eugénie for the Prince Imperial, and this was made in the richest neo-Renaissance manner.

It has been claimed that this style first appeared in France at the exhibition of 1839, and that Aimé Chénavard (whose neo-Rococo exercises we have already noted) merely led a whole group of designers and decorators, but it still seems that the style did not become generally popular before the early years of the second Empire.

Grohé, who became official supplier to the Imperial Court, was perhaps the most spectacular exponent of the neo-Renaissance, but many of the other contemporary furniture-makers that we have already noted as working in the neo-Louis styles were also producing neo-Renaissance pieces. Fourdinois, Jeanselme, Krieger and many other lesser firms all turned out their own interpretations. Neo-Renaissance decoration and furniture were, of course, frequently used in conjunction with other styles in the same house; Baron James de Rothschild's Château de Ferrières, completed in about 1860, had a neo-Renaissance dining-room, sitting-room and central hall, but also a neo-Louis Seize music-room and a neo-Rococo study. The house that Mme Paiva, one of the richest and most notorious figures of the late 1860s, had built for herself on the Champs Elysées in Paris was almost entirely decorated in neo-Renaissance. It took 11 years to build, and the house-warming party did not take place until 1866; the interior is a monument of French neo-Renaissance taste. All the important artists of the day worked on the house, and Carrier-Belleuse even provided a bronze and silver neo-Renaissance console table.

Paul Mauguin, the architect, also designed much of the special furniture, which was ornamented with gilt-bronze plaques set into ebonized surrounds.

The upheavals brought about by the Franco-Prussian war, and France's defeat and the ensuing political troubles, curtailed the development of taste for a time, but Henri Havard, in his influential book *L'Art dans la Maison*, published in 1884, obviously still believed neo-Renaissance to be perfectly acceptable, mingled with a judicious amount of neo-Louis in rooms where he considered it appropriate.

The Exposition Universelle of 1889 was somewhat of a turning-point in French bourgeois taste in that it was firmly forward-looking. The Galerie des Machines and the Eiffel tower served as symbols of a changing cultural attitude, and the revival of floral decoration and the emerging Art Nouveau style were much in evidence.

It should not of course be overlooked that Art Nouveau itself had deep neo-Rococo origins and that these must make it appeal strongly to the public in a country where Rococo was an integral part of its historic culture. Neither should it be assumed that it superseded previous fashions at any one specific moment in time — certainly the neo-Renaissance style continued with gradually diminishing popularity in France until the 1914 war.

Italian interest in neo-Renaissance tended (as might be expected) to favour a sort of 'Dantesque' vision of Italy's past. Again, as might be expected, this style also became associated with the Risorgimento and its own emphasis on Italy's glorious history. As far back as 1840, Cima had proposed designs in a neo-Renaissance style in his *Addobatore Moderno*, and Allessandro Sidoli published examples of his versions of it in the 1850s.

Andrea Baccetti made rich furniture in Florence during the 1860s and 1870s, and received much critical acclaim at the various exhibitions to which he submitted his work.

The Italian furniture-makers usually turned their attention towards the richness of the later Renaissance, and the carver Luigi Frullini was almost alone in following his rather sixteenth-century inspiration. His pieces had a quality of restraint that was noticeably lacking in the productions of his contemporaries, and this was combined with a very architectural character. He was much acclaimed at various exhibitions, including that of 1862 in London.

Enthusiasm for the neo-Renaissance amongst the middle classes continued unabated after Umberto I ascended to the throne of united Italy in 1878, and most bourgeois households had at least one neo-Renaissance room. None of the artistic collections that many Italians were putting together at this period could be considered complete if it did not contain a large proportion of so-called Renaissance objects, many of which of course turned out later to be fakes.

Every European country produced its own version of the neo-Renaissance style; the castle of Peles in Rumania, for example, was started in 1875 and furnished and re-furnished for the royal family in the most elaborate manner right up to 1914. Friedrich and Robert Melzer made neo-Renaissance furniture for the Winter Palace in St Petersburg in 1894. Ibsen's study in his home on the Abendsgate in Oslo, where he lived from 1895 until his death in 1906, contained neo-Renaissance bourgeois furnishings, mixed with overstuffed easy chairs of a more typically mid-century appearance.

The Exotics

The Moorish style A type of decoration which was loosely based on the vocabulary of near-eastern design was popular all through the nineteenth century. Known variously as 'Moorish', 'Turkish', 'Saracenic' or 'Arab', its main characteristics involved the use of the Moorish arch form, highly patterned walls in the manner of Persian tiles, and amorphous pieces of furniture of rather undefined shape, covered with cushions.

The popularity of this exotic fashion is intriguing, but it appears that any function which was considered foreign to conventional nineteenth-century bourgeois ideas was felt to be satisfactorily absorbed when it was in such unusual surroundings. Smoking rooms (with obvious connections), billiard rooms (male preserve), bathrooms (Turkish), were all decorated with versions of near-eastern

Left: John D Rockefeller had a magnificent 'moorish' sitting-room in the house in which he lived on West 54th Street, New York, in the 1880s, but the effect was mostly achieved by the rich joinery (with ivory and mother-of-pearl inlay) and the brilliant colouring. The furniture, although ebonized and splendidly upholstered with embroidered covers, was nevertheless hardly distinguishable from the prevalent neo-Renaissance-cum-Eastlake styles of the period. (Brooklyn Museum)

Below: The 'turkish' style was popular all through the nineteenth century. A typical divan covered in carpet, and with the frame completely concealed, was included in an album of designs for Reiche und Elegante Sitzmöbel by A & L Streitenfeld of Berlin.

detail, and the style was also applied to boudoirs (harem?), garden retreats and, in Lisbon, even a railway station!

During the first half of the nineteenth century, the Moorish style was still mostly employed on follies, pavilions and garden features, and very little furniture was made for such buildings.

In England, Owen Jones, an influential architect and designer, was an enthusiastic exponent of near-eastern decoration, and his *Plans, Elevations and Sections of the Alhambra*, published from 1836 to 1845, created great interest in Islamic practices of polychromy and pattern. Although he designed a lot of buildings and decorative schemes with Moorish details and colours, little evidence survives that he ever produced any furniture. In fact, apart from the overstuffed divan, little furniture in this style seems to have been attempted anywhere much before 1860. Even the famous Arab Hall that the painter Lord Leighton had constructed in his house in London in 1880 had only some fixed seating.

A few pieces with Moorish details were designed by Andrea Baccetti in Italy however, and the incredible Moorish interior of the villa Crespi on Lake Orta, designed by the architect Giovanni Colla in the last years of the century, does seem to have been completely furnished with pieces that made use of near-eastern elements in their design.

The Turkish drawing-room at the Rumanian palace of Peles also had stools and occasional tables with near-eastern decoration, but the specifically oriental look was achieved by the use of overstuffed sofas, and it was upon these objects that most of such schemes relied for their effect, together with coverings of brilliantly patterned carpet and embroidery.

In New York, A A Vantine and Company made a speciality of supplying 'everything that belongs to a genuine Moorish interior' during the 1890s, and the increasing popularity of overstuffed couches, divans and 'Turkish corners' probably reflected the liking for comfort and relaxed informality which were to become such a characteristic of American life. Not that designers in the United States were alone in this trend in the closing years of the century, for firms like Holland & Sons in London were offering a complete 'Turkish' smoking room in one of their catalogues, which had fixed overstuffed divans set on either side of the fireplace and provided the total environment for 'a chamber specially furnished for wakeful rest'.

The Japanese Style The arts of the Far East have fascinated the Western world since the close of the Middle Ages, and during the eighteenth century it became fashionable in most European countries to construct follies and garden buildings in what was loosely called the Chinese style. The English architect Sir William Chambers, in his *Designs of Chinese Buildings, Furniture etc.*, published in 1757, showed suggestions for a number of chairs and tables in his interpreted far-eastern styles, and this kind of piece became extremely popular between 1770 and 1830.

It was not until the opening of Japan to foreign trade in 1854, however, that Japanese art came to be much known in the West, but as soon as this event took place its popularity grew rapidly in Europe and America. While the more advanced aspects of Japanese influence were to be found in the Arts and Crafts movement (to be described in the next chapter), a great many elements of the Anglo-Japanese style filtered down to the middle-level markets during the last 20 years of the century, so that many a bourgeois drawing-room was decorated with 'Japanese' fans, and every suburban boudoir had its 'art' pot containing a spray of peacock feathers.

By the 1880s and 1890s the furniture trade was producing large amounts of Japanese-influenced pieces, some of it using real bamboo for legs and frames (unlike most

Left: Although the celebrated 'Peacock Room' that the painter James McNeil Whistler decorated in 1877 had a strong Japanese flavour, the furniture was either neo-Louis or neo-Renaissance, with a few eighteenth-century antiques. (National Monuments Record, London)

Below: In 1882 Herter Bros of New York provided a complete 'Japanese Parlour' for the 5th Avenue mansion of William H Vanderbilt, including special neo-Japanese furniture.

earlier products which were made of wood with a simulated bamboo finish) and panels of woven grass to decorate doors and table-tops. Most of these pieces were intended as occasional furniture, appreciated for its quaint character, and few rooms would contain more than one or two. Vantine's Emporium in New York imported large amounts of bamboo furniture from China and Japan in the late years of the century, and companies like Nimura and Sato of Brooklyn made up bamboo into furniture in America itself.

Although by 1886 *The Decorator and Furnisher* was able to state that bamboo furniture was always in demand 'among people of artistic tastes', few of these went so far as W H Vandebilt, who commissioned Herter Bros, to design a complete Japanese Parlour in his 5th Avenue mansion.

'National' and 'Old-World' revivals from 1880 to 1914

The increasing nationalism in politics throughout the world towards the end of the nineteenth century, which culminated in the Great War of 1914, was reflected in many aspects of the cultural scene. In furniture design, the trend towards a search for a style which suggested the actual past of the nation concerned, which we have already noted as an aspect of the Renaissance revival, became canalized into revivals which were even more specifically related to national styles, and the production of pieces of furniture intended to reproduce actual antiques with considerable fidelity. In England, from approximately 1880 and certainly at least up until 1914, a con-siderable market grew up for reproductions of English eighteenth-century furniture, and some of these were copied so accurately that it is now very difficult for anyone other than an expert to tell that such pieces are not genuine.

At the upper end of the market, firms like Gillows made so-called Chippendale, Adam, or Sheraton furniture which followed the originals very closely, and in which the standard of craftsmanship was equally high. Indeed this firm had in any case made many of the originals themselves during the eighteenth century (as they pointed out in their catalogues) and their productions might therefore be claimed not even to be copies! Even such a progressive firm as Morris & Company, could turn out furniture in a completely eighteenth-century style, and the bergère chair designed for them by George Jack round about 1895 followed late eighteenth-century precedent so closely as to be indis-tinguishable at first glance from its model. It is also apparent that the snob element in-herent in the increasingly popular activity of collecting antique furniture formed part of the rising demand for accurate copies.

A firm like Maples would have a large show-room in which they offered genuine antiques for sale, mingled with their own reproductions.

At the lower levels of the market, the com-mercial copies of English furniture made by English firms were naturally more convincing than those of Continental styles, but a lot of the output at the end of the century had the curious characteristic of increased size com-bined with a reduction in the individual members. This gave so much late nineteenth-century furniture a strangely spindly look, although the detail might be copied from the model with understanding and accuracy.

The same trends were apparent in America at that time, although 'eighteenth century' across the Atlantic was interpreted as Ameri-can Colonial. By 1884 *Cabinet Making and Upholstery* was able to report that 'the making of antiques has become a modern industry'. The Centennial Exhibition held in Phila-delphia in 1876 to commemorate 100 years of American independence may well have helped to promote a nostalgic interest in a specifically American past with such emotive exhibits as 'a New England kitchen', and in 1888 the *Ladies Home Journal* was telling its readers that 'nice old-fashioned chairs . . . make a parlor look very cosy and old-time'; the centre of the American furniture industry in Grand Rapids soon responded to the demand, and, for instance, Barnard & Simonds of Rochester advertised in the *Grand Rapids Furniture Record* in 1902: 'Furniture of our Forefathers — Colonial Reproduction Chairs'.

By the turn of the century, some firms were even turning out more or less accurate copies of American Empire pieces of the 1830s.

Germany experienced a Biedermeier revival in the last years of the nineteenth century which lasted into the 1920s. Nevertheless, although much use was made of the blond woods and contrasted ebonizing that was such a characteristic Biedermeier feature, and the pieces themselves exhibited a classical severity, the wholesale copying of actual antiques was not nearly as widespread as was the current practice in England or America.

The Munich architects H Helbig and C Haiger designed some furniture between 1898 and 1900 which was almost a neo-Biedermeier pastiche, and even Peter Behrens (a darling of the Modern Movement) produced similar imitations in 1908. In 1913, another architect, Gustav Halmhuber, produced designs for furniture in a neo-German Empire style, reminiscent of the work of Thouret, Raab or von Klenze of 80 years earlier.

In all the German-speaking countries, however, the influence of manufacturing and design associations like the Deutscher Werkbund and the Wiener Werkstätte had, from 1900 or so, begun to turn the course of general

CHIPPENDALE LIBRARY

taste towards a spare, rectangular style which, whilst it had little similarity to Art Nouveau, owed hardly more to nationalistic revivalism. It was a style which was later to be brilliantly exploited by the great French designers of the 1920s and 1930s like Ruhlmann and Leleu, but which was hardly appreciated outside Germany before 1918.

A curious side-effect of nationalism took place in several of the European countries that had a strong tradition of agrarian culture however, and this was a revival of self-consciously 'peasant' styles of furniture. The main features were a wilfully 'primitive' construction, allied to a lavish use of fairly historically accurate, naïve carved and painted ornament, and the principal period of inspiration was usually the late seventeenth century and the eighteenth century. A few such pieces, expressing a highly sophisticated unsophistication had made their appearance in some of the Germanic states as early as the 1850s, but it was not really until the 1880s that the work of designers like J A Malmström in Sweden or Shutov in Russia came to be much appreciated; certainly in Russia this kind of rather self-conscious primitivism had a considerable success.

In certain areas of central Europe peasant furniture had never ceased to be made in accordance with traditional practice until well into the twentieth century, and it was therefore easy for the Hungarians Róberttöl Nádler or Lajos Kosma to take up the tradition where true peasant craftsmen were already abandoning it at the turn of the century. It is an interesting insight into late nineteenth-century trends to realize that such pieces would have been considered to be beneath the notice of an educated clientele until the basic peasant tradition which had produced them was dying, and that the social changes of the nineteenth century seem eventually to have brought a total reversal of aesthetic intention, which has remained with us until the present day.

234

THE REBIRTH OF DESIGN
Arts and Crafts and Art Nouveau

The later part of the nineteenth century saw a succession of attempts to revitalize the applied arts. While the established furniture manufacturers produced their pastiches of traditional or exotic styles, a small number of innovators in both Europe and America tried to break free from bourgeois taste.

In historical terms, Art Nouveau was but one conclusion to the search for originality, unity and moral authority which had begun with designers and theorists such as A W N Pugin in England and Viollet-le-Duc in France during the 1840s. Pugin (1812–1852), the prime mover in the development of a progressive Gothic style in English architecture and design, was aware of the damaging results of uncontrolled mass-production on aesthetics and it was his aim, and the aim of those who followed, to harness the intellectual and material resources of the times to the service of art.

The Aesthetic Movement

Throughout the nineteenth century in England, there were two parallel streams of production and theory. The development of industrial methods caused the mass-production of furniture, metalwork and ceramics in styles borrowed from the past and often debased. As early as 1841, Pugin, in one of his major polemics, *The True Principles of Christian or Pointed Architecture*, could refer in tones of deep disgust to 'those inexhaustible mines of bad taste, Birmingham and Sheffield'.

Six years after this book was written, Henry Cole (1808–1882), using the pseudonym Felix Summerly, founded the firm of Summerly's Art Manufactures, which survived until 1851. During the time this existed, Cole gathered round him a group of men who were to preach the gospel of 'Fitness for Purpose'. This group included Richard Redgrave, Matthew Digby Wyatt, Owen Jones and Ralph Wornum; their aim was, as Cole wrote later in his autobiography:

'To revive the good old practice of connecting the best art with familiar objects in daily use. In doing this, Art Manufactures will aim to produce in each article superior utility, which is not to be sacrificed to ornament; to select pure forms; to decorate each article with appropriate details relating to its use and to obtain these details as directly as possible from nature.'

This view was propounded in the magazine founded by Cole in 1849, *Journal of Design and Manufacture,* which ran until 1852 and in several books written by his circle following the commercially successful but aesthetically disastrous Great Exhibition of 1851. Of this event, Owen Jones remarked in his *Lectures on the Results of the Great Exhibition:*
'No unity; the architect, the upholsterer, the

paperstainer, the weaver, the calico-printer, and the potter, run each their independent course; each struggles fruitlessly, each produces in art novelty without beauty, or beauty without intelligence.'

In his *Manual of Design*, published in 1876, Richard Redgrave put it thus:
'The design for a work must have regard to construction, and consequently to proper use of materials . . . *Utility* must have precedence of decoration.'

Thus, the basic principles behind the movements of the last two decades of the nineteenth century were firmly laid in the 1850s. We recognize instantly the sources of their belief, when William Morris, for example, wrote in 1880, 'Have nothing in your house that you do not know to be useful or believe to be beautiful', or when Ford Madox Hueffer described his father's work in the Arts and Crafts Exhibition Society catalogue produced in 1896: 'Adaptation to need, solidity, a kind of homely beauty and above all absolute dissociation from all false display, veneering and the like. . . .'

Any discussion of new design in English

Left: Pugin's talent is perhaps best expressed in the consistency which unified every part of his work. In the library of the House of Lords at the Palace of Westminster, where he collaborated with Charles Barry between 1844 and 1852, his furniture is exactly matched by the panelling, the bookcases, the ceiling, and even the carpet pattern, to produce that totality which is the peculiar characteristic of a masterpiece. (Palace of Westminster, House of Lords)

urniture in the latter part of the nineteenth entury must, therefore, go back to Pugin and he Gothic revival. Of course, 'gothick' had een an obvious feature of English design from he mid-eighteenth century but the Gothic of 'ugin, Burges and others differed from this arlier manifestation by virtue of its truth to rchaeological sources. Victorian progressive iothic designers did not seek to romanticize heir design but to use its best features as ssential points of reference. This can be seen y comparing A W N Pugin's book *Gothic 'urniture* of 1835 with the work of the same itle by his father Augustus Charles Pugin, ublished in 1820. Pugin's most famous group f furniture was made for the House of Lords n the 1840s in collaboration with the architect f the new Palace of Westminster, Charles 'arry. A recent report by the Victoria & lbert Museum, London, says:

'ugin's greatest involvement was from 1844 nwards in the design of every aspect of the nterior decoration and furnishing. During he next eight years, Pugin literally worked imself to death, providing designs for the ntire internal decoration and all the furniture f major importance. It was Pugin's labours nd attention to the smallest details of rnament that gave the tremendous sense of nity to the interior of the Palace, and at the ame time gave each area its distinctive haracter and each room its particular status.'

There is a great contrast between the sturdy, eautifully functional oak furniture of the Iouse of Lords and Romantic Gothick, of hich Pugin himself had once been a disciple. n *The True Principles* he wrote:

. . your modern man designs a sofa or ccasional table from details culled out of ritton's Cathedrals, and all the ordinary rticles of furniture, which require to be imple and convenient, are made not only very xpensive but very uneasy. We find diminutive ying buttresses about an armchair; every-hing is crocheted with angular projections, nnumerable mitres, sharp ornaments, and urreted extremities. A man who remains any ength of time in a modern Gothic room, and scapes without being wounded by some of its inutiae, may consider himself extremely ortunate . . . I have perpetrated many of hese enormities in the furniture I designed ome years ago for Windsor Castle.'

he majority of the House of Lords furniture as made by the two leading firms of com-ercial cabinet-makers, Holland & Sons of ount Street and Gillow's of Oxford Street. ther pieces, including some of the most nportant, were made in the workshops of ohn Webb and Johnstone & Jeanes, both of ond Street.

Pugin's furniture had considerable influence n English design in the mid-century. His ons, E W Pugin (1834–1875) and Peter Paul Pugin (1851–1904) produced somewhat watered-down pieces based on their father's style. The architect G E Street designed some spectacular pieces for Holland & Sons in the 1860s, and also taught many of the later Gothic designers, who in turn taught the leading members of the Arts and Crafts movement. Another designer, Charles Bevan, was employed by the firm of Marsh & Jones, later Marsh, Jones & Cribb, for whom he designed fine Gothic furniture with inlaid geometric decoration, a typical feature of High Victorian Gothic. The architect William Butterfield designed a small amount of domestic furniture in the Gothic style in the 1850s, usually in walnut inlaid with ebony and sycamore.

In the 1860s, however, there was a revolt against Pugin's ideas and his use of com-mercial firms. The leader of this counter-movement was William Morris. It would be specious, however, to suggest that the various ideas and motives current at the time are necessarily easy to differentiate or indeed that the matter was in the least clear-cut. For side by side with Morris was the Art Furniture movement, which was itself a reaction, how-ever partial, against Pugin but which departed from Morris's ideas on many points. And

Left: Carved, painted and gilt oak washstand designed by William Burges. Made for the Guest Chamber of the Tower House, Melbury Road, London, this piece is signed and dated 1880. The top, bowl and soap dishes are of marble, the back is inset with small mirrors and the taps and fittings are of bronze. (Victoria & Albert Museum, London)

239

somewhere in the middle is the figure of William Burges, who would appear to have had some sympathy with everybody's point of view, but who managed to remain idiosyncratic and unrestricted by any particular movement.

Like most of the leading nineteenth-century furniture designers, Burges was trained as an architect. He had been a pupil of Matthew Digby Wyatt, from whom he would have imbibed many of the principles of the Cole circle, although there is little evidence that they made any great impact on him. He designed many small churches in the thirteenth-century style and the interiors

and furnishings of Cardiff Castle and Castell Coch for the Marquis of Bute, who lavished a vast fortune on these two projects. Burges also designed some remarkable furniture for his own house in Melbury Road, London, which he built between 1875 and 1881 as 'a model residence of the fifteenth century'. Some of the pieces for this house are similar to the ornate painted furniture produced by Morris & Company in the 1860s; the most remarkable of the Burges pieces is the book-case, now in the Ashmolean Museum, Oxford, executed in 1862 and decorated with painted panels by Edward Poynter, Edward Burne-Jones, Simeon Solomon, Thomas Morten, N H J Westlake, W F Yeames, Henry Holliday, Albert Moore, J A Fitzgerald, Frederick Walker and H Stacy Marks. Burges differs from Morris in the strictly archaeological nature of his designs and in his use of commercial manufacturers. None of his designs was marketed commercially, however, and he did lay strong emphasis on craftsmanship.

Burges was also one of the earliest designers in England to appreciate the qualities of Japanese art, drawing a parallel between the honesty of Japanese craftsmanship and that which existed in Europe in the Middle Ages. In much of his work, Japanese motifs mingle with Gothic and Burges forms a natural link between the traditional Western style of Victorian Gothic and the new aesthetics of 'Japonisme'.

The 1860s, then, saw the development of two concomitant approaches to the design and production of furniture and, indeed, to the applied arts in general. The Art Furniture movement developed out of the Gothicism of the 1840s and 1850s and out of the philosophic and practical concerns of Sir Henry Cole and his circle. William Morris, however, took another path, that of a return to a mediaeval idea of individual craftsmanship, although towards the end of his life he recognized the futility of trying to ignore the existence of machinery in the machine age. From the Art Furniture movement developed the Aesthetic movement and from Morris's socialist idealism, the Arts and Crafts movement.

The Art Furniture movement grew naturally out of the philosophy of Henry Cole. It saw the birth of a new breed of artist, the freelance industrial designer. The most famous of these were Bruce Talbert (1838–1881) and Christopher Dresser (1834–1904). Talbert trained as an architect but in 1862 began designing furniture for Doveston, Bird & Hull of Manchester; in later years, he designed for many of the leading commercial manufacturers, including Collinson & Lock, G S Lucraft & Son, Holland & Son, Marsh, Jones & Cribb and Jackson & Graham. Although evidence is lacking, it seems likely that the group of furniture supplied by

Left: Sideboard in oak, with carved boxwood panels and metal hinges designed by Bruce J Talbert and made by Gillows in 1873, in which year it was shown at the International Exhibition in London. This interesting synthesis of Gothic and Japanese forms is typical of the best art furniture. (Victoria & Albert Museum, London)

Gillow's to Bradford Town Hall in 1873 is based on Talbert's designs.

In 1867, Talbert wrote *Gothic Forms applied to Furniture* and followed this seven years later with *Examples of Ancient and Modern Furniture, Tapestries and Decoration*. Like the other leading designers of the Art Furniture movement, Talbert's training in the Victorian Gothic school of architecture was to affect even his most original designs.

Perhaps the most influential critic of this period was Charles Eastlake, whose book *Hints on Household Taste* of 1868 caused a design revolution. He was the first to use the term 'Art Furniture' although, ironically, no piece actually designed by him is known. His ideas for furniture, as seen in his often reprinted work, are in fact more than a little dull. The designer J Moyr Smith, himself a distinctly minor figure, wrote in his *Ornamental Interiors* of 1887 that Eastlake's furniture was 'in construction too much like a packing case'.

The furniture which we would now associate most immediately with the Art Furniture movement is usually of a dark wood, either black or ebonized baywood, basswood or walnut. It has painted decoration and a fair quantity of gilding and brass fittings. The best known firm of commercial manufacturers was Collinson & Lock. This type of furniture was produced in massive quantities throughout the 1870s and 1880s and, as Charles Handley Read pointed out, was largely inspired by the extraordinary cabinet, now in the Victoria & Albert Museum which was designed by the architect T E Collcutt for Collinson & Lock. The eclecticism of the Art Furniture movement is revealed in this piece which betrays Gothic, Japanese, Renaissance and Queen Anne influences but which is nevertheless the first example of an entirely new approach to furniture design in the nineteenth century. It is all the more remarkable for the break it marks with Collcutt's earlier furniture; designed in 1871, this piece is in total contrast to the simple oak furniture which, under the influence of Philip Webb and Bruce Talbert, Collcutt had been designing in the previous years.

The Art Furniture movement produced one furniture designer of outstanding genius, William Godwin (1833–1886). Like Christopher Dresser, Godwin had been one of the first to appreciate the functional, architectonic qualities of Japanese design. Throughout the late 1860s and 1870s, he produced one of the most consistent and convincing bodies of

work of any major designer of this period. His most famous piece remains the ebonized buffet of 1867, which was re-made commercially by the firm of William Watt in 1877. The latter pieces were inset with embossed Japanese leather paper first imported by Liberty's in 1876; the angular design of this piece marks a total and radical break with hitherto accepted European styles.

Godwin designed for a number of firms. He collaborated with Whistler on William Watt's stand for the Paris Universal Exhibition of 1878; the previous year he had designed Whistler's house in Tite Street, Chelsea, and the pieces for Watt were painted with a theme by Whistler called, characteristically, 'Butterfly Suit, Harmony in Yellow and Gold'. He had designed the so-called 'Greek' chair for Watt in 1875 and in 1877 he designed a 'Jacobean' chair for the firm of Collier & Plunckett of Warwick, England. One of his earliest domestic commissions was for the furniture of Dromore Castle, County Limerick, which was designed and built between 1867 and 1869. Godwin's chairs are in oiled wainscot oak with natural calf upholstery; they were made by Godwin's own Art Furniture Company, the first organization of its kind. Apart from the firms already mentioned, Godwin designed for Gillow's, Green & King, W A Smee and Collinson & Lock. Many of his later pieces, as Elizabeth Aslin remarked, were in 'mahogany also ebonized and decorated with a few gold lines in the panels'.

Thomas Jeckyll (1827–1881) was also an aesthetic movement designer of great individuality. He favoured padouk wood and walnut for his furniture and designed some superb cast-iron and brass for the Norwich firm of Barnard, Bishop & Barnard. The two projects with which Jeckyll was connected which have brought him lasting fame were the woodwork for Whistler's Peacock Room, designed for F R Leyland in 1877, the epitome of rich, decorative 'Japonisme', and the furniture for the London house of Alexander Ionides, one of the leading patrons of the Aesthetic movement. Jeckyll's metalwork shows that he had absorbed the decorative aspects of Japanese design. Some of the roundels in the brass and iron fireplaces closely resemble tsuba (sword-guards). An earlier commission than the two previously mentioned, the furniture for Heath Old Hall, Wakefield, designed and executed from 1866 to 1870, shows that, even at this early date, Jeckyll was using Japanese patterns in relief furniture of fairly traditional shape.

William Morris and the Arts and Crafts Movement

The firm of Morris, Marshall, Faulkner & Company was founded in 1861. William Morris (1834–1896) had been articled to the architect G E Street in 1855, where he met Philip Webb (1831–1915), who was to become one of the most important designers for Morris's firm. Prior to entering Street's practice, Morris had been at Exeter College, Oxford, where he had met another significant figure in the history of the firm, Edward Burne-Jones (1833–1898). Through this latter friendship, Morris was brought into contact with two leading members of the Pre-Raphaelite Brotherhood, Dante Gabriel Rossetti and William Holman Hunt.

In essence, Morris's ideas about the quality of design, and his philosophy of improvement, were not much different from those of other leading Victorian figures. He defined two types of furniture, one being 'necessary . . . workaday . . . simple to the last degree' and the other 'state furniture . . . sideboards, cabinets and the like . . . as elegant and elaborate as we can with carving or inlaying or painting'.

Morris's firm first showed its work publicly at the International Exhibition in London in 1862. The pieces exhibited fell into Morris's second category—extraordinary, elaborate, richly painted objects. The King Renée Cabinet, designed by the Gothic architect

Above: Walnut cabinet designed by William Godwin in 1876 for his own use. The four panels of carved boxwood inset into the upright drawers, and the ivory handles, are of Japanese workmanship and were probably purchased by Godwin from Liberty's. (Victoria & Albert Museum, London)

J P Seddon, was painted with imaginary scenes of *The Honeymoon of King Renée*, based on Walter Scott's *Anna von Geierstein*. The artists who undertook this scheme were Ford Madox Brown, Edward Burne-Jones, Dante Gabriel Rossetti and William Morris himself (Morris, it should be emphasized, is not known to have actually designed any furniture). In 1858, Burne-Jones painted the Chaucer cabinet with scenes from *The Prioress's Tale* and in 1861, two further examples, the Chess Player Cabinet and The Saint George Cabinet, the latter painted by Morris, were made by the firm.

Other pieces produced at this early date are more in keeping with the simple idealism which lay behind Morris's socialist principles. As early as 1857, Holman Hunt had made a simple oak table. He designed pieces for the firm in plain shapes, and is credited with the introduction of a green stain which was the sole decoration used on oak tables designed by Philip Webb. Webb also designed the so-called 'Morris' chairs, simple pieces based on rush-seated Sussex chairs.

A report on the Manchester Jubilee Exhibition of 1887 remarked with reference to Morris & Company '. . . it requires a long purse to live up to the higher phases of Morrisean taste . . . .' This comment was certainly true of many of the firm's productions; in general, their clients were drawn from the aristocracy and the rich merchant classes; between 1868 and 1890 they undertook decorative schemes at St James's Palace, at 1 Palace Green for the Earl of Carlisle, at 1 Holland Park for Alexander Alexander Ionides, at Rounton Grange, Northallerton for Sir Lowthian Bell, at Clouds, East Knoyle for the Hon. Percy Scawne Wyndham and at Stanmore Hall for W D'Arcy. Sadly, none of these interiors has survived, but the list makes the point that while Morris may have preached the doctrine of art for everyone, the practical consequence of his idealistic revolt against the machine age was that none but the very rich could afford his work, and, except for the well-educated upper classes, few could appreciate his lofty aestheticism.

The firm began production in 1862 at 8 Red Lion Square, London, moving in 1865 to 26 Queen Square. In 1875, the firm's name was changed to Morris & Company, and two years later showrooms were opened in Oxford Street. In 1881, the workshops were transferred to Merton Abbey, and in 1890, the Pimlico cabinet-making workshops of Holland & Company were taken over. In 1890, George Jack, who had entered Philip Webb's architectural practice in 1880, became chief furniture designer and in 1896, following Morris's death, the designer William A S Benson, who with Morris's encouragement had set up his own workshop in Hammersmith to produce metalwork, became chairman of the firm. Another designer, Mervyn McCartney, produced work for Morris & Company at this time, reverting to eighteenth-century taste. The later pieces were decorated with elaborate marquetry and employed a variety of woods.

Under Morris's influence, the 1880s and 1890s saw the founding of numerous craft guilds and small private bodies dedicated to hand-built furniture and artifacts. One of the first of these was the Century Guild, founded in 1882 by A H Mackmurdo (1851–1942). Typically, it announced its aim as being 'to render all branches of the arts the sphere no longer of the tradesman but of the artist. It would restore building, decoration, glass-painting, pottery, wood-carving and metal to their right place beside painting and sculpture.' Although neither Mackmurdo himself, nor any of the other designers associated with this venture, notably Selwyn Image, Herbert Percy Horne or Clement J Heaton, ever claimed allegiance to that movement which 18 years after the founding of the Guild was to become known as Art Nouveau, at least one of their contemporaries, the designer Reginald Blomfield, pointed out in the *Magazine of Art* of 1904 that many of the stylistic roots could be found in the Century Guild's work: '. . . it [Art Nouveau] started in England some 20 years ago, with the ingenious experiments of

Left: Cabinet in rosewood inlaid with purplewood and ebony, with light metal ('oldsilver') mounts designed by William A S Benson and made by Morris & Company after 1896. Although superbly made, the ornateness and commercialism of this piece is in contrast to the Morris ethos. (Victoria & Albert Museum, London)

Right: William Morris's bedroom, Kelmscott Manor, Oxfordshire. The ornate mediaevalism of this interior typifies Morris's approach to art and design. The bed is sixteenth century, but the embroidery is by Janey and May Morris. The curtains are 'Vine' pattern and the wallpaper 'Willow', both first produced in 1874. (Kelmscott Manor, Oxfordshire)

Exhibition, at the same time decorating the interior of Pownell Hall, Cheshire, for Henry Boddington. He also designed wallpapers for Jeffry's and fabrics for Wardle's.

The Queen Anne style had been popularized in the 1860s by the architect Richard Norman Shaw who had been a pupil of G E Street. Shaw designed Gothic furniture in the early 1860s, and had later become a very successful architect as well as a designer of fabrics and wallpapers for a number of different firms. Shaw's most famous piece of furniture, indeed the only one that can be attributed to him with absolute certainty and a landmark in the development of nineteenth-century Gothic, is a combined writing-desk and bookcase which he designed in 1861 and which was executed for him by the sculptor James Forsyth.

As we said earlier, the founding of the Century Guild in 1882 was the first of many such events, which attempted to perpetuate the spirit of William Morris and John Ruskin. In 1883, pupils of Norman Shaw founded the St George's Art Guild, followed in 1884 by the founding of the Art Workers' Guild and in 1886 by the Art Workers' Guild of Liverpool. In 1888, the same year as the Arts and Crafts Exhibition Society showed its members' work for the first time, the most famous of these groups, the Guild of Handicrafts, was founded by C R Ashbee.

two young architects [Mackmurdo and Horne] with an uncommon share of eccentric ability, who for the first time revealed the numerous possibilities of the "swirl" and the "blob".' Certainly the famous title page of *Wren's City Churches*, or the equally extraordinary chair-back of approximately the same date are prophetic of the 'whiplash' style prevalent on the Continent a few years later but never fully developed in England.

In general, Mackmurdo's significance in nineteenth-century design is a result of his progressive attitude to the aesthetics of his day, rather than to any particular brilliance as a designer. Most of his furniture, in satinwood decorated with inlay, with carved ornament by Herbert Horne, painted panels by Selwyn Image, and hinges by Bernard Creswick, was made by the two firms of Goodall & Company of Manchester and Wilkinson's of Bond Street. Mackmurdo sought his inspiration in past styles, predominantly those of the Italian Renaissance and Queen Anne. His founding of the Century Guild in 1882 was followed by commissions to design a music-room for the International Health Exhibition of 1884, and for a stand with furniture for a firm of tobacco importers, Cope Bros, at the Liverpool International Exhibition of 1886. In 1887, he designed the entrance hall for the Manchester Jubilee

The best known and most gifted designer
connected with the Art Workers' Guild was
Charles Francis Annesley Voysey (1857–1941).
Not surprisingly, he had, like most of his
contemporaries, been articled to a Gothic
architect, in his case J P Seddon. He had set
up his own practice, and with the advice of
his friend, Mackmurdo, designed wallpapers
and fabrics. In 1884, he was a founder member
of the Art Workers' Guild. It is important to
emphasize that Mackmurdo remained the
greatest single influence on his style, and, like
Mackmurdo, Voysey is considered one of the
English designers who pioneered that style
which became known internationally as Art
Nouveau. His own attitude to this distinction
remained ambivalent. He wrote in the
Magazine of Art in 1904: 'I think the condition
which has made Art Nouveau possible is a
distinctly healthy development, but at the
same time the manifestation of it is distinctly
unhealthy and revolting.'

Voysey's wallpapers, such as *Cereus* (1886),
Water Snake (c.1890), *Deer and Trees* (1908),
and chintz patterns such as *Trees and Birds*
(1895), were obviously close in feel, though
flatter and more decorative, to those of
William Morris. They were known widely, as
were Voysey's architecture and designs for
furniture and metalwork, in the rest of
Europe and the United States, having con-

siderable influence on many designers. His
furniture and metalwork, the former usually
of oak and the latter of copper and brass,
display a similar use of light, sinuous shapes,
particularly tree and heart motifs. Voysey
was opposed totally to the somewhat drab
aspects of the Aesthetic movement, combining
his use of delicate motifs with an airy
functionalism considerably before its time.

The Guild of Handicrafts, founded by
Charles Robert Ashbee in 1888 with a capital
of £50, was the organization which was, and
remained, truest to Morris's ideals of honest
workmen producing honest work by hand, to
the spiritual and physical well-being of the
community. In 1890, the Guild leased 'Essex
House' in London's East End and in 1902
moved to the village of Chipping Campden in
the Cotswolds, a move which many other
craftsmen followed and which makes this area
of Gloucestershire still active today in many
branches of the applied arts. The Guild itself
went into voluntary liquidation in 1908,
although many of the craftsmen carried on
working independently, and produced metalwork based on Ashbee's designs until well
into the 1930s.

The Guild's most famous product was
unquestionably metalwork, more specifically
silver. It did produce some furniture, in a
somewhat Gothic English-country-furniture-

via-William Morris style. The principal cabinet-maker employed by the Guild was J W Pyment, and much of the furniture is decorated with embossed leatherwork by Statia Power. More important was the group of pieces the Guild made to the designs of Mackay Hugh Baillie Scott. Baillie Scott had been active as an architect and interior designer in the Isle of Man since 1887, having previously been articled to an architect. In 1898, he was commissioned to furnish the interior of the Grand Duke of Hesse's Palace at Darmstadt, one of the focal points of the Art Nouveau movement in northern Europe, and the most important commission received by any English designer of this period. In terms of his reputation, it placed Baillie Scott on a level with Walter Crane, Voysey and Mackintosh as one of those who had most impact on German and Austrian designers. The furniture and metalwork was executed by the Guild of Handicrafts which itself became revered among German designers.

Baillie Scott, like Voysey, is seen as one of the most important English contributors to the Art Nouveau style; furniture designed by Baillie Scott after the Darmstadt commission and made by J P White of the Pygtle Works, Bedford, in mahogany or oak and inlaid with contrasting woods and metals, is certainly closer in the style of its surface decoration to Continental Art Nouveau furniture than most English designs of this period. In collaboration with Broadwood's,

Baillie Scott designed many 'Manx' pianos, small upright pieces, usually with a plain oak case decorated with elaborate and beautifully designed burnished steel and brass fittings.

The influence of the High Victorian Gothic movement was strong in the firm of Kenton & Company which was founded in 1890 by a number of young architects. Ernest Barnsley and Ernest William Gimson had been pupils of John Dando Sedding, and Sidney Barnsley and Alfred Powell had been pupils of Richard Norman Shaw, while William Richard Lethaby had been principal assistant in Shaw's office. Both Sedding and Shaw were, like Philip Webb and William Morris, pupils of G E Street. These four, together with Mervyn McCartney and Reginald Blomfield, formed Kenton & Company, each putting up £100. They employed four craftsmen but despite producing some splendid pieces, the venture failed in 1892. Lethaby became, with the sculptor George Frampton, first principal of the London County Council Central School of Arts. Gimson and the Barnsleys moved to the Cotswolds. After this move, Sidney Barnsley concentrated mainly on furniture, while Gimson and Ernest Barnsley practised architecture on a wider scale than previously. Nevertheless, Gimson set up a small furniture workshop in Cirencester, which moved to Daneway House, Sapperton, in 1902. Sidney Barnsley designed and made all his own furniture, in a strong rustic style which usually used oak. Gimson designed his pieces only, the manufacture being left to skilled craftsmen, one of whom, Peter Waals, became a cabinet-maker in his own right. Gimson used a variety of rich woods, veneers and inlays. Lethaby's furniture was similar to that of Sidney Barnsley, in oak and firmly rooted in the Arts and Crafts tradition. McCartney and Blomfield were inspired by the eighteenth century, using rosewood and mahogany.

One of the most obvious features of Gimson's furniture is its stylishness, the combination of a beautifully modulated use of form with rich and glowing woods and metal mounts often in silver. In the designs of Charles Rennie Mackintosh (1868–1928), we have the same approach to style, although the use of materials does not play an important part in the work of the Scottish designer, the form always speaking for itself.

Mies van der Rohe described Mackintosh as 'a purifier in the field of architecture', and the influential Art Nouveau dealer and critic Julius Meier-Graefe, in his book *Modern Art* published in 1908, described Mackintosh's interios as 'intellectual chambers garnished for fair souls not for corporeal habitation'. Both descriptions are true; Mackintosh's use of space, incorporating white furniture embellished with sculptural decoration, sinuous lines and inset with panels of pale enamels or stained glass are at once ethereal and functionalist. One uses that last word advisedly for although Mackintosh's work does make a total break with previous design in England, and looks forward to a modern mode of light colours and clean lines, the furniture is frequently by no means 'functional'. It is often poorly made and should be considered more as sculpture.

Mackintosh studied at the Glasgow School of Art under Francis H Newbery. Fellow pupils included Herbert MacNair and the sisters Margaret and Frances Macdonald. Frances married MacNair and in 1900 Margaret married Mackintosh. Mackintosh's early career was remarkably successful. In 1889 he entered the architectural firm of Honeyman & Keppie; in 1896 this firm (although all the designs and plans were Mackintosh's work) won the commission for the new Glasgow School of Art. This magnificent building, unquestionably Mackintosh's finest work, was completed in 1909. In 1897, the designer received the first of his many commissions from Miss Kate Cranston (Mrs John Cochrane) for the decoration of the tearooms in Buchanan Street, Glasgow, the furniture being designed in this instance by George Walton. This was followed in 1901 by the commission to design the interior and furniture for the Ingram Street tearooms, and in 1904 by a similar commission for the Willow tearooms, the last of which was perhaps the most successful of these decorative interiors. From 1902 to 1903, Mackintosh designed and furnished Hill House, Hellensburgh, for Walter W Blackie, the publisher, to whom he had been introduced by Talwin Morris, art director of Blackie's firm and himself the designer of some interesting metalwork in the Mackintosh style. Other important commissions for private houses included Windyhill, Kilmacolm, in 1899, and between 1904 and 1906 the interior of Hous'hill, Nitshill, Glasgow, the home of Miss Cranston. In 1916 and 1917 Mackintosh executed his last important commission, the Bassett-Lowke House in Northampton, but after about 1905 he was ignored by the public and his work was virtually forgotten in Britain.

In his day, Mackintosh's reputation probably stood higher in Germany than it did in his own country. His work was shown widely throughout Europe in the years around 1900, including Vienna in 1900, Turin in 1902, Budapest, Munich, Dresden, Venice and, in 1903, Moscow in an exhibition organized by Sergei Diaghilev. In 1901, he entered the

Left: Upright cabinet in dark stained oak, with stained glass and mother-of-pearl insets, designed by Charles Rennie Mackintosh in about 1905. The geometric quality of the Scottish designer's furniture was the one feature which impressed designers in Austria and Germany.

exhibition organized by Zeitschrift für Innen-Dekoration of Darmstadt, called Haus eines Kunstfreunds. As a result, Mackintosh's work had a considerable influence upon many of the leading northern European designers and architects, including Hoffmann, Olbrich and Behrens in Germany and Austria, the De Stijl group in Holland, and Frank Lloyd Wright in the United States. His style contrasts with the hot, florid forms of French Art Nouveau, but is nevertheless an important part of that movement, rooted in symbolism, which the Germans called Jugendstil.

Most of Mackintosh's furniture is of oak, but some of the later pieces — for instance a table commissioned by W P Douglas in 1912 — were made by the firm of Guthrie & Wells of Glasgow in mahogany. The furniture for the Basset-Lowke House is in both mahogany and ebonized wood, while the fittings for the Glasgow School of Art are in Baltic pine. After 1918, Mackintosh designed some textiles but these were not well received. He also designed carpets for some of his interiors, these being in a style far in advance of its time.

Another leading designer of furniture in Glasgow was George Walton (1867–1903), the brother of the painter, E W Walton. George set up a business as an interior decorator in Glasgow in 1888, and between 1896 and 1897, designed the furniture of Miss Cranston's Buchanan Street tearooms, which was followed in 1897 by a commission to design the interior and furnishings for a café belonging to William Rowntree in Scarborough. He designed a number of domestic interiors, opened a branch of his business in York in 1898, and in the same year moved his headquarters to London. In 1897 and 1898, he designed 'Clutha' glass for the Glasgow firm of James Couper & Sons, as did Christopher Dresser. In 1897, he met George Davison, head of the European division of Kodak and designed a chain of Kodak shops throughout Britain, Belgium, Italy and Austria. His furniture, which comes in a variety of woods including walnut, birchwood, mahogany and ash, is simple in style, close to the English Arts and Crafts tradition, but influenced by Mackintosh. Walton also designed some furniture for the London store of Liberty's.

English furniture in the pure Art Nouveau style, with whiplash lines and flowery inlay, is mainly commercial, produced by such

251

firms as Liberty's and J S Henry. E G Punnett designed good quality pieces for these firms as well as for another firm of commercial cabinet-makers, William Birch. Punnett's pieces are in a geometric style derived from Scottish and Austrian examples. The furniture of the Scottish designers E A Taylor and George Logan, usually in mahogany and often inlaid, is again greatly influenced by Mackintosh. In many English pieces of this type, there is a profusion of inlay — marquetry panels, pewter, mother-of-pearl, enamel, stained glass, and repoussé copper panels. Although some of it is extremely elegant and of fine quality, the majority is obviously of cheap manufacture in a much debased style. Liberty's, which had been founded by Arthur Lasenby Liberty in 1875, commissioned a number of outstanding designers including George Walton, Lindsay Butterfield, Walter Crane, Voysey and Archibald Knox. Their furniture, of which the most famous example is probably the Thebes stool, based on an Egyptian original and first marketed in 1884, is, however, not of the same high level of artistic excellence as their metalwork and fabrics. Ambrose Heal, a member of the Heal furnishing family, designed some excellent

pieces with inlaid metal and wood of contrasting colours.

New Design in the United States

In the United States of America, the development of new design at the end of the nineteenth century followed the same stylistic paths as in Britain but with considerable chronological elision. Most of the various styles which had taken some 50 years to mature in England and Scotland were telescoped into roughly 20 years between 1890 and 1910 in the United States. The influence in the three predominant areas of progressive aesthetics in America — New England, which for the purposes of this essay is taken to include New York State, the Middle West, and the West Coast — was strongly English, with the protagonists of the Arts and Crafts movement, William Morris, Voysey and Ashbee having the greatest impact. Many of the leading American designers had visited England and some of the foremost English designers, including for instance C R Ashbee and Walter Crane, visited America, and some of them finally settled there.

On the Eastern seaboard, the influence of the Gothic revival and the Aesthetic movement was definite but muted. At least one designer, Isaac Scott, made good pieces in walnut in a style closely based on Pugin's, but this work was done in the 1870s, at a time when it would have been anachronistic in England. More interesting is the work of the Herter Brothers of New York, led by Christian Herter, and Henry Hobson Richardson, who worked in the same city. The Herter Brothers' pieces are of very fine quality, usually in ebonized cherry wood, with gilding and marquetry inlay. As with similar furniture in England, the Herter Brothers' work shows a deep awareness of Japanese design.

Henry Hobson Richardson's work was influenced by Richard Norman Shaw, Bruce Talbert and Charles Eastlake. He designed good pieces, usually in oak, with an element of Gothic and Queen Anne. After his death, his firm was taken over by Charles A Coolidge who continued in the same style. One of his major commissions was to furnish the Chicago residence of John J Glessner who was also a patron of Isaac Scott. The Coolidge furniture, in oak, was made by the Boston firm of A H Davenport.

Unquestionably, the most important development was the rise of a mature Arts and Crafts school of furniture-makers and craftsmen, a development which followed the founding of the Boston Arts and Crafts Society in 1897. A number of designers are associated with this movement in the Eastern states, the best known of whom are Elbert Hubbard and Gustav Stickley.

253

Hubbard (1856–1915) started his professional life in the somewhat unpromising capacity of soap salesman. His transition from this occupation to a leading member of the American Arts and Crafts movement was extraordinarily swift, for in 1893 he was a soap salesman and in 1895 he was the publisher of an edition of *The Song of Songs* printed on his own press, modelled on William Morris's Kelmscott press. This was the first work of Hubbard's newly named Roycroft works of East Aurora, New York; needless to say, he had visited England in 1894 and met Morris. The production of books led to that of leather bindings, which in turn led to the foundation of a general workshop for hand-made leather goods, and in 1901, the first furniture was made, mostly in oak, but occasionally in mahogany, and

Left: Walnut and inlaid bookcase designed by Isaac E Scott in 1875. Commissioned by Mr and Mrs John G Glessner of Chicago, this is one of the most impressive American examples of neo-Gothic furniture. Influenced by the English Gothic Revival and by Charles Eastlake it shows none of the provincialism associated with the early arts and crafts movement in the United States. (Chicago School of Architecture Foundation)

tamped with Hubbard's own orb and cross
mark.

Hubbard's idea of furniture was that category which Morris termed 'workaday' and
simple'; Hubbard described his work as
severe and rarely beautiful' and in the recent
exhibition catalogue of the Arts and Crafts
movement in America, the designer is referred
to as having 'popularized a sincere, if somewhat plebeian, version of the ideals of William
Morris'. He employed a number of skilled
designers, including David Hunter, who had
visited Austria and was impressed by the work
being done in Vienna. Hubbard's chief metalwork designer, Karl Kripp, was in fact a
Viennese who brought a touch of Austrian
austerity to the factory's products in copper,
brass and other metals.

Gustav Stickley (1857–1942) must be considered the single most important figure in
the development of new approaches to design
in the United States. One of six brothers, he,
and four of his family, produced good quality
furniture in the Arts and Crafts style but
more significantly, between 1901 and 1916,
he edited the *Craftsman*, the magazine which
more than any other propagated the ideas of
the Arts and Crafts movement throughout
America. Thus Stickley's influence in the
Mid-West and on the West Coast was about as
strong as it was in his own state of New York.
Trained as a stonemason, Stickley started
making furniture with his uncles and other
relatives in the 1880s. In 1898, he founded the
Gustav Stickley Company in Eastwood, Syracuse, New York; he employed two of his
brothers, Leopold and J G Stickley, both of
whom left in 1900 and set up a company of
their own at nearby Fayetteville making furniture closely based on that of their brother.
Through the pages of his magazine, Stickley
was the most vocal of all the progressive
designers active in the United States. His
furniture is almost always of oak, since he
felt that this wood was above all others '. . .
adapted to the massive simplicity of construction'; most pieces are stamped with the
Stickley motto *Als Ik Kan* (All I Can), a
suitable mediaeval boast borrowed from Jan
van Eyck via William Morris. Stickley was
not a good businessman and in 1915 his firm
went bankrupt, the *Craftsman* ceasing publication the following year. Ironically, Leopold
and J G Stickley showed a greater measure of
adaptability to public demand and were in a
position to take over their brother's workshops; the re-organized firm was called the
Stickley Manufacturing Company Inc., and
still exists today.

Surprisingly, the designer who received the
most attention outside the United States was
Charles Rohlfs. Rohlfs opened a workshop in
Buffalo in 1890, employing eight workmen.
His style was simple and functional, but the

work was of very high quality and, unlike
other purist Arts and Crafts designers, he
decorated the strong outlines of his oak
furniture with delicate carving and marquetry
inlays, this work being executed by one of his
craftsmen, George Thiele. It has been said
that this ornament was largely suggested by
Sullivan's exterior decoration for the Buffalo
Guaranty Insurance Building. Rohlfs
exhibited a substantial quantity of his furniture at the Turin exhibition of 1902; the
German, Austrian and English critics were
very enthusiastic, and the American was
elected a member of the Royal Society of Arts
in London. He was also commissioned to
provide some furniture for Buckingham Palace. His mark on furniture is an 'R' within the
rectangular frame of a wood saw.

Whereas the Arts and Crafts movement in
the East faded out during the First World
War, that in the Middle West, centred in
Chicago, led to one of the most significant
architectural movements of the twentieth
century, the Prairie School. The reason for
this is self-evident. Chicago produced two
men of outstanding genius, Louis H Sullivan
(1856–1924) and his one-time employee Frank
Lloyd Wright (1867–1959), around whom the
Prairie School was centred and who gave it
impetus and strength. Without Wright, the
Arts and Crafts movement in Chicago would
probably have suffered the same fate as in
New York.

*Below: Oak settle with
leather cushions designed
by Gustav Stickley and
made in the Craftsman
Workshops, Syracuse, New
York, in about 1908. This
piece first appeared in
Stickley's catalogue of 1909
priced at US $50. It is
interesting to compare its
uncompromising
rectilinearity with the
Frank Lloyd Wright
library table. Nothing
could demonstrate more
clearly the lack of real
imagination apparent in
the majority of East Coast
arts and crafts design.
(Art Institute of Chicago.
Gift of Mr and Mrs John J
Evans Jnr)*

The period between 1895 and 1905 was an
exciting one for designers in the Middle West.
In the former year, the Chalk and Chisel Club
was founded — later the Minneapolis Arts and
Crafts Society — arguably the first organization of its kind in the United States. This was
followed by the Chicago Arts and Crafts
Society in 1897, the Industrial Art League in
1899, the Society of Arts and Crafts of Grand
Rapids, Michigan, in 1902 and the William

255

*Right: Mahogany and
brass long-case clock
designed by George Grant
Elmslie in 1912. Standing
7 feet 4 inches high (nearly
2¼ metres), this is one of
eight pieces commissioned
from the firm of Purcell,
Feick and Elmslie by Henry
B Babson of Riverside,
Chicago. Elmslie had
designed Babson's house in
1907 while working for
Louis Sullivan. The style
of this piece, especially the
finials, is typical of Prairie
School work and is strongly
influenced by Frank
Lloyd Wright. The face-
plate was made and
engraved by Kristian
Schneider and the hands
were made by Robert
Jarvie of Chicago; the
nine-chime movement was
imported from Germany.
(Art Institute of Chicago)*

Morris Society of Chicago, which was founded by an Englishman, Joseph Twyman, in 1903. Twyman was a critic and apologist for the English Arts and Crafts movement, lecturing extensively in Chicago and the Mid-West on Morris and his followers. Walter Crane lectured at the Art Institute of Chicago in 1892, and Ashbee visited Chicago twice; in 1911 he wrote the introduction for a volume of Frank Lloyd Wright's work published in Germany. A number of Chicagoans visited England, and fabrics, wallpapers and furniture by Morris & Company were sold in the major Chicago department stores.

The style and quality of the Prairie School was formed in the late 1880s and early 1890s. The two architects, Louis H Sullivan and J S Silsbee, taught a number of brilliant students and employed a young generation of draughtsmen and designers, which included Frank Lloyd Wright, George Grant Elmslie, Louis J Millet, George L Healey and George Washington Maher. Sullivan had been trained at the Massachusetts Institute of Technology (MIT) and the Ecole des Beaux Arts in Paris. He settled in Chicago in 1875 and formed an architectural practice with Dankmar Adler. Louis Sullivan's conception of bold, stylized ornament as an integral part of his buildings was to have a profound effect on the young designers who worked in his office, and through whom his ideas were carried out. Louis Millet, who was himself trained at the Ecole des Beaux Arts, and George Healey were in partnership from 1881 to 1899, and from 1890 to 1918 Millet was the head of the Decorative Design department at the Art Institute of Chicago.

The characteristic which binds together George Grant Elmslie, George Washington Maher and Frank Lloyd Wright was just this conception of the building and its interior as 'proceeding from main motif to minor motifs, interrelating and to the last terminal all of a piece' and Frank Lloyd Wright, in a famous passage from *In the Cause of Architecture* of 1908, wrote: 'The most truly satisfactory apartments are those in which most of all the furniture is built as a part of the original scheme. The whole must always be considered as an integral unit.' In part, this idea sprang from the notion of the furniture extending and reflecting the lines of the building, and thus emphasizing its essential features but, especially in the case of Lloyd Wright, the concept of the structural importance of the furniture in relation to the whole unit sprang from a deep love and understanding of Japanese art and design, which he had seen for himself when he visited Japan in 1905.

Elmslie was born in Scotland, emigrating to the United States in 1884. In 1887, he entered the office of J S Silsbee, where he met Frank Lloyd Wright and Maher. He moved to the rm Adler & Sullivan two years later, becoming chief designer in 1895. He opened his own practice in partnership with William Gray Purcell and George Feick in 1909, and after Feick's death in 1913, he and Purcell carried n until 1922. Elmslie did not design furniture or all of his interiors, only for the most mportant ones. His designs were less rectilinear and geometric than those of Lloyd Wright, his ornament being more organic and loser in style to that of Sullivan. Most of his urniture is in oak, but occasionally he made nore elaborate pieces in different woods. In 907, he designed the Henry B Babson house n Riverside, Illinois, the furniture being imple and in oak. Five years later, however, vhen he had his own practice, he designed a urther group of furniture for the Babson Iouse in mahogany, including the famous ong-case 'Grandfather' clock now in the arts Institute of Chicago. It is interesting to ote that Babson also owned furniture by justav Stickley.

After a short period in the office of J S ilsbee, George Washington Maher started is own practice in 1888. He travelled to Jurope in 1892 and remained there for five ears, absorbing the major stylistic movenents in England, France, Austria and jermany. On his return to the United States e received a number of important commisions for private residences, the significant haracteristic of which was his conception of he interiors based on a single organic theme. Iis interior for the John Farson house in Oak 'ark (1897) was based on the theme of the lion, hat of the James A Patten House in Evanston 1901) was based on the thistle, while the ollyhock was the theme used for the Harry Lubens house, Glencoe (1902–3). The use of hese thematic designs, which extended hrough the furniture and fabrics used in the ouse, was one way of achieving that sense of nity the Chicago designers required. In 1908, Maher designed the Ernest Magerstadt house, n which the furniture is more geometric and he organic designs more schematic, showing he influence of Frank Lloyd Wright.

After a period in the office of J S Silsbee, 'rank Lloyd Wright became chief draughtsan in the firm of Adler & Sullivan in 1888, emaining in this capacity until 1893. Two of he earliest groups of furniture Lloyd Wright esigned were for his own house in 1895 and or the Isidore Heller house in Chicago in bout 1897. Between 1897 and 1908, when he uilt and designed the interiors of two of his reatest works, the Frederick C Robie house nd the Ray W Evans house, both in Chicago, Vright moved away from the fluid, organic rnament of Sullivan to a strictly geometric, unctional style based on rectangles, slats and at surfaces. As the Princeton Arts and Crafts atalogue remarked, Lloyd Wright's furni-

ture 'must be regarded as architectural sculpture rather than merely utilitarian objects — a part of a larger sculptural whole'.

Not surprisingly, the West Coast of America was a little behind the mid-West and the Eastern states in its appreciation of the Arts and Crafts movement, and the craftsmen and designers who were its main practitioners in California were active between about 1900 and 1910. It would be true to say that, in the regions we have discussed so far, the English style was predominant — at least initially, but on the West Coast, influences from Chicago and New York were probably more decisive. In 1878, the Herter Brothers of New York had designed the interior of the Mark Hopkins house on Nob Hill, San Francisco, and the firm's representative, Edward F Searles, came to San Francisco, married Hopkins' widow and subsequently donated the house to the University of California, when it became the Mark Hopkins Institute of Art. Irving Gill, who had worked in Sullivan's office, settled in San Diego in 1893, the architect Ellsworth Storey of Chicago came to live in Seattle in 1903, George Wharton James, who had been associate editor of Stickley's *Craftsman* in 1904, settled in Los Angeles and in 1909 published the short-lived *Arroyo Craftsman* (only one edition appeared). In 1909, Frank Lloyd Wright undertook his first commission on the West Coast, the George C Stewart house at Montecito.

Below: Oak Library table designed by Frank Lloyd Wright. Made for the Ray W Evans house in Chicago in 1908, this piece is exactly contemporaneous with the stylistically similar furniture of the Frederick C Robie house, also in Chicago. The open geometricity of Wright's style at this time is almost entirely without precedent, although like Godwin's buffet, it owes much to Japanese architecture and design. (Art Institute of Chicago)

The most important firm of craftsmen on the West Coast was Greene & Greene of Pasadena. The brothers Charles Sumner Greene and Henry Mather Greene were born in Cincinnati, and studied architecture at MIT. They would, thus, have been aware of the new developments in aesthetics both in their native city, the centre of the Art Ceramic movement in the United States, and in New England. The Greenes moved to Pasadena in 1893 and in 1901 Charles went to Europe. He was influenced by a strange combination of styles including the English Arts and Crafts movement, Swiss chalet architecture, Japanese designs and the domestic Mission style of architecture, as found in the cool white-walled Mission houses of Spanish America.

In just two years, between 1907 and 1909, the brothers created their major work, four houses in and around Pasadena, for Robert C Blacker, David B Gamble, Charles M Pratt in Ojai Valley, and William R Thorsens in Berkeley. The furniture in Thorsens' house was made by a Scandinavian craftsman in Peter Hall's workshop in Pasadena, and the furniture of all four houses, usually in walnut or teak and inlaid with ebony, fruitwood and semi-precious stones, gave the Greenes a reputation which spread far beyond the boundaries of California. Ashbee visited the state in 1909, and wrote in his memoirs:
'I think C Sumner Greene's work beautiful; among the best there is in this country. Like Lloyd Wright, the spell of Japan is on him, he feels the beauty and makes magic out of the horizontal line, but there is in his work more tenderness, more subtlety, more self-effacement than in Wright's work. It is more refined and has more repose. Perhaps it loses in strength, perhaps it is California that speaks rather than Illinois, . . . as work it is, so far as the interiors go, more sympathetic to me.'

Following the disastrous earthquakes in California in 1906, which destroyed vast areas of building, there was great scope for new ideas in architecture and furniture design. In 1906, the architects Lucia Mathews and her husband Arthur Frank Mathews opened their furniture shop in San Francisco, which lasted until about 1920. Their pieces are in a variety of woods — oak, mahogany, walnut, beech — and are decorated with painted or carved ornament, the former being largely the work of Lucia Mathews herself. The shop, which employed between 20 and 50 craftsmen at a time, undertook both large interior schemes and single commissioned pieces. The style of decoration was influenced by English Arts and Crafts design, but also by French Symbolism and oriental art.

Art Nouveau

In the period between 1890 and 1910, we see the development in Europe of a style which has become known uniformly as Art Nouveau. In fact, this is a term which has been much abused and taken for granted. In strictly historical terms, the *Maison de l'Art Nouveau* was a shop founded in Paris in December 1895 by a dealer-entrepreneur called Samuel Bing. The shop showed work by young, mainly French, designers, in many different media — glassware, furniture, metalwork, prints,

Right: Upright cabinet by Eugène Gaillard, exhibited by Samuel Bing at the Paris, Exposition Universelle of 1900. Gaillard was inspired by French furniture of the Louis Quinze period. This example is of exceptional quality, with well-chiselled bronze fittings following the flowing lines of the wood. (Danske Kunstindustrimuseet, Copenhagen)

Left: Gilt-wood and upholstered sofa designed by Georges de Feure for Samuel Bing and included by the latter in his display at the 1900 Paris Exposition Universelle. Obviously inspired by Louis Quinze furniture, de Feure incorporated rhythmic Art Nouveau forms without relieving the piece of its essential impracticality. (Danske Kunstindustrimuseet, Copenhagen)

258

paintings, ceramics — as well as selling newly imported work from the Far East. The shop was similar to Liberty's in London, although on a smaller and more specialized scale. Bing himself later expressed surprise that his shop should have given its name to a stylistic movement. He wrote: 'At its birth Art Nouveau had no pretensions to being a generic term. It was simply the name of an establishment opened as a rallying point for youth keen to show their modern approach.' And in 1896, the French critic Victor Champier wrote: 'Art Nouveau has only one thing against it; its unduly pretentious precision. It simply indicates an effort.'

In England, the term was, and is still, used largely to describe stylistic developments during the period we have indicated in Europe, and more specifically, France. In Germany, the style is known as *Jugendstil*, in Austria, *Sezessionstil*, in Catalan *Modernista* or *Arte Joven* and in Italy, the London store Liberty gave its name to *Il Stile Liberty*. It is interesting to note that the French periodical *L'Ameublement*, with the furniture of Mackmurdo, Baillie Scott and Voysey in mind, referred to certain characteristics of new furniture design as the *Genre Anglais*. All this might imply that every country was aware of a uniform style but was giving it a different name. In fact, the reverse was true. Every country was indeed aware that the end of the nineteenth century saw a renaissance of artistic ideas, which they naturally wished to characterize by a unifying term but they were also aware of differences. The Austrians and Germans, tied by historic, geographic and linguistic bonds, developed a very similar style, the main characteristic of which is geometricity. They had little apparent sympathy or contact with developments in Paris or Nancy, while France herself maintained an historically consistent insularity towards the development of new styles.

The term Art Nouveau, therefore, can be understood in two ways. It can either be taken as a generic expression of a widespread renewal of artistic ideas in Europe at the end of the nineteenth century, without necessarily implying a stylistic unity, or it can be taken to mean a specifically French and Belgian style of decorative design, characterized by its flowing organic forms, swirls, blobs and whiplash motifs. It is not justifiable historically to use the term Art Nouveau to describe a uniform late nineteenth-, early twentieth-century style in the decorative arts, since it is obvious that no such unified style actually existed. In England and the United States, Art Nouveau in the French style was hardly seen at all.

In France, the major designers of Art Nouveau furniture were Eugène Gaillard, Eugène Vallin, Louis Majorelle, Alexandre

Left: Writing-desk in oak and fruitwood marquetry designed by Emile Gallé of Nancy. Exhibited in the Paris Exposition Universelle of 1900, this piece is a typical mixture of French eighteenth-century forms and late nineteenth-century symbolism. The lid bears an inlaid inscription from a poem by Baudelaire.

Right: Reconstruction of the Pavilion of the Union Centrale des Arts Décoratifs designed by Georges Hoentschell for the 1900 Paris Exposition Universelle. The furniture is by Louis Majorelle and the large painting, L'Ile Heureuse, is by Albert Besnard. (Musée des Arts Décoratifs, Paris)

Charpentier, Emile Gallé, Georges de Feure, Hector Guimard, Georges Hoentschell, Rupert Carabin, Eugène Colonna and Tony and Pierre Selmersheim. There were two distinctive groups of designers, those working with Gallé at Nancy and those who worked in Paris, revolving around Bing. It should not be thought, however, that the new style was accepted in French intellectual circles; in describing the Salon d'Art Nouveau in 1895, Edmond de Goncourt wrote about the 'delirious rantings of ugliness'.

The School of Nancy numbered among its adherents Emile Gallé, Louis Majorelle, Eugène Gaillard and Eugène Vallin. Their work is characterized by a rich use of floral and pictorial marquetry, but is often somewhat commercially made, which reflects adversely on the quality. Also, as several critics have pointed out, the style of the furniture is not particularly original, being closely modelled on Louis Quinze and early Louis Seize Rococo. Much of the naturalism of the Ecole de Nancy's imagery derives from the asymmetrical quality of Japanese art, which influenced French designers in other areas of the applied arts, combined especially in Gallé's case with an affinity with the French Symbolist movement. Maurice Rheims, in his book on Art Nouveau, quotes a long passage written by Gallé to accompany a piece of his furniture made in 1902, called 'Autumn Pathways'. It gives a picture of the inspiration behind much of the School of Nancy's work: '. . . The sense of decoration in this sideboard is extensively based on the deliberate con-

trast between the representation of tangible things and the vision of certain lofty realities, those mysteries which we desire and must divine if we can . . . *Patina*! I have emphasized the antithesis between realistic representation and symbolic adornment by applying a waxy patina only in certain places, where the relief has been heightened by the use of encaustic. Elsewhere, on the other hand, I have taken a daring course which is without precedent in the cabinetmaker's art; the surface of the wood has been left in its natural virgin state without varnish or patina.'

Right: Cabinet designed by Hector Guimard, part of a suite executed in 1900. The rhythmic asymmetry of this piece, derived in part from Japanese naturalism, is typical of the best French Art Nouveau of this date. (Musée des Arts Décoratifs, Paris)

Gallé did not in fact design much furniture, although his first pieces date from about 1885. The major furniture-maker of the School of Nancy was Louis Majorelle (1859–1929), who, although producing many pieces in what might be described as the 'standard' Nancy style, designed a number of magnificent pieces in dark, highly polished woods with ormolu mounts which, both stylistically and in terms of quality, may be compared with the finest eighteenth-century craftsmanship. Most of the Nancy School designers used local fruitwoods, though Majorelle favoured mahogany. Two craftsmen who specialized in pictorial marquetry panels designed by Gallé and Majorelle for use in their furniture, as well as for independent decoration, were Victor Prouvé and Jacques Grüber.

The designers who worked for Bing, including Georges de Feure, Georges Hoentschell and Eugène Colonna, were more eclectic and Symbolist in style than those of the Nancy School and had less interest in naturalism. De Feure and Colonna produced delicate, spidery pieces, the former's being predominantly seat furniture in gilt-wood and with delicate, embroidered silk upholstery. They were somewhat impractical pieces, attempting as they did to emulate the ethereal qualities of Symbolist painting and poetry. De Feure's favoured wood was Hungarian ash. Hoentschell's furniture was more substantial, with a heavier use of sculptural ornament. Many of his pieces were in Algerian plane.

Two French designers of great individuality were Hector Guimard and Rupert Carabin. Guimard was primarily an architect who, as a follower of Viollet-le-Duc, was fascinated by the possibilities of exposed skeletal metalwork in buildings. His architecture aside, he is best known for his brilliant use of such apparently unmalleable materials as cast-iron, which he designed to flow with ease and plastic liquidity. He did, however, create a considerable amount of furniture and *boiserie* (panelling) for his interiors, which show the same concern with fluidity and motion. He tended to use dark woods, such as mahogany. Rubert Carabin was possibly the most Symbolist of all French furniture designers. Just as the work of Mackintosh and Frank Lloyd Wright can be experienced as abstract sculpture without any necessary reference to function, so Carabin's furniture goes to the opposite extreme of vertiginous reality, with that overtone of eroticism which is elemental to the French Symbolist movement. The heavy rich mahogany which Carabin used was sculpted with twisted nudes, masks and foliage with a brilliant, almost oily, patina.

A concern with line similar to that of French architects such as Guimard was apparent also in Belgium. Victor Hortá (1861–1946) designed his first major building, the Maison Tassel in

Brussels from 1892 to 1893, of which one contemporary critic wrote, 'no detail derives from anything at all in existence'. This was followed in the 1890s by the Hôtel Solvay, the Hôtel Van Eetevelde, the Hôtel Deprez, the Maison du Peuple, and his own house, now the Musée Hortá. Both the exteriors and interiors of these buildings are allowed to show their iron, skeletal structures which thus became integral parts of the decorative schemes. The rhythmic flow of the designs, drawn from botanical forms, demonstrates at once the influence of Symbolist art and French eighteenth-century ornamentation. The furniture for some of these houses was also designed by Hortá and is frequently petaloid in form. The majority of Belgian Art Nouveau furniture was designed for specific interiors and was not meant to stand in isolation. The woods most frequently used here, initially, beech, birch and oak, with mahogany and citrus woods imported from the Belgian Congo becoming popular in later schemes.

Gustave Serrurier-Bovy (1858–1910) was a furniture designer who used mahogany and who, apart from occasionally employing stencilled patterns, left his furniture unornamented. Significantly, Serrurier-Bovy had a retail furnishing shop in Liège which

Above: Project for a living room by Bellery Desfontaines, dated 1905. Architect, painter and designer, Bellery Desfontaines in this scheme shows an awareness of current English styles, as well as an obvious respect for designers such as Guimard. (Bibliothèque Doucet, Paris)

Left: Carved mahogany three-legged table designed by Hector Guimard in about 1908. All of Guimard's furniture was made as part of an architectural entity yet its quality allows it to stand alone. The carving on this piece typifies the smooth fluidity associated with the architect's use of organic motifs. (Musée des Arts Décoratifs, Paris)

263

showed English Arts and Crafts furniture. In 1900, he designed collapsible pieces in beechwood.

Henry van de Velde (1863–1957), who spent most of his active life in Belgium, designed beautiful flowing furniture often painted white. He exhibited with Mackintosh on at least two occasions and the Scottish designer's influence was strong in his work. This manifested itself in the general shape of van de Velde's early furniture, his use of white enamelling, his unpainted case furniture, which was frequently inset with pale stained glass, and the chairs he designed, with pale upholstery by the Belgian Symbolist painter, Johann Thorn Prikker. Thorn Prikker also designed chairs himself, in an insubstantial, spidery style. Other Belgian designers whose work was shown at the Salons of *La Libre Esthétique* founded by Octave Maus, which showed the applied arts side by side with painting and sculpture, were Paul Hankar, Paul Cauchie, Georges Hobe, Georges Antoine Peereboom and Antoine Pompe.

Designers in Holland, as in Scandinavia, were influenced equally by the functionalist style of Austria and Germany and the more restless Art Nouveau of France and Belgium. The Netherlands architect, H P Berlage executed his major commission, the Amsterdam Stock Exchange, in 1903, and also designed furniture. His ideas were closest to the Arts and Crafts ethic of William Morris, and his theories on the importance of logical construction and integrity of workmanship enjoyed respect and authority. K P C de Basel, who had been apprenticed to a joiner in The Hague, later worked as an architect in Amsterdam; he designed some furniture which, like his architecture, shows the influence of Assyrian and Egyptian art. C A Lion Cachet was a designer whose work shows one of the strongest influences on Dutch Art Nouveau: batik design from Indonesia. He used woods of contrasting colours, and collaborated with two artists, G W Dijsselhof and Theodoor Nieuwenhuis in founding a studio in Amsterdam.

The influence of French and Belgian Art Nouveau, although strong, was not completely dominant in Italy either. In Turin, Pietro Fenoglio was inspired by Victor Hortá, as were a number of other Italian designers whose work nevertheless tends to vulgarize the original purity of the style. In the same city, however, Giacomo Cometti worked in a style based on the furniture of Mackintosh as interpreted by the Wiener Werkstätte and Eugenio Quarti of Milan, whose strong functional pieces, in mahogany inlaid with mother-of-pearl and metal, show the same stylistic roots.

Pietro Fenoglio's buildings in Turin display the search for unity throughout the architecture, interior metalwork, *boiserie* and furniture that can be seen in the work of Victor Hortá. The Casa Fenoglio has a most restrained and attractive use of flowing metalwork in the balustrades which is echoed on the delicate carvings on the doors and the finely modelled brass fittings. Eugenio Quarti's furniture shows similar restraint, but his is

more geometric. There are pieces bearing carved, floral motifs obviously inspired by the style of French furniture which Quarti had seen and admired in the 1900 Paris Exhibition, combined with a geometricity of outline close to Viennese and German types. Such work shows a keen interest in international developments. In contrast, the work of Ernesto Basile of Palermo is idiosyncratic, with little reference to Art Nouveau or Jugendstil. Massive pieces in mahogany, made by the firm of Ducrot of Palermo and often embellished with sculptural metalwork by Antonio Ugo and painting by Ettore Maria Bergler, seem to hark back to the Italian Renaissance, or even further back to Roman and Etruscan furniture. Not surprisingly, in view of these stylistic antecedents, they are also prophetic of that style of Italian architecture and design which was popularized in Italy during the 1920s and 1930s under Mussolini.

One Italian designer whose work cannot be categorized in this way was Carlo Bugatti (1855–1940). Trained as a painter, Bugatti won a prize for his furniture at the Italian exhibition in London in 1888. The style was extraordinary, being a mixture of Middle Eastern fantasy and Japanese naturalism. Certainly nothing like it had been seen before and, in the Art Nouveau movement as a whole, Bugatti's work remains an amazing eccentricity. Bugatti himself described his furniture as being 'of no special style', although in the Turin exhibition of 1902, the tassels and brass inlays gave way to a more simple, curved style obviously based on the Art Nouveau furniture he had seen in Paris in the 1900 exhibition, in which he was represented. Apart from his use of metal inlays, usually of copper or brass, Bugatti relied for his decorative effects on the inlaying of contrasting woods, ivory and vellum.

Der Jugendstil

The designers and architects of Germany and Austria were in sympathy with the aesthetic ideals of William Morris and his followers, although they were champions of industrial methods. It might also be said that while the more socialist elements of Morris's philosophy — in other words the political aspects of his work — were largely, and probably purposely ignored in the United States, they reached sympathetic ears in Germany and Austria. Between 1890 and 1905, the whole direction of design in northern Europe was changed by a group of exceptionally gifted designers. In Munich, Hermann Obrist, August Endell, Joseph Maria Olbrich, who founded the 'Artist's Colony' in Darmstadt in 1899, Richard Riemerschmidt and Peter Behrens formed a brilliant artistic community and from 1897 to 1898 established the Vereinigte Werkstätten of Munich and Dresden. It is also significant that Henry van de Velde settled permanently in Germany in 1899.

In Vienna, Josef Hoffmann (1870–1956) created the Wiener Secession in 1897 and, in 1903, he collaborated with Koleman ('Kolo') Moser in the founding of the Wiener Werkstätte. In the eighth exhibition of the Wiener Secession, work by the young Austrian designers was shown together with whole rooms designed by Henry van de Velde, the designers of the *Maison Moderne,* a shop in Paris similar to that of Bing which had been founded by Julius Meier-Graefe in 1898, and the British designers Ashbee, Charles Rennie Mackintosh and Mackintosh's wife, Margaret Macdonald. Ashbee and van de Velde had both shown with *La Libre Esthétique* in Brussels in 1894. Ashbee and Mackintosh became firm friends with Hoffmann and Moser, and the Austrians visited England and Scotland; their deep appreciation of the workshop system of the Guild of Handicrafts did much to inspire the formation of the Wiener Werkstätte.

Left: Screen in wood, copper, brass and painted parchment by Carlo Bugatti of about 1910.

Below: Room setting designed by Hermann Gesellius. With Armas Lindgren and Eliel Saarinen, Gesellius was one of the most advanced Finnish architects, and the pavilion designed by these three for the Paris 1900 Exposition Universelle caused great interest. (Hvittrask, Finland)

The most significant work of this latter group is the splendid Palais Stoclet in Brussels, built between 1905 and 1911. One critic, Wilhelm Mrazek, has written recently: 'This house . . . is a *Gesamtkunstwerk*; the *Werkstätte* gave its best there, and made it a monument of *Jugendstil* in applied art. Josef Hoffmann and his co-workers Czeschka, Klimt, Löffler, Powolny, Metzner and Luksch created a house which presents perfect unity in style. Money was no object and they feasted on precious materials. With its play of flat surfaces, the building is a triumph of the geometric principle and of ornamentalism combined with *Sachlichkeit*. All things in the exquisitely furnished interior, vitrines, cup-boards, chairs, lamps, silver and china combine to create an environment which is one great homage to geometric beauty.'

When we read this, and remember the search for unity which dominated the Arts and Crafts movement, the work of Mackintosh and the Glasgow designers and the great architects and designers of the Prairie school, we see this element as one which binds them close to the similar preoccupation of Belgian and French architects such as Guimard and Hortá. We can also appreciate, when we recall Owen Jones' criticism of the Great Exhibition of 1851, quoted earlier, how much had been achieved in the second half of the nineteenth century.

THE TRIUMPH OF STYLE
Art Deco

During the first decade of the present century following the decline of Art Nouveau there was little encouragement for the development of design in furniture. Two main factors for this decline can be found in the writings of contemporary critics of the decorative arts.

The family as an institution was still as potent a social force as it had been in the previous century and proved a strong deterrent, although an unconscious one, against innovations. The average well-to-do family in Europe and America lived in a fairly spacious and comfortable house filled with the accumulated furniture of the last hundred years and the tradition of keeping family furniture with its sentimental associations and comfortable familiarity proved stronger than any desire for novelty. Largely uneducated in artistic matters — there were few magazines with a widespread circulation devoted to interior design in the early years of the century — the buying public was distrustful of investing in anything out of the ordinary and relied largely on the persuasiveness of the salesmen in the big decorating firms in London and New York who through laziness or ignorance found it easier to sell pastiches of Tudor, Queen Anne or Chippendale styles.

The other and perhaps more important factor was adequately summed up in the words of the architect Charles Spooner writing in *The British Home of Today* published in 1904. 'During the last few years', he commented, 'there has been a very large growth in the admiration for old furniture and in the desire to collect it. The admiration is widespread and often uncritical. There is no real desire on the part of many people to buy beautiful things for their daily use, and one is not surprised to find such people turning to old work. It is indeed difficult at the present time to buy a piece of modern furniture with which it would be pleasant to live. The art of furniture making, like many a craft today, is in a depressed condition. It is being carried on by a very few people, and there is as yet but a small demand for it. The great bulk of furniture made today is without art and as long as it is made under the present conditions will remain so.' These conditions Spooner explained as being due to the poor wages paid to men with little or no training. In addition, because the work was subdivided, it became monotonous and deprived the workmen of any pride in their craft. Poor workmanship was concealed by thick coats of French polish and 'what happens afterwards is the purchaser's affair'.

It is noticeable that from this time many firms of reputable antique dealers on both sides of the Atlantic included the significant word 'reproductions' in their advertising. The taste for antique furniture which Spooner recorded obviously could not be satisfied by the comparatively few genuine antique pieces which had survived from the sixteenth to the eighteenth centuries — Regency furniture was considered to be unworthy of collection and was dismissed as 'gimcrack rubbish' — and in consequence both in England and America, and on the Continent, the greater part of the furniture trade was devoted to the production of 'reproductions' of the antique. In many cases these were skilful enough to deceive even an expert eye and in 1906 the firm of Bartholomew & Fletcher advertised that their 'specialité' (sic) was 'reproduction from fine old models'. A coffee-table, or, in the twenties, a radiogram or cocktail cabinet for which there were no historical precedents would have deceived no one, but as late as the 1930s there were many firms like Bartholomew & Fletcher or Nicholls & Janes of High Wycombe whose output consisted of copies, often exact to the last detail, of the eighteenth-century furniture illustrated in Macquoid's *Age of Mahogany* and Macquoid and Edward's *Dictionary of English Furniture* — and in some instances the pieces reproduced were themselves of doubtful authenticity. At the most modest estimate half the antique furniture extant today was actually made in the first three decades of this century both in England and France.

The Demise of Art Nouveau
The Studio Year Book of Decorative Art, an annual publication devoted to the best design in England, America, France, Germany,

Austria and Hungary, made its first appearance in 1906. As far as the English section is concerned, the record of advances in design for many years was a melancholy one. Almost without exception the newly-built houses illustrated were versions of Tudor or Queen Anne originals and, where shown, the interiors were filled with antiques or furniture of so nondescript a character that it is difficult to ascribe it to any particular style. There were a small number of English designers who were making valiant efforts to produce furniture which was not shackled to tradition, but in the absence of any definite contemporary idiom the results were too often timid and unadventurous. Despite their determination to break with the past their forms of furniture were pared-down versions of traditional pieces sparsely decorated with inlaid lines of ebony, boxwood or pewter which did little to enliven the over-simplification.

Ambrose Heal Jnr experimented with hitherto little used woods such as chestnut and, in a number of pieces, used sunken handles on drawer faces or revolving wooden handles, set in circular panels, which when turned released sliding bolts on the inside of drawers. His designs had a refreshing simplicity although on the debit side his side-table for a dining-room illustrated in *The British Home of Today* had no less than 14 legs.

For a few years following its founding in 1893 the Arts and Crafts Society had looked as though it might play a decisive role in improving standards of taste in England and the United States, but by 1906 the quality and originality of its annual exhibitions had deteriorated to the extent that the *Studio* correspondent viewed them with 'a certain feeling of melancholy' with only the furniture of Ernest Gimson giving any hope for the future. Gimson emerged as possibly the most original designer of this period but even his work has echoes of the seventeenth century in its conception. His virtues were simplicity of design with an emphasis on the beauty of the natural grain of the wood accentuated by handwrought handles and decorative hinges by E G Halton and A Gardiner. His use of projecting panels on doors and drawer fronts became almost a signature and in some cases a rectangular panel has an octagonal panel superimposed — in one piece this has a smaller rectangular panel applied to its face with an even smaller octagon superimposed. His seeming lack of invention could have been due to a natural reticence or to the demands of his clients, and the inlaid decorative panels of differently coloured woods and pewter with which he occasionally enlivened an otherwise plain piece of furniture were obviously inspired by Elizabethan and Jacobean embroideries. Although far from being reproductions of the antique, Gimson's furniture could be placed without incongruity into one of the Tudor interiors fashionable at the time and comply with the 'English reticence' so often quoted as an ideal — probably in reaction to the exuberance of French Art Nouveau furniture which had so outraged the traditionalists a few years before.

The influence of Gimson, Sidney Barnsley, George Jack, Peter Waals and others designing in this manner was slight as their output, being entirely handmade, was necessarily small and, in comparison with more commercial products, expensive. Furthermore they tended to work in rural areas where craftsmen with traditional skills could be found and this in turn gave little opportunity for the buying public to become familiar with their work.

In 1908 Aylmer Vallance, writing in *The Studio Year Book*, commented on the developments in cane and wicker-work furniture which had 'arrived at an eminent degree of attainment' at the hands of German and Austrian designers. Very different from the creaking chintz-covered armchairs to be found in many English houses, the new versions of chairs, tables and plant-stands designed by Josef Hoffmann and Wilhelm Schmidt for the Prag Rudniker Werkstätte and by Nicholai in Dresden had a taut elegance which justified their use in drawing-rooms and the winter gardens of hotels. In England the craft of basket-weaving had been centred round Leicester and from basket-weaving the making of cane furniture was a natural progression. Furniture similar to that made on the Continent was made by the Dryad Craftsmen from designs by B J Fletcher. Light and easily cleaned whether left in its natural state or painted, cane furniture became extremely popular for use in restaurants, cafés and public rooms.

The wholesale reproduction of antiques flourished in France to an even greater extent than in England and if anything the skill with which these facsimiles were made was greater. Similarly, there were persuasive and unscrupulous dealers eager to sell for vast sums these spurious antiques — the same dealers who had conducted a campaign of vituperation against Art Nouveau which they considered

Left: Oak dresser designed by Ambrose Heal in 1914. In the early years of the twentieth century English furniture designers strongly resisted such trends as Art Nouveau, and turned for inspiration to the simpler furniture of the sixteenth and seventeenth centuries. Without being a pastiche of an antique, Heal's dresser acknowledges the past while being unmistakably of its time and would harmonize with earlier pieces. Decoration is restrained — a simple carved motif on the edges of the shelves — while the pull-out slide above the drawers provides extra working space. The wooden handle recessed in the circular panels works a concealed fastening.

271

a threat to their livelihood—and remote country-houses were furnished by them with 'family heirlooms' which were sold with a show of reluctance to unsuspecting visitors.

By 1908 Art Nouveau had become so discredited that the critic Achille Ségard described it as 'bizarre, pretentious, abnormal, overwrought and inadequate to any practical object' though *The Studio Year Book* showed that in a modified form several designers remained faithful. Most of the original Art Nouveau designers had abandoned the style very soon after the 1900 Exhibition and its subsequent commercialization. Taste then reverted to an attenuated version of Louis Seize furniture painted white and upholstered in shades of old-rose, which was soon to be found not only in private houses but also in the public rooms and bedrooms of the new hotels which were springing up in the capitals of Europe during the first decade of the century. Irreverently known as 'Louis the Hotel', this type of furniture was popularized by the big decorating firms of Mercier Frères, Maple—which had branches in London and Paris—and Waring & Gillow.

The Advent of Art Deco

In 1910 two events in Paris had a decisive effect and led to the creation of a style which has acquired the recent title of Art Deco. The first was the appearance of Sergei Diaghilev's Ballet Russe and especially the *première* of the ballet *Scheherazade*. Contemporary writings and memoirs abound with descriptions of the astonishing effect this ballet had upon

Left: Chair in white painted oak designed by Charles Rennie Mackintosh for the Rose Boudoir shown at the International Exhibition of Decorative Art, Turin 1902. The chair (and its black painted companion) met with both vitriolic abuse and ecstatic praise. Amid a welter of safely traditional or grotesquely eccentric contributions, the Mackintosh designs were awarded a diploma of honour. (University of Glasgow)

Below left: One of Paul Poiret's contributions to the 1925 Paris Exhibition was the decoration of three barges moored on the Seine. This interior shows Poiret's lasting fondness for the brilliant oriental colours of the Ballet Russe combined with simple shapes reminiscent of the work of the Wiener Werkstätte.

Right: Cupboard veneered in lemonwood forming part of a suite of furniture made in 1907 by Niedermoser of Vienna to the design of Koloman Moser. Moser, together with Hoffmann, was one of the guiding spirits of the Wiener Werkstätte and was similarly interested in designing anything from a complete decorative scheme to a lady's handbag. His work demonstrates the strong links between English and Scottish designers and their Viennese contemporaries. (Museum für Angewandte Kunst, Vienna) its audiences who were transported by the combination of an erotic and sadistic libretto, sensuous music and choreography and, above all, the dazzlingly brilliant *décor* and costumes by Léon Bakst. This sensation was repeated to only a slightly lesser degree when the ballet had it *première* in London in the following year. The pale and subtle nuances of Art Nouveau were superseded by the brilliant oriental colours which were applied to furniture as well as to its upholstery and a

craze for all things Persian pervaded the decorative arts. Large elaborately decorated cushions became a recognized article of furniture piled in heaps in lieu of settees in imitation of those on which Zobeïde, the heroine of *Scheherazade,* and Thamar, the central figure of another exotic ballet designed by Bakst, reclined between orgies.

The second event was the exhibition of decorative arts from the Münchener Werkbund at the Salon d'Automne of 1910. Although badly received by the critics it proved so popular that mounted police had to be brought in to control the crowds clamouring for admission. Little information is available as to the actual exhibits and judging from photographs of other work from the Werkbund it seems improbable that French designers could have been inspired by the rather heavy and characterless interiors — apart from the fact that German taste had never been highly regarded in France and memories of the disasters of the 1870 Franco-Prussian War were still too fresh for many Frenchmen to take an unbiased view. It is more likely that the concept on which the Werkbund was founded — a group of artists and designers working together in conjunction with manufacturers and holding joint exhibitions of their work — appealed to French designers as a practical solution to their artistic problems. The influences which found expression in the pre-war version of Art Deco stem more from the light elegant artifacts of the Austrian Wiener Werkstätte than from the German movement.

During the opening years of the twentieth century the designs of William Morris, Baillie Scott, Charles Voysey, C R Ashbee and Charles Rennie Mackintosh had had considerable influence on German and Austrian designers especially on those of the younger generation desirous of a break with the prevailing taste for ponderous versions of historical styles. Mackintosh, whose work had aroused little interest in England and even less in France, found new admirers particularly in Vienna and his interiors inspired Josef Hoffmann, a brilliant designer of subtle and refined taste. The eccentricities of much of Mackintosh's furniture which tend to give the impression that it was meant more to be admired than used in everyday life were reduced and, combined with reminiscences of the Biedermeier style, resulted in simple and extremely elegant pieces.

In Germany the influence of English designers and critics was tempered by a more practical realization that if furniture of good design were to be brought within the reach of all incomes the slow processes of hand crafts had to give way to the most modern methods of machine production. The Deutscher

Werkbund or German Craft Union was formed in 1907 and within two years had enrolled the active support of 360 designers, 267 manufacturers and 95 influential critics and writers working with the common aim of improving the quality of industrial production. According to *The Studio Year Book* for 1910, the Werkbund was so well organized that its influence had led to a decline in the import into Germany of French and English art productions and the position of Paris as the arbiter of taste in Europe was threatened. The influences which evolved into the pre-war version of French Art Deco can be directly traced, however, to the light, elegant productions of the Wiener Werkstätte rather than to the heavier German counterparts. Just as the Austrian decorative artists had referred back to the Biedermeier period so the French designers, in reaction against the sinuosities of Art Nouveau, returned to the tighter and more disciplined idioms of French furniture of the 1820s — significantly a time when the links with tradition had begun to loosen as a result of the Romantic absorption with the past. In Austrian, French and Italian designs for furniture, textiles and other forms of decoration, the same repertoire of motifs emerged around 1910. Baskets or bowls of formalized flowers appear in oval panels — the oval shape was extensively used for table-tops, mirrors incorporated in dressing-

Left: Dressing-table chair by Follot, about 1910. He was first associated with the French Art Nouveau movement, but by about 1904 he had developed an individual style and was an early pioneer in Art Deco, designing single pieces characterized by the use of precious materials and fine carving. (Musée des Arts Décoratifs, Paris)

Below left: Small commode in shagreen and ebony designed by Paul Iribe. One of the most versatile of Art Deco designers, Iribe first attracted attention with the fashion illustrations he did for Paul Poiret in 1908. Until his departure for the United States in 1914, he created an enormous collection of work for interiors, wallpapers, furniture, fabrics, jewellery and graphics. His favourite motif of a conventionalized rose — the 'rose Iribe' — became the signature of early Art Deco when it was borrowed by other designers. (Musée des Arts Décoratifs, Paris)

Right: French escritoire of about 1920. A typically delicate piece of furniture designed for a boudoir and showing in its lacquered decoration typical Art Deco motifs of oval panels enclosing baskets of conventionalized flowers. This form of ornament shows striking similarities to the work of Italian and Austrian designers; the original inspiration is demonstrably that of Charles Rennie Mackintosh. (The Martins Forrest Collection)

tables or simply as wall-mirrors. Carving in low relief of roses, zinnias and pendant bell-shaped blossoms was applied to the exposed frames of chairs and to mirror frames or used as panels set in doors. A chair by Paul Follot, for example, has an oval panel in the back framing a basket of fruit carved in low relief — the combination of blond fruitwood with ebony reverts to a fashion of about a hundred years before.

The new Art Deco style found an immediate response from the public and its slightly exotic charm which combined novelty with a certain regard for the past was realized to the full by such designers as Paul Follot, Maurice Dufrêne, Clement-Mère, Armand Rateau and others who had previously been in the forefront of the Art Nouveau movement through their association with either Siegfried Bing or Julius Meier-Graefe. Plans were made for an exhibition to be held in 1915 of the decorative arts of all countries, but this had to be postponed indefinitely after the outbreak of the First World War.

Immediately peace was declared the idea was taken up again, for France needed to assert her position as leader of taste in Europe in view of the importance of fashion in every field of the decorative arts to the national economy; and although Europe was shattered and near bankruptcy as a result of the war there were new markets in both North and South America and even eastward in India. Many of the leading French manufacturers threatened to boycott the exhibition if Germany, so recently the bitter enemy of France, were invited to participate. Financial reasons also delayed the International Exhibition of Decorative and Industrial Art until 1925, but in the intervening years the lessons of the Deutscher Werkbund had been driven home, with groups of designers collaborating to present their work in a number of the big Parisian department stores and thus increasing the popular interest in the newest developments of Art Deco.

Twice a year at the Salon d'Automne and the Salon des Artistes Décorateurs, fully furnished rooms were exhibited to the public. These were either actual schemes already commissioned or they could be bought out-right and installed in the client's house. These exhibitions were as much discussed and featured in the press as the collections of the leading couturiers some of whom, Paul Poiret and Jeanne Lanvin for instance, combined dressmaking with the design of interiors. Paul Poiret's *Atelier Martine* was the direct result of his pre-war fashion tours in Germany where he visited the studios of the Werkbund and was so impressed that on his return to France he opened an establishment for the sale of decorative accessories — furniture was not greatly featured in his schemes and where it appears it was obviously inspired by the Wiener Werkstätte.

The 1925 Exhibition

Many critics objected that the furniture at the 1925 exhibition was more a display of luxury and fine craftsmanship than a true reflection of the state of the furniture trade in each country. In fact, a number of the exhibits dated from before the war when the idea of the exhibition had first been put forward. In the meantime, however, Art Deco had undergone modification, was becoming unfashionable and was shortly to disappear in favour of the essentially anti-decorative 'Modernism'.

The designer who had the greatest impact on press and public was Jacques-Emile Ruhlmann whose working life was to span a brief 20 years between his first exhibited work in 1913 and his death in 1933. The Ruhlmann exhibit was spectacularly luxurious and reflected his avowed intention to work only for the richest clients, using the most precious materials and with complete control of the total decorative scheme. As his taste was extremely cultivated and the standard of craftsmanship he exacted from his workers unsurpassed by any standards he found no lack of appreciative clients. His favourite materials were the rarest woods and veneers combined with shagreen, fine leathers, tortoiseshell and ivory, and he used these to clothe the simple but subtle forms of his perfectly proportioned pieces. The individuality and style of his designs were above fashion and consequently changes in taste made no difference to the lavish commissions he received for the decoration of private houses and embassies. The forms of Ruhlmann's furniture were in the tradition of the First Empire or of the Boulle pieces which were popular during the reign of Louis XIV.

In contrast with Ruhlmann's designs, those of André Groult and J Leleu were pared-down versions of the Louis Quinze style with the difference that, instead of intricate inlay and bronze-doré mounts, both these designers veneered the simplified *bombé* — convex — forms with tortoiseshell, macassar ebony or blond shagreen harmonizing with the paintings by Marie Laurençin which Groult included in many of his decorative schemes. Ruhlmann's sombre, rich veneers, relieved by ivory handles and discreet inlays of the same material, were essentially masculine in feeling while Groult and Leleu created interiors and furniture which were eminently suitable as backgrounds for elegant women. Together with Paul Follot, Maurice Dufrêne and Léon Jallot they can be said to be the original exponents of Art Deco in its initial phase.

Working in less conventional materials and often in collaboration with these designers were a number of fine craftsmen whose talents were applied to furniture. Edgar Brandt, Raymond Subes and Paul Kiss, the most esteemed metalworkers of the day, created console tables, the small occasional tables known as 'guéridons', standard lamps, radiator cases and pedestals which interpreted the linear forms of Art Deco in wrought iron. Armand Rateau, whose collaboration with the couturière Jeanne Lanvin has already been mentioned, created bronze furniture which was less inspired by the current Art Deco than by the classical models of Greece, Rome and the Near East, setting them against lacquered walls and screens with the same motifs of birds and flowers.

In the current taste for rich surface textures the techniques of Chinese and Japanese lacquer were revived by Jean Dunand — also a metalworker and acknowledged to be the finest craftsman in contemporary France — and by Eileen Gray and Evelyn Wild. Dunand's

Left: Jacques-Emile Ruhlmann designed this interior for a country-house in the early 1930s. Even in rural surroundings he made no concessions to mock simplicity, the furniture being veneered with rosewood and covered in fine leather.

Below: Cabinet of macassar ebony, inlaid with tortoiseshell and ivory by Ruhlmann. The tapering reeded leg merging into the carcase was his invention. Ruhlmann's work was characterized by simple elegant forms and the use of rare woods combined with delicate ivory inlays. (Collection Galerie Félix Marcilhac, Paris)

urniture, simple in form, was decorated with s many as 20 coats of lacquer and enhanced vith geometrical designs in gold, silver and nlaid eggshells—a revival of a Japanese echnique. The lacquer pieces of Eileen Grey nd Evelyn Wild were plainer, relying on he mirror-smooth surface of the material or effect. After a career as the foremost eweller in Europe working in the Art Touveau manner, René Lalique devoted his ttention to working in glass and there are xtant dining-tables made entirely of etched late-glass held together by almost invisible ietal framings. His glass and marble dining- oom was one of the rather more remarkable xhibits.

If the interiors and furniture by these and any other designers in the different French ictions reflected a taste for luxury and ntasy, the English contribution was in omparison sober, earning only faint, polite ommendation from the compilers of the ficial French catalogue who regretted that e inheritors of the traditions of Ruskin, illiam Morris and Walter Crane could not ive produced something with more iginality. They did, however, praise the tchen furnished by Messrs Easiwork Ltd, d the ensembles arranged by Mrs Maufe nich included a desk finished in silver leaf Edward Maufe. On the other hand the okesman for the English committee found ihlmann's furniture heavy and inclined to erpower the nature of the wood, although was admitted that Ruhlmann's technical skill and craftsmanship were unsurpassed. This adverse criticism did not prevent several English designers from producing direct imitations of his work shortly after. The exhibition gave visitors the opportunity of seeing work from a number of European countries whose productions were little known outside their own borders. It is noticeable that in most cases the trend in design was a pastiche of early nineteenth-century styles with the accent upon national characteristics and trends.

This reversion to the cult of historicism stems from the early years of this century when Italy, politically and economically at a low ebb, had offered little or no encouragement to original furniture design. The only notable name to have survived from this period is that of Carlo Bugatti whose creations, eccentric and frequently grotesque in conception, combined elements derived from sources ranging from North Africa to Japan, executed in inlays of pewter and vellum with lavish use of silk tassels. Very poor as a country, Italy was largely living on tourism and its past glories, selling its many antiques to foreign collectors and replacing them with skilful replicas, the whole of the furniture trade being engaged in this practice. The Milanese designers Emilio Lancia, G de Finetti and Tomaso Buzzi, the latter working for the firm of Labirinto, exhibited furniture with a strong neo-classical influence often with details more or less directly copied from those found on metal furniture excavated at Pompeii and Herculaneum. Giulio Richard, designer for the porcelain firm of Richard-Ginori, inclined more to decorations, inlaid or painted, taken from architectural details of Renaissance buildings, interpreted in a somewhat surrealistic manner. The avant-garde art movement of Futurism which flourished briefly before the First World War was devoted entirely to painting and the issue of vehement manifestoes, both of which involved little financial outlay on the part of indigent reformers. Furniture and the decorative arts necessarily involving craftsmanship and financial investment on the part of the artist were ignored. During the 1930s interest turned to the furniture of the eighteenth and nineteenth centuries which had formerly been despised as falling below the standards of the Renaissance and although genuine pieces of these periods were in plentiful supply, contemporary design was generally limited to copies.

In Denmark Kay Fisher, Aage Rafn and Kai Gottlob also were strongly influenced by the neo-classic furniture of the late eighteenth and early nineteenth centuries. The Swedish exhibit was characterized by the simplicity of the basic forms of the furniture which

betrayed influences of a provincial version of Louis Seize and Empire styles. From the work of Carl Malmston, Carl Bergsten, Horvick, and the firms of Nordiska Kompaniet and Svenska Möbelfabrikorna, critics deduced that the market seemed to be more for a prosperous democratic middle class than for a rich aristocracy.

There were two notable absentees, the United States and Germany. The American designer Paul Frankl wrote in 1930: 'The only reason why America was not represented was because we found that we had no modern decorative art. Not only was there a sad lack of any achievement that could be exhibited but we discovered that there was not even a serious movement in this direction.' Contemporary periodicals give every indication that taste in America was almost exclusively directed toward antiques or reproductions. The early experiments of, for instance, Frank Lloyd Wright, whose 1904 prototype for a revolving writing-chair is now in the Museum of Modern Art, received little encouragement. Advanced contemporary design was confined to architecture — interior decoration was not yet the potent force it was later to become — and the innovations of sky-scrapers which were mainly intended for commercial use were only too often furnished with indifferently designed stock office furniture. With considerable foresight the Metropolitan Museum of Art in New York acquired some of the best of the French exhibits including several fine pieces by Ruhlmann. It was possibly as a result of the display of these objects within a very few years that an interest in contemporary furniture arose in America.

The reasons for the absence of Germany were more complex. The economic situation of a ruined and defeated country was the main cause and the threatened boycott by French manufacturers also played a large part. Added to this, internal difficulties prevented an entry from the Bauhaus which at this time was the only organization of importance which could have represented the new spirit in Germany, working on similar lines to the De Stijl in Holland.

The De Stijl movement, named after the magazine which was the mouthpiece of its various members, had been founded in 1917 by Theo van Doesburg and Piet Mondrian to advance revolutionary theories of 'neo-plasticism' or the stress on horizontal and vertical elements in a design combined with a limited use of primary colours, red, blue and yellow and three neutral colours, black,

Left: Chair designed by Gerrit Rietveld. The avant-garde periodical 'De Stijl' advocated neo-plasticism — a theory of delineating spatial dimension by the use of horizontal and vertical planes combined with the use of only red, blue and yellow and the non-colours, black, white and grey. The early paintings of Mondrian are examples of this theory. Rietveld realized this doctrine in a number of pieces of furniture of which the chair illustrated is the best known example. Although lacking comfort and stability, it represented a genuine attempt to break with outworn traditions. (Victoria & Albert Museum, London)

Above right: Boudoir designed by Louis Sognot for Primavera, the decorative art department of the Parisian store Au Printemps, which was exhibited at the Paris Exhibition, 1925.

white and grey. The 'Berlin' chair designed by G T Rietveld shows the application of these theories to furniture with the various elements of construction joined only by screws and painted to accentuate their individuality. It is easy to see why this chair, known at that time to a limited number of people, should have found little response from the manufacturers for whom it was intended as a prototype for not only was it uncomfortable — as Rietveld himself admitted — but its appearance gave the impression that a single unwary movement would be sure to topple it.

A more modified version of the theory could be found in the furniture designed by S van Ravensteyn which formed part of the Dutch exhibit in 1925. Less aggressive than Rietveld's chair the suite of bedroom furniture appeared to be composed of planks of wood, haphazardly painted in black and white, propped one against another and earned the comment from an Italian critic that it was the 'height of modernistic snobbery . . . mere curiosities'. *De Stijl* was published in Paris in 1920 and the theories it put forward had a considerable influence on the avant-garde designers reacting against Art Deco.

Right: Chair in steel and leather designed in about 1928 by Le Corbusier and Charlotte Perriand. Contemporary with the Bauhaus, a group of French designers were reacting against Art Deco by advancing revolutionary concepts of the relationship between art and the machine, producing interiors and furniture which were often too starkly functional for general acceptance. (Musée des Arts Décoratifs, Paris)

Overleaf: As an architect, Frank Lloyd Wright was an original and highly controversial figure, designing buildings which aroused either fervent admiration or acute dislike. His furniture was often less aesthetically successful than his buildings; Wright tended to think of furniture in terms of architecture, of wood in terms of stone or concrete — with a resulting heaviness. (Victoria & Albert Museum, London)

The International Style

The writings and work of William Morris and his followers had had a great impact on a number of designers in Germany and were one of the contributory causes for the founding of the Deutscher Werkbund in 1907. Its founder, however, Herman Muthesius, after spending several years in England, held the conviction that only by a close collaboration between artists, architects and particularly manufacturers could a new rational style be evolved and that the potentialities of the machine must be utilized rather than ignored as it had been by Morris and his disciples.

In 1919 a programme for training in this integration of art and commerce was realized by the formation of the Bauhaus at Weimar by the architect Walter Gropius with Function and Construction as the keywords of the movement. The anti-academic basis of the training meant a virtual abolition of any decorative ornament in favour of abstract geometrical shapes. Tuition was conducted on two complementary courses, one devoted to techniques and materials, the other to the study of form, both courses being combined in the production of prototypes which could be used by manufacturers in terms of mass-production. In the turbulent political atmosphere of post-war Germany the aims of the Bauhaus, running contrary to established academic standards, were bound to engender hostility and accusations of socialism, and in 1925 the Weimar Bauhaus was closed by the authorities but reopened at Dessau where

it attracted some 600 students from many countries including Japan. Before its final closure by the Nazis in 1933 two directors succeeded Gropius after his departure in 1928 — Hannes Mayer and Mies van der Rohe; the latter, together with Marcel Breuer, was responsible for experimental prototypes of tubular steel furniture from 1925 onward. Mart Stam, a De Stijl associate, had designed a tubular steel chair in 1924, but his version was constructed from lengths of straight tubing joined by curved sections — the Bauhaus types had more elasticity with one continuous piece of tubing bent into shape with no joints at all. The most notable Bauhaus versions were Breuer's 'Cantilever' chair of 1928 and Mies van der Rohe's 'Barcelona' chair dating from 1929.

At the same time a number of French designers were working along similar lines in rejecting the concept of 'Decorative' in favour of 'Functional' furniture. Le Corbusier, Charlotte Perriand, Robert Mallet-Stevens and Pierre Chareau were among those in the forefront of the same movement which the Bauhaus was propagating. The rapid spread of chromium-plated tubular steel furniture throughout Europe was mainly due to the

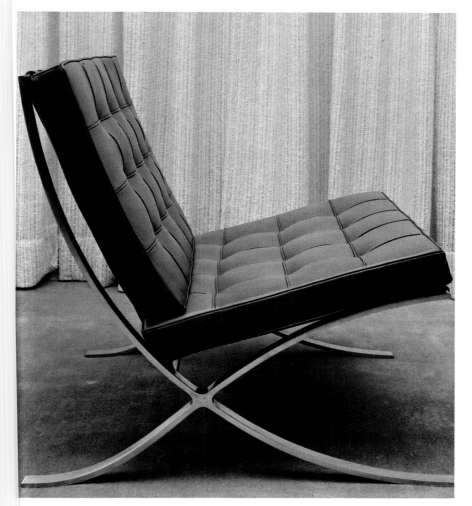

Another extremely significant factor in furniture design in the twenties was the growing use of plywood. This consisted of thin layers of wood with the grain of each layer at right angles to that of the next, glued together under pressure to form a solid board which, if properly made, had none of the disadvantages of a comparable piece of natural wood. It had no tendency to split, warp or twist, was lighter in weight and could be made in sizes far greater than had previously been possible. A heavier version called laminboard or ibus consisted of strips of timber glued together and faced on each side with layers of veneer. Made in even larger sizes than plywood it was used for the sides and doors of large pieces of furniture. Experiments in making plywood had been made in America during the nineteenth century, but the results were unsatisfactory as the adhesive tended to be affected by humidity and the thin sheets of wood, sliced lengthwise across the tree trunk, displayed unsightly joins. A French invention of the 1870s, the rotary cutter, enabled the ply to be cut in a continuous sheet, the log being firmly held at each end and revolved slowly against a long cutting edge gauged to obtain the thickness of veneer required. The development of water-resistant cements in 1890 led to the manufacture of plywood in Russia and Finland. By 1912 Finland was the principal supplier in Europe.

The lightness and great tensile strength of plywood had been utilized in aeroplane construction during the First World War and subsequently in the building of commercial vehicles. During the timber shortages and a consequent scarcity of properly seasoned wood in the twenties, plywood was increasingly used in the construction of domestic furniture and panelling. Employed at first in its natural state it proved invaluable for the backs of large pieces of furniture and mirrors and for drawer bottoms where its resistance to splitting kept out dust. Subsequent technical improvements in facing plywood and laminboard with veneers of rare woods greatly extended its use and by reducing the costs enabled manufacturers to market furniture at far lower prices than hitherto possible. The British Empire Exhibition of 1924, while doing little to advance furniture design in England, had aroused interest in the many rare coloured woods grown in the colonies and extended the range of decorative finishes which had previously been restricted to oak, mahogany, walnut and satinwood. The cut edges of laminboard which exposed the rough inner construction when used for shelves were masked by strips of ebony or rosewood which contrasted with the paler veneer covering the horizontal surfaces and formed a decorative motif characteristic of much furniture of the 1930s.

old-established firm of Thonet which had pioneered the manufacture of bentwood furniture, mass-producing light, elegant and cheap machine-made furniture which could be found in both palaces and cafés. The Thonet techniques were adapted to the manufacture of metal furniture with ease and in fact many of the new pieces bore a striking resemblance to wooden originals created independently over 50 years before.

This new concept of furnishing aroused great controversy when, in addition to chairs, metal was used for tables and cupboards; its detractors claimed it was noisy, uncomfortable and fit only for the surgical wards of hospitals, while its admirers maintained that in an age when the machine was becoming more and more a part of daily life metal furniture was an appropriate symbol of the times. French designers claimed the credit for its invention and softened its starker effects with additions of wooden elements decorated with lacquer or exotic veneers and with upholstery in leather or fur. Introduced in England by the firms of PEL and Cox it was at first marketed as a luxury item, but mass-production reduced its cost and by the early 1930s was a commonplace in hotels, restaurants and canteens.

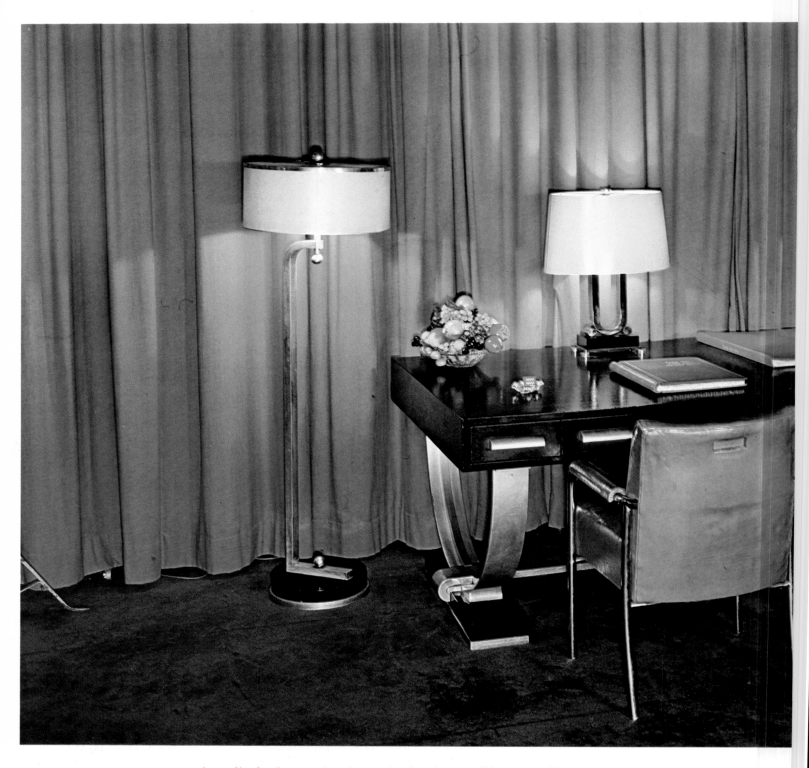

A radical change in domestic furniture design was the result of social changes which followed from the First World War. As a contemporary writer observed, the family pattern was broken up and whereas before the war the tendency was for a family to remain in the same house surrounded by accumulations of furniture and only moving when financial circumstances or a growing family made it imperative, the shortages of money and employment during the twenties forced families — smaller now — to move more often and usually into increasingly smaller houses or flats. Housing shortages forced the splitting of large family houses into as many apartments as possible, and as domestic help became scarcer the tendency was to have the minimal amount of furniture and to avoid a dust-collecting clutter of ornaments. This trend was even more marked in the thirties when, with the increase in cars and outside entertainments, less time was spent in the home.

cupboards made the monumental wardrobes of the nineteenth century unnecessary. Impoverished families could no longer entertain on the lavish scale of the past and, if there were a dining-room at all, it was exceptional to find a dining-table designed to seat more than six people and in some flats no provision was made for dining at all. Dinner parties gave way to cocktail parties — alcohol and particularly gin was inexpensive — and the cocktail cabinet became an important feature of domestic furnishing. Furniture, except in the homes of the very rich, became smaller, lighter, easier to clean, and more importantly became cheaper. A series of bookshelves incorporating a writing-desk and a cocktail cabinet, for instance, were grouped round a divan which also served as a bed and, apart from a low coffee-table and one or two easy chairs, this was the sole furnishing. The design was minimal, block-like and with no unnecessary decoration to collect dust; ornaments and pictures were reduced to a minimum, and the total effect, as photographs of modernistic interiors of the thirties witness, was impersonal and monotonous.

Left: Group of furniture designed by Donald Deskey in 1932 for the private suite of S L Rothafel in Radio City Music Hall. Deskey, one of the leading American decorators of the time, designed this handsome ensemble for the creator of the most palatial, and often outrageous, movie houses ever built. The restrained design reveals the main influences on contemporary American design — Chinese, French and Austrian. (Rockefeller Center, New York)

As rooms in newly-built houses and apartment blocks were smaller than before, less furniture was needed and very often some was built in as part of the structure. The functions of the dining- and living-rooms were combined and consequently the bulky and ornate sideboard, without which no dining-room had been considered adequately furnished, just about disappeared. Similarly technical improvements in plumbing made the antiquated washstand quite superfluous, while built-in

After the Wall Street crash of 1929 and the years of depression which followed until about 1935 the furniture trades of Europe and America suffered as the nouveaux-riches of the twenties were replaced by the 'new poor' — a description which appeared with monotonous frequency during the following decade. The cult of Modernism which had finally ousted the ornamental fantasies of Art Deco in the late twenties was as much a matter of necessity as one of fashion. Catchwords of 'functionalism' and 'fitness for purpose' were really euphemisms for the required low price which put any extraneous ornament out of the question. The 'Great Dullness' as Maurice Dufrêne describes it in his introduction to the 1931 issue of *The Studio Year Book* was the result of 'the uniformity and simplicity of international art'. Dufrêne continued with

Above: Shaped plywood chaise-longue designed by Marcel Breuer in 1936. The upholstery has been removed to show more clearly the basic form. Using similar techniques to those employed by Thonet nearly a hundred years before, designers in the twenties and thirties shaped plywood under steam pressure in their search for new forms capable of cheap mass-production. (John Cox Collection, Brighton)

287

Right: For many years, Heal's was virtually alone in producing modern furniture on a commercial scale. By 1935, a large range of chromium-plated steel furniture was obtainable at relatively modest prices. This illustration from a Heal's catalogue shows an octagonal dining-table with a wood shelf beneath; the armchair has a stretched black hide seat as does the chair on the right which is formed of spring steel tubing.

Below right: Settee by Jean-Michel Frank of 1936, which was derived from Dali's portrait of Mae West. He depicted her as a room setting with a fireplace representing her nostrils, two framed pictures for her eyes, her mouth forming a settee and draperies for her hair. (Royal Pavilion, Art Gallery & Museums, Brighton)

the apt comment that if the photographs in the volume had been presented without captions it would have been impossible to make a correct attribution for the designer or even the country of origin. Two years later John de La Valette, a writer much concerned with the questions of art and industry, claimed in the same publication that in 1933 'we touched bottom in the matter of decorative art'.

Manufacturers were faced with recurring economic crises and the ever present fear of bankruptcy, and they had to produce furniture at the lowest possible cost. Often dispensing

with designers to save money, they made versions of pieces which were themselves anaemic adaptations of originals from the Bauhaus or from avant-garde French designers. The tubular steel chair, now mass-produced and selling at remarkably low cost, appeared in interiors from Austria to California and its over-exposure occasioned caustic comments from writers in decorating magazines. Alternatively, extremely bulky easy chairs upholstered in tweed — one was advertised as capable of seating five people — would provide the only seating accommodation. Another international feature was the use of sycamore as a veneer relieved by machine fluting or by contrasting bandings of a darker wood, ebony or rosewood. In an attempt to relieve the enforced monotony of these pieces, manufacturers resorted to making asymmetrical furniture, for instance a writing-desk with drawers on one side balanced on the other by a plain wooden support.

There were several reasons for the spread of this international and uniform style in interior decoration and furniture. The big decorating firms which had enjoyed great prosperity in the post-war years were severely affected by the depression. Although there were still a considerable number of rich clients their numbers were decreasing as the slump continued with no signs of a return to normal and, in addition, the very lucrative orders for what was termed contract work (decoration of boardrooms, ocean liners and palaces in the Near East) more or less disappeared. Consequently the big firms were obliged to cater for a less wealthy clientele, one both younger and less interested in period *décor*. Their design studios, considerably reduced in number, were forced to work in an unfamiliar idiom and had to acknowledge the hitherto despised modernism.

The increasing number of exponents of the comparatively new profession of interior decorator further threatened the large decorating firms. With little or no professional training — there were no schools of interior decoration as such in the twenties and few in the thirties — they could undercut the big firms and, by using social connections, impose their personal taste on their clients. Very few had the technical ability to design furniture and the majority encouraged the new taste for Regency and Victorian furniture and decorative objects which were considered 'amusing' with the added advantage of being plentiful, owing to the breaking up of many large houses, and, most important, of being extremely cheap. Baroque furniture from Italy and Spain, equally cheap, plentiful, and genuine, was exported in vast quantities to England and the United States where it was ruthlessly stripped of its polish or paint and bleached to harmonize with the currently fashionable pine panelling. It is true to say that a Baroque, Regency or mid-Victorian interior was as typical of taste in the thirties as a modernistic room.

The surrealistic exhibitions in Paris and London extended the trend against modernism and many decorators were quick to utilize its less macabre aspects. Jean-Michel Frank, working in Paris and California, created deceptively simple interiors which were nevertheless very costly. He used furniture in basic shapes completely unadorned but finished in the richest materials — vellum, shagreen or fine lacquer — and to these he added surrealist touches in the form of lamps, tables and ornaments cast in bronze and plaster from designs by Giacometti. Perhaps the most widely known piece of surrealist furniture was the 'Mouth' settee created by Frank after a drawing by Salvador Dali of an interior which metamorphosed as a portrait of Mae West.

Diversity of Styles

The later years of the decade saw a return to more decorative interiors as Europe and the United States gradually recovered from the effects of the depression. The growing number of interior decorators working in intense competition, each relying on the constant presentation of a new concept as much as any couturier in Paris, led to a wide diversity of styles. In practical terms a piece of antique decorative furniture was easier to sell to an unimaginative client as a basis for a building scheme of interior decoration than an idea conveyed by a drawing as the latter always carried the risk that the client might not approve of the furniture when actually made. Although still considerably reduced in size, the furniture trade at both ends of the market probably catered for a wider range of taste than at any time before. On both sides of the Atlantic deplorable versions of Tudor and Georgian originals — anything with a cabriole leg of the Queen Anne style was automatically labelled Georgian — were still mass-produced

Below: Cocktail cabinet in maple, made in England about 1935. The use of plywood and the lack of carved ornament are both measures of economy. The vertical fluting is found in much early thirties furniture and the design of the base shows French influence. (Royal Pavilion, Art Galley & Museums, Brighton)

289

for the hire-purchase trade, and these were so shoddily made that their disintegration after a few years' use was a certainty.

For those with 'taste but limited incomes' — a description much used in advertising in the thirties — there was the birchwood furniture mass-produced by Finmar Ltd, after designs by Alvar Aalto, the Finnish craftsman. This had the attraction of simplicity and lightness, owing to its construction from plywood which was steamed and moulded into pleasing shapes, and was extremely inexpensive. In England Duncan Miller, Betty Joel, Arundell Clarke, Hayes Marshall, Gordon Russell and Alistair Maynard were responsible for furniture which stressed simplicity, good proportions and the use of figured veneers.

From 1935 onwards small occasional tables and cocktail cabinets were covered with sheets of peach-coloured mirror sometimes contrasted with bandings of sapphire-blue faceted mirror. These were indicative of the growing trend to more decorative effects as was buttoned upholstery, a revival of a Victorian fashion, which was extensively used on shaped bedheads, settees and chairs. Endless variations were made on the draped dressing-tables with their skirt of gathered satin or taffeta concealing the drawers and cupboards each side of the kneehole, the fabric-covered top being protected by a sheet of plate-glass. The most popular colours for these were a pale mushroom pink, aquamarine blue and celadon green.

Syrie Maugham, erroneously credited with the invention of the 'all-white' room, originated a number of pieces of furniture which were versions of simple eighteenth-century French pieces altered to suit modern needs, including stands for a telephone with spaces for directories, book tables with sunk compartments for plants and bedside tables to take a lamp and a breakfast tray. These were painted with the crackle finish which was her trademark and were intended to harmonize with the antique French and Italian painted furniture which she included in most of her interiors.

In the thirties there is curiously little mention of the many French designers who had exhibited the fine pieces in the Art Deco manner during the twenties and only a few new designers, André Arbus, Jacques Adnet and Marcel Champion, carried on in the tradition of Ruhlmann (who had died in 1933) — but their furniture is often heavy and inclined to rely on novelty. Taste in France as elsewhere was veering to the antique and decorative.

Many designers had already emigrated from Germany before the advent of the Nazi régime in 1933 and the closing of the Bauhaus in that year saw the exodus of most of its teachers and students to England and, notably, the United States where they had a considerable

Left: Dressing-table and stool designed by Paul Frankl. The decorative motifs on the mirror and the supports for the table show a curious throwback to the already outmoded Art Deco. Frankl did much to propagate a distinctive American style at a time when American manufacturers were solely concerned with reproductions. 'Skyscraper' furniture — cupboards and bookcases piled in vertical shapes echoing the masses of the buildings seen through the windows — illustrated his statement that skyscrapers were the only original works of contemporary art to be found in America. (Sybarites Gallery, New York)

Above right: An example that derives from a French eighteenth-century original of the painted furniture designed in about 1930 by Syrie Maugham. Her interiors achieved their effect by a mixture of furniture of different periods sometimes stripped and bleached but more often painted in off-white or pastel colours with a crackled finish. (Royal Pavilion, Art Gallery & Museums, Brighton)

Right: Syrie Maugham's own drawing-room in about 1933. The stark modernist décors of the depression years gave way to more ornate and decorative designs and under the influence of Syrie Maugham and her celebrated white rooms, the way was opened for more romantic and surrealist interiors. Her use of simple French and Italian furniture combined with off-white walls, mirror screens and masses of white flowers and a sophisticated chic which ensured their imitation.

influence on modern American design. Here, as in England and France, the predominant taste among the richer sections of society was for the past but in the rapidly growing cities modernist decorations and furniture were considered more appropriate in the new buildings. Interior decorators were more highly organized with design studios than in Europe, and Donald Deskey, Gilbert Rhode, Walter Dorwin Teague, Paul Frankl and Hugo Gnam, to mention only a few, designed variations on the limited modernist repertoire of streamlined, veneeered furniture. Their designs made use of asymmetrical forms, curved corners and thick plate-glass tops and shelves with an occasional concession to ornament in the form of lacquered details and motifs derived from Chinese and Japanese sources. It cannot be said that the thirties was a decade remarkable for high standards of originality or invention in furniture or that representative pieces will be as eagerly collected as those of the previous decade.

INNOVATION
Furniture to the present day

The outbreak of war in Europe in 1939 brought to an abrupt halt the stylistic evolution of European furniture design. Through the twenties and thirties, first French Art Deco and, subsequently, the functionalist international Modernist style had made the strongest impact, whilst the thirties had also been years of fascinating and inventive eclecticism. Paris and the German Bauhaus school were the two centres from which had emanated both the most elegant and the most avant-garde ideas.

The disruption of the war, however, shifted the creative centre of furniture design from Europe to the United States, a shift for which the ground had been prepared before the war by the emigration to the States of such influential figures as Mies van der Rohe and Walter Gropius, fleeing the increasingly restrictive regime in their native Germany. Even after the war it was no longer from France or Germany, but from other European countries, that there issued a fresh and exciting new stream of ideas, notably from Italy and from Scandinavia.

The forties, certainly, were years of considerable restriction but they were at the same time years marked by important innovations. In certain instances these innovations were born of necessity, most specifically in the development of new materials. The shortage of certain raw materials, including wood, and the research needs of the war effort led to the development of new synthetics and lightweight alloys which, adapted to peace-time conditions, were to have a major influence on the history of furniture in the post-war years.

The first major influence after 1940 was the American development, led by Charles Eames and Eero Saarinen, of the functionalist tradition but in a new guise which might aptly be dubbed Organic Modernism. In Europe, through the forties and fifties, the story was of a continuing rivalry between innovation and tradition. It was the Scandinavians, and particularly Denmark's designers and manufacturers, who found a harmonious compromise between the need for stylistic evolution and the respect for traditional materials and values. Good traditional craftsmanship and materials and simple, rational forms, new but rooted in the best of the past, became the hallmarks of a Scandinavian style, the influence of which was considerable in the fifties and into the sixties. Meanwhile, however, a sleek reinterpretation of pre-war Modernism came into vogue around 1960 and this neo-Modernist style came to express status and fashionable awareness in business and domestic contexts in the new age of jet travel and prestige skyscraper office blocks.

The sixties witnessed a widespread cultural upheaval which was to make its mark in furniture as in other areas of design. It was the decade in which youth, irreverently, claimed an unprecedentedly significant role as the shaping force in every manifestation of style. New sets of values came into play in furniture design. In the Pop era, the fun factor became a major ingredient. This was the decade of brash new ideas, blow-up or knock-down furniture, disposable furniture in printed cardboard. Plastic became a lively alternative to wood or metal and, above all, it was the era of bright colour.

Through the sixties and seventies, however, and, indeed, into the eighties the dominant thread in the story of furniture design has been the increasing supremacy in the world market of Italian designers and manufacturers, a supremacy which manifests itself in virtually ever facet of furniture design, from the creation of instant classics of sound yet stylish design in noble materials through witty experiment or revolutionary new concepts such as Joe Colombo's prototype living units to the creation of intelligent designs for mass-production in plastics.

The seventies have also been marked by a strong revival of fine craft work in the creation of individualistic pieces of furniture, which contrasts dramatically with the concurrent vogue for 'High Tech' or Industrial Style furnishings, a homage to machine-age functionalism and the spiritual antithesis of the craft tradition.

American Experiments

Architect/designer Charles Eames is without doubt the single most influential force in furniture design to have emerged since 1940. His influence has been international and he must surely rank as one of, if not the, most important furniture designer of the post 1940 era. Eames was born in 1907, studied architecture and, in 1930, opened his own practice. In 1936 he accepted a fellowship at the Cranbrook Academy where, the following year, he became head of the Department of Experimental Design. It was at Cranbrook that he met Eero Saarinen with whom he was to collaborate to produce the prize-winning entries for the 1940 competition, organised by the New York Museum of Modern Art, for 'Organic Design in Home Furnishings.' The competition was inspired by a suggestion from Bloomingdales who saw it as a means of encouraging and promoting the talents of young designers.

The winning entries submitted by Eames and Saarinen involved rationalized, immensely practical solutions to the problems of

Left: The Prototype chaise by Charles Eames, 1948, is an exercise in the new style. Raised on distinctive thin legs, which he had been the first to introduce, this asymmetrical free-form seat, curving in every direction, with an off-centre cutout, might have been the creation of Henry Moore or Barbara Hepworth.

Left: Installation of furniture designed by Charles Eames and Eero Saarinen exhibited at the Museum of Modern Art's 1941 exhibition of Organic Design in Home Furnishings. Their revolutionary new concepts in seating and other living-room furniture won them first prize.

creating adaptable storage furniture and dramatically new concepts in the design of seat furniture. Their modular, infinitely adaptable storage units on low table bases set the pattern for a type of storage system which is still very much in vogue and which was to render obsolete most traditional cabinet furniture and their innovations extended both to forms and to materials. The distinctive new feature of Eames's and Saarinen's chair designs, as with Eames's later independent designs, was the quite separate consideration extended to the seat unit and to the supporting sub-structure. Eames and Saarinen experimented with plywood but went much further than Aalto and sculpted it into seat shells with multi-directional curves and flexibility. Experimentation with fibreglass and synthetics became a natural progression in Eames's sculptural approach to seat furniture design. In 1946 he was honoured with a small one-man exhibition at the Museum of Modern Art. His work as designer to the firm of Herman Miller established a distinctive look, associated most particularly with the contract sector and helped establish Herman Miller as a manufacturing and contract furnishing company of world-wide influence. Eames is best known for his leather-upholstered plywood and cast aluminium Lounge Chair '670' and Ottoman of 1956, an instant classic of modern design. His erstwhile associate Saarinen is acknowledged above all for his gracious 'Tulip'

chairs and matching marble or laminate-topped tables of 1957. Both designers used elegant, ergonomic curves in a fluid, 'Organic' version of functionalist Modernism which was to make a most significant mark on the evolution of furniture in the forties and fifties.

The continuing involvement of the Museum of Modern Art in encouraging the furniture industry's awareness of good design led to a second competition, in 1948, for 'Low Cost Furniture Design.' in which two British designers, Robin Day and Clive Latimer, took the laurels with their first prize-winning design for wall storage units. Day recently acknowledged the extent to which he and others of his generation were inspired by the American examples.

Europe: Invention Versus Tradition

In Europe, through the forties and into the fifties, furniture evolved in a variety of styles, ranging from the inventiveness and stylishness of Italian designs, through the conservatism of many French designs to the contrasting 'Utility' and 'Festival of Britain' phases which characterised British production. Only the Scandinavians seemed able to judiciously avoid extremes, forging a style which was to have a marked influence internationally.

In the United Kingdom, war-time shortages led to the institution of the 'Utility' furniture programme. On July 8 1942 the Advisory

Top: Charles Eames' most celebrated design, his new Classic Lounge Chair 670 and Ottoman 671, designed in 1956 for Herman Miller. Leather-covered upholstery in rosewood, veneered plywood cradle, with cast aluminium brackets and base.

Above : British furniture from the British Utility ranges of 1947. Manufacturers were restricted to designs in these ranges as materials were still subject to controls and goods were therefore made with available rather than the most suitable of materials. Thus manufacturers turned their wartime technology to civilian use by utilising surplus war materials not previously applied to furniture. This tubular metal bed displays in practice many of the theories of low-cost functional simplicity advocated in the 1920's by the Bauhaus.

Committee on Utility Furniture was established in an endeavour to rationalize the British furniture industry, imposing a standradized set of designs, conceived under the aegis of Gordon Russell, who saw the scheme not only as a means of controlling the use of dwindling supplies of raw materials but as an opportunity to instil a sound design sense in British furniture manufacturers. The scheme lasted ten years, and, whilst undoubtedly a most creditable solution to war-time problems, left a legacy of furniture which is as drab as it is soundly designed and which serves only to demonstrate by default that good design involves delighting the eye and the spirit as much as fulfilling a practical function. A new generation of designers helped lift the spirits of the British public with novel furniture designs, characterized above all by slender frameworks in seat furniture, often of steel rod, and by contrasts of masses and slender legs for cabinet furniture. At the forefront of this style, associated with the 1951 'Festival of Britain', were Robin Day and Clive Latimer, Ernest Race and Dennis Young.

Most British designs of the period around 1950 owe much to American and Italian sources and the 'Festival' style was already very much in evidence, as an Italian invention, at the 1948 Milan Triennale. Italian furniture designers, based in the two commercial centres of Milan and Turin, created a distinctive style in the years immediately following the war. For this group, indeed, style was the primary concern; form took precedence over function and the pursuit of stylish form led to the creation of some of the most remarkable furniture of the period, furniture which veered precariously between exaggerated stylishness and eccentricity. Organic, sculptural forms, contrasting with attenuated limbs of a precious refinement characterised the Italian look – a lively, witty mode which was precisely the tonic required after the depressing years of wartime austerity. Carlo Mollino of Turin is today the most highly regarded Italian designer of those years. Amongst his contemporaries, Renzo Zavanella, Ico Parisi, Osvaldo Borsani and Carlo de Carli also deserve mention.

French furniture was never to recover, after the war, the international supremacy which it had enjoyed in the twenties as in previous eras. French supremacy had been founded on the creation of elegant and fashionable furniture of the highest quality for a comparatively small and wealthy market. The French furniture industry was dominated by long-standing traditions of fine cabinet-making. France had produced a number of revolutionary designers in the Modernist ethic, notably Le Corbusier, Pierre Chareau, René Herbst, Robert Mallet-Stevens and Eileen Gray, but their ideas had found only the narrowest following amongst a handful of cognoscenti. The history of furniture since the war has been dominated by an increasingly wide and increasingly aware middle-class market and the traditional French ideals of fine cabinet-work have been rendered obsolete, as, indeed, have so many of the standard items of cabinet furniture which were the mainstay of French tradition, but have no role in the modern home with its built-in storage or modular wall units. Despite their fundamental conservatism, French designers nonetheless launched certain interesting fashions. Amongst the most handsome French pieces of the post war years are the designs of André Dupré Laffon or Jacques Adnet covered in saddle-stitched hide by Hermès. Jean Royère established himself as one of the leading designer/decorators and amongst his specialities was furniture covered in split straw, an idea borrowed from Jean-Michel Frank.

The Scandinavian Influence

The Scandinavians had, in the thirties, rejected the extremes of International Modernism. The coldness of metal and glass furniture and the hard lines of the Modernist style were alien to the Scandinavian temperament. Scandinavian designers sought to be modern but within the framework of traditional values. The Danish designer and teacher Kaare Klint had, before the war, established himself as the spiritual godfather of the moderate Scandinavian style, stressing the need to preserve the arts and crafts tradition and promoting wood as a far more human and inviting material than metal for furniture design.

297

Finnish designer Alvar Aalto had, in the thirties, started the influential experiments with plywood and laminated wood with which he was to persevere with equal success after the war. A deep-rooted respect for the mellow qualities of wood and a leaning towards moderation would in themselves, however, hardly have sufficed to put Scandinavians at the very forefront of furniture design, exporting their products to a wide international market. The success story owes much to official involvement in encouraging good design and craftmanship and in manufacturers' awareness that their success depended on maintaining high self-imposed standards. Danish manufacturers set up their own 'Furniture Manufacturers' Quality Control Board' and in Den Permanente in Copenhagen

established a permanent showcase of the very best Danish design. As early as 1927 Denmark's furniture makers had grouped themselves into an exhibition society under the title of the Danish Cabinet Maker's Guild. In Finland, Ornamo, an association of industrial designers, worked to maintain a strong national image in furniture design as in other areas of manufacture. Sweden's Slöjdföreningen played a similar role and published high-standard guidelines to which designers and manufacturers should aspire. The secret of Scandinavian success was a happy implementation of the Arts and Crafts ideal, a perfect marriage between the interests of designer and manufacturer. International exhibitions, including the 1954 'Design in Scandinavia' show in the United States and the 1956 'Formes Scandinaves' at the Musée des Arts Décoratifs, Paris, helped promote a look of which the most characteristic features were gentle curves, well-crafted, fluid joints, an absence of decoration, coverings and upholstery in natural colours and the use of woods in their natural colours, simply oiled or waxed. Teak was much used by Danish designers and is the wood most popularly associated with the Scandinavian look. Amongst the most notable designers were Alvar Aalto, whose manufacturing firm, Artek, had been set up in 1935, and Carl Malmsten and Bruno Mathsson, both Swedes and both well established before the war. Denmark's most talented designers included Borge Mogensen, Finn Juhl and Hans Wegner, the latter responsible for a piece of furniture, designed in 1949 and known quite simply as 'The Chair' which is a perfect expression of the Danish, and the Scandinavian ideal. It is a perfectly proportioned, restrained and harmonious exercise in Organic Modernism, carved in walnut and mahogany with woven cane seat. Two other distinguished Danish designers deserve mention, Arne Jacobsen and Poul Kjaerholm, though their work, with their fondness for metal frames and bases, leads the way into another phase of post-war furniture design, the re-emergence and re-interpretation of Modernism in the late fifties and early sixties.

The New Modernism

By the late fifties the more extreme styles which had enjoyed a popularity after the war years now looked distinctly unfashionable. The whimsy, the sculptural exaggeration, the studied thinness and amoeboid shapes of the Festival of Britain or Italian styles had exhausted their appeal. The more disciplined, Organic Modernism of Charles Eames' forties experiments and the solid good sense of Scandinavian design had proved their more lasting qualities but the remorseless cycle of fashion demanded a change and the change came with a re-appraisal and reworking of pre-war Modernism. The New Modernism was inspired by the best of pre-war Modernist design tempered by the lessons learnt from the U.S. and from Scandinavia since the war.

The New Modernist phase in furniture design found a quite different market and quite different contexts to those of its precursor. Since the thirties there was an increasing trend towards fluidity in the disposition of living areas in domestic and office architecture. Open-plan was the order of the day. Designers encouraged a sense of spatial continuity between indoor spaces and, where possible, between indoor and outdoor areas. Domestic architects tended more and more to build in storage space, minimising the need for storage furniture. Uncluttered spaces demanded spare and clean-limbed furnishings At the same time the boom being enjoyed by Western ecomomies opened up a whole new corporate and municipal market and created a large demand for prestige contract furnishings. The New Modernist style perfectly expressed the new prosperity, rather through the confident strength of design and materials than through conspicuous opulence. Understatement, indeed, was the very basis of the New Modernism, following Mies van der Rohe's 'less is more' ethic, achieving stylishness by elimination. The most important proponents of the New Modernism included a number of major international designers, and, perhaps more significantly, the large manufacturing and contract furnishing companies for whom certain amongst them contributed designs.

The two most influential firms were the

Left: Herman Miller 1950s design for what was known as the 'Action' Office. The New Modernist phase saw the advent of 'open-plan' space which demanded spare and clean-limbed furnishings, perfectly expressed here.

American companies Herman Miller and Knoll International. Herman Miller had employed Charles Eames since the forties and through the fifties and sixties expanded their operations under the direction of George Nelson, specializing in the contract sector and claiming a major share of this increasingly significant market. In the fifties Eames worked on a new range of designs and in 1958 launched his 'Aluminium' group. In these new

Left: Armchair and marble-topped table by Eero Saarinen, the great master of the modern curvilinear style which he carried through on every scale. He created this range of pedestal furniture for Knoll and it was first manufactured in 1956.

*Right: 'Form' seating
designed by Robin Day for
Hille in 1957, a classic
exercise in the new
modernist vein.*

designs, simple pronged pedestal bases, cast in aluminium, replaced the often complex steel rod bases which he had·used in the forties. The result was a far more sleek silhouette, in keeping with the new fashion for the cleanest possible lines.

Knoll International was founded by Hans and Florence Knoll, former colleagues of Eames at the Cranbrook Academy. Knoll opened branches in France and Germany in 1951 and its British branch, Form International, set up in 1970, has since amalgamated with the leading British post-war contract furnishing company, Hille. Knoll and Herman Miller have transformed the concept of furniture design for office and public contexts and since these firms and their like came to the fore in the fifties one is as likely to find stylishness and design innovation in an office foyer, a college campus or an airport lounge as in a domestic setting.

Metal played an important part in New Modernist furniture, in conjunction with glass, hide, wood or new synthetic materials for desk-tops, facings and panelling. After a lapse of little more than a quarter of a century the masterpieces of the first phase of Modernism were once again in vogue and designs by Marcel Breuer or Mies van der Rohe dating from the late twenties would be judiciously counterpoised with current designs. Knoll International re-issued Mies's 'Barcelona' chair, which acquired a new status as a symbol of a particular approach to design. Designers, meanwhile, were creating their own instant classics. Eames' designs deserve

special credit. The Dane Arne Jacobsen created two remarkable designs in 1958, swivel chairs on cast aluminium pedestal bases with graciously sculpted upholstered seat shells, appropriately called the 'Egg' and 'Swan' chairs. Poul Kjaerholm has created a range of designs of a great austerity of line in flat steel and cane or hide. Robin Day designed for Hille and his clean-lined 'Form' range of 1957 is a classic exercise in the New Modernist vein. Ernest Race, designing for his own firm, Race Furniture, created stylish metal framed domestic and contract designs. New Modernist furniture evolved from the uncluttered, low lined, Contemporary look of the fifties but by the mid sixties had acquired a somewhat different character. Noticeably, chromium-plated tubular steel furniture, the *sine qua non* of Modernism in the thirties was very much in vogue once again, used for chairs, armchairs and the ubiquitous glass-topped coffee table. A new rationalism was also now in evidence in the work of a generation of Italian furniture designers who, abandoning the self-conscious stylistic pursuits of their predecessors, were commanding international attention for the classic simplicity and quality of their products.

'Pop' Styles

Modernism flourished through the sixties and, indeed, still plays a valid role in attitudes to furniture design. In the sixties, however, and since, other forces have come into play and Modernism has become only one of several choices. The sixties witnessed a revolution in attitudes and altogether new values came to dominate furniture design. A new, young market welcomed novel notions which included knock-down furniture, designed for easy transport and capable of being assembled in moments by the purchaser, blow-up furniture in transparent plastic, and even disposable furniture, made up by folding and tucking large sheets of printed card. Traditional ideals of craft were ousted by an ethic which prized wit, fun and invention above quality.

In the sixties, synthetics played an increasingly important role, not, as so often before, merely as more versatile or practical substitutes for natural materials but as exciting materials to be emphasised rather than disguised. At last plastics were welcomed not just as truly remarkable discoveries but as attractive materials in their own right, and forms were evolved to stress the sculptural potential and the strength and resilience of the sophisticated plastics now available. In 1960 Verner Panton designed the first single unit injection moulded plastic cantilever stacking chair, put into production in 1967 by Herman Miller. A bright new palette of bold primaries was used in plastic as in other furniture, most appropriate in the decade of

'Pop' art and American Hard-Edge abstract painting.

Together with the bright, Pop colours came a host of bright, often brash pop ideas and pieces of furniture were created which became an extension of Pop Art sculpture. Many of the most lively ideas came from London, hub of the youthful cultural explosion and, most notably, from the short-lived shop 'Mr Freedom.' English artist Allen Jones created a range of furniture sculptures in the form of life-size, fetishistic female figures. In France sculptor César made a number of amusing pieces in the Pop spirit and sculptor/furniture creator François Lalanne conceived a menagerie of Pop animal furniture – two ostriches were a bar, sheep became stools, sardines in a can a bed and a hippo a complete bathroom. Italian designers came up with their own witty Pop furniture designs which included such ideas as a chair in the form of a giant leather base-ball glove, polyurethane seats with the appearance of boulders, a floor lamp in the form of a palm tree.

Another aspect of sixties invention was a host of futuristic 'space-age' furniture designs inspired by the major breakthroughs and achievements of the decade in space travel. Chairs were designed to look like furnishings

Bottom: English Pop artist Allen Jones sculpted a disturbingly life-like series of fetishistic leather-clad women, glossy fantasies in the form of coat stands, tables and chairs. An Allen Jones table sculpture, 1969.

Left: The 'Cab' chair
designed by Mario Bellin
in 1977 and manufactured
by the Milan based firm,
Cassina. The saddle-
stitched hide covering zips
into place over the skeletal
steel frame.

Far left: Vico Magristretti
chair designed for Artemide
in the late sixties, and
still in production.

Left: One of the most
fantastic designs by Gian
Carlo Piretti for Anonima
Castelli. Known as the
'Pluvium' umbrella stand,
it is moulded in ABS
plastic with six eccentrically
pivoting umbrella rings;
it was manufactured
throughout the 1970's as
part of the PL range.

of a space vehicle and no one design better exemplifies this fantasy fad than Finnish designer Eero Aarnio's 'Globe' chair, a white capsule revolving on a circular white base.

Italy—The New Domestic Landscape

By the mid-sixties and despite the eye-catching and headline-making ideas being generated elsewhere it was becoming increasingly evident that the lead in furniture design was being taken by Italian designers and manufacturers. Italians were as capable as any of producing funky ideas for furniture that was only one step away from sculpture, but the Italians were, at the same time, establishing a solidly based reputation for good design and for good quality of execution.

The success of this new Italian image depended on the vitality of a group of designers, most of whom had design interests far wider than merely the creation of furniture and who saw furniture as just one facet of domestic and industrial design. It depended also on the intelligence of the heads of Italy's furniture manufacturing concerns, always ready to experiment and willing to extend their trust to the designers. If one firm is to be singled out for the influence it has exerted, then it must be the firm of Cassina of Milan.

Cassina has earned an enviable reputation for its consistently high standards of design and manufacture, enlisting the skills of Italy's most gifted designers, including Vico Magistretti, Afra and Tobia Scarpa and Mario Bellini. The Cassina range is distinguished by the discreet luxury of the materials used and by the equally discreet perfectionism of the designs. The thought, the cleverness that go into the concepts are never betrayed by gimmickry; innovation is tempered by sobriety. The Cassina image is associated with contrasts of marble and glass, wood and fine quality hide and the Cassina catalogue of

recent designs has been augmented by the re-edition of twentieth century design classics by such makers as Charles Rennie Mackintosh and Le Corbusier. Cassina is not alone and other Italian firms have produced notable designs, amongst them the firms of Saporiti, Anonima Castelli, Skipper, B&B Italia, Studio Artemide and Kartell, ranging from furniture individually crafted in marble to pieces mass-produced in injection-moulded plastics. Amongst the designers, Gae Aulenti, Cini Boeri, Giovanni Offredi, Enzo Mari, Marco Zanusso, Achille Castiglione and Angelo Mangiarotti stand out for their contribution to this Italian renaissance.

The influence of Italy's designers in shaping the current look of furniture was acknowledged with a major exhibition in 1972 at the Museum of Modern Art – 'Italy, the New Domestic Landscape.' Here could be seen not only the modern classics by Cassina and comparable manufacturers but also the intelligent application of high design standards to mass-production and the remarkable fruits of a spirit of adventure in furniture design which went far beyond the accepted bounds. Perhaps the two most brilliant minds whose talents were spotlighted in the '72 exhibition were Joe Colombo and Ettore Sottsass Jnr.

Colombo's career lasted a mere ten years, cut short by his untimely death in 1971. He made a few outstanding designs for manufacture in plastics and showed a complete sympathy with the medium. His 'Boby' trolley designed in 1968 and still in production is a brilliantly thought-out design and his stacking chairs for Kartell are amongst the best chair designs in plastic. His imaginative approach, however, encompassed many media including synthetic foam from which he constructed variable modular seat furniture, plywood and other materials with which he always found highly personal forms. In the 1972 exhibition, were also shown, posthumously, his advanced concept of living units, cells into which were built solutions to every necessary domestic furniture function. Colombo should rank amongst the most important innovators in modern furniture.

Ettore Sottsass Jnr. is an altogether different prospect, a brilliant industrial designer whose involvement in furniture design can be guaranteed to save the industry from any risk of complacency. In 1972 he showed cabinets in laminated wood which were like monoliths, the furniture counterparts of Hard-Edge abstractionist sculptures.

In 1980, by which date, perhaps, the Italian image was taken for granted and new designs, however good, were following a too predic-

table, safe pattern, Sottsass set up a design partnership, 'Memphis,' and he, and the young designers whose help he enlisted, gave free rein to their imaginations. They produced zany, iconoclastic designs, colourful, eccentric, seemingly unbalanced, which made a startling impact at the 1981 Milan furniture salon, completely undermining accepted standards and injecting a breath of fresh air into an industry which was in danger of becoming too staid.

The Seventies: Crafts Versus Industry
The history of furniture has, over the past decade, been a story of great contrasts. The story of Italian furniture has, arguably, been the most successful, showing the development of a true sympathy between designer and manufacturer. The Italians have found an ideal middle course, always ready to try new ideas on the public, but, at the same time, respecting the needs of the market and producing furniture of great stylishness but also of rational and practical design.

At the same time, others have gone to ideological extremes and the seventies have

Right: Desk for two people designed by John Makepeace and made in his workshops. Hollywood and macassar ebony. Makepeace's perfectionism, his bold choice and mixture of woods and other materials, has set new standards for the creation of highly individualistic furniture in this British-and-American led revival of hand-crafted furniture.

304

Right: A pair of chairs in sycamore with walnut inlay and leather seats, made by Rupert Williamson in 1980.

witnessed two opposed phenomena – the strong revival of interest in the creation, in small workshops, of individualistic, hand-crafted pieces, and, at the other extreme, the fashion for so-called 'High-Tech' or Industrial Style furniture and furnishings, which was celebrated and promoted by the publication in 1978 of the book *High Tech – the Industrial Style and Source Book for the Home* by Joan Kron and Susan Slesin.

The craft revival, which had its strongest roots in the United Kingdom and in the United States, can be understood as a kind of protest against the increasingly industrialized, some might say de-humanized world in which we live. It is a protest against the increasingly impersonal nature of our environment. Contemporary craft furniture is a sophisticated expression of the artisan's joy in his craft, the new craft workshops providing an opportunity for the artist/craftsman to create work which can serve a functional purpose whilst being the vehicle for expressing a philosophical, humanist message. Craft furniture, is, of necessity a luxury industry, perhaps belying the humble sincerity of the spirit which inspires it and the movement has produced craftsmen of considerable skill and invention and individual pieces of great merit.

The British founding father of the movement is John Makepeace, who set up his own workshop in Oxfordshire in 1963 and who, in 1977, was at last able to fulfil his ambition of opening a school for young apprentice furniture designer/craftsmen, at Parnham House in Dorset. Makepeace has inspired a whole generation of young talents, instilling in them a passion for wood and a desire to work it in the most expressive way. Makepeace himself has devised novel forms for furniture and his skills include the use, often in juxtaposition, of a wide range of native and exotic woods, counterpointed by the occasional use of modern synthetic materials or hides.

Amongst the more distinguished practitioners of the craft mode are the British craftsmen Rupert Williamson, John Coleman and Martin Grierson. American Wendell Castle has created extraordinary pieces, sculpted into forms which call to mind the anthropomorphic sculptural exercises of certain more extreme Art Nouveau designers, and he has earned in the United States a place as teacher, and a reputation as craftsman comparable with that held by Makepeace in the United Kingdom. Meanwhile, the proponents of the Industrial Style espouse the impersonal values of the industralized world and adapt industrial designs, from commercial metal shelving to surgical trolleys, for domestic use.

Where the future lies is impossible to predict, but it can be guaranteed that the ever-turning wheels of taste and fashion will inspire further exciting developments in the story of furniture design.

Collections

Austria
Bundes Mobilien Verwaltung, VIENNA
Hofburg, Silberne Kapelle und Hofkirche,
    VIENNA
Kunstgewerbe Museum, VIENNA
Kunsthistorisches Museum, VIENNA
Osterreichisches Museum für Angewandte
    Kunst, VIENNA
Schönbrunn Palast und Park, VIENNA
Technisches Museum für Industrie und
    Gewerbe, VIENNA

Belgium
Hôtel Solvay, BRUSSELS
Hôtel van Eetevelde, BRUSSELS
Musée Horta, BRUSSELS
Musée Curtius, LIÈGE
Musée d'Ansembourg, LIÈGE
Musée de Mariemont, MARIEMONT

Czechoslovakia
Červeny Kamen, ČERVENY KAMEN
Hluboká Castle, ČESKÉ BUDĚJOVICE,
    South Bohemia
National Gallery, PRAGUE
Sychrov Castle, near PRAGUE

Denmark
Danske Kunstindustri Museet,
    COPENHAGEN
Nationalmuseet, COPENHAGEN
Rosenborg Castle, COPENHAGEN

Egypt
Cairo Museum, CAIRO

Federal Republic of Germany
Residenz, BAMBURG
Germanisches Nationalmuseum, BERLIN
Schloss Charlottenburg, BERLIN
Museum Folkwang, ESSEN
Museum für Kunsthandwerk, FRANKFURT-
    AM-MAIN
Museum für Kunst und Gewerbe,
    HAMBURG
Schloss Linderhof, LINDERHOF, Bavaria
Reiss-Museum, MANNHEIM
Bayerisches Nationalmuseum, MUNICH
Residenzmuseum, MUNICH
Landesmuseum für kunst und Kultur-
    geschichte, MUNSTER
Germanisches Nationalmuseum,
    NUREMBERG

Schloss Pommersfelden, POMMERSFELDEN
Residenz, WURZBURG

Finland
Finnish Society of Crafts and Design,
    HELSINKI

France
Château de Compiègne
Château de Ferrières
Château de Fontainebleau
Musée de Lyon, LYON
Musée de l'Ecole de Nancy, NANCY
Musée Thomas-Dobree et Musée archéo-
    logique, NANTES
Musée Condé, Château de Chantilly, OISE
Château de Malmaison, near PARIS
Collection Henriette Bouvier, Musée
    Carnavalet, PARIS
Musée de Cluny, PARIS
Musée des Arts Décoratifs, PARIS
Musée du Louvre, PARIS
Musée Jacquemart-Andre, PARIS
Musée Nissim-de-Camondo, PARIS
Château de Champs, Seine et Marne
Musée de Strasbourg, STRASBOURG
Musée de Versailles et de Trianons au
    Château de Versailles

German Democratic Republic
Historisches Museum, DRESDEN
Museum für Kunsthandwerke, DRESDEN
Schloss Pillnitz, near DRESDEN
Staatliche Schlösser und Gärten,
    POTSDAM-SANSOUCCI

Great Britain
The American Museum in Britain,
    Claverton Manor, near BATH, Avon
Waddesdon Manor, Buckinghamshire
Fitzwilliam Museum, CAMBRIDGE,
    Cambridgeshire
The Bowes Museum, Barnard Castle,
    County Durham
Hardwick Hall, Derbyshire
Glasgow University Collection, GLASGOW,
    Scotland
Dyrham Park, Gloucestershire
Osborne House, EAST COWES, Isle of Wight
The Newarke Houses, LEICESTER,
    Leicestershire
Bethnal Green Museum, LONDON
British Museum, LONDON

Geffreye Museum, Shoreditch, LONDON
Hampton Court Palace, Middlesex
Victoria & Albert Museum, LONDON
Wallace Collection, LONDON
William Morris Gallery, Walthamstow, LONDON
Ashmolean Museum, OXFORD, Oxfordshire
Clandon Park, Surrey
Ham House, PETERSHAM, Surrey
Brighton Art Gallery and Museums, BRIGHTON, Sussex
Corsham Court, Wiltshire
Nostell Priory, Yorkshire
Temple Newsam House, LEEDS, Yorkshire

Italy
Palazzo Rappini, ARPINO
Galleria degli Uffizi, FLORENCE
Museo Horne, FLORENCE
Palazzo Davanzati, FLORENCE
Palazzo Pitti, FLORENCE
Galleria di Palazzo Rosso, GENOA
Palazzo Balbi-Durazzo, GENOA
Galleria del Levante, MILAN
Museo d'Arte Antica: Castello Sforzesco, MILAN
Museo Poldi Pezzoli, MILAN
Palazzo Clerici, MILAN
Museo e Gallerie Nazionale di Capo-dimonte, NAPLES
Museo Nazionale, NAPLES
Galleria Nazionale d'Arte Moderna, ROME
Museo di Palazzo Venezia, ROME
Palazzo Barberini, ROME
Palazzo Colonna, ROME
Palazzo Doria, ROME
Vatican Museums, ROME
Pinacoteca Nazionale, SIENA
Villa La Rocca, SORAGNA
Museo 'Correale di Terranova', SORRENTO
Villa Pisani, Stra
Civico Museo Sartorio, TRIESTE
Museo dell'Arredamento, Stupinigi, TURIN
Palazzina di Caccia, Stupinigi, TURIN
Palazzo Madama, TURIN
Palazzo ex Reale, TURIN
Ca' Rezzonico, VENICE
Palazzo Querini-Stampalia, VENICE

The Netherlands
Rijksmuseum, AMSTERDAM
Stedelijk Museum, AMSTERDAM
Gemeentemuseum, THE HAGUE

Centraal Museum, UTRECHT
Kasteel Duivenoorde, VOORSCHOTEN

Norway
Kunstindustrimuseet i Oslo, OSLO
Nordenfjeldske Kundindustrimuseum, TRONDHEIM

Poland
National Museum, Warsaw

Portugal
Museu Nacional de Arte Antiga, LISBON
Museu-Escola de Artes Decorativas, LISBON
Museu Guerra Junqueira, OPORTO
Museu Nacional de Soares dos Reis, OPORTO
Palacio Nacional de Queluz, QUELUZ

Spain
Museo de Arte Moderno, BARCELONA
Museo Nacional de Artes Decorativas, BARCELONA
Museo Gaudí, BARCELONA
Museo Nacional de Artes Decorativas, MADRID
Palacio Nacional, MADRID

Sweden
Drottningholm Palace, near STOCKHOLM
Historiska Museum, STOCKHOLM
Nationalmuseum, STOCKHOLM
Nordiska Museet, STOCKHOLM
Skokloster Castle, SKOKLOSTER
Royal Palace, STOCKHOLM

Switzerland
Historisches Museum, BASLE
Musée de Valère, SION
Kunstgewerbemuseum und Museum Bellerive, ZURICH
Schweizerisches Landesmuseum Musée National Suisse, ZURICH

USA
Gamble House, Greene and Greene Library, PASADENA, California
Los Angeles County Museum of Art, California
Oakland Museum, OAKLAND, California
The Art Galleries, University of California, SANTA BARBARA, California

Art Institute of Chicago, CHICAGO
Chicago School of Architecture Foundation, CHICAGO
Wadsworth Atheneum, HARTFORD, Connecticut
Yale University Art Gallery, NEW HAVEN, Connecticut
Henry Francis du Pont Winterthur Museum, WINTERTHUR, Delaware
Victoria Mansion (Morse-Libby House), PORTLAND, Maine
Walters Art Gallery, BALTIMORE, Maryland
Boston Museum of Fine Arts, BOSTON, Massachusetts
Greenfield Village and Henry Ford Museum, DEARBORN, Michigan
Nelson-Atkins Gallery of Art, KANSAS CITY, Missouri
Albright-Knox Art Gallery, BUFFALO, New York State
Fine Arts Academy, BUFFALO, New York State
Brooklyn Museum, BROOKLYN, New York State
Cooper-Hewitt Museum of Decorative Arts and Design, NEW YORK
Frick Collection, NEW YORK
The Hispanic Society of America Museum, NEW YORK
Lyndhurst, TARRYTOWN, New York State
The Metropolitan Museum of Art, NEW YORK
The Museum of Modern Art, NEW YORK
Museum of the City of New York, NEW YORK
Philadelphia Museum of Art, PHILADELPHIA, Pennsylvania
Rhode Island School of Design, RHODE ISLAND
Colonial Williamsburg Foundation, WILLIAMSBURG, Virginia
The Virginia Museum of Fine Arts, RICHMOND, Virginia
Governor's House, Colonial Williamsburg, Virginia

USSR
Katalnaya Gorka, Oranienbaum, LENINGRAD
Museum Palaces and Parks in Pavlovsk, LENINGRAD
Palace of Peterhof, LENINGRAD
Palace of Tsarskoe Selo, LENINGRAD
State Hermitage Museum, LENINGRAD

Bibliography

General

Aprà, N *The Louis Styles* (Orbis Publishing, London 1972)

Ayres, J *American Antiques* (Orbis Publishing, London 1973)

Burr, G H *Hispanic Furniture from the 15th century through the 17th century* (Archive Press, New York 1964)

Copplestone, T (Ed) *World Architecture* (Paul Hamlyn, London 1963, 8th impression 1975)

Edwards, R (Ed) *The Dictionary of English furniture—from the Middle Ages to the late Georgian period*, 3 vols (Country Life, Feltham, 2nd revised edition 1954)

Edwards, R *The Shorter Dictionary of English Furniture* (Country Life, Feltham 1964)

Edwards, R & Jourdain, M *Georgian Cabinet-Makers* (Country Life, Feltham, 3rd edition 1955)

Fastnedge, R *English Furniture Styles 1500–1830* (Penguin Books, Harmondsworth 1955)

Fletcher, B *A History of Architecture* (The Athlone Press, University of London 1961)

Gloag, J (Ed) *A Short Dictionary of Furniture* (George Allen & Unwin, London, 2nd edition 1969)

Gonzales-Palacios, A *I mobili nei secoli*, 10 vols (Fabbri, Milan 1969)

Hayward, H (Ed) *World Furniture* (Paul Hamlyn, Feltham 1969)

Honour, H *Cabinet Makers and Furniture Designers* (Weidenfeld & Nicolson, London 1969)

Huth, H *Lacquer of the West: the History of a Craft and an Industry, 1600–1950* (University of Chicago Press, Chicago 1971)

Joy, E, *The Connoisseur Illustrated Guides: Furniture* (The Connoisseur, London 1975)

Kreisel, H (Ed) *Die Kunst des Deutsches Möbels*, 3 vols (C H Beck, Munich 1968–74)

Mercer, E *Furniture to 1700* (Weidenfeld & Nicolson, London 1969)

Philippe, J *Mobilier liègeois, moyen âge—XIXe siècle* (Liège 1962)

Salvy, C *Dictionnaire des meubles régionaux* (Hachette, Paris 1971)

Verlet, P (Ed) *Styles, meubles, décors du Moyen Age à nos jours*, 2 vols (Larousse, Paris 1972)

The Archaeological Record

Baker, H S *Furniture in the Ancient World* (The Connoisseur, London 1966)

Burford, A *Craftsmen in Greek and Roman Society* (Thames & Hudson, London 1972)

Carter, H *Tomb of Tutankhamen* (Barrie & Jenkins, London 1972; Sphere, London 1972)

Lasko, P *Ars Sacra 800–1200* (Penguin Books, Harmondsworth 1972)

Muller-Christensen, S *Alte Möbel vom Mittelalter bis zum Jugenstil* (F Bruckmann, Munich 1957)

Richter, G M A *The Furniture of the Greeks, Etruscans and Romans* (Phaidon Press, London 1966)

The Classical Revival

Bode, W *Die italienischen Hausmöbel der Renaissance* (H Seemann, Leipzig 1902; New York, trans M E Herrick 1921)

Boynton, L O J (Ed) *The Hardwick Hall Inventories of 1601* (Furniture History Society, London 1971)

Brunhammer, Y & de Fayet, M *Meubles et Ensembles, Epoque moyen âge et renaissance* (Larousse, Paris 1966)

Brunhammer, Y & de Fayet, M *Meubles et Ensembles, Louis XIII et Louis XIV* (Larousse, Paris 1966)

du Cerceau, J A *Oeuvres*, 2 vols (Guimard, Paris 1884–91)

Eberlein, H D *Interiors, fireplaces and furniture of the Italian renaissance* (The Architectural Book Publishing Co., New York 1916)

Enriquez, M D *El Mueble Español en los Siglos XV, XVI y XVII* (Panaceos, Madrid 1951)

von Falke, O (Ed) *Deutsche Möbel des Mittelalters und der Renaissance* (J Hoffmann, Stuttgart 1924)

Jervis, S (Ed) *Printed Furniture Designs 1650* (Furniture History Society, London 1974)

Lognon, H A & Huard, F W *French provincial furniture* (J B Lippincott Co., Philadelphia 1927)

Moller, L *Der Wrangelschrank und Die verwandten süddeutschen Intarsienmöbel des 16 Jahrhunderts* (R Linz, Berlin 1956)

Odom, W M *A history of Italian furniture from the 14th to the early 19th centuries*, 2 vols (Doubleday, Page & Co., New York 1918–19; 2nd ed. New York Archive Press 1966–67)

Pedrini, A *Il mobilio, gli ambienti e le decorazioni del Rinascimento in Italia, secoli XV e XVI* (Azienda libraria editoriale, Florence 1948)

Remnant, G L *A catalogue of Misericords in Great Britain* (Oxford University Press 1969)

Salvy, C *Les meubles régionaux en France* (Paris Libraire Gründ 1967)

Schubring, P *Cassoni* (K W Hersemann, Leipzig 1915 and supplement 1923)

Singleton, E *Dutch and Flemish Furniture* (London and New York 1907)

Vogelsang, W *Le meuble hollandais* (Amsterdam 1910)

Wills, G *English Furniture 1550–1760* (Guinness, London 1971)

Wills, G *English Furniture 1760–1900* (Guinness, London 1971)

Wolsey, S W & Luff, R W *Furniture in England: the age of the joiner* (Arthur Barker, London 1968)

Formal Splendour

Lizzani, G *Il Mobile Romano* (Görlich, Milan 1970)

Scarisbrick, D *Baroque—the age of exuberance* (Orbis Publishing, London 1973)

Smith, R C *The Art of Portugal 1500–1800* (Weidenfeld & Nicolson, London 1968)

Symonds, R W *Furniture making in Seventeenth and Eighteenth-century England* (Country Life, London 1955)

Verlet, P *French Royal Furniture* (Barrie & Jenkins, London 1963)

Ward-Jackson, P *English Furniture Designs of the Eighteenth Century* (Her Majesty's Stationery Office, London 1958)

The Line of Beauty

Baccheschi, E *Il mobile veneziano del settecento* (Görlich, Milan 1962)

Baccheschi, E *Mobili intarsiati del sei e settecento in Italia* (Görlich, Milan 1964)

Baccheschi, E *Mobili italiani del Meridione* (Görlich, Milan 1966)

Baccheschi, E *Mobili Tedeschi* (Görlich, Milan 1969)

Beck, D *Book of American Furniture* (Hamlyn, London & New York 1973)

Bjerkoe, E H *The cabinetmakers of America* (Doubleday, New York 1957)

Canonero, L *Barocchetto genovese* (Milan 1962)

Chippendale, T *The Gentleman and Cabinet-Maker's Director* (First edition 1754; third edition 1762; reduced facsimile of third edition, Dover Publications, New York 1966)

Coleridge, A *Chippendale Furniture* (Faber & Faber, London 1968)

Davis, T *Rococo—a style of fantasy* (Orbis Publishing, London 1973)

Downs, J *American Furniture of the Queen Anne and Chippendale periods in the Henry Francis Du Pont Winterthur Museum* (Macmillan, New York 1952)

Feduchi, L *El mueble español* (Ediciones Poligrafa, SA, Barcelona 1969)

Hayward, H *Thomas Johnson and English Rococo* (Tiranti, London 1964)

Kenworthy-Browne, J *Chippendale and his contemporaries* (Orbis Publishing, London 1973)

Mazzariol, G *Mobili italiani del seicento e del settecento* (Milan 1963)

Morazzoni, G *Il mobile veneziano del settecento* (Görlich, Milan 1958)

Verlet, P *French Furniture and Interior Decoration of the 18th Century* (Barrie & Rockliff, London 1967)

Verlet, P *Le style Louis XV* (Larousse, Paris 1942)

Ward-Jackson, P *English Furniture Designs of the Eighteenth Century* (Her Majesty's Stationery Office, London 1958)

Purity of Form

Aprà, N *Empire Style 1804–1815* (Orbis Publishing, London 1972)

Les Ebénistes du XVIIIᵉ Siècle Français (Connaissance des Arts, Hachette, Paris 1963)

Eriksen, S *Early Neo-Classicism in France* (Faber & Faber, London 1974)

Fastnedge, R *Sheraton Furniture* (Faber & Faber, London 1962)

Grandjean, S *Empire Furniture* (Faber & Faber, London 1966)

Harris, E *The Furniture of Robert Adam* (Alec Tiranti, London 1963)

Harris, J *Regency Furniture Designs from Contemporary Sourcebooks 1803–26* (Master Hand Series, 1961)

Jarry, M *Le Siège Français de Louis XIII à Napoleon III* (Office du Livre, Fribourg 1973)

Jourdain, M *Regency Furniture 1795–1820* (Country Life, Feltham 1934)

Ledoux-Lebard, D *Les Ebénistes Parisiens (1795–1830)—les oeuvres et leurs marques* (De Nobele, Paris 1965)

Montgomery, C *American Furniture of the Federal Period* (Winterthur Museum, Delaware 1967)

Musgrave, C *Adam and Hepplewhite and Other Neo-classical Furniture* (Faber & Faber, London 1966)

Praz, M *An Illustrated History of Interior Decoration from Pompeii to Art Nouveau* (Thames & Hudson, London 1964)

de Ricci, S *Louis XVI Furniture* (Heinemann, London 1913)

Salverte, Comte de *Les Ebénistes du XVIIIᵉ Siècle* (De Nobele, Paris 1962)

Verlet, P *French Royal Furniture 1800–1825* (Barrie & Rockliff, London 1963)

Watkin, D *Thomas Hope and the Neo-classical Ideal* (John Murray, London 1968)

Watson, F J B *Louis XVI Furniture* (Alec Tiranti, London 1960)

CATALOGUES
de Bellaigue, G *Furniture, Clocks and Gilt Bronzes in the James A de Rothschild Collection at Waddesdon Manor* (Office du Livre, Fribourg 1974)

F J B Watson *Wallace Collection; Catalogue of Furniture* (William Clowes & Sons Ltd, 1956)

Wrightsman Collection Catalogue, 3 vols (The Metropolitan Museum of Art, New York 1966)

The Machine Age

American Antiques from the Revolution to the Civil War (The American Heritage Publishing Co., New York 1968)

Antiques from the Civil War to World War I (The American Heritage Publishing Co., New York 1969)

Aslin, E *19th Century English Furniture* (Faber & Faber, London 1962)

Brosio, V *Mobili Italiani dell'Ottocento* (Antonio Vallardi, Milan 1962)

The Connoisseur's Complete Period Guides: *The Early Victorian Period* (The Connoisseur, London 1958)

Faniel, S (Ed) *Le XIXᵉ Siècle Français* (Hachette, Paris 1957)

Filomarino, A M C *L'Ottocento—i mobili del tempo dei nonni dal l'Impero al Liberty* (Görlich, Milan 1969)

Janneau, G *Le Mobilier Français* (series) (Vincent, Fréal et Cie, Paris 1967)

Nystrom, B G T *1800-tals Stolar* (Nordiska Museet, Stockholm 1967)

Otto, J C *American Furniture of the 19th Century* (Viking Press, New York 1965)

Stavenow, E *Siden, Sammet, Läder, Lärft* (ICA–Forlaget, Västerås 1961)

Symonds, R W & Whineray, B B *Victorian Furniture* (Country Life, London 1962)

CATALOGUES
19th Century America Exhibition *Furniture and other Decorative Arts* (Metropolitan Museum of Art, New York 1970)

The Rebirth of Design

Aslin, E *The Aesthetic Movement, Prelude to Art Nouveau* (Paul Elek, London 1969)

Bliss, D P *Charles Rennie Mackintosh and the Glasgow School of Art* (Glasgow School of Art 1961)

Bossaglia, R *Art Nouveau* (Orbis Publishing, London 1975)

Champney, F *Art and Glory: The Story of Elbert Hubbard* (New York 1968)

Howarth, T *Charles Rennie Mackintosh and the Modern Movement* (Routledge & Kegan Paul, London 1952)

MacCarthy, F *All things Bright and Beautiful. Design in Britain 1830 to today* (George Allen & Unwin, London 1972)

Macleod, R *Charles Rennie Mackintosh* (Country Life, London 1968)

Macleod, R *Charles Rennie Mackintosh* (Country Life, London 1968)

Naylor, G *Arts and Crafts Movement. A Study of its Sources, Ideals & Influence on Design Theory* (Studio Vista, London 1971)

Pevsner, N *Charles R Mackintosh*—Series: Architetti del movimento moderno (Milan 1950)

Pevsner, N *Pioneers of Modern Design from William Morris to Walter Gropius* (Penguin Books, Harmondsworth 1960)

Pevsner, N *The Sources of Modern Architecture and Design* (World of Art series, Thames & Hudson, London 1968)

Pevsner, N *Studies in Art, Architecture and Design: Vol II—Victorian and After* (Thames & Hudson, London 1968)

Pevsner, N & Richards, J M (Eds) *The Anti-Rationalists* (Architectural Press, London 1968)

Report by the Victoria & Albert Museum Concerning the Furniture in the House of Lords (Her Majesty's Stationery Office, London 1974)

Schmutzler, R *Art Nouveau* (Thames & Hudson, London 1964)

Some examples of Furniture by Charles Rennie Mackintosh in the Glasgow School of Art Collection (Glasgow School of Art, 1968)

Victorian and Edwardian Decorative Arts—*The Handley-Read Collection* (Royal Academy, London 1972)

Watkinson, R *Pre-Raphaelite Art and Design* (Studio Vista, London 1970)

CATALOGUES
The Aesthetic Movement and the Cult of Japan (Fine Art Society's exhibition catalogue, London 1972)

The Arts and Crafts Movement (Fine Art Society's exhibition catalogue, London 1973)

California Design 1910—exhibition catalogue (Pasadena Centre, 1974)

Clark, R J (Ed) *The Arts and Crafts Move-*

ment in America 1876–1916—exhibition catalogue (Princeton 1972)

Victorian and Edwardian Decorative Arts (Victoria & Albert Museum's exhibition catalogues, London 1972)

The Triumph of Style

Dowling, H *A survey of British industrial arts* (F Lewis, Benfleet 1935)

Frankl, P *New Dimensions. The Decorative Arts of Today in Words and Pictures* (Payson & Clarke, New York 1928)

Gloag, J (Ed) *Design in Modern Life* (George Allen & Unwin, London 1934)

Gloag, J *Industrial art explained* (George Allen & Unwin, London 1934)

Gloag, J *Simple schemes for decoration* (Duckworth & Co., London 1922)

Holme, G *Industrial design and the future* (The Studio, London 1934)

Ionides, B *Colour and Interior Decoration* (Country Life, London 1926)

Moreau, C *Intérieures au salon des artistes-décorateurs* (Charles Moreau, Paris 1929)

Les Anées 25 (Musée des Arts Décoratifs, Paris 1966)

L'Art Décoratif Français 1918–1925 (Editions Albert Levy, Paris 1925)

Battersby, M *Art Deco fashion — French designers 1908–25* (Academy Editions, London 1974)

Battersby, M *Art Nouveau* (Colour Library of Art, Hamlyn, London 1969)

Battersby, M *The Decorative Twenties* (Studio Vista, London 1969)

Battersby, M *The Decorative Thirties* (Studio Vista, London 1971)

Battersby, M *Trompe l'oeil: the eye deceived* (Academy Editions, London 1974)

Battersby, M *The World of Art Nouveau* (Arlington Books, New York 1968)

Brunhammer, Y *Lo Stile 1925* (Fratelli Fabri Editori, Milan 1966)

Design in modern industry (Ernest Benn, Kent 1922)

Joel, D *The adventure of British furniture* (Ernest Benn, Kent 1953)

Papini, R *Le arti d'oggi* (Casa Editrice d'Arte Bestetti e Tumminelli, Milan 1930)

Repertoire du gôut moderne (Editions Albert Levy, Paris 1929)

Report on the industrial arts in the international exhibition of Paris 1925 (HM Stationery Office, London 1925)

Shaw Sparrow, W (Ed) *The British home of today* (Hodder & Stoughton, London 1904)

Smithells & Woods *The Modern Home* (F Lewis, Benfleet 1936)

The Studio year book of Decorative Art (The Studio, London 1908–40)

Todd & Mortimer *The new interior decoration* (B T Batsford, London 1929)

de la Valette, J *The conquest of ugliness* (Methuen, London 1935)

Wainwright, S B *Modern Plywood* (Ernest Benn, Kent 1927)

Innovation

Bernard, J R *Le Système Utility* (Paris 1953)

Bonnett, D (Ed) *Contemporary Cabinet Design and Construction* (Batsford, London 1956)

Dexter, A *Charles Eames: Furniture from the Design Collection* (Museum of Modern Art, New York 1973)

Logie, G *Furniture from Machines* (George Allen & Unwin, London 1947)

Magnani, F *Room for the Seventies* (Studio Vista, London 1971)

Modern Interiors (Studio Vista, London 1969)

Møller S E (Ed) *Danish Design* (Danish Institute for Information, Copenhagen 1974)

Russell, G *Designer's Trade* (George Allen & Unwin, London 1968)

Wanscher, O *The Art of Furniture—five hundred years of Furniture and Interiors* (George Allen & Unwin, London 1966)

PERIODICALS
Architectural Review 9 Queen Anne's Gate, London SW1

Design The Design Council, 28 Haymarket, London SW1

Domus 20121 Milano, via Monte di Pieta 15

Industrial Design Whitney Publications, 1 Astor Plaza, New York 10036

Interiors Whitney Publications Inc., 1 Astor Plaza, New York 10036

Mobilia 3070 Snekkersten, Denmark

CATALOGUES
Britain Can Make It—exhibition catalogue (HM Stationery Office, London 1946)

Utility Furniture and Fashion 1941–1951—Catalogue to Geffrye Museum exhibition of 1974 (Inner London Education Authority 1974)

Modern Chairs 1918–1970—exhibition catalogue (Whitechapel Art Gallery, London 1970)

Index

Acknowledgements

We are grateful to the following for permission to reproduce the illustrations on pages:
endpapers Radio Times Hulton Picture Library; frontispiece by courtesy of the Victoria & Albert Museum, London. Angelo Hornak Library; 6 Victoria & Albert Museum, London. TOP—photo R Guillemot; 8-9 Louvre, Paris. Mercurio.

The Archaeological Record
10 © George Rainbird Ltd—photo F L Kenett; 12 © George Rainbird Ltd—photo F L Kenett; 12-13 Ronald Sheridan; 13 IGDA—photo R Pedicini; 14 (top) Scala; 14 (bottom) IGDA—Dagli Orti; 15 Scala; 16 (left) IGDA—photo Pineider; 16 (right) IGDA—photo Ciccione; 17 IGDA—Dagli Orti; 18 Universitete s Oldsaksamling, Oslo; 19 Courtesy of Viscount de L'Isle, Penshurst Place, Kent; 20 (left) Bulloz; 20 (right) National Gallery, Prague; 21 Bulloz; 22-23 IGDA—photo Ciccione; 23 IGDA.

The Classical Revival
24 IGDA; 26 (top) IGDA—Dagli Orti; 26 (bottom) Angelo Hornak Library; 27 IGDA—Dagli Orti; 28 IGDA—Dagli Orti; 29 IGDA; 30 (top) IGDA—Dagli Orti; 30 (bottom) IGDA; 31 Mauro Pucciarelli; 32 IGDA—Dagli Orti; 33 (left) IGDA—Dagli Orti; 33 (right) IGDA; 34 Bulloz; 35 (left) Teigens Fotoatelier; 35 (right) IGDA; 36-7 Ronald Sheridan; 38 (top) Giraudon; 38 (bottom) IGDA; 39 Angelo Hornak Library; 40 IGDA; 41 IGDA—Dagli Orti; 42 Hessisches Landesmuseum, Darmstadt; 43 Landesmuseum, Munster; 44 Uppsala University, Sweden; 45 photo Walter Steinkopf; 46 National Museum, Stockholm; 47 IGDA; 48 Scala; 49 Scala; 50 (top) IGDA—photo Freeman; 50 (bottom) Angelo Hornak Library; 51 Cooper-Bridgeman Library; 52 A F Kersting; 53 Angelo Hornak Library; 54 (top) Cooper-Bridgeman Library; 54 (bottom) Cooper-Bridgeman Library; 55 John Bethell.

Formal Splendour
56 Giraudon; 58 Weidenfeld & Nicolson Library & Archives; 59 (top) Giraudon; 59 (bottom) Europalia; 60-1 John Bethell; 62 J Whitaker; 63 John Bethell; 64 IGDA; 65 IGDA; 66 IGDA; 67 (top) IGDA; 67 (bottom) Angelo Hornak Library; 68 IGDA; 69 IGDA—Dagli Orti; 70-1 IGDA; 72 Wallace Collection; 73 IGDA; 74 IGDA; 75 IGDA; 76 IGDA—C Ciccione; 77 Musée de Versailles; 78 (top) Musée des Arts Décoratifs; 78 (bottom) IGDA; 79 IGDA; 80 Sothebys, London; 81 Rijksmuseum, Amsterdam; 82 Weidenfeld & Nicolson Library & Archives; 83 IGDA; 84 (left) IGDA; 84-5 Angelo Hornak Library; 86 IGDA; 87 IGDA; 88 Angelo Hornak Library; 89 Angelo Hornak Library; 90 Gemäldegalerie, Dresden—photo Gerhard Reinhold; 91 Country Life; 92 Sothebys, London; 93 IGDA; 94 Scala; 95 Rosenborg Castle, Copenhagen; 96 © The Counts Wrangel and Brake—Weidenfeld & Nicolson Library & Archives; 97 Cooper-Bridgeman Library; 98 C M Dixon; 99 IGDA.

The Line of Beauty
100 Edwin Smith; 102 IGDA; 103 The National Trust; 104 (top) IGDA; 104 (bottom) courtesy of F Partridge; 105 (top) IGDA; 105 (bottom) Christies, London; 106 (top) IGDA; 106 (bottom) IGDA; 107 Angelo Hornak Library; 108-9 IGDA; 110 (top) IGDA; 110 (bottom) Metropolitan Museum of Art, New York. Mr and Mrs Charles B Wrightsman Collection. IGDA; 111 IGDA;

112 Musée d'Ansembourg, Liège—photo R Roumat; 113 Musée de Mariemont; 114 IGDA; 115 (top) IGDA; 115 (bottom) IGDA; 116 IGDA; 117 IGDA; 118 MAS; 119 IGDA; 120 BPC Publishing Ltd, London; 121 (left) Schloss Charlottenburg, Berlin—photo Jorg P Anders; 121 (right) Sanssouci, Potsdam; 122 Christies; 123 (top) Kunstmuseum der Stadt Dusseldorf—photo Walter Klein; 123 (bottom) Angelo Hornak Library; 124 Rosenborg Castle, Copenhagen; 125 (top) Rosenborg Castle, Copenhagen; 125 (bottom) Royal Palace, Stockholm—reproduced by gracious permission of HM the King of Sweden; 126 Rijksmuseum, Amsterdam; 127 IGDA; 128 IGDA; 129 (left) IGDA; 129 (right) courtesy of F Partridge; 130 Angelo Hornak Library; 131 Angelo Hornak Library; 132 (top) IGDA; 132 (bottom) Angelo Hornak Library; 133 National Gallery of Ireland; 134-5 Henry Francis Dupont Winterthur Museum, Delaware; 136 IGDA; 137 (left) Henry Francis Dupont Winterthur Museum, Delaware; 138 (right) Henry Francis Dupont Winterthur Museum, Delaware.

Purity of Form
138 Hermir Verlag; 140 IGDA; 141 IGDA; 142 TOP—photo R Guillemot; 143 Christies, London; 144 Sothebys, London; 145 IGDA—Dagli Orti; 146 (top) IGDA; 146 (bottom) Sothebys, London; 147 TOP—photo R Bonnefoy; 148 IGDA—photo Freeman; 149 (top) Sothebys, London; 149 (bottom) Sothebys; 150 (top) TOP—photo R Guillemot; 150 (bottom) Christies, London; 151 IGDA; 152 Giraudon, Paris; 153 (top and bottom), 154 (top) IGDA—photo Dagli Orti; 154 (bottom) Musée des Arts Décoratifs, Paris; 155 IGDA; 156-7 A F Kersting; 158 IGDA; 159 IGDA—Dagli Orti; 160 A F Kersting; 161 IGDA; 162 Christies, London; 163 IGDA; 164 IGDA—photo Dagli Orti; 165 (top) IGDA; 165 (bottom) IGDA; 166 Mary Evans Picture Library; 167 (top) IGDA; 167 (bottom) IGDA; 168 National Trust; 169 Jonathan Bourne; 170 Angelo Hornak Library; 171 (top) IGDA; 171 (bottom) Malletts, London; 172 Sothebys, London; 173 Schloss Charlottenburg, Berlin—photo Jorg P Anders; 174 Schloss Charlottenburg, Berlin. Weidenfeld & Nicolson Library & Archives; 175 (top) Museum für Kunsthandwerk, Frankfurt; 175 (bottom) Residenzmuseum, Munich. Victoria & Albert Museum, London; 176 Weidenfeld & Nicolson Library & Archives—photo Edwin Smith; 177 (top) Swedish Royal Collection. Victoria & Albert Museum, London; 177 (bottom) Rijksmuseum, Amsterdam; 178 Royal Institute of British Architects. Weidenfeld & Nicolson Library & Archives; 179 (top) Biblioteca Vaticana; 179 (bottom) Sothebys, London; 180 Weidenfeld & Nicolson Library & Archives; 180-1 IGDA—photo Dagli Orti; 182 Soprintendenza ai Monumenti del Piemonte, Turin; 183 Scala; 184 (left) Metropolitan Museum of Art, New York—gift of Mrs J Insley Blair. IGDA; 184 (right) Jonathan Bourne; 185 The Henry Francis du Pont Winterthur Museum, Delaware; 186 (left) IGDA; 186 (right) IGDA; 187 Metropolitan Museum of Art, New York—gift of Mrs Russell Sage & others. IGDA.

The Machine Age
188 Baron Guy de Rothschild. TOP—photo R Guillemot; 190 IGDA; 191 Orbis—photo Angelo Hornak; 192 Country Life Publications, Derby; 193 Orbis—photo Angelo Hornak; 194 National Trust—photo Chris Newsholme; 196 A F Kersting; 197 Orbis—photo Angelo Hornak; 199 Giraudon; 200 Giraudon; 201 Oranje-Nassau Museum, Delft; 203 George Rainbird Ltd—photo Werner Neumeister; 204-5 Nordiska Museet, Stockholm; 205 Musei Civici di Brescia; 206 The American Museum in Britain, Bath; 207 IGDA; 208 Novosti; 209 Weidenfeld & Nicolson Library & Archives—photo Edwin Smith; 210 (top) Musée des Arts Décoratifs; 210 (bottom) Harriet Bridgeman Ltd; 211 Cooper-Bridgeman Library; 212 Mansell Collection; 213 (top) Private collection; 213 (bottom) Lyndhurst, Tarrytown, USA—photo Louis H Froh-

man; 214 National Trust; 215 IGDA; 216 (top) Metropolitan Museum of Art, New York—gift of Mr and Mrs James B Tracey. Harriet Bridgeman Ltd; 216 (bottom) Harriet Bridgeman Ltd; 217 Mary Evans Picture Library; 218 (left) Malletts, London; 218-9 Stadtische Museen Vienna; 219 (bottom) Mary Evans Picture Library; 220 Radio Times Hulton Picture Library; 221 Orbis—photo Angelo Hornak; 222-3 The Metropolitan Museum of Art, New York—gift of Frederic H Hatch; 224 The Metropolitan Museum of Art, New York. The Edgar J Kaufmann Charitable Foundation Fund 1968; 225 Harriet Bridgeman Ltd; 226 Orbis—photo Angelo Hornak; 227 IGDA—photo Rizzi; 228-9 Brooklyn Museum, New York; 229 (right) Orbis—photo Angelo Hornak; 230 National Monuments Record; 231 IGDA; 232 Harriet Bridgeman Ltd; 233 (top), 233 (bottom), 234 (left) Orbis—photo Angelo Hornak; 234-5 Cooper-Bridgeman Library.

The Rebirth of Design
236 IGDA; 238 Perfecta Publications; 239 Angelo Hornak Library; 240 Victoria & Albert Museum, London; 241 Picturepoint; 242 Angelo Hornak Library; 243 Angelo Hornak Library; 244 Angelo Hornak Library; 245 A F Kersting; 246 (top) Angelo Hornak Library; 246 (bottom) Michael Holford—reproduced by courtesy of the William Morris Gallery, Walthamstow; 247 Mary Evans Picture Library; 248 (top) Octopus Ltd; 248 (bottom) Leicester City Museum & Art Gallery; 249 Angelo Hornak Library; 250 (left) Sothebys, London; 250-1 Annan, Glasgow; 251 (right) Sothebys, London; 252 (top) Heal & Son Ltd, London; 252 (bottom) Angelo Hornak Library; 253 Angelo Hornak Library; 254 Chicago School of Architecture Foundation. Gift of Mrs Charles F Batchelder. Picturepoint; 255 Chicago Institute of Art. Gift of Mr and Mrs John J Evans; 256 Chicago Institute of Art—gift of Mrs Theodore D Tieken; 257 Chicago Institute of Art—gift of Mr and Mrs F M Fahrenwald. IGDA; 258 IGDA; 259 IGDA; 260 Sothebys, London; 261 Cooper-Bridgeman Library; 262 Bulloz; 263 (top) Bibliothèque Doucet, Paris; 263 (bottom) IGDA; 264 (left) IGDA; 264 (right) IGDA; 265 IGDA; 266 Sothebys, London; 267 TOP—photo Guillemot.

The Triumph of Style
268 Robert Walker Collection. TOP—photo Guillemot; 270 Sunday Times; 271 Heal & Son Ltd; 272 (top) Cooper-Bridgeman Library; 272 (bottom) Martin Battersby; 273 Sunday Times; 274 (top) Musée des Arts Décoratifs, Paris; 274 (bottom) Musée des Arts Décoratifs, Paris; 275 Angelo Hornak Library; 276 Orbis—photo Angelo Hornak; 277 (top) Martin Battersby; 277 (bottom) Collection, Galerie Félix Marcilhac, Paris; 278 (top) Collection, Galerie Félix Marcilhac, Paris; 278 (bottom) TOP—photo Guillemot; 279 (left) Musée des Arts Décoratifs, Paris; 279 (right) Royal Pavilion, Art Gallery & Museums, Brighton; 280 Orbis—photo Angelo Hornak; 281 (top) Martin Battersby; 281 (bottom) Musée des Arts Décoratifs, Paris; 282-3 Victoria & Albert Museum, London; 284 (top) Royal Pavilion, Art Gallery & Museums, Brighton. Loaned by Martin Battersby. Orbis—photo Angelo Hornak; 284 (bottom) Design Council, London; 285 IGDA—photo Titti; 286-7 Angelo Hornak Library; 287 (right) Orbis—photo Angelo Hornak; 288 (top) Heal & Son Ltd; 288 (bottom) Orbis—photo Angelo Hornak; 289 Orbis—photo Angelo Hornak; 290 Angelo Hornak Library; 291 (top) Orbis—photo Angelo Hornak; 291 (bottom) Mary Evans Picture Library.

Innovation
292 foto Memphis; 294-295 P. Garner; 296 (top) Design Council; 296-297 Private Coll; 298 (top) Private Collection; 298 (bottom) Design Council; 299 P. Garner; 300 Hille; 301-302 P. Garner; 303 (top) P. Garner; 303 (bottom) The Observer/Design Council; 304 Courtesy of J. Makepeace; 305 P. Garner.